W9-BYL-231

Criminal Conduct &
Substance Abuse Treatment for
Women in Correctional Settings

Criminal Conduct & Substance Abuse Treatment for Women in Correctional Settings

Female-Focused Strategies for Self-Improvement and Change
Pathways to Responsible Living

Adjunct Provider's Guide

Harvey B. Milkman
Metropolitan State College of Denver

Kenneth W. Wanberg
Center for Addictions Research and Evaluation, Denver

Barbara A. Gagliardi
Metropolitan State College of Denver

Los Angeles • London • New Delhi • Singapore

Copyright © 2008 by SAGE Publications, Inc.

All rights reserved. No part of this book may be reproduced or utilized in any form or by any means, electronic or mechanical, including photocopying, recording, or by any information storage and retrieval system, without permission in writing from the publisher.

For information:

SAGE Publications, Inc.
2455 Teller Road
Thousand Oaks, California 91320
E-mail: order@sagepub.com

SAGE Publications Ltd.
1 Oliver's Yard
55 City Road
London EC1Y 1SP
United Kingdom

SAGE Publications India Pvt. Ltd.
B 1/I 1 Mohan Cooperative Industrial Area
Mathura Road, New Delhi 110 044
India

SAGE Publications Asia-Pacific Pte. Ltd.
33 Pekin Street #02-01
Far East Square
Singapore 048763

Printed in the United States of America

Library of Congress Cataloging-in-Publication Data

Milkman, Harvey B.
Criminal conduct and substance abuse treatment for women in correctional settings: adjunct provider's guide : female-focused strategies for self-improvement and change—pathways to responsible living/Harvey B. Milkman, Kenneth W. Wanberg, Barbara A. Gagliardi.
    p. cm.
Includes bibliographical references and index.
ISBN 978-1-4129-0593-0 (pbk. alk. paper)
    1. Women prisoners—Substance use. 2. Women prisoners—Mental health. 3. Women prisoners—Rehabilitation.
4. Female offenders—Substance use. 5. Female offenders—Mental health. 6. Female offenders—Rehabilitation. 7. Women drug addicts—Rehabilitation. 8. Substance abuse—Treatment. I. Wanberg, Kenneth W. II. Gagliardi, Barbara A. III. Title.
[DNLM: 1. Substance-Related Disorders—therapy. 2. Crime—psychology. 3. Prisoners—psychology. 4. Sex Factors.
5. Women—psychology. WM 270 M644g 2008]

RC451.4.P68M55 2008
365'661082—dc22   2008010389

This book is printed on acid-free paper.

08   09   10   11   12   10   9   8   7   6   5   4   3   2   1

Acquisitions Editor:	Kassie Graves
Editorial Assistant:	Veronica K. Novak
Production Editor:	Astrid Virding
Copy Editor:	Pam Suwinsky
Typesetter:	C&M Digitals (P) Ltd.
Proofreader:	Dennis W. Webb
Indexer:	Judy Hunt
Cover Designer:	Candice Harman
Marketing Manager:	Carmel Schrire

Contents

List of Figures

List of Tables

List of Reflection Poems

Preface

Criminal Conduct and Substance Abuse Treatment: Strategies for Self-Improvement and Change (SSC)—*Pathways to Responsible Living: The Participant's Workbook*, 2nd edition (Wanberg & Milkman, 2006) and *Provider's Guide*, 2nd edition (Wanberg & Milkman, 2008) are designed to deliver state-of-the-art cognitive-behavioral treatment to substance-abusing judicial clients. The treatment curriculum is intended for judicial clients, 18 years of age or older, who manifest co-occurring problems with substance abuse and criminal conduct. Expected treatment outcomes for those who complete the program are the ability to engage in meaningful life experiences while not regressing into recidivism and relapse.

To date, more than 75,000 clients, in court-supervised outpatient, residential community corrections, and prison settings, have participated in the SSC treatment curriculum. Analysis of both client and provider satisfaction has been very positive. After consultation with authors, research scientists, agency supervisors, and treatment practitioners who provide alcohol and other drug (AOD) treatment services to female judicial clients, we find an overwhelming consensus that treatment effectiveness is enhanced by increasing focus on the specific needs of women. Extensive review of the scientific literature fully supports gender-focused treatment for substance abuse and criminal conduct.

Three cognitive-behavioral skill sets are critical to successful SSC implementation across gender: *mental self-control, relationship sensitivity,* and *social responsibility.* The treatment process is skill based and multimodal, recognizing the client's movement through identifiable stages of change. Motivational enhancement as well as relapse and recidivism prevention strategies are generic paradigms for both men and women. Treatment is delivered in both individual and group settings using modeling, role playing, interpersonal (treatment provider and group participant), and quantitative feedback relevant to the client's disclosure of thoughts, attitudes, and beliefs concerning substance abuse and criminal conduct.

Multidimensional assessment of the specific areas of perceived benefit and disruption resulting from substance abuse and criminal conduct is interwoven throughout the 50-session curriculum.

Sections I and II of this *Adjunct Provider's Guide* offer a discussion of the theoretical and research basis for gender-sensitive and female-relevant content and exercises. Of central importance is that treatment providers develop a *contextual awareness* of the biological, psychological, and social underpinnings of female substance abuse and crime and understand the salient differences from the experiences of most men.

This volume has general applicability for female-focused treatment of substance abuse and/or criminal conduct. The therapeutic principles and philosophical orientations are relevant to any program that seeks improved treatment outcomes with women who have criminal involvement and/or substance abuse issues.

Section III of this *Guide,* while utilizing the content and exercises presented in the SSC treatment curriculum, details specific gender-focused adaptations for each of the modules and sessions in the three-phase SSC model: (1) challenge to change, (2) commitment to change, and (3) ownership of change.

Qualified implementation of the SSC treatment curriculum requires training in the basic *Criminal Conduct and Substance Abuse Treatment* model, with full utilization of the *Provider's Guide* (Wanberg & Milkman, 2008) and *Participant's Workbook* (Wanberg & Milkman, 2006). *Adjunct Guide,* coupled with gender-focused training, is designed to enhance treatment efficacy by adding increased specificity and sensitivity for women.

ACKNOWLEDGMENTS

Karen Storck has made invaluable editorial and research contributions to this volume as well as having authored Chapter 5: Understanding Posttraumatic Stress Disorder.

We are also grateful to Monica Zilberman for coauthorship of Chapter 3: Mental and Physical Health Issues in Female Criminal Justice Clients.

We would like to express our appreciation to the *Adjunct Provider's Guide* Advisory Group, which provided vital feedback throughout the development of this project. Special thanks to Trudy Laskey, Kim Williams, and Regina Davis from The Haven, Jim Rowan and Chana Alles from Arapahoe House, and Maureen O'Keefe from the Colorado Department of Corrections, whose discussion added depth and focus to many aspects of this *Guide*—especially in establishing treatment guidelines for dealing with issues of trauma and abuse. We also wish to give our heartfelt thanks to the women at The Haven who openly and courageously shared their insights and life experiences, moving us forward in our goal to honor the special strengths and needs of female judicial clients with co-occurring substance abuse and criminal conduct. We thank the Colorado Alcohol and Drug Abuse Division for their encouragement and support of this project.

Finally, Drs. Milkman and Wanberg would like to state our respect and appreciation for the vital female voice and scholarly expertise that Barbara Gagliardi has imparted to this work.

Harvey B. Milkman
Kenneth W. Wanberg
Barbara A. Gagliardi

Introduction

CHAPTER OUTLINE

OVERVIEW AND PURPOSE

DISCUSSION OF THE *PROVIDER'S GUIDE FOR CRIMINAL CONDUCT AND SUBSTANCE ABUSE TREATMENT: STRATEGIES FOR SELF-IMPROVEMENT AND CHANGE [SSC]— PATHWAYS TO RESPONSIBLE LIVING* (2ND EDITION)

WHY A SPECIAL NEEDS FOCUS FOR WOMEN?

SOCIOCULTURAL AND COGNITIVE CONSIDERATIONS

BIOLOGICAL CONSIDERATIONS

A PLATFORM FOR UNDERSTANDING LEARNING AND CHANGE

EMPIRICAL SUPPORT FOR GENDER-FOCUSED TREATMENT

TREATMENT CONSIDERATIONS

A STRENGTHS-BASED PERSPECTIVE

INCREASING THE RELEVANCE OF COGNITIVE-BEHAVIORAL TREATMENT FOR WOMEN

SOCIAL RESPONSIBILITY THERAPY

HOW THIS ADJUNCT PROVIDER'S GUIDE IS ORGANIZED

Section I: Understanding the Causes and Context of Female Substance Abuse, Crime, and Mental Disorder

Section II: Essential Elements in the Education and Treatment of Female Judicial Clients

Section III: Gender-Specific Adaptations for Women

LEARNING OBJECTIVES

▶ To explain the purpose of the *Adjunct Provider's Guide* and explain its relationship to the *Provider's Guide* and *Participant's Workbook* for *Criminal Conduct and Substance Abuse Treatment: Strategies for Self-Improvement and Change [SSC]— Pathways to Responsible Living*, 2nd edition (Wanberg & Milkman, 2006; 2008)

▶ To review some of the major principles that are presented in the *SSC Provider's Guide*

▶ To assert that the principles of cognitive-behavioral treatment can be used to improve treatment for female clients

▶ To present the need for gender-specific programming

▶ To elucidate ways in which the lives of female judicial clients are affected by their general experiences as women

▶ To provide an overview and chapter summary of the content of the *Adjunct Provider's Guide*

OVERVIEW AND PURPOSE

Until recently, the focus on women and substance abuse was overshadowed by the understanding and treatment of substance abuse by men. As suggested by Cook, Epperson, and Gariti (2005), suppression of women and their subsequent lack of social power may be a contributor to the small amount of knowledge concerning women's issues and substance abuse. In the field of human services, however, there has been increasing acknowledgment that gender plays a prominent role in the development of social behavior and cognition and presents profound implications for the processes of growth and change. More specifically, there has been a recent call for broad-based development of a woman-focused treatment protocol for professionals working with female judicial clients (for example, Ashley, Marsden, & Brady, 2003; Bloom, 2000; Bloom, Owen, Covington, 2005; Bloom, Owen, Covington, & Raeder, 2003; Chesney-Lind, 2000; Covington, 2000; Kassebaum, 1999; Whitaker, 2000; White, 2001). The current work arises in response to this call and proceeds in the direction of:

▶ Documenting the need for gender-specific programs

▶ Reviewing the literature to examine the effectiveness of such programs

▶ Developing a woman-focused treatment curriculum for those who manifest co-occurring substance abuse and criminal conduct

This *Adjunct Provider's Guide* has two main goals: The first is to provide a broad perspective on psychological, social, and biological issues regarding intervention and treatment for women who manifest co-occurring problems with substance abuse and criminal conduct (for example, personal safety, reducing guilt and shame, coping response to sexual abuse and trauma, and parenting skills) (Peters & Wexler, 2005).

The primary purpose of this *Adjunct Guide* is to provide a gender-focused treatment for women that corresponds to the *Participant's Workbook* and *Provider's Guide for Criminal Conduct and Substance Abuse Treatment: Strategies for Self-Improvement and Change [SSC]—Pathways to Responsible Living*, 2nd edition, henceforth referred to as the *SSC Provider's Guide* and *Participant's Workbook*

(Wanberg & Milkman, 2006, 2008). These volumes address the treatment needs of both men and women who have a history of substance abuse and criminal conduct. The purpose of this *Adjunct Guide* is to enhance the *SSC* curriculum where needed, with reference to the specific needs and issues of the female judicial client.

Qualified implementation of the *SSC* curriculum requires, first and foremost, mastery of the material developed in *Criminal Conduct and Substance Abuse Treatment: Provider's Guide* and *Participant's Workbook*. The modules and sessions in the *Workbook* are delivered with complete fidelity to the concepts and procedures presented in the *Provider's Guide*. However, for increased relevance, the gender-focused enhancements presented in this *Adjunct Guide for Women in Correctional Settings* should be used to complement the session outlines as presented in the *Workbook*. The intent and purpose of this volume is to supply the contextual awareness for increasing the female focus of each session in the curriculum. Treatment effectiveness is enhanced by imbuing each session with recognition of, and sensitivity to, the client's cultural values, socialization experiences, competencies, and strengths. In most cases, *SSC* for women will be delivered in all-women groups (for example, prison, jails, and residential community corrections). In some cases (for example, outpatient services associated with probation or parole), treatment may be delivered in mixed-gender groups. In either case, the material presented in this volume should be utilized to enhance provider awareness and proficiency in treating female clients.

DISCUSSION OF *THE PROVIDER'S GUIDE TO CRIMINAL CONDUCT AND SUBSTANCE ABUSE TREATMENT: STRATEGIES FOR SELF-IMPROVEMENT AND CHANGE— PATHWAYS TO RESPONSIBLE LIVING*

The *SSC Provider's Guide* has three sections. Section I provides a summary of the foundational theories and models that underlie the *SSC* curriculum. Section II provides operational and delivery guidelines for the *SSC* treatment curriculum, and Section III provides a comprehensive guide to the delivery of the *SSC* phases, modules, and sessions.

The *SSC* treatment approach is based on 10 core strategies and principles:

1. Developing a therapeutic relationship through motivational enhancement and a therapeutic alliance

2. Multidimensional assessment based on convergent validation

3. Integrating education and therapeutic approaches

4. Facilitating learning and growth and the stages of change

5. Cognitive-behavioral approach

6. Relapse and recidivism prevention

7. Focusing on moral responsibility to others and the community

8. Integrating the therapeutic and the correctional

9. A cohesive group that elicits a prosocial identity

10. Reentry and reintegration into the community

SSC providers have broad roles, including being teachers, therapists, coaches, counselors, and skills trainers.

Readers are referred to *Criminal Conduct and Substance Abuse Treatment: History, Research, and Foundational Models: A Resource Guide* (Wanberg & Milkman, in press) for a full review of cognitive-behavioral principles as they are applied to the causes, consequences, and treatment choices for substance abuse and criminal conduct. This *Resource Guide* will be a companion to the *SSC Provider's Guide.*

WHY A SPECIAL NEEDS FOCUS ON WOMEN

While effective treatment for both men and women judicial clients is predicated on the strategies and principles discussed previously, women's treatment needs are in many ways different from men's. One difference stems from women's social position, which reflects inequality in relationships, the workplace, and in the general social hierarchy that confers to males privilege and to females subordination. (Bem, 1996; Cook, Epperson, & Gariti, 2005; Crawford & Unger, 2000; Gergen & Davis, 1997; Lorber, 1994; Miller & Stiver, 1997). Gender-enhanced relevance is therefore required.

To improve services for women in correctional settings, it has become helpful to incorporate into treatment policies and curricula a special needs focus (Bloom, Owen, Covington, & Raeder, 2003; Covington, 2000; Henskens, Mulder, Garretsen, Bongers, & Sturmans, 2005; Kassebaum, 1999; White, 2001). This is especially important in view of the fact that during the past 30 years, the rates of female arrest and imprisonment have been on the rise (Covington, 2000; Harrison & Beck, 2005; Kassebaum, 1999; Pollock, 1998). In fact, women make up a fast-growing portion of the criminal justice population (Chesney-Lind, 2000; El-Bassel, Gilbert, Schilling, Ivanoff, Borne, & Safyer, 1996; Harrison & Beck, 2005; McQuaide & Ehrenreich, 1998).

In the years between 1990 and 1998, there was an increase in the number of women on probation, in jail, on parole, and in prison. Between 1977 and 2004, the number of women serving sentences of more than a year grew by 757 percent, more than twice the rate of the male prison population, which increased by 388 percent during the same period (Frost, Greene, & Pranis, 2006). Since the prison boom began in the late 1970s, the total number of people incarcerated in prisons and jails has risen to about 2.3 million, 7 percent of whom are women (Harrison & Beck, 2005). As significant as these statistics may be, the reader is cautioned to keep in mind that low base rates of female offending turn very small increases in absolute rates of criminal processing into large total percentage increases (Miller, 1986). In fact, as Bloom et al. (2003) reported, women account for 17 percent of all offenders under some form of correctional sanction, or one million women in the year 2001. Eighty-five percent of them are under community supervision, usually probation.

There are multiple factors reflecting sociocultural, legal, and policy changes (Chesney-Lind, 2000; McMahon, 2000) that contribute to the large percentage increase of women in correctional settings. The Center for Substance Abuse Treatment estimates the co-occurrence of substance abuse and female offending to be as high as 80 percent (Kassenbaum, 1999). Recent changes in the law regarding mandatory minimum sentencing for drug-related activity have had an impact on the increased rates of female versus male incarcerations (Chesney-Lind, 2000; Covington, 2001; Curry, 2001; Kassebaum, 1999; McMahon,

2000; Phillips & Harm, 1998). Increasing economic hardship may also be producing some of these changes (Curry, 2001; Willis & Rushforth, 2003).

Little evidence exists to suggest that this increase in the number of women in corrections is due to an actual swelling in the frequency or severity of female crime (Chesney-Lind, 2000). Arrest rates are telling in this regard: while the total number of female arrests increased by 38.2 percent (1989–1998), the number of women experiencing correctional supervision during this time rose by 71.8 percent (Chesney-Lind).

SOCIOCULTURAL AND COGNITIVE CONSIDERATIONS

The course and etiology of criminal conduct and substance abuse follow different trajectories for women and men (Bloom, 2000; Chesney-Lind, 2000; Covington, 1998a; Kassebaum, 1999; Whitaker, 2000; White, 2001). A wide range of factors, many of which characterize women's experiences in general, contribute to the specific patterns of criminal conduct in women and the types of crime women generally commit. These factors include violent trauma through sexual and physical abuse (Acoca & Austin, 1996; Bloom, Chesney-Lind, & Owen, 1994; Kassebaum, 1999; Sandrine, Sharon, Kang, Angarita, & Gastfriend, 2005; Veysey, DeCou, & Prescott, 1998), socioeconomic hardship (McMahon, 2000), gender oppression and sexism (Covington, 2000; Kassebaum, 1999), relationship and family issues, mental and physical health problems, and the more generalized socialization experiences of growing up female in American society (Kassebaum). The impact of these experiences can be seen in many aspects of women's criminal conduct, including:

▶ A common pathway into crime through helping a male partner

▶ Relational motivations for crime

▶ Negative evaluations of self-worth

▶ Lack of moral development and sociopathy

▶ Psychosocial schemas and scripts that underlie unhealthy gender norms for behavior, especially with regard to expectations for interpersonal relationships

▶ Psychological, cognitive, and emotional deficits frequently found in female judicial clients due to a high prevalence of victimization and violent trauma in their lives

▶ The need for a treatment curriculum that provides healthy relational experiences in order to maintain successful outcomes in recidivism reduction

Effective intervention in the processes that underlie female crime will be served by programs that address the multiple needs and common skill deficits of women judicial clients. Where absent or limited, these programs need to be developed and more extensively applied (Kassebaum, 1999; Pollock, 1998).

BIOLOGICAL CONSIDERATIONS

Biological factors play a crucial role in explaining several important mechanisms involved with addiction cycles in women. Because women judicial clients generally have experienced more violent victimization than men, physiological reactions to trauma are important considerations when working with them in treatment. There are two basic trajectories of injury to the nervous system that may appear in the aftermath of violent trauma and chronic threat, particularly when that trauma occurs during the developmental processes of early childhood (Niehoff, 1999). The first trajectory produces an overreactive stress response from assault to the nervous system that may result in elevated levels of norepinephrine and cortisol as well as a failure of maturation in the startle response. This type of injury may underlie a diagnosis of posttraumatic stress disorder (PTSD) (Niehoff, 1999), which is found more frequently in women than in men (Blume, 1990; Covington, 2000). Posttraumatic stress disorder could be due, in part, to trauma experienced in early life (Nemeroff, Bremner, Foa, Mayberg, North, & Stein, 2006). People with PTSD tend to startle easily; to reexperience traumatic events in nightmares, flashbacks, and memories; are easily retraumatized by reminders of the trauma; and tend to be hypervigilant to threat or danger (American Psychiatric Association, 1994). Figure 0.1 represents this pathway of overreactive stress response that may develop in response to violent trauma.

Figure 0.1   Posttraumatic Stress Disorder Versus Normal Fear

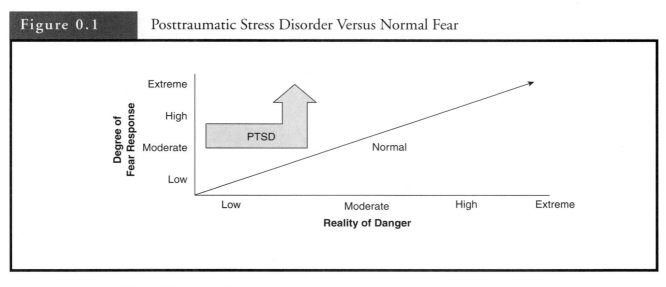

Source: Based on Cox, Hallam, O'Connor, and Rachman (1983).

Reproduced with permission from *British Journal of Psychology* ©The British Psychological Society.

The second type of pathology that may develop in the aftermath of trauma appears to produce opposite results. Constant exposure to threat may desensitize the body's response to violence, resulting in a dissociative response that is more common in women (Acoca & Austin, 1996; Hidalgo & Davidson, 2000; Veysey, DeCou, & Prescott, 1998). Disassociation is characterized by a sense of observing the abuse from a distance, as if having left the body that is being abused.

In more severe cases, this trajectory may result in a diagnosis of antisocial personality disorder (Niehoff, 1999), which is characterized by low levels of norepinephrine, low levels of reactivity overall, and a syndrome sometimes dubbed "without a conscience," as perpetrators feel no regret for their crimes. Antisocial personality disorder is more frequently found among men than women (Hidalgo & Davidson, 2000; Najavits, Weiss, & Shaw, 1997).

In addition, physiological problems related to substance abuse may undergo a different course of development in women than in men. Biological differences between men's and women's bodies underlie a "telescoping" process in women, speeding the development of substance-related problems, so they sometimes appear earlier in women and with lower levels of consumption. Bioavailability of substances also varies within the bodies of men and women. Because females have less water content than men, alcohol absorption and metabolism is reduced in the gastric tract. At equal levels of consumption, and correcting for differences in body weight, women reach higher blood alcohol content (BAC) than men (Wilsnack, 1995).

A PLATFORM FOR UNDERSTANDING LEARNING AND CHANGE

The cognitive-behavioral model for learning and change is widely recognized as a significant treatment option in dealing with criminal justice clients who have a history of substance abuse problems. Application to women is of particular value because many of their needs and issues are situated within distorted beliefs and expectations about self, others, and relationships that are different from men's in addition to a lack of sufficient cognitive and psychosocial skills to live a stress-free, substance-free existence. Distorted or negative beliefs about the self and the world are seen to impede growth and change.

A woman's appraisal of herself and her world frequently include maladaptive expectations about what a woman should be (Crawford & Unger, 2000;

Denmark, Rabinowitz, & Sechzer, 2000). Further, traumatic stress may amplify and perpetuate the stereotypes to which a female may feel necessary to adhere (Krause, 2004). Social constructs of gender, ranging from obligations of female care to assessments of female beauty, to the division of labor, to expectations regarding emotion, all influence how women perceive themselves and their lives. Norms, stereotypes, and stigmas frequently underlie the maladaptive self-perceptions common among women judicial clients (Bem, 1996; Crawford & Unger, 2000; Miller & Stiver, 1997). Each of these may be reflected in the automatic thoughts that frequently underlie substance use and relapse and criminal conduct and recidivism.

Attributions that women make about their lives are often counterproductive and self-defeating. Women generally have more of an external locus of control than men (Crawford & Unger, 2000; Rubinstein, 2004), an orientation that has been linked to feelings of powerlessness and low self-efficacy. Women often cite the lack of options for earning a legitimate wage as motivation for their crimes. Attributions regarding success and failure are particularly problematic in women since they are much more likely than men to attribute their successes to external causes and their failures to internal causes (Covington, 2000). This pattern of attribution has been found to undermine self-confidence and produce counterproductive, self-defeating behavior among women in general. The cognitive processes discussed here, as well as the beliefs and attitudes that underlie them, provide a major target for change in successful and continued recovery.

EMPIRICAL SUPPORT FOR GENDER-FOCUSED TREATMENT

Wanberg (2008), using 10 different samples, compared 20,612 male judicial clients with 6,097 female judicial clients across the scales of the Adult Substance Use Survey—Revised (ASUS-R) (2006) and selected subscales and the total score on the Level of Supervision Inventory—Revised (LSI-R) (Andrews & Bonta, 2003).

The ASUS-R (Wanberg, 2006) is a self-report, differential screening survey, designed to assess alcohol and other drug (AOD) use involvement and disruption,

psychological and mood adjustment problems, social and legal nonconformity, motivation and treatment readiness, defensiveness, and self-perceived strengths. The scales of the ASUS-R can provide guidelines for making service and treatment referral decisions and treatment planning.

The LSI-R is a survey of attributes, behaviors, attitudes, and situations designed to help define the judicial client's risks and needs relevant to determining levels of judicial supervision and treatment planning (Andrews & Bonta, 2003). The LSI-R draws information from the official record and self-reports of the judicial client. The results and a comprehensive discussion of the study are shown in the Appendix.

From a general perspective, the cognitive-behavioral approaches to developing self-control, effective interpersonal relationships, and community responsibility as presented in SSC will be effective for both male and female judicial clients. However, the findings of this study, and the literature reviewed throughout this guide, provide substantive information concerning how treatment should be adjusted for the female criminal justice client. These are summarized here:

▶ Females in the up-front stage of the judicial system (probation) will benefit more from a psychosocial emphasis in treatment, whereas males at this level in the judicial system need greater concentration in the treatment of antisocial and criminal thinking and behavioral patterns. Within the deeper components of the judicial system, for example, prison settings, females will need more concentration in correcting antisocial and criminal thinking and behavioral patterns, and males may need a greater emphasis in the psychosocial areas. Females in the prison setting will be more hard core with respect to criminal involvement.

▶ Females at all levels will need more intensive concentration in the psychosocial and psychological areas of treatment. It is clear: females at all levels of the judicial system are more psychologically disrupted. More concentrated psychological therapies, addressing not only past and present traumas but many of the formal diagnostic categories of mental disorders, are needed. Clearly, females will need more concentration and individual attention in dealing with the sources of psychological and mood adjustment problems, having had greater exposure to psychophysical and psychosocial traumas than the average male.

▶ The fact that female clients are more open and disclosing about psychological problems may be interpreted as a positive factor in treatment. However, the negative of this is that females have lower ego defenses and are more apt to open up critical areas that they are not adequately prepared to deal with. Thus, providers need to be alert to the fact that the female judicial client may self-disclose too much, too soon. This will require more structured and supportive therapies to deal with areas of vulnerabilities and affective material for which clients may not have the ego strength to deal with.

▶ Female judicial clients will need therapies to teach skills and attitudes that empower them in relationships and in society. One of the primary reasons for the use of drugs among female clients is to achieve that sense of empowerment. The empowerment skills need to be relationship directed more so than in male clients, who seem to have a sense of empowerment in relationships, albeit misdirected.

▶ Related to the guidelines mentioned, female criminal justice clients are clearly more disrupted and deficient with respect to their economic and educational positions in society. Employment, job, and economic skills training is essential for most female judicial clients who are unable to compete with their male counterparts in finding employment and economic status in the community. This is not to say that males do not have deficits in this area. There are many barriers for both female and male clients that block efficacious reentry and reintegration into stable employment and a stable job role in society.

▶ Again, related to the issue of relationship and society empowerment, female judicial clients clearly indicate greater upset and disruption in the marital and family domains. Skills in the area of interpersonal closeness, family support, parenting skills, and stable and meaningful intimacy involvements are critical for the female criminal justice client. Male clients often have the skills to find supportive relationships outside of intimate and close interpersonal involvements. Females have difficulty in establishing these relationships outside of a physically intimate relationship.

The guidelines presented indicate that the female criminal justice client will need, on the average, more resources for individual-oriented and specialized treatment (for example, treatment of posttraumatic stress) as they progress through the correctional system. As well, this summary provides guidelines with respect to adjusting correctional treatment not only for the female judicial client but also for the male client. As we reflect on the different approaches for the female judicial client, we will also gain insight into the unique and specific needs of the male client.

TREATMENT CONSIDERATIONS

The holistic model presented in this *Adjunct Guide* addresses many of the contextual issues (biological, psychological, affective, sociocultural) that have been noted, discussed, and critiqued by several authors who have explored gender-specific issues (for example, Covington, 1998a, 1998b, 2001; Harrison, Jessup, Covington, & Najavits, 2004; Kassebaum, 1999; McMahon, 2000).

Some female-focused topics (for example, safety and sexual abuse) may have relevance to men who have developed similar problems in response to similar experiences. For example, although men's response to childhood sexual abuse may be quite different from women's, there are some areas of overlap. Men who have learned to take a submissive role in interaction with others (especially with stronger, more dominant men) may have similar psychological deficits and corresponding treatment needs as women. In general, however, these experiences and orientations tend to be gender specific, with widely divergent probabilities of occurrence in either gender.

Most existing services for female judicial clients follow one of two patterns: (1) traditional programs that treat women using strategies originally designed for use with male clients (Covington, 1998b; Kassebaum, 1999; Sun, 2006); or (2) programs that include special programming for women concurrent with traditional programs.

The first of these strategies assumes a "one size fits all" approach, providing a generic approach to common needs and concerns of substance abuse and criminal conduct, but it does not always address the specific needs of individual clients or special groups.

"Identical treatment is not necessarily equitable" (Whitaker, 2000, p. 5). A woman's sense of self develops differently in all-female versus mixed-gender groups (Bloom & Covington, 1998; Bloom, 2000).

The second strategy for treating women clients often involves multiple treatment sources; a judicial client may have to seek out for her substance abuse, trauma-related issues, and mental health needs from different agencies and treatment services. This could result in contradicting results across various treatment components (Covington, 1998a). Hence, treatment components are fragmented and sporadic, lacking the comprehensive networking of community services and programs that women need for reorientation and transition into a substance- and crime-free life (Kassebaum, 1999).

Both approaches fail to include a realistic assessment of the obstacles women face during reentry into the community: needs for affordable and safe housing and problems achieving financial self-sufficiency without skills.

Sun (2006) asserted that women in mixed treatment groups, especially those in which men outnumber women, are frequently eclipsed by the needs of men and find it difficult to concentrate on their own needs and feelings. After having examined the rates of posttreatment recidivism in both men and women, Messina, Burdon, Hagopian, and Prendergast (2006) found that each gender tends to take a different path in the approach to treatment, leading to recommendation for separate treatment programs.

There is mounting research evidence that treatment outcomes for women can be enhanced when they participate in gender-specific programs (Bloom et al., 2003; Carten, 1996; Covington, 2001; Kassebaum, 1999; Sorbello, Eccleston, Ward, & Jones, 2002). Success in woman-focused treatment programs is measured by lower rates of relapse and recidivism than among women in existing mainstream programs. Success has also been measured in lower rates of inpatient care following treatment, greater job constancy, and better parenting relationships that resulted in higher rates of child custody (Kassebaum, 1999).

Evidence shows that effective treatment programming does empower these addicted women

offenders to overcome their substance abuse, to lead a crime-free life, and to become productive citizens.... Effective women-centered treatment... represents a small investment but enormous savings for U.S. society and further encourages all correctional systems, in states and local communities, to adopt this comprehensive approach for women in their jurisdictions. (Kassebaum, 1999, p. 3)

According to Kassebaum (1999), long-term residential female-focused programs in community settings are lacking. These programs have been found particularly relevant for meeting different treatment needs of women criminal justice clients. Greenfield, Burgdorf, Chen, Porowski, Roberts, and Herrell (2004) found that women who received long-term (6 months or more) treatment have higher success rates in abstinence from drugs than those who received short-term treatment. However, fewer than 9 percent of women clients receive this type of treatment (Kassebaum, 1999). Programs that include family and parenting components are sorely deficient. Programs that provide women with continuing service upon leaving custody to help them reenter the community, maintain abstinence, and avoid criminal conduct are very few, despite research demonstrating the effectiveness of such aftercare for reducing recidivism (Kassebaum; McQuaide, & Ehrenreich, 1998). Although the number of gender-specific treatment programs has been rising, it has not kept pace with the ever-growing number of females in the judicial system. In fact, the ratio of women in need to women who receive appropriate treatment is estimated to be no different than it was the late 1970s (Kassebaum, 1999).

The Center for Substance Abuse Treatment, a division of the U.S. Department of Health and Human Services, Substance Abuse and Mental Health Services Administration (SAMHSA), is currently funding several treatment programs in prisons and jails specifically designed for women with acute alcohol or drug abuse problems. Kassebaum (1999) emphasizes the need for a three-pronged approach to the treatment of substance abuse in women, including (1) a theory of addiction, since most females in the judicial system have severe problems with substance abuse; (2) a theory of women's psychological development, addressing how women heal; and (3) a theory of trauma, since most female judicial clients have had severe experiences with violent victimization. The principles noted as essential in the design and implementation of these new programs are as follows:

▶ Treatment that is rooted in a profound understanding of how women grow and develop and how these factors influence addiction processes

▶ Creative use of sanctions to reinforce the treatment goals of assuming responsibility for one's actions while maintaining motivation for ongoing participation in treatment

▶ Continuity of treatment through aftercare, to aid in successful transition into the community, including networking with community services for affordable housing, counseling programs, and parenting education

Further, Kassebaum (1999) asserts that treatment should be delivered in community-based programs, when possible, allowing the woman's family to remain intact. This is especially true for children and the contact they receive with the mother while the children are in the care of a relative (Smith, Krisman, Strozier, & Marley, 2004).

According to the National Survey of Substance Abuse Treatment Services (N-SSATS) report issued by the Drug and Alcohol Services Information System (DASIS) (2005):

▶ Forty-one percent of substance abuse treatment facilities that accepted women provided special programs or groups for women.

▶ Larger facilities were more likely than smaller facilities to offer special programs for women.

▶ Facilities with special programs or groups for women were more likely to offer special programs or groups for other types of clients than were facilities without special programs for women.

Among the 13,371 treatment facilities that responded to the 2005 N-SSATS survey, 13 percent did not accept women as clients. The report looked only at the 11,578 facilities that accepted women. Figure 0.2 shows the comparison between those that offered special programs or groups for women with facilities that did not offer gender-focused programming.

A STRENGTHS-BASED PERSPECTIVE

The treatment curriculum developed in this *Adjunct Guide* assumes a strengths-based approach, meaning that many of the factors found in women judicial clients, formerly regarded as deficits, are actually

Figure 0.2   Facilities Accepting Women

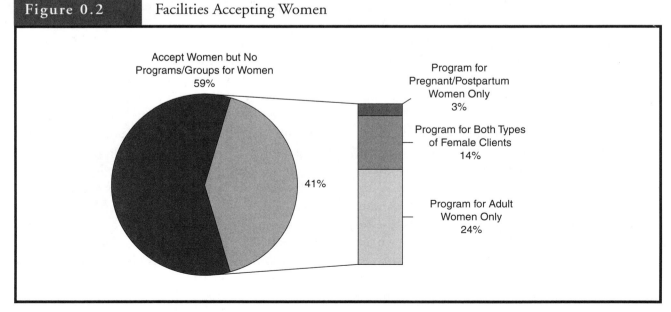

Source: National Survey of Substance Abuse Treatment Services (2005).

strengths from which to build support systems and motivating factors for maintaining recovery. For example, a woman's relational orientation when coupled with the ability to set boundaries becomes a valuable capacity rather than a deficit in relationships of codependence (Miller & Stiver, 1997). A female judicial client who comes to appreciate the importance of boundary setting in healthy relationships has made a powerful step toward building a sense of efficacy. When a woman realizes that she can combine healthy and realistic choices with her expectations for love and support, she may become cognizant of warning signs in others' behavior that this care may not be forthcoming. This may help her to make wiser choices about whom to trust and encourage her to establish and maintain a support network of friends and relationships. Treatment for substance abuse perpetuates this phenomenon by assisting the female in understanding she has support from those around her. Additionally, she is more willing to accept assistance from those who care about her after receiving treatment (Richardson, 2002). Further, the relational orientation that underlies a woman's desire to be reunited with her children and to be a good mother to them may serve as a powerful motivator for her to enter and maintain treatment in order to avoid relapse and recidivism.

Thus, *relationality*, or the ability and desire to bond, is a factor quite consistently found among women and may be a resiliency factor that supports recovery for women (Covington, 2000; Kassebaum, 1999; Jordan, Kaplan, Miller, Stiver, & Surrey, 1991). A second component of this strengths-based philosophy is the recognition that many cognitive and emotional deficits found in women judicial clients are not due to an inability to learn or to the disruptions of mental illness. Rather, they reflect a developmental lag that was brought on by early childhood and adolescent experiences with violent trauma and victimization, substance abuse in their families of origin, poverty and malnutrition, chronic threat, and other conditions. In fact, Bugental and Shennum (2002) indicate that women abused as children perceive themselves to have less self-control. Thus, the remedy for these deficits in women is most often found by providing a woman with a safe and reliable environment, within which she can experience the essential elements of

trust, bonding, and intimacy that will further her maturational process in these areas (Harrison et al., 2004; Kassebaum, 1999). It is important to recognize that many women whose childhood experiences include hardship, abuse, and suffering do not follow a path of substance abuse and criminal conduct.

The correctional setting may actually be the first time in a female judicial client's life that she has had the time, space, and safety to explore essential issues of identity and maturation. Not having had the chance to try out options elsewhere, a female judicial client may need time to explore a wide range of feelings and behaviors (both positive and negative) in the correctional setting before she can rationally begin to evaluate the contingencies between behavior and outcome and make choices about the life she hopes to lead (Kassebaum, 1999). This experimentation may occur within many contexts. It may occur within the context of personality characteristics (testing the limits of gentleness and trust), testing the boundaries of a healthy relationship (including comfort with differing levels of self-disclosure), sexual life choices (including experimentation with lesbian feelings and lifestyles), belief systems (especially with regard to religious and spiritual beliefs), mood and emotion, and the development of character and prosocial attitudes and behavior.

INCREASING THE RELEVANCE OF COGNITIVE-BEHAVIORAL TREATMENT FOR WOMEN

The techniques involved in cognitive-behavioral treatment (CBT) (Beck, 1995; Clark & Steer, 1996; Leahy, 1997; Wanberg & Milkman, 1998) can be effectively utilized with women. In particular, cognitive-behavioral treatment has been shown effective in reducing PTSD (Zlotnick, Najavits, Rohsenow, & Johnson, 2003). Training in *relaxation* (Jacobson, 1938), *stress inoculation* (Meichenbaum, 1985), and the use of *systematic desensitization* in treatment (Wolpe, 1958) can all help to bring a woman's stress level under rational control and reduce the power of triggers for relapse. Similarly, *anxiety management* techniques, such as *behavioral self-control* (Franks & Wilson, 1973; Kanfer, 1970) and *thought stopping* can further reduce a woman's stress and allow for a more coherent and prosocial response to environmental contingencies, one which is predictive of positive outcomes and more in keeping with her own self-interest. Each of these strategies fosters self-reinforcement, resulting in a strengthening of adaptive patterns of thinking, feeling, and acting. Thus, small cognitive and behavioral changes will reinforce one another, gradually increasing a sense of well-being.

Other CBT approaches, such as *directive self-instructional training* (Arnkoff & Glass, 1992; Leahy, 1997; Meichenbaum, 1985); *social skills training* (Lange & Jakubowski, 1976); and *training in problem solving* (Spivack & Shure, 1974), develop skills to manage a crime- and substance-free life by providing behavioral alternatives and engendering an internal locus of control (Rotter, 1966). *Systematic rational restructuring* (Goldfried, Dencenteceo, & Weinberg, 1974), which helps a woman see new ways of thinking about her life and her options, can modify cognitive distortions, irrational beliefs (Ellis, 1975; Ellis & Harper, 1961), maladaptive assumptions, and automatic thoughts (Beck, Wright, Newman, & Liese, 1993; Leahy, 1997). While maladaptive cognitions trigger AOD use and criminal conduct, new ways of thinking help the client to reanalyze these thought patterns in terms of their usefulness and consequences.

Role playing and behavioral rehearsal can strengthen the availability and habituation of critical coping responses. All of these factors may have an impact on the development of self-efficacy. It is essential that these new ways of thinking are relevant to a woman's culture, socioeconomic realities, and personal life situation. With time, a woman judicial client can learn to check new patterns of thought against her actual experience and identify obstacles in her environment and relationships that may prevent her from using these alternatives (Salkovskis, 1996). The aim of treatment is to help the female judicial client expand her perception of options, so she can see for herself that there are *more constructive strategies of survival beyond substance abuse and crime.* Since raising self-esteem and a sense of self-importance is such an important issue in women's recovery (Covington, 2000; Miller & Stiver, 1997), treatment should not imply that her

previous attempts at survival were wrong. Many females have lived in hostile environments involving violence, abuse, and discrimination. Estimates regarding the frequency of experience with some type of physical or sexual abuse among women clients range from 70 percent (Coll, Miller, Fields, & Matthews, 1997) to more than 90 percent in Center for Substance Abuse Treatment (CSAT)-funded programs (Kassebaum, 1999). Another study found that only 14 percent of women judicial clients reported no experience with trauma and abuse at all (Kerr, 1998).

Depression is a particularly debilitating problem among female judicial clients (McMahon, 2000; Wanberg, 2008). In addition, more substance-abusing women reported depression than men (Wanberg, 2008). Nineteen percent of women judicial clients are diagnosed with depressive disorder (Covington, 2000). A. Beck (1963, 1976) and J. Beck (1995) have investigated the relationship between negative thought patterns and depression, asserting that it is the interpretation of events, and not the events themselves, that cause a depressive response. In particular, women classified as depressed appear to have difficulty interpreting social cues, for example, the meaning of eye contact (Lee, Harkness, Sabbagh, & Jacobson, 2005). Therapy can facilitate new possibilities for appraising events and assessing their options. It is especially useful for a woman to see how many of the stresses and difficulties in her life reflect the general social position of women (Bem, 1996; Crawford & Unger, 2000; Miller & Stiver, 1997).

The next part of this chapter draws on female life experiences and summarizes cognitive-behavioral principles with specific application to female criminal justice clients. Although not all experiences of women in corrections can be represented here, the most prominent patterns are identified. Although the common features of CBT are relevant to both men and women, the following summary is directed at application more specifically to women.

Individuals are actively involved in the construction of their realities. These realities are constructed from a constellation of factors operating in women's lives, such as social constructs regarding the meaning of *womanhood* and personal experiences with regard to:

▶ Power and powerlessness

▶ Abuse and violation versus respect and courtesy

▶ Caring for others (men, children, relatives) versus self-care

▶ Sense of male entitlement and privilege that fosters female submission

People respond to their cognitive assessment of their environment rather than to the environment itself. Once a woman has experienced poverty, low wages, sex discrimination and disrespect, physical or sexual violence, the burden of single parenting, and so on, the meaning of her world, her trust in its responsiveness to her, and her perception of her own needs and desires may be profoundly altered. Women frequently take a submissive posture to such violation, such as the learned helplessness (Seligman, 1975) experienced among battered women who stay with abusive partners and become isolated in their houses (Walker, 1989). Another route is to strike out and fend for oneself in a hostile world. Thus, substance abuse and criminal conduct can be seen as attempts (albeit maladaptive ones) to survive under harsh conditions.

Feelings, thoughts, and behaviors are interactive and interrelated. As this process of substance abuse and criminal conduct becomes repetitive, a woman may fail to perceive alternative behaviors that she could employ or alternative environments in which she could live. She is likely to return to places that are familiar, despite the fact that they are often abusive and foster the development of substance abuse, criminal conduct, and other self-destructive behaviors. Disturbances in emotion and behavior are the result of disturbances in thought and perceptual processes.

Gradually, the process may develop from failure to see alternatives to expectations of inevitability. A woman's negative self-identity (as "gun moll," "drug mule," "wise-ass") may underlie feelings of well-being as a result of successful criminal behavior and outcome expectancies for such in the future. Her automatic

thoughts may include heightened threat perception and the need to strike back (Niehoff, 1999).

Assessment of women's psychological and emotional problems is based on their underlying patterns of cognition. Attitudes may develop to support the belief that women who "submit" to society are naïve and that their perceived "submission" can only bring on degradation (McQuaide & Ehrenreich, 1998). Women may not, however, perceive the connection between degradation and their own substance abuse and criminal conduct. Outcome expectancies that maintain a perception that the use of substances and engagement in criminal conduct produce positive outcomes, satisfaction, and rewards may develop. A host of external attributions (for example, cruelty by men, unequal opportunity) underlie rationalizations that may allow women to believe they were driven into criminal conduct rather than having chosen it, and that without substance abuse and criminal conduct, they could not survive.

The emphasis in therapy should be on identifying and changing dysfunctional thoughts and beliefs. The gender-focused *SSC* curriculum helps women to see that many of their problems are neither personal nor their fault, nor is the world out to get them, but rather they are the result of the social condition of women and minorities in modern times (McMahon, 2000). Women discover the ways in which substance abuse and criminal conduct conspire to further their difficulties rather than resolve them. They learn to place specific financial, family, and relationship issues in the broader context of women's lives, so they can begin to appreciate the strength in women's survival and look to other women in recovery and in the broader society as friends and support systems and as role models for adaptive behavior. This may reduce self-blame and self-hatred and engender self-acceptance. It may help increase feelings of self-efficacy in perceiving the possibility of overcoming problems through more constructive means. This is the philosophical framework for much of feminist therapy (Crawford & Unger, 2000; Denmark, Rabinowitz, & Sechzer, 2000).

Changes in thoughts, feelings, and behavior should be met with self-reinforcement in order to maintain recovery.

Women can develop an internal process whereby they acknowledge the little steps that initiate change, feel a sense of accomplishment in making these small changes, and see how small changes become large as they accumulate over time. Sometimes just helping a woman to mail a letter to her child and receive a response can provide a basis for building the sense that things can change. This is an educational as well as a therapeutic process. Counselors and treatment providers fulfill the function of evaluation, education, consultation, coaching, and support. They may also serve as role models who demonstrate effective means of coping, stress management, and social interaction. In these ways, they may help a woman to understand how she engages in counterproductive thought patterns that may underlie her self-destructive response to the environment. Female judicial clients should be encouraged to see their criminal conduct and substance abuse in the context of this maladaptive response.

Relapse and recidivism prevention in women involves a continuum of care. In order to maintain abstinence and prevent relapse and recidivism, women need an environment with support structures to help them accomplish their goals. This environment needs to be encouraging of abstinence and reinforcing when abstinence is achieved. However, often they return to an environment that is disrespectful and abusive (Bloom, Chesney-Lind, & Owen, 1994; Coll, Miller, Fields, & Matthews, 1997; Kassebaum, 1999), to relationships that place the burdens of a "woman's role" upon them, and to the demands of male entitlement to female care (Blume, 1998; Markarian & Franklin, 1998; Wilsnack, 1995). They must often contend with inadequate housing, at best an indifferent social response that interferes with regaining custody of their children (McMahon, 2000), a work world that undermines their chances of earning a decent wage to support themselves and their children (Wilson & Anderson, 1997), and the added stigma of being "a woman" in the criminal justice system. In order to succeed at recovery, a woman must be specifically fortified to deal with these realistic components of her life, as they will arise during her reentry process. Alongside these demeaning and difficult experiences, she must have a place to go for support and rekindling of relationships.

Providing aftercare as an integral part of treatment can help her deal with these experiences in an ongoing manner. Support structures must be available in the community that can successfully advocate for a woman's needs in transition in order to help her avoid relapse and recidivism. She must be informed of and taught how to use these community resources (Kassebaum, 1999).

SOCIAL RESPONSIBILITY THERAPY

Social responsibility therapy (SRT) is a core component of *SSC* and represents an essential dimension for both women and men in corrections. It focuses on character building, social and moral responsibility, developing prosocial attitudes and behaviors, managing anger and preventing violence, settling conflicts, and understanding and practice empathy. It is discussed in more detail in Chapter 8.

HOW THIS *ADJUNCT PROVIDER'S GUIDE* IS ORGANIZED

Section I: Understanding the Causes and Context of Female Substance Abuse, Crime, and Mental Disorder

This section describes the theory and empirically based research that provides the foundation for implementing women-focused treatment programs.

Chapter 1: Women and Crime

Chapter 1 examines the scope of the problem of female offenses, addressing general patterns of criminal conduct among women, characteristics of female judicial clients, risk factors for criminal conduct in women, and the kind of crimes that women generally commit. It then addresses the relationship between female offending and substance abuse, examining criminal conduct in women with alcohol-related problems as well as female incarceration and illicit drug use. The chapter concludes by discussing the relationships among female substance abuse, criminal conduct, underlying psychosocial issues, and implications for treatment.

Chapter 2: Connecting Female Substance Abuse, Cognition, and Crime

Chapter 2 further explores vulnerability factors for substance abuse and criminal conduct in women and describes gender-related addiction cycles. First, biological influences on the etiology of substance abuse in women are examined. Then, social and interpersonal factors that are frequently found in the lives of women who offend are investigated, with experiences of violent trauma being important. These patterns and trends are compared to those commonly found among women's lives in general, and issues such as the use of prescription drugs to manage the memory and pain of these experiences are identified as factors that may contribute to a high incidence of multiple drug use among women criminal justice clients. The chapter proceeds to a discussion of key features that characterize the development of women's self-concept, including cognitive and relational factors that often stem from the social construction of the female in American society. Chapter 2 concludes by investigating key targets for education and cognitive and behavioral change, with special attention to social skills deficits that women may have developed as a result of the issues mentioned.

Chapter 3: Mental and Physical Health Issues in Female Criminal Justice Clients

This chapter provides an in-depth discussion of the specific psychological issues and diagnoses found in female judicial clients that may differ from their male counterparts. This list includes:

▶ High incidence of trauma from physical and sexual abuse, both historical and ongoing, which contributes to higher rates of posttraumatic stress disorder

▶ High rates of dual diagnoses that are quite different from patterns found in male criminal justice clients, including chronic depression, suicide and other mood disorders, anxiety disorders, and personality disorders

▶ Health problems of women in the criminal justice system, including sexuality issues, hepatitis, cancer, and HIV/AIDS

▶ Ethnic considerations in health care

▶ Different patterns of AOD disruption in women

Chapter 4: Adolescent Girls and Delinquency: The Route Into Correctional Settings

This chapter examines some of the life circumstances commonly experienced by adolescent females who become involved in criminal activity. It explores the role of gender norms as young girls begin to form their gender identity and analyzes how disruptive experiences at home, combined with gender identification and development of a relational orientation, may make girls susceptible to a pathway into crime often initiated by their boyfriends or other male figures. This trajectory is extended into the lives of women who offend and demonstrates how girls who begin offending at an early age progress within correctional systems. The experiences of girls within the correctional setting are investigated, and treatment recommendations for adolescent females are drawn from these factors and considerations.

Chapter 5: Understanding Posttraumatic Stress Disorder

Posttraumatic stress disorder and posttraumatic stress symptoms are identified as one of the main factors in the origins and perpetuation of female substance abuse and criminal offending. Chapter 5 begins by tracing the evolution of PTSD from its initial associations with "shell shock" and devastating war experiences to the current conceptualization as deriving from any catastrophic stressor, usually, but not always, outside the range of ordinary human experience. After presenting data on the incidence and prevalence of PTSD and associated symptoms, the chapter describes vulnerability factors that may distinguish those who develop the disorder from others who are more resilient. A discussion of methods for assessment and criteria for diagnosis is followed by the description of gender differences in incidence and patterns of co-occurring disorders. The chapter then moves to a discussion of the relationships among PTSD, running away, substance abuse, prostitution, drug sales, robbery, and other patterns of criminal offending. The recovery process is examined, along with the profound difficulties in providing a safe environment within the constraints of contemporary prison settings. Cognitive-behavioral treatment for co-occurring substance abuse and PTSD is described in terms of five key principals for effective treatment.

Section II: Essential Elements in the Education and Treatment of Female Judicial Clients

When faced with recidivism, women are found to have different coping skills than men, likely due to a lower sense of self-efficacy (Pelissier & Jones, 2006). This section develops a contextual awareness of gender-specific biological and socialization experiences, with corresponding recommendations for assessment and treatment with women clients.

Chapter 6: Assessment of Women in Correctional Settings

Chapter 6 provides an overview of the many aspects of assessment that are useful in treatment with females who have a history of substance abuse and criminal conduct. Based upon the literature review provided in the previous section, Chapter 6 discusses the following elements and considerations for effective gender-focused assessment:

- Summary of factors important in the assessment of female judicial clients
- Need for different norms for psychometric instruments for men and women
- Initial screening and assessment
- Client Master Profile and Master Assessment Plan

- Treatment matching
- Involvement of the female judicial client in the development of the treatment plan, and
- The continuum of care

The chapter begins with an overview of the assessment process and how this assessment fits into the overall *SSC* curriculum. Specific areas of assessment unique to females are then delineated. Screening and in-depth assessment are discussed, and various tools are identified that are designed to address specific areas of female assessment. The assessment process is related to the Master Profile and the Master Assessment Plan completed by clients upon culmination of Phase I of the *SSC* curriculum. The importance of collaboration between the provider and client is discussed, along with the critical importance of planning for a continuum of care.

Chapter 7: Gender as Culture and Other Diversity Considerations

Chapter 7 begins with an expanded view of culture to include the context of values within which a person has lived and formed their primary experience of themselves. Counseling itself is discussed as a cultural identity with notable differences in values and expectations from traditional cultures, for example, keeping a schedule of appointments, self-disclosure, openness, and intimacy. This chapter provides the conceptual framework for increasing awareness around issues related to gender, race, and ethnicity. Some of the socioeconomic issues that women judicial clients may face, such as inadequate housing, lack of job skills, low wages, and job discrimination, are explored in terms of how these experiences can generate maladaptive perceptions and cognitions. These include believing that dependence on a man—even an abusive man—and/or criminal behavior constitute the "only possible options" in making a living. Economic factors are considered in the context of successful community reentry along with the importance of financial self-sufficiency in maintaining treatment goals of relapse and recidivism prevention. Treatment motivation and critical targets for intervention services are covered, in terms of dealing with external circumstances such as poverty and housing; thoughts and feelings about taking care of children; and disappointments and aspirations regarding pregnancy, children, and the responsibilities of mothering.

Chapter 8: Gender-Specific Strategies and Models for Treatment

This chapter begins by presenting a philosophical framework for gender-specific treatment programming, identifying specific conceptual approaches to education and therapy with women. It then investigates issues involved in the establishment of an effective therapeutic alliance. A discussion of developing an effective group process with women ensues, emphasizing the importance of developing trust within the treatment community in order to establish a base for social support, mutual aid, and role modeling. Chapter 8 reviews key adaptations for women when using cognitive-behavioral treatment. The chapter concludes with discussion of commonalities among an array of existing programs that provide gender-focused treatment services for women in correctional settings.

Section III: Gender-Specific Adaptations for Women

The material presented in Section III of this *Adjunct Guide* is used to supplement Section III of the *SSC Provider's Guide*, which presents in-depth discussion of the research support along with methods and approaches for delivering each session of the *SSC* curriculum. The intent and purpose of this section are to supply the contextual awareness for increasing the female focus of each session in the *SSC* curriculum. The material in this section is critical in that treatment effectiveness is enhanced by imbuing each session with awareness and sensitivity to the client's cultural values, biological characteristics, socialization experiences, competencies, and strengths.

SECTION I

UNDERSTANDING THE CAUSES AND CONTEXT OF FEMALE SUBSTANCE ABUSE, CRIME, AND MENTAL DISORDER

CHAPTER OUTLINE

LEARNING OBJECTIVES

▶ To describe the population of women judicial clients and the nature of the crimes that women generally commit

▶ To examine common characteristics of female judicial clients

▶ To elucidate the relationship between alcohol- and other drug-related behaviors and criminal conduct in women

▶ To identify factors that place women at risk for engaging in substance abuse and criminal conduct, and to explore each of these factors regarding the frequency and general trends within them

▶ To examine the impact of diversity among women and their rates of imprisonment

▶ To explore the factors involved in relapse and recidivism among women

SCOPE OF THE PROBLEM: WOMEN IN THE CRIMINAL JUSTICE SYSTEM

Women make up a fast-growing portion of criminal justice populations (Bloom, Owen, Covington, & Raeder, 2003; Covington, 2001; McQuaide & Ehrenreich, 1998; Women's Prison Association, 2003). In the 6 years between 1989 and 1995, there was a 460 percent rise in the female prison population, compared with an increase of 241 percent for men over the same time period. As of June 30, 2006, the number of women under the jurisdiction of state or federal prison authorities increased 4.8 percent from midyear 2005, reaching a total of 111,403. The number of men rose 2.7 percent, totaling 1,445,115 during the same time period (Bureau of Justice Statistics, 2006).

The accelerated rate of growth in the female prison population is due to many factors. It is difficult to determine how much of this growth can be attributed to an actual shift in female behavior or how much is due to changes in law and social policy. Changes in welfare policy have reduced the number of legal alternatives by which women can access financial resources (this is particularly true for women with dependent children). This may underlie some of the increase in the number of imprisoned women (McQuaide & Ehrenreich, 1998). Increased severity in response to drug-related charges and sentencing has also had a disproportionate impact on women as compared to men (Covington, 2001; Kassebaum, 1999; McMahon, 2000; Phillips & Harm, 1997). Substance abuse is strongly linked to probation, imprisonment, and parole violation among women (Covington, 2001). These and other factors are believed to have led to triple the number of incarcerated women in the past decade (Covington, 2001).

Women Judicial Clients and Substance Abuse

Substance abuse is the most commonly diagnosed disorder among female judicial clients. Close to 80 percent of female judicial clients have substance abuse problems, and many fall into the category of having severe and long standing problems (Kassebaum, 1999). Nearly 64 percent are classified as drug abuse/dependent and 32 percent as alcohol abuse/dependent (Covington, 2000). Substance-abusing females are imprisoned in the United States at 6 to 10 times the rate of American women in general (Covington).

Substance abuse is a significant contributor to criminal behavior in general. Brennan and Austin (1997) found that more than 50 percent of men and women report that drugs or alcohol were involved in the crimes that led to their current imprisonment. Women judicial clients are more likely than their male counterparts to be impaired by drugs at the time of their crimes (Covington, 1998b).

Substance abuse issues are at the top of the list of problems for women judicial clients. Of those women deemed drug dependent, a full 86 percent meet the criteria for residential treatment. At entry into prison, women's drug abuse is generally more advanced and severe than men's at this time and generally requires longer treatment (Covington, 1998b). Drug dependence appears to be one of the major pathways into crime for females. Interviews with female judicial clients who started engaging in criminal activity in their twenties found that many of these women entered into crime as a way to support a drug habit. In most cases, drug abuse began in response to a major life event such as the death of a loved one, depression and grief, or a sharp reduction in financial stability (Pollock, 1998). (For information regarding pathways into crime for females who began their criminal careers as juveniles, see Chapter 4 of this *Guide*.)

GENERAL PATTERNS OF CRIMINAL CONDUCT AMONG WOMEN

Pollock (1998) reported that the types of crimes women currently commit are similar to those women have committed in the past. The economic motivations for these crimes remain consistent as well. Many crimes committed by women are economically driven, related to alcohol and other drug (AOD) use, poverty, or both (Covington, 2001). This is supported by the observation that men's crimes are more often affective, while women's crimes are as likely to be committed for instrumental as well as affective reasons (Pollock). Table 1.1 presents a comparison of male and female judicial clients regarding the features of criminal conduct.

Table 1.1

Ten-Year Arrest Trends by Sex, 1996–2005

8,009 agencies; 2005 estimated population 178,017,991; 1996 estimated population 159,290,470

OFFENSE CHARGED	MALE						FEMALE					
	Total			Under 18			Total			Under 18		
	1996	2005	Percent change	1996	2005	Percent change	1996	2005	Percent change	1996	2005	Percent change
TOTAL[1]	6,773,900	6,261,672	–7.6	1,258,168	897,305	–28.7	1,845,799	1,982,649	+7.4	445,332	381,643	–14.3
Murder and nonnegligent manslaughter	8,572	7,114	–17.0	1,290	664	–48.5	992	875	–11.8	98	75	–23.5
Forcible rape	18,512	14,924	–19.4	3,153	2,332	–26.0	233	205	–12.0	49	60	+22.4
Robbery	73,192	60,096	–17.9	22,962	15,118	–34.2	7,788	7,745	–0.6	2,356	1,673	–29.0
Aggravated assault	260,469	224,080	–14.0	36,972	28,312	–23.4	54,936	57,923	+5.4	9,152	8,655	–5.4
Burglary	195,124	153,888	–21.1	76,490	41,672	–45.5	25,674	27,085	+5.5	8,758	5,744	–34.4
Larceny–theft	595,297	421,828	–29.1	212,281	105,513	–50.3	310,666	270,765	–12.8	106,880	77,300	–27.7
Motor vehicle theft	86,405	67,522	–21.9	36,188	16,172	–55.3	13,913	14,638	+5.2	6,769	3,583	–47.1
Arson	9,972	8,114	–18.6	5,794	4,230	–27.0	1,626	1,602	–1.5	712	685	–3.8
Violent crime[2]	360,745	306,214	–15.1	64,377	46,426	–27.9	63,949	66,748	+4.4	11,655	10,463	–10.2
Property crime[2]	886,798	651,352	–26.6	330,753	167,587	–49.3	351,879	314,090	–10.7	123,119	87,312	–29.1
Other assaults	597,763	554,044	–7.3	99,610	95,555	–4.1	158,366	183,431	+15.8	38,240	47,402	+24.0
Forgery and counterfeiting	45,250	43,068	–4.8	3,388	1,768	–47.8	26,853	27,670	+3.0	2,045	832	–59.3
Fraud	137,874	104,201	–24.4	4,536	3,065	–32.4	117,288	89,338	–23.8	2,411	1,714	–28.9
Embezzlement	5,545	5,979	+7.8	486	419	–13.8	4,607	6,108	+32.6	394	332	–15.7
Stolen property; buying, receiving, possessing	78,156	66,459	–15.0	23,140	11,540	–50.1	13,676	16,312	+19.3	3,507	2,362	–32.6
Vandalism	163,890	139,529	–14.9	78,226	54,939	–29.8	26,179	28,837	+10.2	9,681	8,758	–9.5

OFFENSE CHARGED	MALE						FEMALE					
	Total			Under 18			Total			Under 18		
	1996	2005	Percent change	1996	2005	Percent change	1996	2005	Percent change	1996	2005	Percent change
Weapons; carrying, possessing, etc.	113,685	103,184	−9.2	28,657	24,052	−16.1	9,331	8,870	−4.9	2,410	2,782	+15.4
Prostitution and commercialized vice	20,524	14,615	−28.8	303	202	−33.3	28,412	27,026	−4.9	420	668	+59.0
Sex offenses (except forcible rape and prostitution)	52,296	48,112	−8.0	9,829	9,437	−4.0	4,188	4,298	+2.6	791	1,000	+26.4
Drug abuse violations	688,006	832,707	+21.0	100,568	86,895	−13.6	142,678	202,137	+41.7	16,832	19,255	+14.4
Gambling	5,541	2,942	−46.9	528	378	−28.4	811	504	−37.9	35	17	−51.4
Offenses against the family and children	68,211	55,393	−18.8	3,089	1,894	−38.7	16,248	17,230	+6.0	1,750	1,173	−33.0
Driving under the influence	745,658	658,705	−11.7	9,191	8,187	−10.9	132,069	157,538	+19.3	1,809	2,363	+30.6
Liquor laws	286,425	255,746	−10.7	66,537	49,116	−26.2	78,367	93,228	+19.0	29,149	27,640	−5.2
Drunkenness	391,721	284,892	−27.3	12,156	6,999	−42.4	55,046	50,838	−7.6	2,665	2,095	−21.4
Disorderly conduct	324,503	279,714	−13.8	83,418	78,552	−5.8	95,729	99,725	+4.2	29,279	37,870	+29.3
Vagrancy	12,893	13,752	+6.7	1,654	1,082	−34.6	3,531	3,624	+2.6	344	313	−9.0
All other offenses (except traffic)	1,651,922	1,751,008	+6.0	201,228	159,156	−20.9	410,986	518,699	+26.2	63,190	60,894	−3.6
Suspicion	3,209	2,211	−31.1	1,118	254	−77.3	816	358	−56.1	335	106	−68.4
Curfew and loitering law violations	84,194	61,069	−27.5	84,194	61,069	−27.5	35,213	26,589	−24.5	35,213	26,589	−24.5
Runaways	52,300	28,987	−44.6	52,300	28,987	−44.6	70,393	39,809	−43.4	70,393	39,809	−43.4

Source: Crime in the United States (2006).

*8,009 agencies; 2005 estimated population 178,017,991; 1996 estimated population 159,290,470

[1] Does not include suspicion.

[2] Violent crimes are offenses of murder, forcible rape, robbery, and aggravated assault. Property crimes are offenses of burglary, larceny—theft, motor vehicle theft, and arson.

The Uniform Crime/Incident-Based Reporting system uses general offense categories that were developed by the Federal Bureau of Investigation (FBI) to standardize reporting across states. The Index crimes were chosen on the basis of their seriousness and frequency of occurrence, and they are used to gauge trends in the overall volume and rate of crime. The Index crimes defined by the FBI include the following:

Violent Crimes

▶ **Murder**. The willful killing of one human being by another. Excluded from this category are deaths caused by negligence, suicide, or accident, justifiable homicides, and attempts to murder, which are classified as assault.

▶ **Rape**. The carnal knowledge of a person against his or her will. Attempts to commit rape by force or threat of force are also included; however, statutory rape (without force) and other sex offenses are excluded.

▶ **Robbery**. The taking or attempting to take anything of value from the care, custody, or control of a person or persons by force or threat of force or violence and/or by putting the victim in fear.

▶ **Aggravated Assault**. The unlawful attack by one person upon another for the purpose of inflicting severe or aggravated bodily injury. This type of assault is usually accompanied by the use of a weapon or by means likely to produce death or great bodily harm and also includes attempts to commit murder.

Property Crimes

▶ **Burglary**. The unlawful entry of a structure to commit a felony or theft. The use of force to gain entry is not required to classify an offense as burglary.

▶ **Larceny**. The unlawful taking, carrying, leading, or riding away of property from the possession or constructive possession of another. It includes crimes such as shoplifting, purse snatching, bicycle thefts, and so on, in which no use of force, violence, or fraud occurs. This offense category does not include offenses such as embezzlement, forgery, or bad checks.

▶ **Motor Vehicle Theft**. The theft or attempted theft of a motor vehicle, including automobiles, trucks, buses, motorcycles, and snowmobiles.

The Nature of Female Crimes

In general, women's crimes are AOD-related property crimes such as larceny, shoplifting, or writing bad checks (Covington, 2001). In a study of the California prison system, 71.9 percent of women (versus 49.7 percent of men) were convicted of these types of crimes, reflecting trends nationwide (Bloom, Chesney-Lind, & Owen, 1994). Common criminal offenses among women are prostitution, fraud, and drug-related activities (Pollock, 1998).

Many women are incarcerated for drug-related offenses alone. They are far more likely to be involved in "gender entrapment," that is, caught up with drug-dealing through a relationship with a man (Richie, 1996). Females generally act as subordinates to the males in drug distribution (Davis, Johnson, Randolph, & Liberty, 2005), often taking on the low-status role of the courier (Harper, Harper, & Stockdale, 2002). However, the position of courier puts women at great risk for involvement with the law. When women do engage in drug selling on their own, this activity is far more likely to involve petty sums of money—women's drug selling is on the level of small trade, earning about $10 per sale. Because of this, they are often involved in as many as 20 transactions per day, both exposing them to a higher risk of detection and supplying minimal financial remuneration in return (Chesney-Lind, 2000).

As shown in Table 1.1, the biggest increase in women's crimes between 1996 and 2005 included embezzlement, buying, receiving, and possessing stolen property, drug abuse violations, driving under the influence, and liquor law violations.

Women's crimes often display a relational component (Richie, 1996), that is, women generally engage in their first crime by helping a male partner to commit an offense (Pollock, 1998). This involvement in criminal conduct then leads women to act on their own. More than 50 percent of women judicial clients have partners who also offend, and 25 percent of their partners are currently serving time (Bloom, Chesney-Lind, & Owen, 1994).

Women's crimes are less violent than are men's. One study found that 11 percent of women inmates were arrested for a violent offense (Jordan, Schlenger,

Fairbank, & Caddell, 1996). Another study found that 10 percent of the arrests and 41 percent of the imprisonment of women were for violent offenses (Dawson, 1994). There has recently been a rise in the rate of arrest for assault by women (increasing from 6 percent in 1988 to 16.5 percent in 1998) (Chesney-Lind, 2000). This increase, however, has closely paralleled policy changes that require mandatory arrest in domestic violence incidents (Chesney-Lind). Arrests of males have also increased dramatically in these situations. Men are arrested for murder at 10 times the rate of women (Bartol, 2002).

Substance abuse appears to be a major factor in violent crime among women. As noted, Bloom et al. (2003) reported that approximately 80 percent of incarcerated women have substance abuse issues. Among women who commit homicide, rates of AOD abuse or dependence were 50 times higher than in the general population (Eronen, 1995). Additionally, violent female judicial clients were found to have personality disorders in conjunction with substance abuse problems (Weizmann-Henelius, Viemero, & Eronen, 2004). The low incidence of violent crime committed by females as compared to males is consistent with recent research regarding women's and men's attitudes toward the use of violence. While men generally perceive the use of aggression as a way of gaining control in their lives, women more generally perceive the use of aggression as a loss of control (Campbell, 1993). These differences may underlie a major difference in the affective consequences of aggression for the perpetrator, in that men are more likely to feel pride in the aftermath of violence, while women are more likely to feel shame and self-blame (Campbell).

Of women who are in prison for a violent offense, about 33 percent have assaulted or killed a relative or partner (Dawson, 1994); 30 percent of men have killed a female partner. Of those who commit homicide, their victims are most likely to be family members: either spouses (41 percent) or children (55 percent) (Dawson). In spousal murder, there has generally been a prolonged history of physical abuse perpetrated by the victim, against whom the woman retaliates (Chesney-Lind, 2000). Fifty-nine percent of the women committed for killing their partners have suffered physical abuse at the hands of their victims (Chesney-Lind, 2000; Huling, 1991). Of the women who have killed women, anger and/or fights have been cited as instigation. These statistics clearly reflect the relational nature of female crime.

Research in the area of female serial killers appears to be sparse. This lack of research may be because only a very small portion of female judicial clients are serial killers (Arrigo & Griffin, 2004). Though serial murder appears to be rare among women, when it does occur, there are clear features that distinguish it from the crimes of their male counterparts. Women tend to inflict less physical damage on their victim, rarely engage in torture, lure their victims (rather than stalk, which is characteristic of male serial murderers), and use poison (which is rare in men) to inflict death. Women generally stay in one location, whereas male serial killers tend to wander from state to state (Keeney & Heide, 1994). Both male and female serial murderers are likely to come from dysfunctional families as well as to have experienced physical or sexual abuse, or both (Pollock, 1998). Table 1.2 provides a summary of trends in serial murder by women versus men.

Characteristics of Female Judicial Clients

The majority of women in corrections are poor, undereducated, unskilled, and isolated from an adequate support system. Fifty-one percent of incarcerated women have no prior offense, as opposed to 39 percent of males. Fifty percent of women and 37 percent of men had an immediate family member who had been incarcerated. One quarter of imprisoned women reported physical or sexual abuse by a family member. Forty-two percent of women in prison grew up in homes with only one parent, typically the mother. Nearly 17 percent of women judicial clients lived in foster care or in a group home during their childhood (Bloom, Owen, Covington, & Raeder, 2003).

Female judicial clients are often single parents or have dropped out of school due to pregnancy, and many are involved in dysfunctional relationships with men and abuse substances (Covington, 2001; Reed & Leavitt, 2000; Pollock, 1998). Sixty-four percent of female judicial clients have not completed high school (Curry, 2001). Few have experienced a positive relationship with a man (Pollock, 1998). Most

Table 1.2

Serial Murder: Characteristics of Female Versus Male Offenders		
	Women	**Men**
Serial murder	More rare compared to men	Rare
	Less physical damage to victim	More physical damage to victim
	Rarely engage in torture	Torture common
	Lure victim	Stalk victim
	Use poison	Kill with hands/object
	Stay in one location	Move around
	Dysfunctional family	Dysfunctional family
	Physical/sexual abuse	Physical/sexual abuse

Sources: Keeney & Heide (1994); Pollock (1998).

have experienced some form of physical or sexual abuse, either in childhood or as an adult (estimates range from 70 to 90 percent) (Bloom et al., 1994; Coll, Miller, Fields, & Matthews, 1997; Kassebaum, 1999). Many women who commit violent offences have witnessed abuse between their parents, had parents who were AOD dependent and/or engaged in criminal conduct while they were young, and have grown up in poverty (Kassebaum, 1999; Sommers & Baskin, 1993). They are also more likely to suffer from other significant mental health difficulties concurrent with substance abuse (Ditton, 1999) and to be engaged in multiple drug use (Kassebaum & Chandler, 1994; Kerr, 1998).

Compared with their male counterparts, women in prison are generally older (early thirties as compared to male clients, who are, on average, in their late twenties), have less extensive criminal histories, and are more likely to have children. Although both men and women justice clients tend to come from disruptive families of origin, this may be more the case with women (Fletcher, Shaver, & Moon, 1993). Fewer men than women experience financial dependence on a substance-abusing or offending spouse, and they do not experience anything that parallels the extensive

and profound programming that women receive to "stand by your man." Very few men enter the criminal life based on their relationship with a woman, but many women find men to be their vehicle into crime (Pollock, 1998). Just as women enter crime through their relationships with men, males who commit crime may also embark on their criminal pathways through relationships with other men. It appears that males instigate the lead into crime for both genders.

Women judicial clients are a diverse group: females account for 31 percent of juvenile offenders (Acoca, 1998a; Snyder & Sickmund, 1999); women who are pregnant or have given birth within the past few months account for 25 percent (McMahon, 2000); and women who are suffering under a dual diagnosis number 24 percent (Ditton, 1999). Although women judicial clients come from all cultures and socioeconomic backgrounds, a disproportionate number come from minority populations. In one study, 35 percent were African American, 16.6 percent Latina/Hispanic, 33 percent Anglo American, and 13 percent other minorities (Covington, 2001).

The Impact of Diversity on
Women, Crime, and Substance Abuse

Although much of the research on women and crime has been conducted within prison populations, there are significant ways in which this population may differ from women in general (Pollock, 1998). Paralleling the statistics on men, women who are sentenced to prison are disproportionately from minority populations and are more likely to have family histories of alcoholism, drug abuse, and criminal conduct. They are likely to be less educated than are women judicial clients who are not sentenced to prison time. White women in the middle class do commit crimes (generally shoplifting and embezzlement), and some go to prison, but generally they are sentenced to probation and community service (Pollock).

Minority women are disproportionately imprisoned (Kassebaum, 1999). As discussed by Primm, Osher, and Gomez (2005), nonwhites represent 62 percent of the prison population yet represent only 25 percent of the general U.S. population.

African American women are overrepresented in prison populations. Race is an even stronger predictor of African American female prison terms than those of African American men. In California, African American females comprised 35 percent of the prison population; 17 percent were Latina/Hispanic (Bloom et al., 1994). In a nationwide survey done in 1994, the rate of African American female incarceration was 7 times that of white women (Kassebaum). Between 1986 and 1991 alone, the number of African American female inmates rose by 828 percent (Mauer & Huling, 1995, cited in Kassebaum, 1999). Nationally, African American women comprise 46 percent of all female inmates (Snell, 1994). In a report titled *Compelled to Crime: The Gender-Entrapment of Battered Black Women,* Richie (1996) comments on the disproportionate number of African American and Latina/Hispanic women engaged with the criminal justice system.

RISK FACTORS AND DYNAMIC PREDICTORS OF CRIMINAL CONDUCT IN WOMEN

This part of the chapter presents several factors that place women at greater risk than men for engaging in substance abuse and criminal conduct, and reports frequencies and general trends found in female judicial clients. Further exploration concerning the psychological mechanisms that may be involved is provided in subsequent chapters.

Female Incarceration and Illicit Drug Use

As stated earlier, substance abuse is a major contributor to criminal activity in women, serving either as a motivator to obtain money to support a habit or as a physiological factor that undermines judgment. Sixty-one percent of women in U.S. federal prisons are there for drug-related violations (Snell, 1994). Substance abuse in women is embedded within a complex package of oppressive experience, such as violence and victimization, concurrent poverty, unsafe housing or homelessness, denial of anger, desperation for escape, concurrent mental illness, and lack of an adequate support system.

Of incarcerated women who are currently serving time for drug offenses, 35.9 percent were charged solely with possession (Covington, 2001). Among the reasons given for the high rate of women in prison is the rise of crack cocaine use among women (El-Bassel, Gilbert, Schilling, Ivanoff, Borne, & Safyer, 1996). A 1991 study of New York State drug-dependent female inmates found that 51 percent had used crack, 28 percent heroin, and 4 percent other drugs. Crack cocaine users were 3 times more likely than other users to have carried out their crimes to obtain money for drugs.

More recent research (National Institute of Justice [NIJ], 2004) shows the powerful impact of the methamphetamine epidemic on female judicial clients. According to data from the Arrestee Drug Abuse Monitoring (ADAM) Program (NIJ, 2004), a median of 4.7 percent of adult male arrestees and 8.8 percent of adult female arrestees tested positive for methamphetamine at the time of arrest in 2003. The adult male samples were compiled from 39 U.S. sites, and the adult female samples were compiled from 25 sites.

It is estimated that women who relapse are 7 times more likely to be rearrested than women who abstain in the months following incarceration (Kassebaum, 1999). Women judicial clients who receive substance abuse treatment are less likely to recidivate than those who do not (Hubbard, Craddock, Flynn, Anderson, & Etheridge, 1997).

Comparing Alcohol and Other Drug Use Patterns of Men and Women

Drinking norms among women in the general public have undergone much change in the past 50 years. The age of onset for alcohol use by women decreased by 2 years from the middle 1960s through the middle 1990s (Markarian & Franklin, 1998). Women judicial clients generally start using alcohol and other drugs in their early teens (Reed & Leavitt, 2000). This is earlier than girls on the average and may be used as a sign of impending risk for abuse and criminal conduct in a girl's development.

The study cited in the Introduction of this *Guide* (see "Empirical Support for Gender-Focused Treatment") comparing large samples of men and women in the judicial system provides insight into how these two populations differ (Wanberg, 2008). Following is a brief summary of the findings:

▶ The two groups do not differ as to overall AOD involvement; however, within specific drug use categories, men report higher involvement in marijuana and alcohol and women report higher involvement in cocaine and amphetamines.

▶ Women report higher levels of AOD disruption and negative outcomes.

▶ Women indicate higher levels of psychophysical disruptions from AOD use.

▶ Women show significantly greater levels of psychological, family, and economic problems and disruption, based on both self-report and an instrument that uses self-report and judicial scores.

▶ Men show significantly greater involvement in criminal conduct, both in self-report and judicial records.

▶ Although the two groups do not differ as to motivation and readiness for AOD treatment, women are less defensive about reporting personal-emotional issues.

In the Introduction, these data were used to identify guidelines for the treatment of female judicial clients.

The incidence and pattern of AOD-related problems also differ between males and females. Table 1.3 provides a comparison of women and men with regard to AOD problems.

Even though many women are involved with the criminal justice system for their substance abusing behaviors alone, many are there for the commission of much more serious crimes, ranging from larceny to violent assault and homicide (as explored previously in "The Nature of Female Crime"). With regard to these crimes, substance abuse may play a role, but providers are cautioned not to assume that addressing substance abuse issues alone will stop criminal conduct. Criminal behavior in women is related to a wide range of factors such as rage, the need for escape, feelings of revenge, mental illness, and desperation due to poverty and victimization.

Table 1.3

AOD Problems: Frequencies Among Male Versus Female Judicial Clients		
At Entry Into Corrections		
	Women	**Men**
Stage of AOD use	More advanced	Less advanced
Severity of AOD use	More acute	Less acute
Suicide risk	Higher	Lower
Medical complications	More acute	Less acute
Correlation Between AOD Activities and Crime		
	Stronger	**Weaker**
Commit crimes under the influence	More frequently	Less frequently
Conviction for possession alone	36%	5–15%*

Sources: Bartol (2002); Blume (1998).

*Distinction based on jail versus prison

Trauma and Criminal Conduct in Women Judicial Clients

The incidence of violent trauma among women judicial clients is much higher than in the general population of women (see Chapters 3 and 4 of this *Guide*). Research shows that 46 percent of all female judicial clients with drug abuse issues had been raped, and as many as 44 percent had suffered incest. More than 90 percent of women offenders in Center for Substance Abuse Treatment (CSAT)-funded programs had experienced either physical or sexual assault at some time in their lives (Kassebaum, 1999). While some male offenders also report sexual assault in childhood, there are several major factors that are necessary to fully understand the extent of these experiences among women and girls. For 31.7 percent of women judicial clients, abuse started during childhood and continued through into adulthood. Although it may be equally disruptive when it does occur, only 10.7 percent of male offenders report such abuse in childhood, and this abuse rarely continues into adulthood. Twenty-five percent of women clients report that their abuse started in adulthood, as opposed to only 3 percent of male offenders. Only

5.3 percent of male offenders report an experience of abuse in adulthood (Chesney-Lind, 2000).

Other studies report that at least 80 percent of female judicial clients have experienced some form of physical or sexual abuse (Bloom et al., 1994; Veysey, DeCou & Prescott, 1998). Acoca and Austin (1996) report that trauma-related victimization is one of the most "universally shared attributes" among incarcerated women (p. 58). Among women who participated in a 1996 National Center on Crime and Delinquency (NCCD) research study, more than 92 percent reported some form of physical, sexual, or emotional trauma in their lives (Acoca, 1998b). A study carried out by the Correctional Service of Canada found that only 14 percent of women offenders in Canadian correctional facilities did not report a history of abuse (Kerr, 1998). This study reports that 81.3 percent had experienced physical abuse, 82.5 percent reported emotional abuse, 76.2 percent reported sexual abuse, and 70 reported having experienced all three types of abuse at some point in their lives.

The devastating effects of sexual assault may be further illustrated in the observation that 26 percent of rape involved three or more rapists acting together. Indeed, 55 percent of convicted rapists admitted participation in a gang rape (Crawford & Unger, 2000). The incidence of violent assault of substance-abusing female judicial clients is even higher (Covington, 2000), as research shows that substance abuse increases women's level of risk for such assault (Covington, 2000; Markarian & Franklin, 1998; Wilsnack, 1995). Research with adolescent female judicial clients indicates that there is an interaction among trauma and abuse experiences and criminal conduct. Girls frequently enter crime as a means of survival on the streets. Being cast out or running away from abusive homes places many girls into street life with limited skills and few legitimate alternatives for earning money. Involvement in drug selling and prostitution to obtain money to survive often becomes a pathway into the criminal life (Acoca, 1998b).

Psychological Issues in the Lives of Female Judicial Clients

Regarding mental health issues in general (Chapters 3 and 4 of this *Guide* provide detailed analyses of female mental health issues), women in the judicial system are more likely to suffer from chronic depression, anxiety, and suicidal thoughts than are their male counterparts. Twenty-four percent of female judicial clients have received a mental illness diagnosis (schizophrenia, mania, or major depression) (Ditton, 1999), versus 9.5 percent of males (Bartol, 2002). Nineteen percent of female judicial clients were diagnosed with schizophrenia, bipolar disorder, or chronic depression (Teplin, Abram, & McClelland, 1996). Compared to women in the general population, women judicial clients have higher rates of antisocial personality disorder and borderline personality disorder (Kassebaum, 1999). Kassebaum also reported that 80 percent of women offenders have chronic and severe substance abuse disorders.

Covington (2001) reflects upon four major areas that become disrupted in the lives of female judicial clients:

1. **Disorders of Self.** "The chronic neglect of self in favor of something or someone else" (p. 87)

2. **Unhealthy Relationships.** Involve the use of substances to maintain contact with using partners, to compensate for the absence of relationship, or to deal with the trauma of abuse (Covington & Surrey, 1997)

3. **Sexuality.** Including dysfunction, shame, guilt, fear, sexual abuse, prostitution, and sexual identity issues

4. **Spirituality.** A fragmentation within self, lack of wholeness or connection among body, emotions, social world, and spirituality within the self

Table 1.4 summarizes these mental health factors.

Family Relationships Among Women Judicial Clients

Depending on the type of facility, between 67 and 80 percent of women in correctional settings have children, compared to about 60 percent of male offenders (Covington, 2001; Kassebaum, 1999). These women are often single mothers with primary responsibility for their children and little help with child care from others. Many experience severe guilt and worry over not being with their children or of

Table 1.4

Mental Health and Criminal Conduct in Women Versus Men		
	Women	**Men**
Mental illness diagnosis	24%	9.5%
Chronic depression	More common	Less common
Anxiety	More common	Less common
Suicidal thoughts	More common	Less common
Antisocial personality disorder	Less common	More common
PTSD	34%	Less common
On medication for mental distress	More common	Less common

Sources: Bartol (2002); Covington (2000); Ditton (1999); Kassebaum (1999); Teplin, Abram, and McClelland (1996).

Table 1.5

Family and Relationship Issues in the Lives of Women Versus Men Judicial Clients		
	Women	**Men**
Pregnancy/postnatal period	25%	—
Children	64%–80%	59%
Single parent/little help with childcare	Majority	Minority
Relationships with men:		
Abusive spouse/partner	60%	5.3%
Partner involved in criminal activity	> 50%	Unknown
Partner incarcerated	25%	Unknown

Sources: Chesney-Lind (2000); Covington (2001); Curry (2001); McMahon (2000); Pollock (1998).

losing custody (Phillips & Harm, 1997). As stated previously, 25 percent of women are either pregnant or have given birth in the months just prior to the time of incarceration (McMahon, 2000). Table 1.5 provides the frequencies of relationships in the lives of women judicial clients.

Socioeconomic Hardship and Criminal Conduct Among Women Judicial Clients

The majority of women in correctional facilities are poor, undereducated, and unskilled. More than 60 percent of women were unemployed at the time of their arrest, compared to less than a third of their male counterparts (Collins & Collins, 1996). Underemployment, low pay, and unskilled work are also more common among women than among their male counterparts. Even when employed, women judicial clients live in poverty, as their jobs tend to be minimum wage, entry-level positions (Covington, 2001; Pollock, 1998; Reed & Leavitt, 2000). Socioeconomic hardship among women is reflected in the observation that economic factors play a larger role in the motivation of female than male crime (McMahon, 2000; Pollock, 1998).

Homelessness is also a prominent factor in female drug-using judicial clients, especially among female crack users (found in 12.5 percent crack users versus 5.1 percent of other drug users) (El-Bassel et al., 1996). The exchange of sex for money or drugs also has greater prevalence among crack users than other drug users.

"The widespread practice of exchanging sex for money or drugs...has evolved into a particularly degrading and dangerous form of prostitution" (El-Bassel et al., 1996, pp. 52–53). Prostitution drastically increases the probability of rape. The added dangers of living on the streets for women as compared to men are important factors to consider in understanding the increased trauma experienced by homeless women. Table 1.6 provides a review of these economic factors.

Relapse and Recidivism

Women generally return to prison less frequently than men, although recidivism rates can be as high as 66 percent. However, there are a number of barriers to a woman's continued recovery and maintenance of a substance- and crime-free life that can lead to relapse and recidivism upon reentry into the community. These include:

⟩ *Lack of job skills and a criminal history* that carries an added stigma attached to being a female offender produce a low probability of securing the

Table 1.6

Socioeconomic Hardship and Criminal Conduct in Women and Men*	Women	Men
Unemployed (at legitimate job)	49%–63%*	< 33%*
Job skills	Generally lacking	Generally present
On public assistance	22%	Unknown
Prostitution	33%	15%
Drug selling (involvement)	16%	67%–85%**
Financial dependence on a SA/offending partner	Common	Rare
Added stigma of being a female judicial client	All	

Sources: Bartol (2002); Bloom, Chesney-Lind, and Owen (1994); Covington (2001); Curry (2001); El-Bassel, Gilbert, Schilling, Ivanoff, Borne, and Safyer (1996); Pollock (1998); Reed and Leavitt (2000).

*Upon entry into the correctional system

**Distinction based on jail versus prison

economic self-sufficiency that is crucial to maintenance of abstinence (Wilson & Anderson, 1997).

▶ *Lack of safe and reliable housing* for women (McMahon, 2000) sets them up for continued exposure to the very risk factors that initially led into substance abuse and criminal behavior.

▶ *Social policy* often mitigates a woman's success. Since they generally cannot afford housing without public assistance, they are unable to receive such assistance unless their children are living with them (McMahon, 2000). Phillips and Harm (1997) report that the 1996 felony drug law denies Title IV-A assistance and food stamps to individuals with a history of a drug-related conviction.

▶ A *poor state of health* may serve as a significant factor in relapse and recidivism. Women offenders are generally in a poor state of health. Women's mental and physical health often suffers more and differently than men's (Blume, 1998). A Massachusetts study found 35 percent of women offenders to be HIV positive (Covington, 2001). (An added burden of

telescoping in the biological progression of substance-related disease processes within women is covered in Chapter 3 of this *Guide*.)

▶ *Women are less likely than men to have a strong support system* to help them meet their many needs and responsibilities upon release (Veysey et al., 1998).

Addressing issues of relapse and recidivism is crucial in effective treatment for women. More than two thirds of female judicial clients are incarcerated for repeat offences, and one third of women who have been released return to prison within three years (Dawson, 1994). Yet we can only speculate on the factors that may be involved in relapse and recidivism for women, as little research has been done to investigate the specific psychosocial dynamics at the root of repeat offending in women. Indeed, even if all of these factors were to be elucidated, few programs have the resources to provide comprehensive care after release, that is, focus attention on the full range of issues confronting women in recovery, such as safe housing, help with child care and parenting classes, job placement, family counseling, and continued education about dealing with cravings and urges (McQuaide & Ehrenreich, 1998).

THEORIES OF FEMALE CRIME

Androcentric models place the root of criminal conduct in the offender's deeply felt desires for power and control. Such models are not only androcentric in that their major assumptions stem from a male model of development based on separation and autonomy, but they are also ethnocentric in that it is rooted in the traditional Western focus on individualism and self-assertion (geocentricism). Female judicial clients are generally involved in crime for entirely different reasons (Covington, 2000; Pollock, 1998). An important basis for female crime is economic and/or relational motivation. A desire for acceptance from others, the ability to maintain relationships, and conditions of poverty and disempowerment are the most common motivations cited by women for committing their crimes (Pollock). Thus, theories of female criminality must be reconstructed to account for the real-life situations that drive females into crime. Accomplishing this goal requires the deconstruction of assumptions underlying theories of male criminality and the inclusion of theories of female criminality so that female clients are no longer placed into models that had been developed for men (Bloom, 2000; Chesney-Lind, 2000; Covington, 2000; Kassebaum, 1999; Whitaker, 2000; White, 2001).

The specific characteristics that differentiate female judicial clients from their male counterparts must be extensively applied in developing effective therapy regarding female criminality. Consideration must be given to understanding female psychological development in the context of the real-world circumstances of women offenders' lives. Early theories of female criminality tended to neglect these crucial components. For example, an early stage of theorizing about female crime occurred during the late 1960s to early 1970s, when the United States was experiencing an earlier phase of increased participation of women in crime (Miller, 1986). Two theories emerged that linked the rise in female crime to the then-occurring women's movement: (1) Adler (1975) linked criminality in females to significant changes in female attitudes and behavior to more like those of the male offender population; (2) Simon (1975) linked female crime to women's increased exposure to the workplace, which brought them into contact with the means and opportunity to engage in white-collar crime (Miller, 1986). But there was little evidence to support either of these two assertions.

Simon's (1975) thesis about women's increased exposure to the workplace giving them direct access to opportunities to engage in (white-collar) crime is seriously challenged by the fact that most of the property offenses committed by women at the time were not white-collar crime. Women, then as now, tended to be unemployed and to engage in petty street crime with an economic motivation. In addition, then, as now to a great extent, women's expansion into the workplace was primarily into traditional female arenas such as the service professions, sales, and clerical work, where access to large sums of money is rare. When we look more closely at the specific type of crimes that women committed in each category, a significant pattern begins to emerge. Most fraud by women is credit card fraud, most larceny is shoplifting, and most forgery is on stolen personal checks written for small sums of money (Miller, 1986). Since this type of detail is not found in Federal Bureau of Investigation (FBI) crime reports, the petty nature of female crime is frequently overlooked. This information is still relevant today, as the nature of female crime has changed little over the past several decades and the economic motivation for female crime has remained constant as well (Pollock, 1998).

Adler's (1975) theory of a dramatic shift in female crime following changes in attitudes brought on by the 1970s women's movement is also flawed. Chronology of events is crucial. The increase in female crime that led to such theorizing occurred before the feminist movement hit most segments of society (Miller, 1986). In addition, the rise in crime appeared only in property offenses; surely if there had been a large-scale shift in attitudes, there would have been a parallel increase in violent crime as well. Simon (1975) and Adler failed to take into account the nature of female judicial clients' lives and the psychological characteristics of the female judicial clients themselves. Service providers with female judicial clients will do well to work within paradigms that take into consideration the important factors that propel women and girls into crime, contribute to recidivism, and undermine chances of recovery.

What is important in theorizing about the etiology of criminal conduct in women is to recognize that there are many causal factors—economic, relational, experience of trauma, and so on. There is no single factor that accounts for the variance to explain criminal conduct in the female judicial population as a whole. And, within the female judicial group, as within the male judicial group, there are different explanatory types and patterns. Understanding the factors that may contribute to criminal conduct within any one female judicial client is an important component of the comprehensive screening and assessment process.

IMPLICATIONS FOR TREATMENT AND POLICY: WHAT FACTORS REDUCE RECIDIVISM AMONG FEMALE JUDICIAL CLIENTS?

This chapter underscores the importance of providing intensive substance abuse treatment as a major component of gender-focused services with female judicial clients. Substance abuse treatment must be specifically directed to help women judicial clients recognize the relationships among:

- ❯ Substance-related activities and increased probabilities of losing their freedom to correctional facilities

- ❯ Substance-related activities and increased probabilities of experiencing violent trauma

- ❯ Unhealthy relationships, substance abuse, and criminal prosecution in their lives

In addition, substance-related treatment must address:

- ❯ The underlying psychological issues (including dual diagnosis) in the lives of female judicial clients

- ❯ The underlying psychosocial issues in the lives of female judicial clients

- ❯ Destructive patterns within the families and relationships of women

- ❯ Economic issues faced by women that may motivate their involvement in illegal substance-related activities

This last issue would be addressed with the goal of helping women to develop constructive alternatives for securing a living.

CHAPTER REVIEW

This chapter has described the population of women judicial clients, the nature of women's crime, and the relationship between AOD use and criminal conduct in women. It presented a number of factors found to place women at risk for criminal behavior, and supplied associated statistical information regarding the incidence of these factors among female judicial clients. Addressing both sociocultural and biological issues in the etiology of criminal conduct in women, it developed a platform from which to understand the need for gender-focused programming.

The remaining chapters in Section I further explore vulnerability factors for criminal conduct in women, especially women judicial clients with substance abuse problems. The cognitive-behavioral mechanisms underlying these risk factors are elaborated upon and discussed. Implications for treatment will then be explored in Section II of this *Adjunct Provider's Guide*.

CHAPTER 2: Connecting Female Substance Abuse, Cognition, and Crime

LEARNING OBJECTIVES

▶ To examine sex differences in the course of AOD development and consequences, and to trace these differences to biological factors in male and female physiology

▶ To continue in the exploration of vulnerability factors for substance abuse and criminal conduct in women

▶ To relate these factors to more general patterns and trends in women's lives

▶ To explore elements of a relational orientation as they may apply to the etiology of substance abuse and criminal conduct in women and identify some of the underlying maladaptive cognitions that this orientation may entail; aim is toward understanding these cognitive elements as targets for therapeutic change

▶ To explore some of the self-image issues commonly found among women substance-abusing clients and identify specific cognitive targets for change

▶ To explore addiction cycles in women that may influence the trajectory of criminal conduct and identify specific cognitive targets for change in these cycles

▶ To emphasize the connection between substance abuse and crime in women

▶ To elucidate the usefulness of cognitive-behavioral techniques in corrections with women judicial clients

▶ To understand women as perpetrators as well as victims

INTRODUCTION

This chapter explores the connections among substance abuse, cognition, and crime in women judicial clients. These factors are essential because:

▶ Substance abuse provides a major route into criminal behavior for women.

▶ Substance abuse is especially implicated in women's violent crime.

▶ At time of arrest, women generally test positive for at least one drug (McMahon, 2000).

▶ Twenty-five percent of women report having committed their crimes to obtain money for drugs, compared to 16 percent of men who make such a claim (Snell, 1994).

▶ Prostitution is a common form of crime committed by women to obtain drug money (Grella, Scott, Foss, Joshi, & Hser, 2003).

GENDER DIFFERENCES IN SUBSTANCE USE

Although different patterns of AOD abuse between men and women have been recognized for quite some time (e.g., Horn & Wanberg, 1973; Wanberg & Horn, 1970; Wanberg & Knapp, 1969) only recently have these issues gained consideration in treatment (Becker & Gatz, 2005). It has widely been reported that drinking in women is far less common than in men. Yet a longitudinal study of alcohol abuse in the general population found that although women scored lower than men on physiological symptoms and binge drinking in the late 1960s, these differences had virtually disappeared a decade later (Horn & Wanberg, 1973). Moreover, women constituted as many as 50 percent of those in treatment, up from 15 percent in the 1960s sample (Horn, Wanberg, & Foster, 1987). Today, at-risk drinking found in primary care settings for men and women is probably about equal (Lewis, 1997), despite the fact that physicians are more likely to look for, notice, and advise treatment for substance abuse problems in men. For women, referral for substance abuse remains low (Wilsnack, 1995).

There are noticeable gender differences in the symptom pattern of addictive disorders: some report that women are less likely to be problem drinkers than are men across all ethnic groups, and when they do drink they tend to drink less (Markarian & Franklin, 1998). Although ethnic groups are similar in this male/female differential, Caucasian women are more likely, and black women are less likely, to use alcohol, with Hispanic women intermediate between the two (Markarian & Franklin, 1998). Additionally, African American women begin drinking later than Caucasian women, and the drinking process proceeds more rapidly than it does in Caucasian females (Johnson, Richter, Kleber, McLellan, & Carise, 2005). Although women enter treatment at about the same age as males, with about the same degree of alcohol dependence, they begin heavy drinking at a later age and their age of first drunk is significantly later than men's (Gomberg, 1986; Schmidt, Klee, & Ames, 1990; Wanberg & Horn, 1970; Wanberg & Knapp, 1969). Women are also more likely than men to suffer physical symptoms from drinking (Nolen-Hoeksema, 2004). This suggests a more rapid development of alcohol dependence in women (Smith & Cloninger, 1981). While alcoholic women may drink less than their male counterparts, they are more likely to use other sedative drugs in tandem with alcohol. Several studies suggest that there are three distinct patterns of substance use that differentiate men from women:

1. Women tend to fit the solo, isolative pattern of use more than do men (Gomberg, 1986; Horn & Wanberg, 1973; Horn et al., 1987; Schmidt et al., 1990). However, this difference has clearly attenuated over the past 20 years, and the prevalence of gregarious, convivial drinking is a common pattern now found among women.

2. Women tend to use alcohol and other drugs (AOD) *to manage moods and psychological distress* more than men do, and they score higher on emotional and psychological disruption from AOD use (Blume, 1991; Horn & Wanberg, 1973; Horn et al., 1987; Wanberg, 2008). This same finding was found among adolescent females with AOD problems. Girls scored significantly higher on the psychological problems scale than boys (Wanberg, 1992a, 1992b).

3. Women tend to indicate less social role disruption due to AOD use. For example, women score lower than men on the Alcohol Use Inventory—Social Role Maladaptation Scale. This is certainly

congruent with fewer women in the criminal justice system (Wanberg, 2008).

In addition, with more women now entering treatment facilities for AOD abuse, standard instruments for risk assessment such as the Statistical Information on Recidivism Scale (SIR) (Nuffield, 1989) seem unable to predict patterns of recidivism for women as reliably as they do for men (Bonta & Hanson, 1994). Thus, it appears that different factors may predict recidivism among men than among women. A study of females who were incarcerated in 1997 found that 55.7 percent had alcohol abuse issues, 84 percent had drug abuse issues, and 53.1 percent of their crimes was due to AOD influence (Curry, 2001).

Wanberg's 2008 study of 20,612 male offenders and 6,097 female offenders utilizing the Adult Substance Use Survey-Revised (ASUS-R) provides strong empirical support for gender-focused approaches to treatment and rehabilitation.

PSYCHOSOCIAL ISSUES AND SUBSTANCE ABUSE IN WOMEN

Psychosocial factors play an especially important role in the development of addictive disorders among women (Blume, 1998) and are important predictors of the extent of substance use. Grella et al. (2003) found substance-abusing females had higher rates of posttraumatic stress disorder than did substance-abusing males. In a longitudinal study by Timco, Finney, and Moos (2005), women initially scored higher then men in psychosocial stressors while having fewer family resources.

Gender norms, which exert a strong impact on a woman's sense of self, elucidate the development of the automatic thoughts that may serve as triggers and expectancies for AOD use among women. Palacios, Urmann, Newel, and Hamilton (1999) found that specific problems and motivations associated with addictive disorders are reflective of the differences in social demands placed upon them. These differences appear in both self-report and clinical observation. Women are less frequent to report "acting out" or "feeling out of control" when under the influence (Ames, Schmidt, Klee, & Saltz, 1996).

Women are less likely than men to use drugs with a thrill-seeking motivation but are more likely to use them to deal with emotional pain and distress. In a long-term follow-up study of college drinking, risk factors for problem drinking were different for women than for men. In stating their reasons for substance use, women tended to focus on relief from shyness, getting along better with others, and feeling happy (Covington, 2000). Pelissier and Jones (2006) found that women are more likely to engage in substance abuse in relation to a lower sense of self-efficacy than men.

These motivational differences suggest that women may be at greater risk for the psychological aspects of substance abuse than are men, especially with regard to interpersonal relationships (Blume, 1998). In fact, among women, abuse-related consequences tend to be psychological (feelings of guilt, shame, depression, and low self-esteem) and interpersonal (social isolation) (Wanberg, 2008). In both cases, these consequences are generally more severe for women than for men (Makarian & Franklin, 1998). Pelissier and Jones (2006) hypothesized that women becoming involved in drugs more rapidly than men may explain lower levels of self-confidence, which perpetuates the cycle of addiction. El-Bassel, Gilbert, Schilling, Ivanoff, Borne, and Safyer (1996) found that female drug users who reported poor coping skills were more likely to use crack cocaine than any other drug. Women who perceived themselves as lacking social support were also more likely to be crack users. Table 2.1 presents psychosocial issues that are commonly observed among female substance abusers.

Substance Abuse and Cognition in Women

Wanberg and Milkman (1998, 2008) examined cognitive processes as major players in the development and maintenance of AOD use and criminal conduct in both men and women. The methods of cognitive-behavioral treatment can be improved when they are placed within contexts and procedures that are relevant to women's experiences. Automatic thoughts often precede cravings and urges and act as triggers for use. Self-reported motivations associated with addictive disorders tend to differ for women and men (Covington, 1998b). The motivating factors for

Table 2.1

Psychosocial Issues and Substance Abuse in Women Compared to Men		
	Women	**Men**
Characteristics		
Self-esteem	Lower	Low
Motivating Factors		
Thrill seeking	Less common	More common
Dealing with emotional pain and distress	More common	Less common
Relief from shyness	More common	Less common
Improved performance in relationships	More common	Less common
Consequences		
Relationship problems	More common	Less common
Report guilt and shame, low self-esteem	More common	Less common
"Act out"; feel "out of control"	Less common	More common

Sources: Ames, Schmidt, Klee, and Saltz (1996); Blume (1998); Covington (2000); Makarian and Franklin (1998).

AOD use cited by women offer significant insight into triggers and their accompanying AOD expectancies. Table 2.2 summarizes elements of cognition associated with high levels of substance abuse among female criminal justice clients.

Women frequently incorporate the previously noted motivating factors as rationalizations for substance abuse. Ironically, women who use substances are actually at greater risk of developing psychological and social difficulties than are men and other women, especially with regard to interpersonal relationships (Horn et al., 1990; Wanberg, 2008; Wanberg & Knapp, 1969). Education in treatment settings that provides a more realistic portrayal of the consequences of substance use may help women to alter their distorted beliefs and expectancies, increasing resistance to cravings and urges and thereby decreasing the likelihood of relapse.

Table 2.2

Cognitive Elements Associated With Female Substance Abuse	
• *Relationship issues*	They anticipate that AOD use will relieve shyness, make it easier for them to perform on dates, and improve their sexual function
• *Social issues*	They perceive that AOD use will allow them to mix socially
• *Psychological issues*	The need to numb feelings associated with self-blame and low self-esteem or to "deal with" anger, expecting that AOD use will relieve depression and make them feel more "happy"
• *Trauma-related issues*	The need for escape, especially from the pain of psychological and physical trauma; crime victims with posttraumatic stress disorder are especially likely to report alcohol abuse and dependency
• *Skills deficits*	Women judicial clients report poor coping skills, believing there are no alternatives to AOD use

PATTERNS AND TRENDS IN WOMEN'S LIVES

Relational Orientation

Socialization experiences of girls and women stress the value of communality and connection in relationships (Bylington, 1997; Covington & Surrey, 1997; Miller & Stiver, 1997). Interpersonal interaction is often at the center of a woman's sense of self as well as her life decisions (Covington, 2000; Finkelstein, Kennedy, Thomas, & Kearns, 1997; Palacios et al., 1999).

Theoretically, girls perceive themselves to be more similar than different to their earliest maternal caretakers, so they do not have to differentiate from their mothers in order to continue to develop their identities. This is in contrast to boys, who must develop an identity that is different from the mother's in order to continue their development.... Consequently, defining themselves as similar to others through relationships is fundamental to women's identities. (Bylington, 1997, p. 35)

Psychological growth in females, therefore, requires an extension of relationships. Miller and Stiver (1997) call this general orientation toward connection with others a "relational orientation" and explain how it underlies and elucidates much of women's behavior in general, including that of female substance-abusing offenders.

Relationality is an important strength in women, one that may be built upon in treatment with a female client to bring mutuality, empathy, and a growth-fostering support system into her life as well as helping motivate her to maintain recovery. As Covington (1998a) asserts, psychological problems among women can be traced to disconnections or violations within relationships. A "depressive spiral" or disconnection may result, according to Miller (1990). This is characterized by low self-worth, confusion, and a gradual turning away from relationships. Each of these factors may cause a woman to withdraw from healthy options in her life and toward solace in the use of substances to self-medicate or escape.

Some women perceive substance use as a way to make and keep relationships with other people. Most women offenders are introduced to drugs and crime through boyfriends (Blume, 1998; Pollock, 1998) or male relatives (Markarian & Franklin, 1998). Relationality may cause a woman to follow a man's lead about friends and appropriate behavior as well as whether and how much to drink or use drugs. Relationality may also be manifested in choices that keep a woman in abusive and dangerous relationships with men (the "Stand by your man" ethic). The thought processes that underlie women's trust in these relationships, and their expectancies for love within them, are clear targets for change in treatment. Coll, Miller, Fields, and Mathews (1997) assert that women may be more easily influenced than men, especially when they perceive others as supportive. They found that women are more apt to attribute their failures to their own uselessness, thus hampering their ability to recognize the destructive effects of significant others. A possible explanation is that women have a tendency toward a lesser sense of self-control than men (Ross & Mirowsky, 2002), which becomes more pronounced with age. This may lead a woman to attribute negative situational outcomes to herself; that is, whatever happened must somehow have been her fault.

Covington proposes that addiction in women can itself be considered a type of relationship "characterized by obsession, compulsion, non-mutuality, and an imbalance of power. It is a kind of love relationship in which the object of addiction becomes the focus of a woman's life" (Covington & Surrey, 1997, p. 338). The same level of focus that a woman would normally give to relationships with others is now given to the substance. Addiction becomes more severe when a woman begins to replace interpersonal relationships with a relationship to her substance of choice (Covington, 1998a, b). Addiction becomes the "organizing principle" of her life and activity (Covington, 1998a, b). Covington notes the frequent use of "relational imagery" in women's discussions of their substance use, speaking of "passionate affairs" with their substance(s) of choice. In this context, women's comments such as "Alcohol was my friend and then it betrayed me" and "Drugs were the only ones who soothed me" become understandable. This personalizing of the relationship with substance may provide a powerful cognitive mechanism that may underlie the onset, and sometimes maintenance, of substance abuse and dependency by women.

Caretaking at the Expense of Self-Care

Other cognitive factors that place women at risk for substance abuse and criminal conduct can also be traced to general patterns in women's lives. As a direct consequence of the demands of relationality, the major focus of female socialization is on caretaking. Many women have learned that taking care of others supersedes and replaces the need to take care of self. This neglect of self-care in favor of the needs of others is at the root of much substance abuse in women and has been defined as "a chronic neglect of self in favor of something or someone else" (Covington, 1998a). In fact, many women do not recognize that they have a *right* to care for themselves, and acts of self-care may take on self-blaming associations for being "selfish."

The adaptation of negative personal roles by a female can lead to depression, making it harder for a woman to recover (Stenius, Veysey, Hamilton, & Anderson, 2005). Experiences with violent trauma may undermine a developing woman's sense of self and thereby contribute to a neglect of self-care. Sexual assault in particular (and especially at an early age) that satisfies the desires of another person more powerful than she is while totally defeating her own desires may have this effect. These experiences may teach her to view her body as a vehicle for the satisfaction of others (Butler, 1978; Herman, 1992). Therefore, recovery for many women may also involve the primary need for a safe environment, one that allows her to feel unthreatened from without but also allows her to learn self-soothing techniques that will increase her sense of safety within the integrity of her own body (Covington, 1998b).

Trauma

Women in the general population are many times more likely to experience sexual or physical abuse than are men (Bachman & Saltzman, 1995; Covington, 2000). Sexual and/or physical abuse appears far more frequently in the life history of female offenders than among their male counterparts (Blume, 1998; Chesney-Lind, 2000). Research has found that rates of experience with physical or sexual assault among women offenders in prison are four times the rates found in their male counterparts (Chesney-Lind, 2000). Increased risk for violent assault has also been found among female substance users (Covington, 2000; Markarian & Franklin, 1998). Demaris and Kaukinen (2005) found assault victims to engage more often in binge drinking than non-assault victims. Women who report such experiences are four times as likely to report serious alcohol-related problems (Wilsnack, 1995). A study of female offenders who use crack cocaine also found an increased risk of violence. According to Falck, Wang, Carlson, and Siegal (2001), 83 percent of the women who reported rape were high on crack cocaine when the attack occurred. Thus, a self-perpetuating pattern of victimization and substance dependence may develop a trauma-related onset of substance abuse, placing woman at increased risk for further trauma. Treatment programs need to consider these high levels of victimization encountered by drug-addicted women who become embroiled in

criminal justice processing (Falck et al., 2001). Chapter 5 of this *Adjunct Provider's Guide* presents a comprehensive summary of the effects of trauma on women and some promising strategies for treatment. Chapter 8 contains a section on providing support to counselors who may experience vicarious trauma associated with identifying with their clients.

The Effects of Disconnection in Women

Female judicial clients frequently live lives characterized by abuse, disconnection, and isolation. By virtue of their substance abuse and criminal activity, these women often become separated from children, family, and friends who live within law-abiding and conventional frameworks. Table 2.3 shows some psychosocial consequences that can ensue from disconnection.

Economic Issues

Economic issues are also very different for women and men. Most men are not dependent on women for economic support, yet it is a common experience for a woman to be dependent upon a man. Women who enter the workplace face many sources of discrimination. They generally occupy lower-paying and unskilled positions, often in service-oriented and child-oriented arenas (Covington, 2001; Pollock, 1998; Reed & Leavitt, 2000). Along with increasing work responsibilities come greater performance expectations. Pay is often not commensurate with job duties. Failure to reach external and self-defined criteria for success can lead to a lower sense of self-worth becoming manifested as anger and aggression (Palermo, 2003). Although poverty affects many male criminal justice clients, underemployment or unemployment disproportionately affects women. Women are also more likely than men to cite transportation to and from work, need for child care, and other demands for caretaking at home as major obstacles to their ability to obtain gainful access to the work environment (McMahon, 2000).

STIGMAS AND STEREOTYPES OF WOMEN AND SUBSTANCE ABUSE

Social norms regulating substance use by women date back to the earliest stages of human history.

Table 2.3

Psychosocial Consequences of Disconnection Among Women Judicial Clients	
Psychological Isolation	She may question her own needs, feelings, and thoughts due to lack of validation from a healthy support system. She may become dependent on the definition supplied to her by an abusive partner or other prominent person (usually male) in her life. This may undermine her sense of autonomy as well as her ability to resist the demands of someone who encourages her to use substances or who goads her into criminal activity for their own gain.
"Condemned Isolation" (Miller, 1990)	She may feel that she is the problem and that her isolation is punishment for her faults ("I'm bad"). Self-blame such as this is strongly associated with substance abuse.
Lack Empathy for Self	This is reflected in her diminished ability for self-care through constructive avenues.
Lack Empathy for Others	This may manifest in theft, robbery, and other types of criminal behavior.
Shame (Jordan, 1991)	She may take responsibility for the problems in her relationships, believing that "something is wrong" with her, and subsequently focus energy on changing herself to be more pleasing to others. The problem arises when these attempts lead her into substance abuse and criminal behavior in order to meet the demands of destructive relationships with others who fail to have her interests in mind.
Depression	All of the above may contribute to the "depressive spiral" (Miller, 1990) described earlier and to withdrawal from other healthy outlets in life.

Blume (1998) notes that laws differentially regulating substance use based on sex are found in the Code of Hammurabi around 2000 B.C. In ancient Rome, alcohol use by women was severely sanctioned: the Law of Romulus permitted a sentence of death for women found drinking (Wilsnack, 1995). Wilsnack attributes this to deep-seated fears that substance use by women would render them unable to perform as wives and mothers, and that uncontrolled sex by women would destabilize the male-dominated balance of power. Despite these long-standing attitudes toward women and substance use, the modern advertising industry has targeted women as a growth market; marketing schemes link alcohol and cigarettes with images of youth, sensuality, charm, and overall success. Cigarette advertisements express "slimness and liberation." These marketing campaigns may make engaging in these behaviors more acceptable to girls and women (Wilsnack, 1995).

Attitudes and stereotypes regarding women and the use of substances involve a double standard. Drinking behavior that is acceptable, even expected, in men appears to many as reprehensible in women (Covington, 1999). While these social attitudes may serve as protective factors for some, the powerful stigma that associates substance use with promiscuity and moral ruin generates psychological trauma for women who use substances.

Markarian and Franklin (1998) discuss the "stereotypical association of sexual promiscuity that is attached to addicted women" (p. 400). Such stereotypes make women appear more acceptable as targets for sexual aggression. Dovetailing with the stereotype that drinking activates the female libido is the belief that when a (drinking) woman says "No," she really means "Yes" (Blume, 1998). Even the substance-abusing woman herself may have come to believe this. According to Smith, Davis, and Fricker-Elhai (2004), trauma victims reported a sense of greater benefit and lower risk associated with marginal behavior such as drug use and risky sexual activity. Rapists frequently give "the woman's drinking" as justification for assault, especially for date rape. Research that investigated perceptions of rape among the general population found that young adults attributed less responsibility to an intoxicated rapist, while they gave more responsibility to an intoxicated victim (Blume, 1998). Rates of violent assault—especially rates of rape and domestic violence—climb higher when a woman is using alcohol or other drugs (Miller & Downs, 1986). A woman who drinks in a bar experiences greater risk of becoming a victim of crime than a man who drinks in bars or a woman who is not drinking (Miller & Downs, 1986). There is clearly a link between the stigma accompanying female substance use and an increased probability of victimization.

Women's Response to Stigmas and Stereotypes

How do individual women respond to the social norms and substance use regarding women just discussed? One significant response is that women feel shame and guilt, often because they internalize the fears of society that substance use by women will render them unable to perform properly as wives and especially as mothers (Covington, 1998a). Research has documented these responses among women judicial clients, particularly when substance abuse is combined with incarceration and women are forced to be away from their children for long periods of time (Phillips & Harm, 1997).

Defensiveness, traditionally referred to as "denial" (unwillingness to recognize or admit AOD-related problems) is another consequence of these social norms and stigmas (Blume, 1998; Wilsnack, 1995). Because the idea of women using substances has such a negative connotation, others who are significant in the woman's life often minimize the signs of her substance abuse and may actually discourage her from seeking treatment (Kerr, 1998; Wilsnack, 1995). Women are generally identified at a later stage in their substance abuse when entering treatment than are men (Blume, 1998). Guilt, shame, and the fear that family members might recognize their substance-related problems make women more likely to sneak and engage in substance use alone (Covington, 1998a). This explains much of the often noted "invisibility" of women's drinking. These negative feelings also cause women to present to physicians with issues of depression and anxiety. This frequently results in prescriptions for medication, adding to the high rate of multiple-use dependence in women (Kassebaum & Chandler, 1994; Kerr, 1998). Late recognition of substance abuse problems leads to more severe health consequences as well as higher risks for HIV and unwanted pregnancy (Blume, 1998). The mental and physical consequences of substance abuse in women are discussed comprehensively in Chapter 3.

Another response to the stereotypes regarding the "uncontrollable" nature (including promiscuity) of a woman's behavior when she steps outside of conventional norms (the "fallen woman") is to abandon these norms altogether. This attempt at self-assertion, however, often draws her into contact with people and situations in which substance abuse and criminal conduct are likely to occur. For instance, adolescent girls may start to hang out with older males who are more likely than the girls' same-age peers to bring them into contact with drugs and alcohol (Acoca, 1998b). Cognitive-behavioral treatment is of key importance in helping a woman see more productive avenues of self-assertion and in developing positive expectancies regarding these behaviors and situations.

The belief that drinking activates the female libido and thus enhances sexual experience is widely accepted among female offenders (Blume, 1991). This is in direct contradiction to the actual effects of substance abuse on female sexual functioning, which include the reduction in libido and orgasmic function. Education regarding sex and other health issues associated with AOD use in women may help a woman offender to make decisions more in keeping with her own goals and needs.

THE INTERACTION OF WOMEN'S SOCIAL ROLES AND RELATIONSHIPS

Age, Marital Status, and Alcohol and Other Drug Use Among Women

According to Ostermann, Sloan, and Taylor (2005), it is the *discrepancy in alcohol consumption* between partners that leads to divorce rather than the amount of alcohol consumed. However, women with alcohol problems experience a greater probability of divorce than do men with alcohol problems. More women than men who enter therapy are divorced. Alcoholic women who are married are more likely to have an alcoholic spouse than their male counterparts. Within the marriages of alcoholic women, there is an increased probability of marital discord, and they receive less help with child care from their spouses (Brown, Kokin, Seraganian, & Shields, 1995). Women who were single or never married were 8.3 times more likely to be regular users of crack cocaine than were women in other relationship configurations. This type of social isolation, often found among crack users, may be attributed to a difficulty in forming and sustaining relationships due to the habits of lying and theft that often accompany the use of crack cocaine (El-Bassel et al., 1996).

In research designed to identify risk factors for substance abuse in women, Blume (1998) found a relationship between marital status and age. Blume's study found a complex association between high risk for AOD abuse in women and marital status. Table 2.4 summarizes the interaction of age and marital status as associated with a high risk for substance abuse. For example, women ages 21 to 34 who had never been married, were unemployed, and had no children were at higher risk for substance abuse.

Thus, being *without a prominent role,* having *lost a significant role,* and being *trapped within a role* are all positively correlated with increased risk of substance abuse in women, depending on age (Blume, 1998). Clearly, there is important and ongoing interaction between women's social roles and age norms in our society. Unmarried but cohabiting women are also at increased risk for substance abuse (Blume, 1998). Proposed causes for this association include possible uncertainty in these women's lives, having no clear role definition for themselves in these situations, as well as possible tensions in a relationship that this uncertainty might perpetuate. On the other hand, women who enter cohabiting relationships may have some different characteristics from women who

do not and perhaps are less tied to social norms in general, including those norms that traditionally curtail drinking in women.

While divorce and separation are related to higher rates of substance abuse among women (as they are in men), this tendency has declined in recent years. Changes in gender norms (that is, destigmatization of divorce) may account for the fact that many women who participated in problem drinking within marriage experienced a *drop* in these problems upon divorce or separation. This finding is congruent with the findings of Zins, Guegen, Leclerc, and Goldberg (2003) that women drank more in the year before marriage and four years into the marriage. However, alcohol abuse was reported to subside in the year after a divorce. Contrary to general trends observed in the past, this relief from alcohol-related problems occurred most dramatically with women who had been married to a frequently drinking partner or when the relationship had been characterized by sexual difficulties (Blume, 1998; Wilsnack, 1995).

A relational orientation in women is also reflected in the observation that a spouse's drinking behavior is predictive of a woman's alcohol use. Close association between a husband and wife's drinking behavior has been observed, although it is difficult to sort out just how this mutual influence exerts itself. "It does seem clear that marriage affects how women drink, whether through modeling, social pressures, or changes in drinking opportunities" (Wilsnack, 1995, p. 405). Drinking-related problems may be exacerbated by an imbalance in drinking patterns within a relationship: heavy use by only one partner predicted a degree of marital discord. What's more, this imbalance in drinking behavior appears to predict heavier drinking and more alcohol-related problems in women (Wilsnack, 1995). Perhaps an imbalance in substance use by partners symbolizes more general incompatibilities between them.

Women are at greater risk for domestic violence and rape when they are involved with an AOD-abusing man. Their risk also increases when they themselves are users. Treatment programs are beginning to incorporate intimate partner violence treatment into substance abuse programs because the two are so commonly linked (Fals-Stewart & Kennedy, 2005).

Table 2.4	
Interaction of Age and Marital Status Associated With Higher Risk of Substance Abuse	
Age	**Marital Status**
21–34	Never married, childless, and unemployed (role-less)
35–49	Divorced or separated, children not living with them, unemployed (lost role)
50–64	Married, children not living with them, unemployed (role entrapment)
All ages	Unmarried but cohabiting with a partner

Source: Blume (1998).

Men perceive women who are drinking as more vulnerable to dominance; that is, when women step out of the prescribed norms for female behavior, they are perceived as more sexual and deviant. The effect is reciprocal, creating an increased risk of trauma and substance dependence. Women who report having experienced domestic violence or sexual assault are four times as likely to develop severe alcohol-related problems (Wilsnack, 1995).

Complex interactions between substance abuse and age have also been found. Higher rates of drinking-related problems are found among women in young adulthood. For women, alcohol consumption was found to increase throughout the early adult years and peak at the age of 21 (Casswell, Pledger, & Hooper, 2003). In keeping with a relational interpretation, frequency and quantity of use tended to fluctuate with the comings and goings of male partners, the behavior of peers, changes in places to "hang out," marital status, and other social events. Lifetime prevalence of drug dependence is higher among women in midlife, reflecting the higher occurrence of prescription drug dependence in women (Blume, 1998). In men, lifetime drug dependence is higher in adolescence and young adulthood, reflecting the strong influence of male peers at this time in their lives. Male peers often spend time on the streets, where access to drugs is more readily found. This underlies the observation that men are more likely than women to use "street drugs," while women are more likely to obtain drugs through medical channels (Bush-Baskette, 2000). All of these observations underscore the influence that gender norms exert on judicial client behavior and criminal conduct. Gender norms change with age and social role; patterns of AOD use can follow these changes.

In summary, shifts and perhaps uncertainty within role definitions across age and marital status may underlie some of the AOD-related problems that develop in women. An imbalance in substance use by partners contributes to increased risk for AOD abuse in women. Other configurations, such as having a substance-abusing or abusive spouse, also place women at greater risk. Clearly, there is important interaction among social roles, relationships, and substance abuse in women. Focus is drawn to the importance of understanding gender-specific

patterns of stress in order to provide enhanced treatment services.

Multiple Drug Use in Women

Research presented in the Introduction of this *Guide* across large samples shows that men and women do not differ with respect to general involvement in the use of multiple substances (Wanberg, 2008). One difference shown, however, is that women are more involved in the abuse of prescription tranquilizers. In addition, there is a high rate of multiple substance use among women in midlife stemming from the tendency for women to be prescribed medication when presenting to physicians with symptoms of depression and anxiety (Covington, 1998b). Women who abuse alcohol are more likely to engage in prescription polydrug use than are male substance abusers (Markarian & Franklin, 1998). Most of the amphetamines (80 percent) and antidepressants (71 percent) that women take are prescribed by doctors (Galbraith, 1991). Women are more likely than men to use drugs for self-medication (men cite thrill seeking and recreational pleasures more often) (e.g., Belknap, 1996). In particular, minorities such as African Americans may be at greater risk for self-medication, as they cite both negative life events and racism as reasons for substance abuse (Ehrmin, 2002).

Multiple drug patterns are very prevalent among female judicial clients. The multiple drug use patterns of women (60 percent of women prisoners were diagnosed with multiple substance abuse), when compared to male counterparts, are distinguished by widespread abuse of prescription drugs (Kassebaum & Chandler, 1994; Kerr, 1998). Male offenders are more involved in illicit multiple substance use, for example, marijuana, cocaine, alcohol (Wanberg, 1997, 2008).

The practice of self-medication reinforces tendencies among women to blame themselves and remain passive about sexual and physical abuse as well as about social inequities and injustices. As she internalizes these problems, a woman may become trapped within them and become hampered in understanding that she can alter her situation by empowering herself to make different choices about relationships, jobs, and housing. This requires developing a sense of empowerment (see Chapter 8, Gender-Specific Strategies and Models for Treatment).

The Social Support Network

Women who drink often experience isolation. Markarian and Franklin (1998) found that the following factors conspire to produce this outcome, especially within minority populations:

- Guilt, shame, and depression
- Negative views of women who drink
- Arguments from family
- Increased vulnerability to sex crimes when intoxicated
- High incidence of addictive disorders among family members

Boyd, Guthrie, Pohl, Whitmarsh, and Henderson (1994) found that 65 percent of women crack cocaine abusers had a substance-abusing parent, and sibling use and partner use were likely to be high; women experience more arguments from family and friends about their drinking than do men (Markarian & Franklin, 1998). In fact, women frequently enter therapy because of relationship and family issues. A major therapeutic goal is to help a woman develop a supportive network of friends and relatives to help her in recovery. The mothers of women offenders are often important figures in their recovery (Strauss & Falkin, 2001). Therefore, special attention to the role of surrogate mothers might enhance the development of social support networks for women (Markarian & Franklin, 1998). Surrogate motherhood could be fostered in the client-provider relationship as well as among the women themselves.

Women Judicial Clients Who Have Children

Sixty-seven to 80 percent of women judicial clients have children (Covington, 2001); 70 percent of these children are under the age of 18 (Bush-Baskette, 2000). Most of these women are the sole support of these children at the time of incarceration. While 65 percent of male offenders also have children, less than 50 percent of these men had primary responsibility for their care at the time of incarceration; most children of male offenders are cared for by the children's mother while the fathers serve out their sentences (Bush-Baskette, 2000). This is a rare situation in the lives of female offenders. Children of incarcerated female offenders are generally cared for by their grandmothers or other relatives, are in foster care, or have been placed under the care of the state.

Women offenders suffer an added burden of emotional difficulty in these situations. Incarcerated women were found to experience more depression when less contact was made with their children as compared to incarcerated women who had more contact (Poehlmann, 2005). Initial trauma due to separation from children when the female was sentenced to prison was found to be an additional cause of distress for the incarcerated mother. Deep shame for being a "bad mother" haunts them, as they worry about their inability to be present while their children are growing up and feel guilt for having imposed this burden on their children (Phillips & Harm, 1997).

Child care is frequently cited as a barrier to obtaining substance abuse treatment for women who have primary responsibility for their children (Markarian & Franklin, 1998). The isolation associated with substance abuse renders women with children bereft of opportunities to either seek or attend treatment services. This perpetuates involvement in substance abuse, which increases the likelihood for criminal conduct in women in order to provide for their families while satisfying their substance-related needs.

A significant consequence of substance abuse in women is losing custody of a child. Losing a child is especially likely among female crack users. El-Bassel et al. (1996) used interviews to examine the relationship between the psychological trauma of losing a child and crack cocaine abuse among incarcerated women. They found that losing custody of a child (found in 58 percent of crack users compared with 20.5 percent of other drug users) was associated with increased crack use among drug-addicted women offenders. Specifically, women who lost custody of their youngest child were 3.2 times more likely to be classified as regular crack users than other drug-addicted women.

Substance Abuse and Pregnancy

Twenty-five percent of female judicial clients are either pregnant or in the first months following birth. They are generally in a poor state of health and have received inadequate or no prenatal care (McMahon, 2000). In a national analysis across all 50 states, the percentage of women of childbearing age who drink is approximately 50 percent, with an estimated 13 percent who binge drink (Tsai, Floyd, & Bertrand, 2007). Among pregnant women aged 15 to 44 years, 3.9 percent reported using illicit drugs in the past month based on combined 2004 and 2005 National Survey on Drug Use and Health (NSDUH) data. This rate was significantly lower than the rate among women aged 15 to 44 who were not pregnant (9.9 percent). The 2002–2003 combined rate of current illicit drug use among pregnant women (4.3 percent) was not significantly different from the 2004–2005 combined rates (Substance Abuse and Mental Health Administration, 2006).

As a result of the "war on drugs," there has been a recent trend toward prosecution of pregnant women for "prenatal child abuse." Assessment of these practices, however, reveal that they are *more likely to deter a pregnant substance user from seeking treatment*, including prenatal services, than they are to deter drug use (Blume, 1998).

GENDER NORMS AND SENSE OF SELF

An important source of maladaptive cognition in women may be found in gender norms. A woman's belief system regarding "what it means to be a woman" (that is, to suffer and to support husband and family at all costs) generally guides her perception of herself, her relationships, and her world (Bem & Bem, 1971). Combining personal life experiences with the sociocultural myths and scripts underlying gender norms, she creates a narrative for understanding her life (McQuaide & Ehrenreich, 1998). Gendered perceptions interact with her sense of herself in relation to her age, race, social class, and ethnic identity to produce her own particular narrative. This narrative delineates reasons and justifications for her behavior. How well a woman can adjust to prison or participation in community corrections, how much she dedicates herself to treatment programming, how she will anticipate discharge, and how able she will be to manage recovery and resist relapse and recidivism are all determined, in part, by the cognitive evolution of this narrative (McQuaide & Ehrenreich, 1998). Development of and growth within this narrative, therefore, is an integral part of the recovery process while she is involved with the correctional setting. Validating the notion that cognitive evolution is key to recovery, Messina, Burdon, Hagopian, and Prendergast (2006) found that psychological impairment was the strongest predictor of recidivism among offending women.

At the same time that we acknowledge the almost universal effect of gender norms in women's lives, we must maintain an emphasis on the personal and individual. To say that all women are affected by gender norms does not imply that women are all affected to the same degree or in the same ways. Correctional personnel should "avoid the search for a unified and coherent self or voice" (Stewart, 1994, p. 29) to represent that of female offenders in general. The multifaceted nature of personality and the well-documented fact that different situations bring out different behaviors, personas, or voices from people make it imperative that we allow each woman to speak for herself in revealing how gender norms have affected her. McQuaide and Ehrenreich (1998) advocate using a qualitative approach to listen to women's voices and hear the stories that they tell.

By listening to a woman recount her experiences and current situation, by hearing the words that she uses and attending to the ways that she uses them, we can detect how a woman perceives the context and meaning of her crimes. In these ways, we can discern the underlying patterns of cognition that ultimately produce her AOD expectancies, her more general control expectancies, and her justifications for her criminal activity. We can also identify the triggers that activate these cognitions. As a woman speaks, she tells stories of survival. These stories reveal the strengths and personal qualities that have allowed her to survive (McQuaide & Ehrenreich, 1998). Resiliency factors and coping mechanisms are also deeply embedded within the cognitive scripts involved in her narrative. Finally, it is important to remember that a woman in prison is able to express only a part of her being. "To see her only as a prisoner is to falsify her and reduce her to her current social status" (McQuaide & Ehrenreich, 1998, p. 243). Each of these elements is essential when developing a suitable individualized treatment plan for a woman offender.

This "listening" to the accounts of women offenders is just as important in the treatment of male judicial clients. The process is the same, though the story will be different.

The Relational Self

A significant gender effect is observed in the development of a relational orientation among girls at an early age (Covington & Surrey, 1997). Boys and girls, as well as men and women, often vary with regard to the centrality of relationships, communication, and intimacy in their lives. Centrality of intimacy and harmony in relationships are often found at the root of a woman's sense of self (Kassebaum, 1999). A woman may judge herself using the criteria of how well she lives up to standards for female conduct, including her beauty and attractiveness, her ability to give of herself selflessly to others, her ability to be a good mother, and so on. Self-chastisement can be harsh; she may berate herself for failing (especially since it is impossible for any woman to comply with all of these demands), and this diminishment complicates self-esteem issues that may already be operating. This may lead women to make self-destructive choices in an attempt to satisfy the demands of these norms. Table 2.5 summarizes some destructive choices made by women judicial clients in the service of establishing or maintaining a supportive relationship and in attempting to live up to normative expectations of women.

Scholars who study women's issues strongly assert that in treatment, a woman must come to recognize the patterns and trends that characterize women's lives in general (Covington, 2001; Covington & Surrey, 1997; Kassebaum, 1999). They must be helped to identify the social and economic roots of many of their problems, perceiving the norms and biases that underlie them. Being ready for treatment in addition to being motivated is a key component to a female's ability to achieve success (Longshore & Teruya, 2006). By placing their problems in this

Table 2.5

Unhealthy Relationship Choices Made by Female Judicial Clients

- *Staying in an abusive relationship* in an attempt to live up to the vows and promises she has made. These choices are supported by a culture that asks her to "work harder," "try to help him," "love him better" and accuses her, "You made your bed hard, now you sleep in it."

- *Hanging out in bars and trusting men to be drinking cronies,* often without evaluating the increased risks of assault that these choices may bring. Women are especially at risk when they perceive others to be supportive.

- *Following a male partner's lead regarding substance use behavior.* Research has found a pattern of influence between male and female partners' AOD behavior and criminal conduct. Women are usually introduced to substances, and to crime, through a boyfriend or other male.

- *Following a man's lead in choice of friends and recreational activities,* which often exposes her to increased opportunity for drug and alcohol use.

- *Expecting love from a man, in return for her love,* without insight into the engrained social patterns of dominance and submission that frequently accompany male-female relationships.

- *Placing all of the responsibility for her problems on herself and her personal situation* makes her unable to recognize the social influences that underlie these dynamics.

broader social context, they may begin to see other women as allies and role models and as support systems in helping to manage life more constructively. These features are a necessary component in a woman's growth toward empowerment and, in turn, success in treatment.

Self-Image Issues

Self image issues for women exert a major influence on cognition in general and addiction cycles in particular. The negative impact of stereotypes as well as dysfunctional life experiences frequently combine to produce feelings of worthlessness (Covington, 2000; Kassebaum, 1999). This generally stems from the internalization of negative stereotypes (Bem & Bem, 1971), which may manifest as:

) Low self-esteem (Wilke, 2001)

) Self-defeating attributional patterns (Yarkin, Town, & Wallston, 1982)

) Poor body image and eating disorders (Pike & Striegel-Moore, 1997)

) Depression and the denial of anger (Oliver & Toner, 1990)

) High suicide risk (Blume, 1998)

Accompanying feelings of powerlessness may further fuel poor self-image. Criminal conduct may appear as a respite from some of these problems.

Self-Esteem

Low self-esteem and substance abuse appear to be reciprocal in effects and especially prominent among female substance abusers. Some suggest (for example, Covington, 1998a; Wilke, 2001) that our understanding of recovery in women must be reconstructed to include this important component of self-functioning. In this view, recovery is seen as occurring on at least two planes: (1) higher levels of self-esteem would be seen as equal in importance to resolution of substance abuse problems; (2) the roles that women consider superior to others are a source of self-esteem, a key component in a positive treatment outcome (Stenius et al., 2005). "Those who have higher levels of self-esteem but unresolved AOD problems and those with resolved AOD problems but lower self-esteem would both be defined as experiencing an incomplete recovery, with neither group being superior to the other" (Wilke, 2001, p. 495). This reconstruction would have important clinical implications: affirmation of a woman's choices and decisions about treatment goals would be essential to encourage her development of self as an agent of constructive action. The emerging self who is the initiator of this action would provide a significant step toward higher levels of self-worth and -respect (Wilke, 2001). Greater self-esteem is a source of confidence and is highly correlated with happiness (Stenius et al., 2005).

Self-Efficacy

How might a woman's sense of self, the demands of a relational orientation, and the various elements of poor self-image influence a woman's cognitive tendencies to produce substance abuse and criminal behavior? There are two pathways that should be noted: (1) self-efficacy and (2) locus of control. Unable to support herself and her children (and her AOD habit), and perceiving the workplace as a path leading to low wages and disrespect, a woman may find herself in a dysfunctional relationship of abuse and degradation. Bad relationships generally worsen her substance abuse habits and undermine her and her family's safety (and vice versa). Desperation to "get out" may lead to criminal conduct. Anticipation of economic relief can play a larger role in the motivation of women toward crime.

As she continues to engage in cycles of substance abuse and criminal conduct, the substance-abusing woman may eventually come into contact with the correctional system, where she faces a deepening severity of consequences. Because she harbors such low expectancies for success on her own, the conditions of financial and substance dependence may exert a powerful hold as she rationalizes staying in unhealthy relationships and considers recidivism. Treatment programs, therefore, should provide realistic training in job skills and placement, aimed toward helping her to increase self-efficacy and develop an internal locus of control.

Social Skills Deficits

Social skills deficits have been found in a wide range of content areas, including, but not limited to the following:

) Assertiveness skills

) Relationship expectancies, that is, recognizing patterns of dominance and submission

) Trigger identification for AOD use

) Coping skills

) Parenting skills

) Life management skills

Problems of self-efficacy, as well as each of the other areas listed, are explored in subsequent chapters.

PERSONAL RESPONSIBILITY AND THE SOCIOCENTRIC PERSPECTIVE

We have looked at how the role of women in our society, their exposure to abusive relationships, and the traumas resulting from those roles and relationships contribute to the development of substance abuse and criminal conduct. These roles and relationships have contributed to vulnerability and victimization. Certainly, effective intervention and treatment must consider these factors. Yet, treatment of female judicial clients has the primary purpose of focusing on the perpetration of criminal conduct resulting in individuals and society becoming the victims. Thus, treatment is correctional as well as therapeutic. Although the majority of women in criminal justice settings have suffered grave injustices, mostly at the hands of men and the greater society, this undeniable truth cannot in any way be construed as justification to inflict harm on innocent victims.

An important part of the treatment process is helping the client understand the cycle of victimization, in that being a victim often leads to the victimization of others. In the case of the offender, this takes the form of criminal behavior. Yet, even more important is helping the client to understand her role in being the perpetrator of victimization and in facilitating the knowledge, awareness, motivation, and skills to learn and practice morally responsible behavior in the community. This component of cognitive-behavioral treatment—the development of social and moral responsibility toward others and the community—is of equal importance to that of helping clients develop self-control through cognitive restructuring and control in relationships through interpersonal skill building. Thus, as mentioned in the Introduction to this *Guide*, social responsibility therapy (SRT) is an important component of the cognitive-behavioral treatment of the female judicial client.

IMPLICATIONS FOR TREATMENT AND POLICY: WHAT FACTORS REDUCE RECIDIVISM?

This chapter underscores the need for treatment programs for women that are gender focused and specific. A strong focus on psychoeducation (Covington, 1998b)—about the effects of substance abuse on women's bodies and psychology, about the effects of female socialization on development of a woman's psyche, about the high incidence of violent trauma in a woman's life and its aftermath—can go a long way toward helping a woman to develop the motivation for entering and maintaining herself in treatment (Covington, 1998b). Encouraging women to recognize the environmental context of their problems and to experience the full range of emotions that are stirred by realization of this context provide important pathways to healing in women (Marecek & Hare-Mustin, 1991).

Also important to successful treatment is a focus on the relational orientation (with partners, children, parents, friends, community) of many women criminal justice clients. The relational focus of treatment is a theme that runs throughout female-focused education, counseling, and psychotherapy and is addressed in Section III of this *Guide*, Gender-Specific Adaptations for Women). Prominent treatment issues concerning female relationships include:

▶ Addressing ways in which unhealthy relationships may undermine a woman's psychological stability and/or serve as triggers to subsequent substance abuse and criminal behavior

▶ Addressing ways in which a woman's relational orientation may serve as protective factors in relapse and recidivism prevention

▶ Address how healthy relationships may serve to raise self-esteem, which contributes to healing and recovery

▶ Finding ways in which healthy relationships may be solicited and organized into a support system to help a woman recover

In addition, cognitive-behavioral interventions must address strong thought habits that are barriers to change. Some common patterns of negative cognition include:

▶ A woman's belief that she is able to control her substance use must be replaced with the recognition that she has lost this control to the addictive process (Covington, 1998a).

▶ Although a woman may perceive that criminal conduct has given her more control in her life, treatment must help her to recognize that she has actually lost this control, both to addictive processes and to unhealthy relationships that challenge her ability to make decisions based on good sense and self-interest (Covington, 1998a).

▶ Recovery from substance abuse may involve an equally imperative need to break a woman's fixation on unhealthy relationships that undermine her abilities of self-care.

Recovery and the prevention of recidivism for a woman may involve both an extension of her life away from the use of substances, as well as an extension of her sense of self, into one that recognizes her rights to self-care and to healthy relationships that can provide her with care from others (Covington, 1998a). Facilitating an awareness among female judicial clients of how their criminal conduct has caused harm to others and to society are importance focuses of treatment for women in correctional settings; that is, effective treatment includes a strong emphasis on moral and community responsibility.

CHAPTER REVIEW

Chapter 2 has presented an overview of some general patterns related to substance abuse among women. Gender differences in substance abuse were explored, along with some general patterns and trends in women's lives that may underlie many of the cognitive processes related to female substance abuse. The chapter also identified specific patterns of thoughts, feelings, and actions that have bearing on the development of substance abuse and criminal conduct in female judicial clients. Analysis of these general patterns placed them into the context of women's social relationships as well as into social expectations for female behavior.

Psychological and correctional services for women require attention to the multiple ways in which the more general conditions of women's lives may contribute to a woman's substance abuse, mental health, and criminal behavior. Further, in the interest of supporting a woman's recovery once she has left the correctional setting, basic skills must be established to facilitate:

▶ Effective coping in demanding environments

▶ Building of healthy relationships

▶ Improvements in self-image

▶ Detection of the factors that make relationships unhealthy as well as the ways they may undermine a woman's recovery and resistance to recidivism

▶ Continued building of self-efficacy

▶ Vocational rehabilitation and job placement, to provide realistic assistance for her ability to earn a legitimate living on the outside

▶ Developing skills of moral responsibility in the community

CHAPTER 3: Mental and Physical Health Issues in Female Criminal Justice Clients

CHAPTER OUTLINE

OVERVIEW OF MENTAL HEALTH ISSUES IN FEMALE SUBSTANCE-ABUSING JUDICIAL CLIENTS

DUAL DIAGNOSIS IN WOMEN: COMMON PSYCHIATRIC DISORDERS FOUND AMONG WOMEN JUDICIAL CLIENTS

Depression and Other Mood Disorders

Personality Disorders

Psychotic Disorders

Anxiety Disorders

Suicide

WOMEN AND VIOLENT TRAUMA

Posttraumatic Stress Disorder

The Psychological Consequences of Violent Trauma: Behavioral Disturbances

THE SPECIFIC CAUSES OF VIOLENT TRAUMA

Childhood Sexual Abuse

Sexual Assault in Adulthood

Domestic Violence

Institutional Abuse

Trauma and Criminal Conduct in Women

MEDICAL CHALLENGES FOR WOMEN JUDICIAL CLIENTS

Health and Overcrowding

Hepatitis

HIV and AIDS

Cancer

Pregnancy

Fetal Alcohol Syndrome

Substance Abuse and Women's Health

ETHNIC CONSIDERATIONS IN HEALTH CARE

IMPLICATIONS FOR TREATMENT AND POLICY: WHAT FACTORS REDUCE RECIDIVISM?

CHAPTER REVIEW

LEARNING OBJECTIVES

▶ To investigate the range of psychological disorders that is found among women judicial clients

▶ To identify and explain the specific psychiatric diagnoses frequently found in women judicial clients

▶ To explore the range of violent experiences in the lives of girls and women that underlies posttraumatic stress disorder and other psychiatric symptomatology in women

▶ To identify specific correlates and consequences of these traumatic experiences

▶ To assess the impact of violent domination on adult manifestation of substance abuse and other psychiatric disorders

▶ To explore the relationship between these experiential and psychiatric factors and women's criminal behavior

---

This chapter was coauthored by Monica Zilberman, M.D., with editorial suggestions by Sheila Blume, M.D.

OVERVIEW OF MENTAL HEALTH ISSUES IN FEMALE SUBSTANCE-ABUSING JUDICIAL CLIENTS

As noted at several points in this text, the number of women in U.S. prisons has increased dramatically in the past 25 years. We have also observed a significant drop in their age of incarceration; approximately 30 percent of these females were imprisoned for drug-related crimes (Gunter, 2004). While some women in correctional facilities display few overt psychological symptoms, others have displayed a wide range of psychiatric symptoms and have been diagnosed with psychiatric disorders. It is estimated that more than 60 percent of incarcerated women might present a lifetime diagnosis of a psychiatric disorder (Haywood, Kravitz, Goldman, & Freeman, 2000). Forty-five percent present a current psychiatric diagnosis, and 40 percent of these inmates have substance-related disorders (Jordan, Schlenger, Fairbank, & Caddell, 1996). Unfortunately, only a small portion of those female detainees in need of psychiatric care receive treatment: approximately 24 percent in one survey (Teplin, Abram, & McClelland, 1996). While some researchers report lower or equal rates of mental illness in female versus male judicial clients (Watkins, Shaner, & Sullivan, 1999), others suggest that women judicial clients may more frequently present with psychological symptoms than do male judicial clients, and they more commonly receive a dual diagnosis (Veysey, DeCou, & Prescott, 1998). Substance use disorders are much more common in women judicial clients than in women in the general population (Bloom, Owen, Covington, & Raeder, 2003). The rate of dual diagnosis attributed to women in jails is as high as 60 percent (Acoca, 1998a), and the need for specific mental health services has been estimated at 45 percent for women judicial clients overall (Acoca & Austin, 1996). Markarian and Franklin (1998) report a similar tendency among alcohol-abusing female nonjudicial clients, who are more frequently diagnosed with depression and anxiety disorders than are alcohol-abusing male nonjudicial clients. Consistent with the statistics on trauma reported in Chapter 2, more than 50 percent of female substance abusers with severe mental illness report experiences of sexual assault before the age of 18, a significantly higher level than do men with substance abuse disorders or other women with severe mental illness but without concurrent substance abuse (Alexander, 1996).

Twelve percent of women judicial clients have been hospitalized for psychiatric treatment prior to incarceration, and 36 percent of incarcerated women have attempted suicide. Suicide attempts are much higher among substance-abusing women than among their non-abusing counterparts, and the rate of suicide death is 23 times the rate among non-substance-abusing women in the general population (Markarian & Franklin, 1998). Nevertheless, 31 percent of women taking medication for a mental health disorder remain without any supervision for their prescription drug intake while incarcerated (Acoca, 1998a).

"While researchers vary in their estimates of the rate of psychiatric disorders among women in jails and prisons, most agree that diagnostic and treatment services are generally inadequate and in some cases nonexistent for this population" (Acoca, 1998a, p. 57). Disturbing patterns appear, including lack of adequate procedures for screening mental health symptomatology in women; serious deficits in psychologist-to-inmate ratios (recorded at 1:2,900 inmates in 1993); limited availability of mental health staff, who are present on an irregular and sporadic basis; inadequate supervision of medication intake; and supervisory staff who are unable to distinguish behaviors associated with mental illness from those that involve deliberate disruption of prison procedures. This last factor has led to instances where inappropriate discipline, isolation, confinement, and other punitive consequences have been used in response to psychiatric symptoms (Acoca, 1998a). Women have thereby been denied adequate services to help them resolve their mental health issues, a factor of major importance in supporting recovery. Instead, they may be exposed to consequences that feel disturbingly similar to the environmental contexts that contributed to the development of their symptoms in the first place.

In general, higher rates of substance abuse and dependence have been found among the mentally ill, regardless of other demographic or population dynamics (RachBeisel, Scott, & Dixon, 1999). Reported incidence of substance abuse and/ or dependence stands at about 50 percent among people with severe psychiatric diagnosis, and progression of mental illness in these instances involves greater impairment in psychosocial abilities, less compliance with treatment, poorer prognosis, and more use of emergency services than among people with similar diagnosis but without substance abuse. Thus, inadequate attention to mental health symptoms in correctional facilities may actually contribute to relapse and recidivism, thereby slowing the processes of recovery that are necessary for an offender to resist reengagement in criminal offense. What's more, the continued use of emergency services comes at quite a cost to society.

Understanding the specific nature of psychiatric disorders in women judicial clients, the ways that psychiatric symptoms may differ in women as compared to men, and the etiology of their development in women can provide treatment providers with specific foci in individualized programming for the female dually diagnosed population. The more we understand about how these disorders manifest in women, about how they are produced, and the specific cognitions, emotions, or physiological processes that underlie them, the more prepared we are to provide treatment services that are directly related to these psychiatric targets.

DUAL DIAGNOSIS IN WOMEN: COMMON PSYCHIATRIC DISORDERS FOUND AMONG WOMEN JUDICIAL CLIENTS

Gender differences have been reported to occur in dually diagnosed populations of women and men. These differences are found with respect to specific disorders, the frequencies of these disorders presenting clinical symptomatology, and attitudes toward treatment within each gender (Watkins et al., 1999). The following sections of the chapter present differences in the kinds of diagnoses that female and male judicial clients generally receive.

Depression and Other Mood Disorders

Women are more likely to be diagnosed with chronic depression than are males (Acoca, 1998b; Covington, 1998a) and are more likely to be taking prescription medication for depression. Female judicial clients are more often diagnosed with depression than are

individuals of both genders in the general population (Gunter, 2004). Excluding substance-related disorders, major depression is the most frequent current psychiatric diagnosis among women in jail, from 5 percent (Baillargeon et al., 2003) to 11 percent (Jordan et al., 1996). Alcohol abuse or dependence co-occurred with major depression in 19 percent of women judicial clients, four times the rate in men and three times the rate in the general population of women (Covington, 2000). Women judicial clients also experience mood disorders and eating disorders more frequently than their male counterparts (Kerr, 1998). Both dysthimia and bipolar disorders are more often diagnosed among incarcerated women than among incarcerated men, respectively nearly two times and three times as frequently (Baillargeon et al., 2003). Interestingly, a gender difference that appears repeatedly among the general population does not show up in judicial clients. While women in general are more likely than men to seek medical care, this does not hold true for women in corrections with concurrent substance abuse and other psychiatric diagnosis (Watkins et al., 1999). Thus, these women often remain undiagnosed until a major event, for example, criminal arrest, brings them into contact with authorities.

Personality Disorders

Borderline personality disorder may be commonly misdiagnosed in women, as some of its symptoms mimic the effects of violent trauma (Root, 1992). Approximately one third of incarcerated women fulfill criteria for borderline personality disorder (Jordan et al., 1996).

Antisocial personality disorder (ASPD) is less common among female judicial clients than their male counterparts. Twelve percent of incarcerated women present a diagnosis of ASPD (Jordan et al., 1996). In another study, 10 percent of women with alcohol problems met criteria for this diagnosis (Blume, 1990; Covington, 2000). It is estimated that the rate of ASPD among female judicial clients can be as much as 12 times higher than the rate among women in general. A study of female opiate injectors found that 27 percent met the criteria for ASPD (Lightfoot, 1997). Early onset of alcohol abuse and related problems among women may be associated with impulsive behavior and antisocial personality disorder, as they are in men (Wilsnack, 1995).

Psychopathic symptoms are prevalent among 15.5 percent of the population of female judicial clients in a jail setting (versus 25–30 percent estimated for men) (Bartol, 2002). Other studies have found a rate of psychopathy at 12.9 percent of female inmates (Salekin, Rogers, Ustad, & Sewell, 1998). Research suggests that female psychopaths may exhibit different presenting behaviors than their male counterparts. They may be less violent than their male counterparts (Mulder, Wells, Joyce, & Bushnell, 1994) and may return to prison for recurrent crime less often than male psychopaths and nearer to the rate of incarcerated females without this diagnosis (Salekin, Rogers, & Sewell, 1997).

Bartol (2002) reports that psychopathy is frequently associated with alcohol and other drug abuse, as well as a history of sexual abuse in childhood, prostitution, and the likelihood of having been married to a psychopath or alcohol abuser or alcohol-dependent male. Bartol cautions, however, that past use of the label "psychopathy" with women may have reflected the broader societal bias against female sexuality and may "have been attached indiscriminately to women who were believed to engage inappropriately in sexual activity" (Bartol, 2002, p. 98). Separating out sexuality from other behavioral responses, Bartol found that female and male psychopaths have similar presenting dynamics. Two broad types have been described in women. The first is women who appear to experience no regret, empathy, or guilt, are frequently bored, and engage in lying and thrill-seeking behaviors. The second type, whose symptoms tend to appear earlier in life, engage in promiscuous sexual and antisocial (but not violent) behaviors (Bartol, 2002). No significant racial differences or trends were found among female psychopaths (Vitale, Smith, Brinkley, & Newman, 2002).

Psychotic Disorders

Gender differences have been found in the symptoms of schizophrenia as well (Franzek & Beckmann, 1992). For example, females tend to exhibit more affective symptoms and persecutory delusions, a more favorable profile in terms of course of illness, but increased side effects from antipsychotics. Among incarcerated women, prevalence rates of 0.7 percent for schizophrenia (1 percent for men), 0.9 percent for schizoaffective disorders (0.5 percent for men), and 0.5 percent for other psychotic disorders were found (0.6 percent for men) (Baillargeon et al., 2003).

Anxiety Disorders

Levels of anxiety disorders are also high in this population. Phobic disorders are found in 31 percent of women judicial clients (versus 15 percent of male judicial clients, and double that of women in general), and panic disorders are found in 7 percent of women judicial clients (versus 2 percent of men) (Covington, 1998b). Another study revealed lifetime prevalence rates of 2.7 percent for generalized anxiety disorder and of 5.8 percent for panic disorder among female judicial clients, whereas current diagnoses were estimated at 1.4 percent for generalized anxiety disorder and 5 percent for panic disorder (Jordan et al., 1996).

Suicide

Both the number and frequency of suicidal ideations and attempts are higher among women judicial clients. Due to higher rates of substance abuse or dependence and psychiatric comorbidity, young female judicial clients are significantly more likely to attempt and complete suicide than are young men (Dyer, 2003). Another study found that suicide rates in prison are at least similar between genders and proportional to the jail population (Way, Miraglia, Sawyer, Beer, & Eddy, 2005). This is surprising given that both in the general population and among nonincarcerated substance-abusing individuals, males more frequently complete suicide. It implies that incarcerated women need to be thoroughly assessed concerning suicidal ideation. Another difference is the method of choice for suicide. Both nonincarcerated substance-abusing women and women in the general population employ less lethal methods when attempting suicide (using medicines, for instance), whereas men usually attempt suicide through violent methods (guns, knives, and hanging). While in jail, there is no gender difference in the method of choice for a suicide attempt, hanging being the most common one for both genders (Gunter, 2004).

Table 3.1 presents a summary of some differences in common diagnoses among women versus men.

Table 3.1

Most Common Diagnoses in Male Versus Female Judicial Clients		
	Women	**Men**
Chronic depression	19%	5%
Suicidal ideation and attempts	More frequent	Less frequent
Eating disorders	More common	
Phobic disorders	31%	15%
Panic disorders	7%	2%
Antisocial personality disorder	10% + alcohol	27% + opiates
Psychopathy	9–15%	25–30%

Sources: Acoca (1998a); Bartol (2002); Covington (1998a, 1998b, 2000).

WOMEN AND VIOLENT TRAUMA

As discussed earlier, an issue that is central to understanding women's mental health is found in the high rates of victimization and violent trauma they have experienced. Although violent trauma occurs at quite high rates in the lives of girls and women in the general population (Crawford & Unger, 2000), the incidence of violent trauma among women judicial clients is much higher than in the general population of women. Women judicial clients are also more likely to have experienced violent trauma than their male counterparts, and dually diagnosed women experience higher levels still (Alexander, 1996). Ninety-seven percent of homeless, mentally ill women (who exhibit a rate of 50 percent for substance abuse or dependence) report at least one incident of physical or sexual assault in their lifetime (Goodman, Dutton, & Harris, 1995; Watkins et al., 1999).

These experiences place women at high risk for developing a wide range of psychological and social problems, including substance abuse or dependence and criminal behavior. Women who seek treatment for substance-related difficulties are more likely to be victims of violent assault than are women in general, and a strong correlation between assault experience (especially in childhood) and subsequent alcohol and other drug abuse has been found (Steele, 2000). Watkins et al. (1999) conclude that "victimization and violence are normative experiences for many dually-diagnosed women, while they are not normative experiences for dually-diagnosed men" (pp. 116–117).

Posttraumatic Stress Disorder

A frequent result of violent trauma, *posttraumatic stress disorder* (PTSD), is seen at a very high rate in women judicial clients. In one study, 33.5 percent of women judicial clients were diagnosed as having PTSD due to rape or other violent assault (GAINS Center, 1997; Teplin et al., 1996), and many service providers suggest that this figure is even higher when one considers the continuum of traumatic consequences. Women judicial clients experience higher rates of PTSD than their male counterparts; and substance-abusing women have higher rates of PTSD than women in the general population (Hidalgo & Davidson, 2000; Najavits, Weiss, & Shaw, 1997). A comprehensive review of PTSD in substance-abusing women judicial clients is the scope of Chapter 5.

The Psychological Consequences of Violent Trauma: Behavioral Disturbances

Trauma may manifest in several other ways when a female offender comes in contact with the criminal justice system. For example, a history of abuse may create increased sensitivity to situations involving the use of force or coercion (Veysey, DeCou, & Prescott, 1998). A woman offender may perceive the surroundings and routine of correctional settings as menacing and unsafe, as they may recapture the feelings of entrapment she may have experienced during her abuse. This pervasive perception of threat may trigger a wide range of responses, from withdrawal and fear to rage and violent outburst, and deterioration in mental health can be expected. A woman may act out against such experiences, through self-injury, attempts at suicide, or worsening substance abuse (Veysey et al., 1998). Clearly, such trauma-related feelings of peril experienced by women judicial clients can become major obstacles to effective treatment with this population. Veysey et al. assert, "Some, if not a majority, of the problems officers and administrators confront in supervising female inmates may be attributed to female detainees' perceptions of danger and their responses to that threat" (p. 51).

Veysey et al. (1998) go on to identify several specific factors that may exacerbate the problems of women with trauma-related issues. Any experience that rekindles memory of her abusive history has the potential to retraumatize such a woman. These trauma reminders bring her back into the frame of the abusive event and trigger equally intense emotions as during the actual experience. Among these trauma reminders, the authors name:

▶ Interacting with persons who remind them of the violent perpetrator, such as authority figures or men in general (also uniforms)

▶ Being physically restrained, kept in locked rooms or spaces

▶ Isolation

▶ Being unclothed, as during strip searches or medical exams

▶ Lack of privacy, as during psychiatric observation

▶ Loud noises

▶ Darkness

▶ Being without information regarding what will happen to them next

A provider's awareness of these issues, and anticipation of the events that may trigger them, may improve services across the entire treatment continuum. From arrest through intake, incarceration, and release, a service provider who provides support and understanding concerning these issues may reduce their impact and deter deterioration. Alternatives include supplying a woman with information so she can anticipate what her experiences might be, using female staff to perform strip searches and attend to a woman's health care needs, addressing child care concerns soon after arrest in order to communicate interest and concern for the woman offender's family, allowing her to ask for help or support, and providing supportive staff members to accompany her through difficult correctional procedures. These cost-effective and simple interventions can markedly reduce the fear, anger, and resentment that may underlie violent or irrational outbursts during correctional procedures (Veysey et al., 1998).

THE SPECIFIC CAUSES OF VIOLENT TRAUMA

Childhood Sexual Abuse

Childhood sexual abuse is commonly found among female substance abusers as well as among women with histories of concurrent or independent psychiatric symptomatology. A national survey of women's drinking habits in the United States investigated the lives of 1,099 women to examine patterns among childhood sexual abuse and other substance-related and psychological difficulties. This study found that women with a history of childhood sexual domination were more likely to report alcohol dependence and alcohol-related problems and to experience symptoms of clinical depression and anxiety. A higher frequency of depressive episodes was found among these women, as well as self-reports regarding nervousness and anxiety. More than one third of the women who had experienced sexual abuse in childhood reported lifetime use of one or more illicit drugs. These women were also more likely to report lifetime use of prescription psychoactive medications as well as illicit drugs (Wilsnack, Vogeltanz, Klassen, & Harris, 1997). This study concluded that sexual abuse in childhood is among the dominant factors in the etiology of substance abuse and psychiatric diagnosis in women. Possible explanations for these relationships between childhood sexual abuse and later substance abuse and psychopathology share a common denominator: substance abuse is either used to counter, or block, negative feeling states brought on by the abuse or to improve the woman's social and sexual response. Abuse in the home, perpetrated by a trusted other, especially a parent, involves a devastating violation of trust, including multiple levels of betrayal, as well as the experiences of invasion and terror found in other relationships of abuse (Butler, 1978; Crawford & Unger, 2000; Denmark, Rabinowitz, & Sechzer, 2000). Betrayal is frequently furthered by the "conspiracy of silence" (Butler, 1978; Crawford & Unger, 2000), that is, the aura of secrecy and disbelief that a female child or woman encounters when she speaks of this abuse. Denial and secrecy in the response of others, or alternatively a "voyeuristic" probing for details, can render a female child or woman virtually unable to trust or reach out for help. Family denial, which serves to keep the abuse a secret, may leave her with feelings of guilt upon disclosure for "betraying a family secret" or for speaking badly about her parents (Crawford & Unger, 2000). These multiple issues of trust and betrayal must be dealt with delicately in the treatment process (see Chapter 7).

Sexual Assault in Adulthood

As mentioned previously, sexual assault is a prominent factor in women's lifetime risk of addictive disorders. Alcohol abuse or dependence occurs among women who have been assaulted at three times the rate of women with no history of assault, and drug abuse or dependence occurs at four times the rate than among non-abused women (Blume, 1998; Koss & Dinero, 1989). Rates of violent trauma in addicted women are far higher than those experienced by addicted men.

Most rapes involve people who know each other, that is, date, acquaintance, and marital rape. Only 20 percent of all rapes are performed by strangers (Denmark et al., 2000). Among women judicial clients, prostitution provides another important route for the occurrence of sexual assault (Falck, Wang, Carlson, & Siegal, 2001). Increased exposure to men who may be abusing substances (in bars, clubs, the "drug scene," and so on), as well as the stigma-related associations between women using substances and sexual availability (discussed in Chapter 2), increase risk of sexual assault among women who engage in criminal conduct.

Domestic Violence

Domestic violence is another important source of trauma among women that may be complicated by substance use. It includes any sort of physical, sexual, or emotional abuse perpetrated by one partner to another, as well as abuse toward children and the elderly. Substance use (by the perpetrator, the victim, or both) is involved in as many as 92 percent of reported episodes of domestic violence. Alcohol use seems to be involved in up to 50 percent of the cases of sexual assault. Substance use may also be involved in domestic violence in more subtle ways, such as arguments over financial matters (the substance user takes money from the spouse or diverts money that should be used to pay household bills to buy drugs, for example) and conflicts related to seeking and splitting drugs (Zilberman & Blume, 2005).

A full 81 percent of women judicial clients report experiencing physical assault in their lives, 29 percent of them in childhood and 60 percent in adulthood, generally by a partner (Bloom, Chesney-Lind, & Owen, 1994; Kerr, 1998). Repeated experiences of emotional or physical violence perpetrated by an intimate partner, along with its psychological consequences for the woman's self-esteem, may produce exaggerated perception of threat and the associated defensive and attack postures commonly observed in women judicial clients (Niehoff, 1999).

Institutional Abuse

Unfortunately, abuse may also occur within treatment settings. Women judicial clients who have been abused by service providers feel a sense of betrayal as well as powerlessness, and they often feel that there is no safe place for them to go. Needless to say, this abuse undermines the effectiveness of the treatment setting, as it imbues this setting with suspicion and fear, secrecy, and a sense of betrayal. The woman offender who has been abused within a treatment setting may feel that it is impossible for her to speak out about this abuse, as she may fear retaliation and punishment. This secrecy mimics the "conspiracy of silence" involved when abuse occurs within the family. Individuals who have been entrusted to help her instead contribute to her problems and difficulties. It is important that women judicial clients be educated regarding the illegality of this type of abuse as well as empowered with mechanisms of redress should this abuse occur.

Institutional abuse is not confined to treatment settings. Unfortunately, cases are documented with regularity that involve abuse by doctors, church officials, police officers, employers, teachers, baby-sitters, social workers, halfway house directors—just about anyone in a woman's life may have perpetrated a violating and invasive act upon her body. It is important that service providers be aware of the potential for this type of abuse in a woman's life and address the extreme sensitivity to danger that may develop when a woman perceives there to be "no safe place" for her to go. Being able to feel ownership of the space one occupies is a necessary ingredient for the empowerment necessary to achieve successful recovery and resistance to recidivism.

Trauma and Criminal Conduct in Women

A vicious cycle of victimization, chemical use, slowing of emotional development, limited stress resolution, more chemical use, and heightened vulnerability to further victimization may also involve criminal behavior, contact with corrections, incarceration, release, relapse, and recidivism (Steele, 2000). Women judicial clients tend toward less violence than their male counterparts. Their criminal behavior often arises through experiences with trauma and subsequent substance abuse or dependence and/or contact with the drug culture.

Particularly, women who engaged in juvenile criminal behavior, or criminal behavior before the onset of drug use, tend to experience polydrug problems. Emotional abuse has been experienced by 57 percent of these women, physical abuse by 49 percent, and sexual abuse by 40 percent (Palacios, Urmann, Newel, & Hamilton, 1999).

MEDICAL CHALLENGES FOR WOMEN JUDICIAL CLIENTS

Women in correctional facilities have a wide range of unique health needs and difficulties (Acoca, 1998a). Yet the "gender-based disparity in medical response is perhaps most evident in the nation's prisons and jails, where…women receive inferior health care compared to their male counterparts" (Acoca, 1998a, p. 51). Acoca and Austin (1996) report that

61 percent of female judicial clients are in need of medical treatment for one or more health problems. Also, women generally have more health concerns, different types of medical problems, and require health care at four times the rate of men. Continuing treatment and follow-up of women offenders' health concerns once they do receive care is minimal. For instance, 42 percent of women judicial clients who take medications for medical problems are not under supervision. Overmedication is common, as are resulting side effects and physical decline (Acoca, 1998a). Two factors have recently been associated with self-reported poor health among incarcerated women. Women reporting recent use of heroin and a history of physical assault are three times more likely than men to present with deteriorated health (Fickenscher, Lapidus, Silk-Walker, & Becker, 2001).

Health and Overcrowding

Other health care concerns that directly relate to conditions of imprisonment result from the overcrowding and lack of clean air that are often characteristic of these environments. Institutional vehicles for transportation of inmates are often crowded and stuffy, and negative air pressure rooms, which might reduce the risk of infection from an individual with a contagious disease, are in short supply. These conditions foster circumstances conducive to the spread of airborne contagious disease such as influenza and tuberculosis (Acoca, 1998a). Routine assessments upon intake do not generally include screening for such conditions. In recent years, the prevalence rates of tuberculosis have increased in correctional facilities, estimated as 8 percent in 2000, double the rate in the U.S. general population. It has been estimated that incarcerated individuals are also at higher risk for having latent tuberculosis infection and later developing tuberculosis (McNiel, Binder, & Robinson, 2005). As women are generally less violent than men, they are frequently kept in even more crowded conditions than are male inmates, many sleeping 6–8 to a cell (Acoca, 1998a). Fast identification of contagious cases through rigorous screening might reduce potential exposure to tuberculosis (Saunders et al., 2001). Without a continuing program of care to supervise medication, dosage requirements frequently go unfilled, and medications may be stopped before the necessary terms of effectiveness have been reached. Drug-resistant strains are thus bred within the nation's prisons and may be transmitted into the general population upon release (Acoca, 1998a).

Hepatitis

Other sexually transmitted diseases (STDs), such as hepatitis B and C, are also transmitted through the pathways of intravenous drug use, unprotected sex, and tattoos. Contrary to rates within the general population, various studies have found the prevalence of hepatitis C among incarcerated women to be higher than among incarcerated men (Baillargeon et al., 2003). In California state prisons, 54 percent of women inmates test positive for hepatitis C (versus 39 percent of males) (Acoca & Austin, 1996). Among reincarcerated women in Rhode Island in 1996–1997, the prevalence of hepatitis B was as high as 29 percent, and hepatitis C was even higher, 40 percent. Self-reported risk behaviors included substance use (84 percent), previous incarceration (68 percent), sexual behavior (44 percent), and injecting drug use (40 percent) (Macalino et al., 2004).

Despite high rates of HIV/AIDS and other STDs (syphilis, gonorrhea, chlamydia, and papillomavirus infections) among women in prisons, and in contrast to health care resources that are available to male judicial clients for such problems, health-related facilities specifically designed to deal with these health problems in women are "limited or nonexistent" (Acoca, 1998a, p. 53). Effective interventions in jails include hepatitis C testing, hepatitis B vaccination, and education (Macalino et al., 2004).

HIV and AIDS

AIDS is an important health problem in jails. Of the total cases of AIDS in the United States in 1996, 4 percent were found in incarcerated individuals. The AIDS rate for incarcerated persons is estimated to be six times the overall U.S. rate. Although cases of AIDS are still more common in incarcerated males (89 percent) as compared to females (11 percent), among persons incarcerated at the time of their initial AIDS diagnosis, rates were higher for females (Dean-Gaitor & Fleming, 1999). Incoming female inmates in Texas criminal justice in 1999 presented higher rates of HIV infection compared to males (Wu et al., 1991). Other recent studies show that rates of HIV for incarcerated females were higher than for males, probably due to elevated rates of women with substance abuse and dependence. Risk factors for HIV in prisons include substance use or dependence, sharing injecting equipment, sexual activities—heterosexual and homosexual, consensual or not—prostitution, tattooing, and body piercing (Hellard & Aitken, 2004).

HIV and AIDS are among the most prominent (25–30 percent) medical conditions in women judicial clients (Acoca, 1998a). Seventy percent of women infected with the virus acquire their HIV infection either through drug injection or sex with a man who injects drugs (Blume, 1998). Just under a third of incarcerated women report sharing needles at some time in their drug use history, 10 percent reporting they had shared needles with 50 or more users (Acoca, 1998a). In addition, 86 percent of incarcerated women in this study reported engaging in unprotected sex, with 10 percent of these women reporting 50 or more sexual partners. Exchanging sex for drugs (and outright prostitution) are major routes whereby female judicial clients who use either crack cocaine or heroin become infected (Blume, 1998).

People with chronic mental illness and comorbid substance use disorders are at increased risk for contracting HIV; estimates have reached 10–76 times greater than the general population (Lerner, 2001). This wide range is probably due to the fact that individuals with co-occurring substance abuse and mental disorders are difficult to track and to test randomly for HIV infection. As described previously, intravenous drug use is a major route for infection; however, another, very prominent risk factor is high-risk sexual behavior. A study of sexual behaviors among people with severe psychiatric diagnosis revealed that sexual encounters involved low rates of condom use, trading sex for drugs (or cash, a roof over their heads, or other basic needs), sex with many partners, sexual assault, and sex between women and bisexual men (Lerner, 2001).

HIV/AIDS hits certain populations especially hard. Rates among incarcerated African American women and Latinas are especially high (Acoca,

1998a), reflecting rates among women in the general population, where the rate of AIDS is 13 times greater for African American women and 8 times greater for Latinas than for white women (Acoca, 1998a). Dually diagnosed individuals also face increased risk for contracting HIV; they become infected at a rate 10–76 times greater than the general population (Lerner, 2001). In addition to the risk factors named previously, low rates of condom use, trading sex for drugs, money, and a place to stay, coerced sex, and women having sex with bisexual men increase their level of risk.

Specific prevention programming has been explored in some countries, but attempts are sparse. Some of the initiatives that have been tested include syringe exchange programs, bleach programs, and condom distribution.

Cancer

Cancer risk factors—including alcohol, tobacco, and other drug use, as well as viral infections, including HIV and hepatitis B and C—are known to be highly prevalent in incarcerated populations. Survival rates among incarcerated women with cancer are lower than those for women in the general population. The most common types of cancer among female inmates are cervical cancer, followed by breast and lung cancers (Mathew, Elting, Cooksley, Owens, & Lin, 2005).

Pregnancy

Pregnant substance-using women judicial clients pose a significant challenge in terms of health care in jails. Imprisoned women are more likely to have premature labor and low birth weight (Knight & Plugge, 2005; Mertens, 2001). Drug use in the perinatal period is associated with a variety of obstetric and postpartum complications, including *abruptio placentae*, meconium staining, premature rupture of membranes, and reduced birth weight and height. Poor nutrition and lack of appropriate prenatal care further complicate pregnancy outcomes (Zilberman & Blume, 2005).

Fetal Alcohol Syndrome

Fetal alcohol syndrome represents the third most common cause of mental retardation in the United States, after Down syndrome and spina bifida. It is completely preventable through abstinence from alcoholic beverages during pregnancy. Because of the high use of alcohol among female judicial clients, their risk for having children with these problems is also high. The estimated prevalence in the general population is 1 to 3 cases per 1,000 live births, with increased risk associated with binge drinking, increased maternal age, and increased parity. The full syndrome is characterized by pre- and postnatal growth retardation, central nervous system abnormalities (including microcephaly), facial dysmorphisms (with maxillary hypoplasia, shortened palpebral fissures, and epicanthic folds), and cardiac abnormalities. Other fetal alcohol effects include spontaneous abortion, reduced birth weight, and behavior changes (Zilberman & Blume, 2005).

Substance Abuse and Women's Health

Health care problems are frequently exacerbated by substance abuse or dependence. Once again, recall that many medical complications due to substance abuse develop more rapidly in women and become more severe, even at lower levels of consumption. This "telescoping" of female alcohol-related problems relates to a wide range of medical complications, many of which are reproductive. Among these we find breast cancer and sexual dysfunction (Blume, 1998). Acoca (1998a) reports that women who have experienced violent sexual or physical trauma require medical services at twice the rate of nonvictimized women; their medical problems include surgical, gynecological, and gastrointestinal difficulties, as well as the by-products of suicide attempts. Of course, these women are also more likely to require mental health services.

Chronic and heavy alcohol consumption may underlie sexual dysfunction in women, in that it may suppress both sexual arousal and orgasmic function. This is contrary to widely held beliefs of women judicial clients who frequently assume that alcohol will boost their sexual pleasure. Sixty percent of female alcohol users report that they believe alcohol enhances sexual responsiveness, and women who consume alcohol at higher levels are more likely to hold this belief. Research has also found that these sexuality-related alcohol expectancies are correlated with high-risk sexual behavior in women. There may be a bidirectional relationship; however, as clinical studies suggest, sexual dysfunction may also contribute to substance abuse problems in women (Wilsnack, 1995).

Health care clinicians may help women reduce their alcohol consumption and their risk for HIV infection by explaining that their drinking has suppressed rather than enhanced their sexual responsiveness. Women may be educated to understand that, in fact, they may enjoy sex more during sobriety than they do while drinking (Blume, 1998). A great opportunity for providing women with education regarding reproductive health, safe sex, and family planning is missed due to the lack of specialized health care for women judicial clients. Acoca (1998a) reports, "There are no consistently applied policies regarding contraception, abortion, and general reproductive education and counseling for incarcerated women" (p. 56).

ETHNIC CONSIDERATIONS IN HEALTH CARE

McQuaide and Ehrenreich (1998) found that, as with men, a disproportionate number of incarcerated women are from minority groups. In 1991, 14.2 percent were Hispanic women (while Hispanics made up only 7.3 percent of the general female population at that time), and 46 percent were African American women, compared to 12.5 percent of the general female population.

Health care concerns, which are disproportionately found among African Americans, include diabetes, certain kinds of heart disease, hypertension, and sickle cell anemia. These diseases often receive no special attention in prisons' health care systems (Acoca, 1998a).

IMPLICATIONS FOR TREATMENT AND POLICY: WHAT FACTORS REDUCE RECIDIVISM?

Acoca (1998a) recommends gender-specific interventions in the health care of women. Differences in the mental and physical health needs of male and female judicial clients require specific services designed to address the issues found within each gender. Investigators into the health needs of the incarcerated women assert that successful treatment of chemically dependent women with a history of violent trauma

should include simultaneous components to address their co-occurring disorders of substance abuse and mental illness. Careful attention should be paid to sorting out the source and etiology of a woman's psychological difficulties, as experiences with trauma, substance abuse or dependence, and posttraumatic stress disorder may all present with symptoms that mimic other psychiatric diagnoses. Mental and physical health care services in correctional facilities must be expanded to allow for accurate screening, assessment, and treatment of these gender-related difficulties (Acoca, 1998a; Steele, 2000).

In addition, access to the few medical and mental services that are available may be blocked by ethnic and linguistic differences. It was estimated that 20 percent of incarcerated women spoke little or no English or were more comfortable speaking in their own language. At the same time, few members of the correctional, mental health, or medical staff at correctional facilities were bilingual (Acoca & Austin, 1996). Thus, there is a great need to reorganize mental and physical health care services in correctional settings so that they are both gender- and culture-responsive (Acoca, 1998a).

CHAPTER REVIEW

Chapter 3 has described a full range of both medical and psychological difficulties found at high incidence among the female incarcerated population. Issues regarding psychiatric diagnosis have been explored, as has the adequacy of prison services to meet these needs. Substance use problems as well as accompanying psychological and mental health difficulties in women judicial clients have been found to stem from experiences with violent trauma. Specific sources of this trauma were explored and were found to occur at very significant rates among female judicial clients. Finally, the aftermath of trauma was examined with relation to behavioral disturbances, posttraumatic stress disorder, and dual diagnosis. Some key findings are outlined below:

◗ The number of women in U.S. prisons has increased dramatically in the past 25 years.

◗ It is estimated that more than 60 percent of incarcerated women present a lifetime diagnosis of a psychiatric disorder.

▶ Forty-five percent of incarcerated women present a current psychiatric diagnosis, and 40 percent of these inmates have substance-related disorders.

▶ Only a small portion of those female detainees in need of psychiatric care receive treatment.

▶ While researchers vary in their estimates of the rate of psychiatric disorders among women in jails and prisons, most agree that diagnostic and treatment services are generally inadequate and in some cases nonexistent for this population.

▶ Excluding substance-related disorders, major depression is the most frequent current psychiatric diagnosis among women in jail, from 5 percent to 11 percent.

▶ Alcohol abuse or dependence co-occurred with major depression in 19 percent of women judicial clients, four times the rate in men and three times the rate in the general population of women.

▶ Phobic disorders are found in 31 percent of women judicial clients (versus 15 percent of male judicial clients, and double that of women in general).

▶ A frequent result of violent trauma, posttraumatic stress disorder (PTSD), is seen at a very high rate in women judicial clients. In one study, 33.5 percent of women judicial clients were diagnosed as having PTSD due to rape or other violent assault and many service providers suggest that this figure is even higher when one considers the continuum of traumatic consequences.

▶ Domestic violence is another important source of trauma among women that may be complicated by substance use. A full 81 percent of women judicial clients report experiencing physical assault in their lives, 29 percent of them in childhood and 60 percent in adulthood, generally by a partner.

▶ Sixty-one percent of female judicial clients are in need of medical treatment for one or more health problems. Also, women generally have more health concerns, different types of medical problems, and require health care at four times the rate of men.

▶ Despite high rates of HIV/AIDS and other STDs (syphilis, gonorrhea, chlamydia, and papillomavirus infections) among women in prisons, and in contrast to health care resources that are available to male judicial clients for such problems, health-related facilities specifically designed to deal with these health problems in women are limited.

▶ HIV and AIDS are among the most prominent (25–30 percent) medical conditions in women judicial clients.

▶ Pregnant substance-using women judicial clients pose a significant challenge in terms of health care in jails. Imprisoned women are more likely to have premature labor and low birth weight.

CHAPTER 4: Adolescent Girls and Delinquency: The Route Into Correctional Settings

LEARNING OBJECTIVES

- To investigate primary risk factors that predict entry of adolescent girls into the juvenile justice system
- To describe common characteristics found in the trajectory of development from juvenile to adult offending among females
- To explore the role of violent trauma as a dominant factor in female offending
- To investigate female participation within gangs
- To explore experiences of girls within the juvenile justice system
- To examine key issues that hamper female adolescents' reentry into society
- To address the specific needs of female adolescent criminal justice clients in order to improve outcomes, reduce recidivism, and prevent their children from participating in cycles of drug abuse crime and violence

INTRODUCTION

Childhood experience with violent trauma among female judicial clients is associated with substance abuse and criminal activity. Criminal offense may take several forms, including participation in gangs and the drug culture. Correlates of criminal offense in adolescent females, such as school failure, destructive dating norms, teen pregnancy, and poor mental and physical health, are widely reported. Analysis of conditions within the juvenile justice system indicates a need for gender-specific programming.

GENDER DIFFERENCES BETWEEN ADOLESCENTS IN AOD TREATMENT AND JUVENILE JUSTICE SETTINGS

A study of three large samples of adolescents indicates robust differences between female and male clients who were admitted to substance abuse treatment (Wanberg, 2008). Within a sample of 3,557 adolescents admitted to adolescent substance abuse treatment in Colorado, females scored higher on self-report scales that measured family disruption and mental health symptoms (anxiety, depression, self-harm histories, and so on). Males scored higher on scales measuring deviancy and delinquency and school adjustment problems. These findings support the literature showing that male substance-abusing clients are more apt to manifest conduct disorder and antisocial behaviors and do more poorly in school. Females are more intensely involved in and impacted by problems in the family and their interaction with these problems, which result in more severe mood and psychological adjustment problems. Congruently, Pelissier and Jones (2006) found that, compared to their male counterparts, female adolescent substance abusers are apt to be more dependent on social support for their rehabilitation.

These same analyses were conducted with two samples of juvenile offenders: 2,535 juveniles in the probation system who had been referred for substance abuse problems and 2,197 juvenile offenders committed to incarcerated settings and identified as needing treatment for substance abuse. Across both offender samples, girls scored higher in reporting *family disruption* and *mental health symptoms*. However, the gender difference on criminal conduct found in the general adolescent treatment population was not as clear with the offender samples. In both offender samples, on the general criminal conduct scale, girls and boys did not differ. However, on the scale measuring more serious criminal conduct and deviancy, boys scored higher.

These findings suggest that female adolescent judicial clients are more sensitive to and affected by disruptive and traumatic family experiences, which are correlated with a high degree of mental health problems. Male counterparts do not seem to identify their families as being as disruptive and tend to act out their problems, resulting in higher levels of deviant and antisocial behaviors. These findings support the impact of relational factors on females in the development of substance abuse and criminal conduct problems as well as the development of psychological symptoms. It also indicates the importance of the relational focus in the intervention and treatment of both adolescent and adult female criminal justice clients.

ADOLESCENT GIRLS AND DELINQUENCY

Females constitute the largest-growing segment of the juvenile justice population (Acoca, 1998b). In the past decade, girls have been arrested for nearly every type of offense at a greater rate of increase than boys (Snyder, 1997). This includes arrests for violent crime, where research has long revealed far lower rates among females than males. Snyder (1997) reports that 723,000 girls younger than age 18 were arrested in 1996 alone. Thirty-one percent of juvenile arrests are female. Males are more likely to be rearrested than females (46 percent of males versus 27 percent of females) (Snyder & Sickmund, 1999). Males and females differ in the seriousness of their crimes as well. Only 16 percent of females had been arrested for a serious offense, versus 42 percent of males. Chronic offending (more than four referrals) occurs in 52 percent of male offenders versus 19 percent of female offenders (Snyder & Sickmund, 1999). Females and males, however, enter the criminal justice system at about the same age: 14. Those who came into contact with criminal justice earlier ("early onset offenders") were more likely to chronically engage in serious offenses (Snyder & Sickmund, 1999).

Leve and Chamberlain (2004) found the mean age of first arrest for females to be somewhat younger than for males, at 12.5 years of age. The authors identify two main predictors that may account for earlier female onset: (1) parental transitions (regarding family environment) and (2) the criminality of the biological parents.

THE NATURE OF FEMALE ADOLESCENT OFFENSE

As stated by Staton, Walker, and Leukefeld (2003), it appears that age does not hold significance when considering drug use and sexual activity in female criminal justice clients. Forty-six percent of women who have been convicted for criminal activities report their first arrest before the age of 18 (Acoca & Austin, 1996).

Female adolescents constitute the largest percentage of arrests for status offenses (Acoca, 1998b; Belknap, Holsinger, & Dunn, 1997; Covington, 1998a; Snyder & Sickmund, 1999). Status offenses are defined as actions that would not be offenses if they were committed by adults, such as promiscuity, truancy, or running away. Most runaways are teenage girls (58 percent) who are between 16 and 17 years old (68 percent). Of these girls, 29 percent found themselves without a familiar or safe place to stay. Children on the streets for at least a time may also be "throwaways," referring to "a child who was told to leave home, or whose caretaker refused to let come home . . . , or whose caretaker made no effort to recover the child when the child ran away, or who was abandoned" (Snyder & Sickmund, 1999, p. 38). Status offenses and throwaway status are likely to be related to physical and sexual abuse (Covington, 1998a). Additionally, sexual abuse can greatly impact an adolescent's life in a number of ways, including prompting the adolescent to run away. Once on the streets, females were found to be more likely than to engage in risky drug use, including the use of cocaine, which is often used by those who had been sexually abused (Chen, Tyler, Whitbeck, & Hoyt, 2004).

While females participate in the same kinds of delinquent acts as males, the degree of this participation varies by sex. Criminal behaviors of delinquent girls closely mirror the patterns of adult female crime, generally being in the realm of property crime, and much less likely to be violent (Covington, 1998a).

Except in some areas—notably assault—differences between male and female participation in criminal conduct are generally constant across race and ethnicity. The arrest ratio of male juveniles varied across race and ethnicity, but arrest ratios for females are relatively constant across race and ethnicity. Five percent of white, 6 percent of black, and 7 percent of Hispanic female juveniles had ever experienced arrest (in contrast to 9 percent of white, 13 percent of black, and 12 percent of Hispanic male juveniles.

Male juveniles seem to fight more than female juveniles (46 percent versus 26 percent in the previous year). This difference appears at all grade levels. Males were also more likely to carry a weapon to school (13 percent male versus 4 percent female). Juvenile drug users were more likely than nonusers to report breaking the law. Fifty percent of juveniles commit their crimes with other juveniles or adults, a pattern that holds true among both male and female juveniles and is twice the rate for adults (Snyder & Sickmund, 1999). Social norms may contribute to a lower rate of female fighting. Females who fight are seen as deviant. Consequently, fear of being an outcast acts as a deterrent (Ness, 2004).

The number of female adolescents who perpetrated a murder remained stable from 1980 to 1997. This figure is reported to be about 130 juvenile females per year, constituting only a small fraction (7 percent) of the homicides committed by juveniles in total. The rate of murder committed by males, however, steadily rose from 1980 to 1997, more than tripling before it reached a peak in 1993. Males are more likely to use firearms when committing murder (73 percent who used firearms versus 14 percent who used a knife), while 32 percent of females used a knife and 41 percent used a firearm in carrying out their murders (Snyder & Sickmund, 1999).

When they kill, males and females tend to kill different kinds or types of victims: 54 percent of males killed an acquaintance, 37 percent a stranger, and only 9 percent of male juveniles killed a family member. By contrast, 39 percent of females killed a family member, and only 15 percent killed a stranger. Age of victim was also significantly different for male and female homicide perpetrators. While only 1 percent of males who killed were involved in the murders of children less than 6 years of age, 18 percent of females who committed murder killed children in this age range. Women, in general, are more likely to kill children, mainly their own, though not always (Messing & Heeren, 2004). However, because males kill at such a higher rate than females overall, approximately equal numbers of juvenile males and females are responsible for killing young children.

JUVENILE VICTIMS OF CRIME

Murder

One of the leading causes of mortality among juveniles is murder. Of all the murders committed in 1997, 11 percent were of victims under age 18. Murder is the fourth leading cause of death among children between 1 and 4 years, third among children between 5 and 14, and second among those ages 15–24 (National Center for Health Statistics, 1997). Younger children (under 13 years) who are murdered are equally likely to be male or female. At 14 years of age, however, the percentage of male and female murder victims diverges; at this age, murdered juveniles are more likely to be male. Data compiled for 1980–1997 showed that by 15 years of age, males were three times more likely to be murdered, and by age 17, males were more than four times as likely to be murdered as females. Nevertheless, females accounted for 29 percent of murdered juveniles from 1990 to 1997. In addition, 33 percent of murdered juveniles were younger than 6, and 50 percent were ages 15–17. Forty-seven percent of juvenile murders were of black victims, a rate five times that of white juveniles (Snyder & Sickmund, 1999). Of the murders that were solved and cleared, the perpetrators in 40 percent were family members; in 45 percent the perpetrators were acquaintances, and 15 percent were strangers. Family members were more than twice as likely to be implicated in the murder of a juvenile female as of a male (Snyder & Sickmund).

Assault

In a recent survey, only 29 percent of the youth interviewed had not experienced direct or indirect victimization (Finkelhor, Ormrod, Turner, & Hamby, 2005). Young people are at highest risk for rape, robbery, and aggravated assault, with rates peaking between the ages of 12 to 17 and 18 to 24. The differences between these age groups appeared in the severity of assault type. Young adults (18–24) were more likely than juveniles to experience serious assault, while juveniles were three times more likely than young adults to experience simple assault. The perpetrators of serious violent assault against juveniles were acquaintances (18 percent), relatives (11 percent), friends (34 percent), or strangers (36 percent) (Snyder & Sickmund, 1999).

Assault of juveniles under age 12 constitutes 5.5 percent of all reported violent crime. Sexual assault is, by far, the major form of assault experienced by juveniles under age 12, constituting 32 percent of all reported assaults of juveniles. Snyder and Sickmund (1999) reported that 33 percent of sexual assault victims are under the age of 12. Females constitute 96 percent of all adult sexual assault victims, 92 percent of those experiencing sexual assault between the ages of 12 and 17. However, 26 percent of those sexually assaulted under age 12 are male (Snyder & Sickmund).

Juvenile offenders perpetrate a sizeable portion of sexual assault of juveniles and most of these assaults are perpetrated by juveniles known to the victimized children. Forty-seven percent of the perpetrators of sexual assault against children under age 12 are family members, 49 percent are acquaintances, and just 4 percent are strangers (Snyder & Sickmund, 1999).

RISK FACTORS FOR JUVENILE OFFENDING AMONG FEMALES

Poverty

Poverty has been named as a significant risk factor for juvenile crime among both females and males. This could be due, in part, to the findings of poverty being a correlate of aggression (Anooshian, 2005). Twenty percent of all juveniles lived in poverty in 1997. Although juveniles constitute 26 percent of the U.S. population, they account for 40 percent of those who live below the poverty line. Percentages that live below poverty level are disproportionate to racial and ethnic population distribution. Blacks and Hispanics made up 37 percent of those living in poverty, compared to 16 percent of whites and 20 percent of Asian juveniles (Snyder & Sickmund, 1999).

Family of Origin

Pollock (1998) reports on the results of extensive interviews with female offenders concerning their family environments during childhood. These were women who had begun their criminal activity as juveniles. Two basic family patterns emerged:

Little Love or Affection. These women felt that they had been a "disappointment" to their parents, who were strict disciplinarians, controlling the family through the use of fear and intimidation. Use of severe punishment was not uncommon in these families, and neglect of the child's needs and perspectives was the rule (Pollock, 1998). "Far from being insulators against delinquency, these families are instigators of delinquency, addiction and criminality" (Pollock, 1998, p. 52).

Overburdened Parent. Forced to hold several jobs to feed the family, these parents were unable to spend time with their children, often leaving them alone, with other relatives, or on the street. AOD use was often a way of life in these families, and loss of relatives and friends to murder and gang-related activities was common. Girls in these families were likely to run away, often with the motivation of helping to relieve the burden on their parents, who had "too many mouths to feed" (Pollock, 1998).

Another study indicated that there are two distinct patterns of family dysfunction and problems among juvenile offenders (Wanberg, 1992a): (1) family distance, where there is minimal involvement and support among family members, and (2) overt family disruption, including economic problems, abusive and rejecting behavior, parental arguing, and so on. The former is similar to Pollack's (1998) "Little love or affection pattern."

Substance Abuse

AOD use among juvenile justice clients tends to correlate with other criminal behaviors, such as carrying a handgun, gang membership, and drug selling (Snyder & Sickmund, 1999). While 20 percent of non-drug users reported theft from a store, this figure rose to 40–50 percent of drug users, depending on frequency of use. According to Snyder & Sickmund (1999), drug use was a little more common among males than females, especially with regards to LSD, crack, cocaine, steroids, and heroin. Use rates of stimulants, barbiturates, and tranquilizers were more similar. Wanberg (2008) compared adult criminal justice clients across gender. Males showed greater involvement in the use of alcohol and marijuana, whereas females showed greater involvement in cocaine and amphetamines. Females may use drugs (such as cocaine and amphetamines) that will enhance their sense of power and energy in relationship with others. Males may be more apt to use those drugs that will mitigate anxiety and fear of engaging in criminal conduct and fear of getting caught (alcohol and marijuana) and in enhancing their sense of power over others (alcohol). Wanberg (2008) describes a trend in which male criminal justice clients have a history of greater involvement in hallucinogens and female counterparts have a greater involvement in tranquilizers. According to Wanberg (2008), even though there is no significant gender differentiation across general drug involvement, female criminal justice clients report having greater life disruptions resulting from AOD use.

Teen Pregnancy

The Center for Disease Control and Prevention (Martin et al., 2007) reported that although the birthrate for teenagers 15–19 years fell in 2005, teenage childbearing is "an ongoing public health and public policy concern. Infants born to teenage mothers are at risk for poor birth outcomes ... [and] teenage mothers have limited educational levels, resulting in fewer economic resources for themselves and their children" (p. 5). Martin et al. reported that a recent study found public costs of teenage childbearing in the United States to be about $9.1 billion annually.

Table 4.1	
Teen Birth Rate Among Girls Ages 15 to 19 for Year 2005	
All races	40.5
White, non-Hispanic	25.9
Black, non-Hispanic	60.9
American Indian or Alaska Native, total	52.7
Asian or Pacific Islander, total	17.0
Hispanic	81.7

Source: Martin et al. (2007).

Note: Per 1,000 females

According to Martin et al. (2007), 83.3 percent of females ages 15–19 who gave birth were unmarried. Vulnerability factors that place juveniles at risk for teen pregnancy are early school failure, early behavioral problems, family dysfunction, and poverty (Snyder & Sickmund, 1999). Additionally, interpersonal processes in an adolescent female's life were found to influence the desire to have a child (Grant et al., 2002). A poor relationship with parents was found to correlate with a greater reliance on a boyfriend. This, in turn, was connected to a stronger desire for a child. The child can be viewed, perhaps, as the "missing link" in the troubled adolescent's life. These conditions may also place girls at greater risk for criminal behavior. Acoca (1998b) reports that 29 percent of the girls in the National Center on Crime and Delinquency (NCCD) study reported at least one pregnancy, and 16 percent went through pregnancy during confinement in a correctional facility.

School Failure and Delinquency

Another factor that is frequently found among female juvenile justice clients is a pattern of school failure, as defined by being left back in school, expelled from classes, or placed in remedial or disciplinary environments (Acoca, 1998b). Chesney-Lind and Sheldon (1998) found that school failure is a predictor of delinquency in girls; the strength of this correlation is higher among girls than among boys. There is a direct correlation between emotional, physical, and sexual abuse and school failure. The greater the number of abuse experiences, the more likelihood of failure in academics (Acoca, 1998b).

Experiences With Violent Trauma in Childhood: A Major Route Into Criminal Conduct

"Gender matters in the forces that propel women into criminal behavior" (Chesney-Lind, 2000). Although adolescent male offenders also report a high incidence of abuse, the prevalence of these experiences, especially emotional and sexual abuse, is much higher in girls than in boys (Acoca, 1998b). In fact, the abuse histories of adolescent girls in corrections are very similar to those of adult women criminal justice clients (Covington, 1998b). On the basis of interviews with convicted adolescent females, Dixon, Howie, and Starling (2005) found that 37 percent had characteristics of posttraumatic stress disorder (PTSD), with 70 percent of those having experienced sexual abuse.

In developing a profile of the characteristics frequently found among female adolescent offenders, the National Council on Crime and Delinquency (NCCD) Acoca (1998b) placed experiences with some form of violent trauma (emotional, physical, or sexual abuse) as nearly universal in these girls. Many report that abuse experiences in childhood were "the equivalent of first steps leading to offending as juveniles" (Acoca & Austin, 1996). Acoca (1998b) recounts an adolescent's entry into criminal conduct:

> Growing up in a home bereft of even the basics for survival, this girl engaged in street begging for food at age 10; by age 12 her profits had increased through the sale of crack cocaine. She gave the money to her mother to buy food for the family. This girl had repeatedly been the witness of violence in her home, fights between her parents, abuse of her brother and she, herself, had suffered child abuse, including beatings and stabbing. (p. 568)

Table 4.2 reports a breakdown of abuse types as experienced by adolescent female offenders.

Table 4.2		
Types of Abuse Suffered by Convicted Adolescent Females		
Type of Abuse	Percentage of Offenders Reporting Experience	Average Age of Occurrence
Emotional abuse	88	
Verbal threats of physical harm	46	
Accusations of worthlessness	60	
Physical/sexual abuse	81	
Beaten/burned 5 or more times	> 45 31	11–13 years
Shot/stabbed	25	13–15 years
Sexual abuse of these, molested/fondled	> 56 > 33	5 years
Rape or sodomy	40	
Forced to leave home	~ 32	12–15 years
Witnessed violent fights at home	58	
Neglect (made wards of the state)	25	12–14 years

Sources: Acoca (1998b); Acoca and Dedel (1998).

Emotional abuse included hearing shouting that frightened them, being forced into isolation or prevented from attending school or work, accusations of worthlessness, and more. Witnessing domestic violence among members of their family was also included; this was reported by 58 percent of the female juvenile justice clients (Acoca, 1998b). Aggression and delinquency have been named as prominent among the consequences of this type of experience in childhood (Saunders, 1994).

Physical and/or sexual abuse was reported by 81 percent of the girls in the NCCD study. Forty-five percent reported having been burned or beaten by the age of 13. This type of abuse generally occurred

at the hands of boyfriends (20 percent), mothers (19 percent), and others (16 percent). Twenty-five percent reported being shot or stabbed at least once in their lives; these crimes usually occurred outside of the girl's home, and the perpetrators were generally acquaintances: gang members (36 percent), strangers (19 percent), family members (8 percent), friends or neighbors (8 percent), and boyfriends (8 percent) (Acoca, 1998b). From these statistics, we can infer that in addition to the high rates of violence these girls are experiencing inside their homes, the communities in which these girls live are also characterized by high rates of violence.

Fifty-six percent of the girls reported experiences with sexual abuse (Acoca, 1998b). Forty percent reported being raped or sodomized, 17 percent more than once. This type of assault also occurred most frequently between the ages of 12 and 15; the greatest number occurred at age 13. The perpetrators named in these assaults were acquaintances (28 percent), boyfriends (15 percent) and dating partners (14 percent), family friends and neighbors (14 percent), and strangers (15 percent). A third of the girls who reported sexual abuse reported molestation at the age of only 5 years on average. Molesters tended to be friends or neighbors (32 percent), acquaintances (31 percent), stepfathers (8 percent), and strangers (7 percent).

Female juvenile justice clients had frequently been forced to leave their homes, usually between the ages of 12 and 15 years. Mothers were the most frequent parent to initiate this expulsion (Acoca, 1998b). Many of these girls were forced to live on the streets, where they came into contact with the drug culture and other destructive elements of street life. Neglect was also widely reported. A full 25 percent had been made wards of the state due to parental neglect, with 13 years being the most vulnerable age for this occurrence (Acoca, 1998b).

PSYCHOLOGICAL CONSEQUENCES OF VIOLENT TRAUMA IN ADOLESCENCE

Studies consistently find that these early experiences with violence and assault are strongly associated with severe psychological disturbance among adolescent girls. Women in general are more likely than men to experience adverse effects, such as more pronounced and prolonged symptoms and poor quality of life, as a result of PTSD after a traumatic event (sexual in nature or otherwise) (Seedat, Stein, & Carey, 2005). Among these disturbances are eating disorders, depression, suicidal ideation and attempts, risk taking, and substance abuse (Acoca, 1998b). And in this list, we also find delinquent activity. This section of the chapter describes patterns across certain types of abuse and specific delinquent behaviors that were identified in the NCCD study. Among these behaviors can be found the use of multiple drugs, participation in gangs, school failure, having sex with many partners, and early pregnancy. The presence of these behaviors is found to correlate with arrest and engagement with the juvenile justice system among female adolescents (Belknap & Holsinger, 1998; Chesney-Lind & Sheldon, 1998; Owen & Bloom, 1997).

When a young girl learns early to find her solutions in substance abuse, she is entering a path of learning deficits, poor coping abilities, and deteriorating mental and physical health. As her needs for coping and maintaining psychosocial balance become more demanding, the "solution" becomes a major source of problems in itself, which compounds the psychosocial distress she may be feeling from other events in her life. Multiple drug use is a behavior often found in these situations. This appears to be related to the following (Acoca, 1998b):

> Number of emotional abuse experiences (18–23 percent of girls who experienced one to three types of emotional abuse engaged in multiple use; 43 percent of those who experienced four or more types of emotional abuse)

> Number of sexual abuse experiences (35 percent of girls who had experienced at least two types of sexual abuse used multiple drugs)

> Number of physical abuse experiences (those who experienced at least three types of physical abuse were more likely to be multiple drug users)

GENDER NORMS AND ADOLESCENCE

Adolescent Dating and Sexuality: The Effect of Social Norms

The history of abuse found in the lives of girl offenders takes many forms and occurs in a wide variety of contexts. Often co-occurring with abuse in the family and/or dating environment, sexual harassment in their schools and on the streets of their communities is reported by convicted female adolescents. One study showed that as many as 81 percent of high school girls reported sexual harassment at school (Sadker & Sadker, 1994).

Girls who engage in physical violence cite frequent experience with threatening taunts and harassment at bus stops, in schools, on the streets, and many other places. This is especially true for girls who are either slow or fast in the maturation of female secondary sex characteristics. For example, underdevelopment or overdevelopment of the breasts in adolescence makes girls vulnerable to taunts and teasing by others. Social norms and demands to be self-reliant in adolescence often undermine a girl's ability to seek help for her problems at school or through another authority figure (Pollock, 1998).

GIRLS AND GANGS

Female adolescents constitute a small fraction of all gang members, with statistics estimated at 7 percent (Pollock, 1998) through 10 percent (Snyder & Sickmund, 1999). Yet the NCCD study found that 47 percent of convicted female adolescents reported involvement with gang activity and 71 percent of these reported that they were "very involved" (Acoca, 1998b). The majority of the neighborhoods in which these girls lived were described as having active gangs. Self-report statistics regarding level of involvement in a gang, however, are difficult to interpret, due to the phenomenon of "wannabes." It is important to note, for example, that self-reported participation by females is much higher than law enforcement statistics would reveal, sometimes reaching as high as 38 percent (Snyder & Sickmund, 1999).

It has been estimated that adolescent females engage in less (and less severe) criminal activity than males when they are in a gang. Generally speaking, girls use gangs as social "hangouts," a group of peers and a place to meet, to get together, tell stories, and dance. Some indicators suggest that the presence of girls in gangs may even lessen the degree of violence among male gang members (Pollock, 1998). Female gang participation, however, tends to be concentrated in smaller cities where gang-related violence tends to be less violent and serious (Snyder & Sickmund, 1999). However, females are more likely to participate in prostitution as their position in the gang, often choosing this as a source of income for the group (Knox, 2004).

Gangs often serve as surrogate families for their members, males and females alike. But the importance of support and protection derived from this "family" can reach much greater proportions when a girl seeks refuge from an abusive or conflict-ridden home (Acoca, 1998b; Pollock, 1998). Often, a gang may appear to be a refuge from the harshness of a girl's former experiences. Acoca (1998b) reports the number one reason girls join gangs is "protection from harm" (p. 573). Many of the girls who join gangs have suffered violent trauma (Acoca, 1998b). Gang membership is found in the 65 percent of girls who have suffered two sexual assaults versus 45 percent who have not. Gang membership is found at a rate of 50 percent in girls who have experienced two forms of physical abuse, and in 63 percent of those who have experienced three or more types (versus 35 percent who report no experience with physical abuse) (Acoca, 1998b).

Except for the violence and serious criminal activity enacted by their male counterparts, girls' participation in gangs mirrors the behavior of boys. A difference between male and female gang participation emerges, however, when we look at age. Females tend to join gangs at a later age than do males; one study found that a third of female gang members were older than 26 years of age (Pollock, 1998).

Female gang participation may occur through a girl joining a predominantly male gang or through the formation of "girl gangs." Interviews with females in girl gangs from Detroit provide insight into the girls' perception of their own behavior. Taylor (1993) reported that these girls perceived their gangs as "posses," the equivalent of other criminal organizations. Their attitudes toward men were very independent: they felt that males were "nice to have around, but not necessary." Living a crime-free life, in their expressed opinions, was "for jerks and honkies" (Taylor, 1993). Four types of gangs have been identified, with females participating in all types (Pollock, 1998):

1. **Scavenger.** Sporadically engaging in crime if the opportunity arises.

2. **Territorial.** Exerting control over a certain area with boundaries

3. **Commercial.** Engaging in the supply (and sometimes manufacture) of a product (usually drugs) to sell for profit.

4. **Corporate.** Organized as a criminal syndicate; prominent players in the drug trade and make large sums of money; least likely to abuse substances.

FEMALE ADOLESCENT DETENTION

As mentioned previously, adolescent females constitute the largest percentage of arrests for status offenses (Acoca, 1998b), and many of these girls find themselves in correctional facilities. This occurs despite the fact that a section of the U.S. Department of Justice issued a report to prevent status offenders from being "held in secure confinement" (Acoca, 1998b, p. 575). In general, adolescent female offenders commit much less serious crimes overall than do their male counterparts (Acoca, 1998b). Nevertheless, they are confined in the same type of juvenile detention facilities and are generally treated with the same security measures as are male juveniles. Female adolescent detainees often do not have similar privileges for outdoor recreational opportunities as males. As girls are generally less violent than boys, they are more often housed in overcrowded rooms with poor ventilation than are males (Acoca, 1998b), increasing risk for both physical and psychological deterioration.

An increasing number of female adolescents are being confined in adult correctional facilities (Acoca, 1998b). Among these detainees were girls who had experienced a history of abuse and neglect as well as clinical depression. Incarcerated women were found to experience depression as one of the most common psychological disorders (Rau, 2002). Often, no special programming is provided for juveniles in adult correctional facilities, and what educational resources are available are generally geared to the adult, at a level that makes them inaccessible to the average juvenile offender (Acoca, 1998b). This may provide some explanation as to why the rate of suicide among girls housed in adult facilities is 7.7 times higher than the rate for those housed in juvenile detention facilities (Chesney-Lind & Sheldon, 1998). Adult women in these correctional facilities expressed fear for the girls' safety (Acoca, 1998b).

EXPERIENCES OF GIRLS IN THE JUVENILE JUSTICE SYSTEM

The National Council on Crime and Delinquency (NCCD) also investigated the nature of girls' experiences within the juvenile justice system (Acoca & Dedel, 1998). Databases, case files, and interviews with the girls were scrutinized to determine prominent needs and risk factors that might arise for this population within the juvenile justice system itself. These investigations revealed that the procedures used in the juvenile justice system often lack considerations of the special needs of female juveniles, despite the fact that this group constitutes the largest growing portion of the juvenile population. Many girls report incidents of emotional, physical, and sexual mistreatment that rekindled memories of previous abuses. In fact, some of the interviewers observed such behaviors while conducting the study (Acoca, 1998b).

Housing, feeding, health care, and other important areas in correctional settings for juvenile offenders were often not carefully monitored (Acoca, 1998b). The U.S. Dept of Justice Human Rights Watch (1995) reported that "there is no general monitoring of the conditions in which adjudicated children are confined" (Acoca, 1998b, p. 575). Clothing that is unclean, loosely fitting, or doesn't fit at all is common fare for girls in juvenile facilities. Inadequate hygiene and personal care products were named as responsible for a high incidence of dry and damaged skin, head lice, and scabies among young female offenders (Acoca, 1998b).

Besides being uncomfortable, these factors may contribute to the low self-esteem and feelings of worthlessness that are frequently found among female offenders in general. Many systems have corrected and found solutions to these problems.

No gender-specific policies have been incorporated into the procedural practices of the juvenile justice system (Acoca, 1998b). Thousands of female adult and juvenile detainees are under the direct supervision of male staff. Under these circumstances, the specific health and emotional needs of female adolescent offenders are likely to be missed. Health screening, adequate food, hygiene, and living space are essential to this population of females, who frequently enter the juvenile justice system with deteriorating health and a high probability of pregnancy or motherhood (Acoca, 1998b). Twenty-nine percent of the girls in the NCCD study reported having been pregnant, and 16 percent experienced this pregnancy while confined in a correctional facility (Acoca, 1998b). Of these, 29 percent reported experiencing some form of restraint during pregnancy, a punishment that left them in fear of falling and hurting the baby or of being unable to obtain adequate medical attention should they require it. Another important factor to consider is the occurrence of "multiple additional violations" that adolescent girls may suffer once they are involved with the juvenile detention system (Acoca, 1998b).

Girls in juvenile detention reported the occurrence of demeaning comments (such as being called "sluts" and "hookers"), shouts and threats of physical violence, and the use of bad language as common means used by staff to gain their compliance and enforce their silence. Intimidation is reported in cases where the girls attempt to file grievances about abuses or inappropriate touching that they have seen or experienced. The girls report these incidents to be sexually demeaning, anxiety producing, and damaging to feelings of self-worth (Acoca, 1998b).

Unfortunately, female adolescents also report instances of physical and sexual abuse within the juvenile justice system (Acoca, 1998b). Chesney-Lind & Sheldon (1998) report that occurrences such as male observation of strip searches and showers, gynecological exams carried out with improper procedures, and the use of mace (Acoca, 1998b) are relatively common. Body cavity inspection may be demanded anytime a breach of rules is suspected or after routine visits from those outside the facility (Acoca, 1998b). These are just a few of the invasive correctional procedures that increase the burden of trauma, shame, and depression among female juvenile offenders. Many of the girls have become used to being treated in this manner.

I'm real used to doing that.

Interview with a female detainee
(Acoca, 1998b, p. 579)

In other words, these experiences seemed to reinforce the girls' perception, born for many with their experiences of sexual violation at home and in the streets, that they did not have the right or the power to protect their physical boundaries (Acoca, 1998b, p. 579).

Acoca (1998b) found an absence of standardized methods in the facilities and systems they reviewed for gathering data about the more serious abuses that may occur in the juvenile justice system. She asserts that these experiences within the juvenile justice system may compound injuries that female juveniles have experienced during earlier life experiences with abuse and thereby undermine the potential for girls to benefit from juvenile correctional procedures. Further degeneration of mental health (such as PTSD symptoms), increased engagement with substance abuse (due to attempts at self-medication), and lowering of self-efficacy (regarding the ability to protect herself) may all contribute to higher rates of recidivism.

Reentry Into the Community

Female juvenile justice clients, as with male juvenile justice clients, are generally returned into the very environments that victimized them in the first place, often with little correctional intervention or preventive measures evoked to prevent reoccurrence of violent trauma. Caught in a cycle of abuse and detention, these girls may develop a sense of the inevitability of invasion. Many never learn that they have the right to protect themselves or their bodily integrity; substance abuse is often used to self-medicate the feelings that stem from continued abuse; and a progression of abuse, recidivism, and incarceration may ensue (Acoca,

1998b). Sadly, there are many "missed opportunities" to enhance the "developmental potential not only of this generation of girls but of future generations" (Acoca, p. 563). With this, she refers to the fact that many female juveniles have children or are pregnant at the time of contact with the criminal justice system.

IMPLICATIONS FOR TREATMENT AND POLICY: WHAT FACTORS REDUCE RECIDIVISM?

In the conclusion to her comprehensive review of the conditions for girls in juvenile correctional facilities, Acoca (1998b) asserts that the goals of the juvenile justice system would be more effectively addressed with implementation of the following gender-specific policies:

▶ Programs that provide alternatives to incarceration for female adolescent offenders and their children

▶ Specific educational strategies designed to disrupt the generational cycle of child abuse

▶ Parenting skills development

▶ Maternal health services, including prenatal care when needed

▶ Child care services and family systems support

▶ Competency-based educational programming to provide training in coping and life skills

▶ Programs that help female juvenile offenders develop skills of moral responsibility to the community and society

As well, the information in this chapter points to the need for comprehensive services that address mental health issues in the female juvenile justice population.

CHAPTER REVIEW

This chapter has reviewed the juvenile justice system as female adolescents may experience it. Special attention has been paid to the specific needs of teenagers as well as to areas of continuity between the problems of juvenile and adult women who are involved in the correctional system. A specific trajectory of development from childhood experience with violent trauma to substance abuse and criminal activity has been identified. The various forms that criminal offense may take among adolescent females have been investigated, including participation in gangs and the drug culture. Correlates of criminal offense in adolescent females, such as school failure, destructive dating norms, teen pregnancy, and poor mental and physical health have been noted. Finally, conditions within the juvenile justice system have been analyzed, leading to treatment recommendations for gender-specific programming.

CHAPTER 5: Understanding Posttraumatic Stress Disorder

LEARNING OBJECTIVES

▶ To provide historical and etiological perspectives on Posttraumatic Stress Disorder

▶ To describe criteria for the diagnosis of Posttraumatic Stress Disorder and complex Posttraumatic Stress Disorder

▶ To discuss gender-sensitive assessment tools for diagnosing Posttraumatic Stress Disorder

▶ To distinguish between Type I and Type II traumatic events

▶ To explore the connection between criminal behavior and traumatic life experiences

This chapter written by Karen Storck, Center for Interdisciplinary Services, Inc., Denver, Colorado.

- To discuss the co-occurrence of Posttraumatic Stress Disorder and other mental disorders

- To present a three-stage model for recovery from trauma: safety, remembrance, reconnection

- To describe the basic tenets of *Seeking Safety*, the most studied model for Posttraumatic Stress Disorder treatment

- To discuss additional intervention strategies including psychopharmacology, exposure, hypnosis, and eye movement desensitization and reprocessing

- To discuss relationships among therapist personal experiences, job satisfaction, and treatment outcomes

- To explore whether effective trauma therapy is feasible for community providers

INTRODUCTION

This chapter is intended to provide a summary of the research related to the causes, symptoms, and treatment approaches associated with traumatic life events, specifically as they relate to women in corrections. Treatment of posttraumatic stress disorder (PTSD) requires specialized training and professional supervision. The information in this chapter is intended to sensitize providers to the prevalence of PTSD in the judicial population, promote awareness of issues involved in assessment and diagnosis of PTSD, and provide an inventory of resources available for client care. The information in this chapter should not in any way be construed as a primer for developing the necessary skills to effectively treat PTSD.

HISTORY OF POSTTRAUMATIC STRESS DISORDER

Earnest research concerning PTSD began after the Vietnam War as a result of the profound psychological problems experienced by the war's veterans, both men and women. PTSD-like symptoms have, however, been observed in all veteran populations, including both World Wars, the Korean conflict, in United Nations peacekeeping forces deployed to other war zones, as well as the Gulf War and the War in Iraq. Similar symptoms also occur in veterans from other countries, including Australia and Israel (Beall, 1997). Written accounts of PTSD symptoms are documented from the Civil War, when it was known as "Da Costa's Syndrome," based on his paper written in 1871, where it was described as "soldier's heart" or "irritable heart." Holocaust survivors are also discussed in medical literature as having similar symptoms, as are survivors of railway disasters and atom bombs on Hiroshima and Nagasaki. Most recently, PTSD has come to the forefront of psychological interest as the survivors of the September 11, 2001, terrorist attacks in New York City and Washington, D.C., exhibit PTSD symptoms; survivors of the 2004 tsunami in southeastern Asia and eastern India, and 2005 survivors of the earthquake in Pakistan and hurricanes in the southeastern United States will undoubtedly suffer PTSD as well.

What we now know as PTSD was, in the 1800s, grounded in hysteria. Freud, Janet, Charcot, and Breuer suggested that hysteria was precipitated by environmental events (Beall, 1997). Detractors of this theory looked for organic causes, including:

▶ Damage to the spinal cord, such as from railway injuries

▶ Microsections of exploded bombs entering the brain, particularly in World War I

▶ Brain damage resulting from starvation, such as in Holocaust survivors

Other theories included those with a psychological attribution, such as malingering or preexisting unstable personalities that were prone to develop neurosis.

Before the third edition of the *Diagnostic and Statistical Manual of Mental Disorders (DSM-III)*; (American Psychiatric Association [APA], 1980) defined this as a disorder, the syndrome had numerous monikers, including "shell shock," "war neurosis," "traumatic neurosis," "operational breakdown," "combat trauma," " fright neurosis," "nuclearism," and "battle fatigue." Due to the persistence of forensic psychiatrists and psychologists, PTSD gained credibility in the *DSM-III* as a subcategory of anxiety disorders rather than its previous categorization of dissociative disorder.

Also evolving has been the definition of *trauma*. In the *DSM-III* (American Psychiatric Association, 1980), *trauma* was defined as a "recognizable stressor that would evoke significant symptoms of distress in almost everyone" and as a "psychologically traumatic event that is generally outside the range of usual human experience," and, as the revised third edition of the *Diagnostic and Statistical Manual of Mental Disorders (DSM-III-Revised)* (American Psychiatric Association, 1987) adds, "Outside the range of such common experiences as simple bereavement, chronic illness, business losses, and marital conflict."

The fourth edition of the *Diagnostic and Statistical Manual of Mental Disorders (DSM-IV)* (American Psychiatric Association, 1994) , reclassified PTSD as a stress response, giving it respect as a clear disorder and pointing to the importance of specific research and appropriate treatment options. The current definition of a traumatic event requires that both of the following are present: "(1) The person experienced, witnessed, or was confronted with an event or events that involved actual or threatened death or serious injury, or a threat to the physical integrity of self or others (criterion A1), and (2) the person's response involved intense fear, helplessness, or horror (APA, 1994, pp. 427–428).

PTSD is no longer considered a disorder only of war veterans; it occurs in men and women, adults and children, Western and non-Western groups, and at all socioeconomic levels. Only a small minority of people appear to be invulnerable to extreme trauma. These stress-resistant individuals appear to be those with high sociability, a thoughtful coping style, and a strong perception of their ability to control their own destiny, or possessing an "internal locus of control" (Herman, 1992).

At the core of PTSD diagnosis is a traumatic event that is outside the individual, as opposed to a weakness or flaw within the individual (Bayse, 1998). The traumatic event was described in the *DSM-III* (APA, 1980) as a catastrophic stressor that was outside the range of usual human experience. At that time, reactions to such events as divorce, failure, rejection, and so on would have been diagnosed as adjustment disorders rather than PTSD. As Herman (1997) points out, however, rape, battery, and sexual and domestic abuse are so common they can hardly be described as outside the range of ordinary experience. Military trauma, too, affects millions; thus, Herman asserts that traumatic events are extraordinary not because they are rare but because of the way in which they affect human life.

Included in the *DSM-IV* and its text revision (APA, 1994, 2000) as categories of traumatic events are those *within* the range of usual human experience, such as automobile accidents and deaths. The *DSM-IV* specifies that the individual must have an intense emotional reaction to the traumatic event, such as panic, terror, grief, or disgust (Bayse, 1998). Herman (1997) uses the *Comprehensive Textbook of Psychiatry*'s description of trauma: "intense fear, helplessness, loss of control, and threat of annihilation" (p. 33).

POSTTRAUMATIC STRESS DISORDER POPULATION STATISTICS

The National Center for Posttraumatic Stress Disorder (NCPTSD, 2007) reported that about

8 percent of the population will have PTSD symptoms at some time in their lives. Approximately 5.2 million adults have PTSD during a given year; however, this is only a small portion of those who have experienced a traumatic event. About 60 percent of men and 50 percent of women experience a traumatic event at some time in their lives.

Women are more likely to experience sexual assault and child sexual abuse. Men are more likely to experience accidents, physical assault, combat, or disaster or to witness death or injury. About 8 percent of men and 20 percent of women who experience a traumatic event will develop PTSD (National Center for Posttraumatic Stress Disorder, 2007). Sexual assault is more likely than other events to cause PTSD (Vogt, 2007).

Approximately 30 percent of men and women who served in war zones experience PTSD symptoms. An additional 20 percent to 25 percent have had some symptoms. More than 30 percent of male and 26 percent of female veterans of the Vietnam War experienced PTSD symptoms at some time during their lives (Beall, 1997). As many as 10 percent of the first Gulf War veterans, 6 percent to 11 percent of Afghanistan veterans, and 12 percent to 20 percent of the Iraq War veterans are expected to have experienced PTSD (National Center for Posttraumatic Stress Disorders [NCPTSD], 2007).

According to the National Center for Posttraumatic Stress Disorders (2007), individuals most likely to develop PTSD are:

▶ Those directly exposed to a traumatic event as the victim or as a witness

▶ Those who were seriously injured during the event

▶ Those who experienced a trauma that was long lasting or very severe

▶ Those who believed their lives were in danger

▶ Those who believed that a family member was in danger

▶ Those who had a severe reaction during the event such as crying, shaking, vomiting, or feeling separated from the surroundings

- Those who felt helpless during the trauma, not being able to help themselves or family member(s)

- Those who had an earlier life-threatening event, such as being abused as a child

- Those with another mental health problem

- Those with family members with mental health problems

- Those with minimal support from family and friends

- Those who recently lost a loved one, particularly if it was unexpected

- Those who have had recent, stressful life changes

- Those who drink alcohol in excess

- Those who are women, poorly educated, or are younger

The National Center for Posttraumatic Stress Disorders (2007) also reported that African Americans and Hispanics may be at higher risk than whites to develop PTSD and that one's culture or ethnic group may affect how one reacts to PTSD symptoms; people from groups that are open and willing to talk about problems may be more willing to seek help.

While one person may have few problems adjusting and returning to a normal state after a traumatic event, others may be debilitated for years; two people exposed to the same event will have different levels of reaction. It is impossible to predict or measure the potential effect of a traumatic event on different people, but certain variables seem to have the most impact, including:

- The extent to which the event was unexpected, uncontrollable, and inescapable

- The level of perceived extent of threat or danger, suffering, upset, terror, or fear

- The source of the trauma: human-caused trauma is generally more difficult than an event of nature

- Sexual victimization, especially when betrayal is involved

- An actual or perceived responsibility for the event

- Prior vulnerability factors, including genetics or early onset as in childhood trauma

Herman (1992) agrees that no two people will have identical reactions to the same trauma, despite PTSD's constant features. She reported a study of veterans with PTSD whose symptoms were related to their individual childhood history, emotional conflicts, and adaptive style. Those who had displayed antisocial behavior before going to war showed symptoms of irritability and anger. Those who had high moral expectations of themselves and compassion for others were more likely to have predominant symptoms of depression.

SYMPTOMS OF POSTTRAUMATIC STRESS DISORDER

Chronic PTSD typically involves periods of increase in symptoms followed by a remission. Some individuals experience symptoms that are unremitting and severe, while others report a lifetime of mild symptoms, with significant increases in symptoms following major life events such as retirement, medical illness, or reminders of military service such as reunions or media attention to anniversaries of events.

Generally described, the symptoms of PTSD include (Dryden-Edwards & Stoppler, 2007; Kinchin, 2005; Smith, Jaffe, & Segal, 2008):

- Reexperiencing the trauma
  - Flashbacks
  - Nightmares
  - Intrusive memories and exaggerated emotional and physical reactions to triggers that remind the person of the trauma

- Emotional numbing
  - Feeling detached
  - Lack of emotions, especially positive ones
  - Loss of interest in activities

- Avoidance
  - Avoiding activities, people, or places that are reminders of the trauma

- Increased arousal
  - Difficulty sleeping and concentrating
  - Irritability
  - Hypervigilance
  - Exaggerated startle response

PTSD also creates physiological changes in the body, including:

- Neurobiological changes
  - Alterations in brainwave activity
  - Changes in the size of brain structures, including decreased size of the hippocampus and abnormal activation of the amygdala
  - Changes in functioning, such as memory and fear responses
- Psychophysiological changes
  - Hyperarousal of the sympathetic nervous system
  - Increased startle reaction
  - Sleep disturbances
  - Increased neurohormonal changes resulting in heightened stress and increased depression
- Physical manifestations
  - Headaches
  - Stomach or digestive problems
  - Immune system problems
  - Asthma or breathing problems
  - Dizziness
  - Chest pain
  - Chronic pain or fibromyalgia

Psychological outcomes can include the following:

- Depression, major or pervasive
- Anxiety disorders such as phobias, panic, and social anxiety
- Conduct disorders
- Dissociation
- Eating disorders

Social manifestations include:

- Interpersonal problems
- Low self-esteem
- Alcohol and substance use
- Employment problems
- Homelessness

- Trouble with the law
- Self-destructive behaviors
  - Substance abuse
  - Suicide attempts
  - Risky sexual behaviors
  - Reckless driving
  - Self-injury

To be diagnosed with PTSD, according to the *DMS-IV* (American Psychological Association, 1994, 2000) the stressor must be of an extreme nature and considered life threatening; however, in adjustment disorder, the stressor can be of any severity and includes divorce or job loss. Symptoms of avoidance, numbing, and increased arousal that are present before exposure to the stressor do not meet the criteria for PTSD diagnosis and should be considered as a mood disorder or another anxiety disorder.

Other diagnoses to rule out include brief psychotic disorder, conversion disorder, major depressive disorder, acute stress disorder, obsessive-compulsive disorder, and malingering. As emphasized by Armstrong and High (1999), "It is important to carefully assess causality, intentionality, and motivation as well as traumatic events and symptoms" (p. 46) when considering an appropriate diagnosis. Simple recounting of a traumatic event or listing of symptoms by a client and accepting a client's presentation of the problem is not a strong enough basis for PTSD diagnosis. Armstrong and High further stress that the client's state of mind at the time of the critical event should be thoroughly considered. PTSD sufferers are able to describe the horror, helplessness, and/ or dissociation they experienced. To ensure proper diagnosis, these authors suggest careful observation of the client's physical responses when discussing the traumatic event.

COMPLEX POSTTRAUMATIC STRESS DISORDER

Complex PTSD is considered to be a form of PTSD that includes impaired affect regulation, dissociation, and severe difficulties in interpersonal relationships, along with the main features of reexperiencing the trauma, avoidance, and hyperarousal (Kimerling, Prins, Westrup, & Lee, 2004). Kimerling and associates note that *affect regulation* has been defined as the "ongoing process of an individual's emotional patterns in response to moment-by-moment contextual demands" (Kimerling et al., p. 573). These individuals show low-threshold and highly intense emotional reactions with a slow return to baseline. They are easily upset, have trouble calming down, and feel overwhelmed by negative emotions.

Affect disregulation, a symptom of complex PTSD, is a more common occurrence in women with PTSD, probably because of the differences in how men and women experience emotion. Women are more likely than men to utilize emotional coping strategies and are more likely to report negative emotions such as shame, sadness, and guilt (Kimerling et al., 2004). In addition, affect regulation is developed when young; when trauma occurs in childhood, the ability to experience, identify, and talk about emotions can be disrupted.

Another component of complex PTSD, dissociation, ranges from simple daydreaming to depersonalization or derealization. Trauma during childhood, particularly that perpetrated by family members or those in authority, is indicative of the more severe forms of depersonalization (Kimerling et al., 2004). As with affect disregulation, dissociation is most often found after exposure to events that are more common among women.

The interpersonal relationships of those with complex PTSD are problematic. Individuals with complex PTSD have difficulty assessing and receiving social support and have issues relating to social stigma associated with the event (Kimerling et al., 2004). The symptoms of PTSD themselves can cause problems in existing relationships. Male veterans with PTSD exhibit more problems with marriage and intimacy and are more likely to separate or divorce than veterans without PTSD. Interpersonal violence is also linked to PTSD in men. Kimerling et al. reported that research with women, which has not been as extensive as with males, has focused mainly on exposure to child sexual abuse and adult sexual assault. It has been shown, however, that sexually abused or assaulted women are less likely to be married and more likely to be single mothers. Less satisfaction with relationships, specifically with trust and

communication, are frequently reported, as is violence with intimate partners.

POSTTRAUMATIC STRESS DISORDER ASSESSMENT METHODS

While the questioning of clients who have experienced recent acute trauma allows for a fairly straightforward diagnosis, those who have suffered prolonged, repeated trauma are not as easily diagnosed (Herman, 1997). Presentations are often disguised, particularly in complex PTSD. Physical symptoms, insomnia, depression, or anxiety may be initially reported, but without explicit questioning it can be difficult to determine that an individual has actually lived in fear of very real violence. Prolonged childhood abuse is more complicated to detect, as the client may not have full recall of the history. In addition, the client most likely will not connect the childhood trauma with current symptoms and particularly not with criminal behavior (Herman).

Herman (1997) encourages clinicians who suspect a diagnosis of PTSD to share this with the client. By giving the client words to describe and attach to her feelings and experiences, the client can feel not alone, not crazy, and can even expect to recover as others have.

Caution, however is strongly recommended. Sharing such assessment and diagnostic impressions must be carefully thought out and should be given as a reflection of the client's story that directly indicates such a diagnosis. It is best that reflective feedback be couched in the client's own words, and it should be given within the context of how data from the client match formal diagnostic criteria, such as from the *DSM-IV* (American Psychiatric Association, 1994). These criteria and the clinical evidence should be reviewed with and confirmed by the client. It should also be made clear that diagnosis only provides a guideline, but does not offer a complete understanding; that understanding only evolves in the course of continued assessment and treatment Wanberg, K., personal communication, March 5, 2008).

Assessment tools for PTSD fall into two categories: those that measure trauma history and those that measure symptom history. Norris and Hamblen (2004) suggest the use of one tool from each category in order to properly understand the full impact of each individual's circumstance.

Kimerling et al. (2004) discuss the importance of using assessment methods that sustain reliability and validity measures in the context of gender. They list three general concepts that will affect the use of trauma exposure measures when considering gender issues:

1. The behaviorally specific language that is used and its ease of being understood,

2. The extent to which specific characteristics of traumatic events are measured, and

3. The inclusiveness of the events being examined.

Studies have shown that some women, although they had experienced the legal definition of rape, may answer "No" to the question, "Have you ever been raped?" Kimerling et al. (2004) encourage the use of gender-sensitive measures such as the Life Stressor Checklist, Revised (LSC-R) by Wolfe and Kimerling (1997b). This 30-item questionnaire includes unique assessments for abortion, death of a child, domestic violence, sexual assault, and rape. As Kimerling et al. point out, this checklist includes a measurement for stressors that usually do not meet the *DSM-IV* (American Psychiatric Association, 1994, 2004) criterion A for PTSD but are very relevant to women. These include unwanted separation from their children, care giving for a disabled or ill family member, and severe financial strain.

Kimerling et al. (2004) also support the use of the Potential Stressful Events Interview (PSEI) by Kilpatrick, Resnick, and Freedy (1991). Using sensitive, plain language, the PSEI is appropriate for use with both men and women. Exposure characteristics such as age at time of event and severity are also considered.

The reason for the importance of collecting information, such as age at the time of trauma, the severity, and chronicity, is that these factors define the parameters of exposure that may explain gender differences in PTSD prevalence and comorbid symptoms. One tool that meets these criteria is the Trauma History

Questionnaire (THQ) by Green. This tool is able to differentiate multiple incidents of physical assault from repeated and chronic partner violence or physical abuse (Kimerling et al., 2004).

The Traumatic Life Events Questionnaire—(TLEQ) by Kubany et al. (2000) also utilizes specific terms to describe 21 potentially traumatic events, including gender-specific ones such as miscarriages and abortions. It also includes an open-ended question to assess other highly disturbing events.

POSTTRAUMATIC STRESS DISORDER AND GENDER

According to Herman, in her 1992 book *Trauma and Recovery: The Aftermath of Violence—From Domestic Abuse to Political Terror,* the study of psychological trauma is dependent upon the political movement of the time. She demonstrates how Sigmund Freud found the source of hysteria in female patients to be childhood sexual abuse. At that time, however, because the "patriarchal world" was not ready to accept this reality, he retracted his theory and instead asserted that women with hysteria fabricated stories of childhood sexual abuse (Beall, 1998). With the feminist movement of the 1960s, the study of rape and other sexual-based trauma was given credibility.

As Beall (1998) reports, Lenore Walker's *Abused Women and Survivor Therapy: A Practical Guide for the Psychotherapist* (1994) shows how the effects of interpersonal violence in women's lives, including experiences such as physical, sexual, and psychological abuse, cause profound changes in abused women, including PTSD symptoms. According to Kimberling et al. (2004), gender itself plays a part in the type of trauma to which an individual is exposed; hence the original studies of two specific populations: male combat veterans (shell shock) and female sexual assault survivors (rape trauma).

Women, have, however served at war. As Beall (1998) reports, this small group of women is unacknowledged as victims of war and is often misdiagnosed with borderline personality disorder. They often receive inadequate treatment by male therapists who are not equipped to deal with the psychological difficulties of women. In the early 1970s, a pattern of psychological reactions following rape was identified and called "rape trauma syndrome." As reported by Herman (1997), researchers Burgess and Holmstrom found that women viewed rape as a life-threatening event, fearing mutilation or death during the attack. Insomnia, nausea, startle response, nightmares, and numbing symptoms followed. A link was then drawn between rape victims and combat veterans.

Stemming from the feminist movement, this research on rape was followed by studies on domestic violence and sexual abuse of children. Lenore Walker (Beall, 1998) defined "battered women syndrome" as having the same symptoms as rape trauma and shell shock.

Kimerling et al. (2004) point out that research shows that men are more likely to experience traumatic events in their lifetimes, yet women are more than twice as likely to develop PTSD. Studies conducted in the United States have indicated that approximately 61 percent of men and 51 percent of women report at least one lifetime traumatic event, with the majority experiencing multiple events. Men, on average, reported 5.3 events and women reported 4.3 events. Women were more likely to report sexual assault in childhood or adulthood; men were more likely to report having been shot or physically assaulted or having experienced motor vehicle crashes or combat.

Kimerling et al. (2004) also suggest that there may be an underreporting of traumatic events by women. They cite evidence that assessment tools may not possess content validity or gender sensitivity; for example, trauma lists do not include "sudden miscarriage" or "stillbirth." Further, references to "rape" or "sexual assault" often will miss early childhood experiences of sexual abuse, which is more common for women. In addition, these authors point out that the broad categorization of traumatic events can encompass a single, brief event with a stranger as well as prolonged physical abuse by an intimate partner, making the category of "physical assault" not an accurate descriptor.

Kimerling et al. (2004) also report that, in addition to being twice as likely to suffer from PTSD

as men, women experience more chronic forms of the disorder. This may be explained by the fact that women typically experience trauma at an earlier age, and the trauma is typically in the form of sexual assault. Kimerling et al. hypothesize that factors beyond the specific exposure, such as differences in cognitive processes, social roles, and relationships, also help define the differences in response between men and women.

Comorbidity

Kimerling et al. (2004) reported on a 1995 study that showed differences between men and women and their patterns of comorbidity: Fifty-nine percent of men and 43.6 percent of women were shown to have three or more additional diagnoses. Most common in men were alcohol abuse or dependence (52 percent), major depressive disorder (MDD) (48 percent), and conduct disorder (43.3 percent). Women experienced major depressive disorder (48.5 percent), simple or social phobia (28–29 percent), and alcohol abuse or dependence (28 percent). Kimerling et al. emphasize that comorbidity has a major effect on the severity of PTSD and is therefore an important aspect of assessment and treatment.

Physiological Diseases and Disorders

Bender (2004) reported that women with PTSD experience more adverse medical conditions such as arthritis, lower back pain, obesity, emphysema, and hypertension than women in general or those with depression only. Depression has long been known to be associated with poor physical health, but women with PTSD exhibited even worse health, based on a 1999 survey of 30,000 female veterans. Nearly 90 percent of women with a diagnosis of PTSD experienced at least one medical condition, which, in addition to the conditions mentioned previously, included low energy, chronic pain, and poor physical functioning. According to this study, women with PTSD also experienced more physical pain than women with depression or with neither diagnosis. Bender states that the study suggests that trauma may be linked to "chronic neuroendocrine dysregulation" as well as to poor personal habits such as smoking, drinking, or drug use and cautions those in the mental health care field to be aware of the need for additional treatment for comorbid medical conditions.

Kimerling et al. (2004) concur that both men and women with PTSD have a greater incidence of functional impairment as well as a poorer course of disease. These include cardiovascular disorders (a significant finding since heart disease remains the leading cause of death among women in the United States), gastrointestinal disorders including liver disease, viral hepatitis, irritable bowel syndrome, and gastroesophageal reflux disease (commonly known as heartburn).

Women with PTSD who experienced childhood sexual trauma are also commonly found to have sexually transmitted diseases, suggesting that trauma exposure serves as a risk factor for infection, particularly HIV. Sexual trauma exposure is a direct risk factor for sexually transmitted diseases. Kimerling et al. (2004) reported that a 1996 study of HIV-infected women showed that 43 percent of them had been sexually assaulted at some time in their lives. It was also reported that the disease progresses more rapidly among women with PTSD than among those without.

Studies also show that, in victims of trauma, there are physical changes, specifically volume reduction in the hippocampus, the learning and memory center of the brain. The hippocampus works in tandem with the medial prefrontal cortex, the area that regulates emotional response to fear and stress, thus indicating a physiological relationship to PTSD symptoms (Bremner, 2002). Combat veterans were found to have an 8 percent reduction in hippocampal volume, yet no differences were found in other parts of the brain. Interestingly, Bremner also reports that the hippocampal volume reduction is specific to those with PTSD but not associated with closely related disorders such as anxiety or panic disorder. Further, the hippocampus has the ability to regenerate neurons; however, stress has been found to stop or slow neuron regeneration. Bremner suggests that this change in size of the learning and memory center of the brain among PTSD sufferers may explain the delayed recall or "recovered memories" that many victims of childhood abuse experience. He explains that the abuse caused damage to the hippocampus, leading to a distortion or fragmentation of memories.

The changes in the function of the prefrontal regions of the brain may explain the pathological emotional responses in those with PTSD (Bremner, 2002). Bremner reports that studies of veterans with PTSD showed a decreased blood flow to this area when viewing combat-related scenes and sounds. This did not occur in veterans without PTSD. Similar results were found when comparing women who experienced childhood sexual abuse and suffer PTSD as opposed to those with childhood sexual abuse and no PTSD symptoms.

Depressive Disorders

As noted previously, major depressive disorder (MDD) is a frequent partner of PTSD, with studies showing similar rates of occurrence in both genders. As Kimerling et al. (2004) pointed out, this is an interesting phenomenon, since women's risk for MDD in the absence of PTSD is greater than men's. Their explanation is that PTSD "may create a vulnerability toward depression in men that suppresses the protective effect of male gender" (p. 579).

Due to the overlap of MDD and PTSD symptoms (diminished interest in activities, sleep and concentration disturbances), assessment and diagnosis can be difficult. In an attempt to distinguish the two disorders, Kimerling et al. (2004) report that clinicians have outlined several methods of determining the difference between the two diagnoses. The symptom of diminished interest in activities in PTSD is specific to cues of past trauma exposure; in MDD, it is generalized and characterized by loss of energy and hopelessness. PTSD sleep difficulties are characterized by nightmares and hypervigilance that occur only after the traumatic event. Difficulties in concentration with MDD are more global, whereas with PTSD they are dissociative and result from trauma-related memories. Kimerling et al. also assert that because prolonged childhood trauma is more common in women than in men, and because there is a closer relationship between childhood maltreatment and adult psychopathology in women then men, gender tends to be a confounding factor in the process of diagnosing PTSD and MDD.

Substance Abuse

A 1990 study found that approximately 74 percent of men and 29 percent of women with PTSD had a lifetime diagnosis of alcohol abuse (Ouimette, Wolfe, & Chrestman, 1996). Kimerling et al. (2004) report that approximately 30–50 percent of men and 25–30 percent of women with lifetime PTSD also are substance abusers. It has been shown that a comorbid diagnosis of PTSD and substance use disorder (SUD) is associated with poorer substance use outcomes: those with PTSD relapse more quickly, drink more on days when they do drink, have a greater percentage of heavy drinking days, and suffer greater negative consequences due to their substance abuse than do non–PTSD abusers (Brown, 2000).

Interestingly, women are more likely than men to develop substance use disorders after exposure to a traumatic event and symptoms of PTSD, with approximately 65–84 percent of women experiencing PTSD before developing substance use disorders. This supports the "self-medication" hypothesis as an important component of PTSD/SUD comorbidity among women, in which women use alcohol or drugs to cope with trauma-related symptoms. In contrast, men are more likely to experience trauma due to their behaviors linked to substance use, which then results in PTSD symptoms (Kimerling et al., 2004). Kimerling et al. highly suggest that clinicians routinely screen clients for SUD when PTSD is suspected.

POSTTRAUMATIC STRESS DISORDER AND CHILDHOOD TRAUMA

Estimates of childhood sexual abuse are varied, ranging from 16 percent to 30 percent of women and 10 percent to 15 percent of men in the general population (Bremner, 2002; Courtois, 1995; Whealin, 2003). These estimates follow years of reports of incest and sexual molestation having been obscured by the taboo surrounding them. Courtois believes this taboo applies to disclosure and discussion of the events rather than the actual occurrence of them.

Volpe (2005) discusses Terr's description of "Type I" and "Type II" traumatic events. While single, short-term events such as rape, assault, or a severe beating are referred to as Type I trauma, repeated or prolonged exposure such as child sexual abuse is referred to as Type II. It is suggested that Type II trauma has a greater impact on an individual's functioning than Type I.

Today, sexual abuse is considered to be a major public health problem with numerous personal and societal implications. All forms of child abuse are considered to be risk factors for psychological, social, and physical effects, both short term and long term in nature for both men and women (Courtois, 1995). Short-term effects often take the form of children acting out, agitated behavior, being cruel to others, showing seductive or sexual behavior that is inappropriate for their age, and experiencing frightening dreams. Some injure themselves or attempt suicide (Whealin, 2003).

Long-term effects, with symptoms persisting into adulthood, include PTSD, anxiety, depression, sexual anxiety, poor body image, low self-esteem, and unhealthy behaviors such as alcohol and drug abuse, self-mutilation, and eating disorders (Whealin, 2003). Beall (1997) refers to Dusty Miller's book, *Women Who Hurt Themselves,* where the phrase "trauma reenactment syndrome" (TRS) was coined. Miller (1994) denotes women in this category as being "at war with their bodies" and struggling for control. This quest for control within a woman can be one explanation for the development of criminal behavior. As Marcus-Mendoza and Wright (2004) report on Dougherty's work in 1998, even though feeling internally powerless, abused women in the judicial system will create an external toughness and commit crimes to survive. The abused woman also minimizes the effect that the abuse has had on her.

POSTTRAUMATIC STRESS DISORDER AND THE FEMALE JUDICIAL CLIENT

Kubiak (2004) expresses concern that trauma is rarely considered in relation to incarceration, either as a cause of imprisonment or the result thereof. Zlotnick, Najavits, Rohsenow, and Johnson (2003) indicate that the rates of PTSD and SUD are higher for incarcerated women than the general population of women, with PTSD and SUD being the most common disorders among female detainees who are awaiting trial. Zlotnick et al. report that the prevalence of PTSD in the female prison population occurs at a rate of 33.5 percent for lifetime experience of PTSD symptoms and 22.3 percent for current PTSD symptoms. This, they note, is more than twice as high as the rate among nonincarcerated women.

Marcus-Mendoza and Wright (2004) assert that the majority (up to 90 percent) of women prisoners in the United States have suffered physical, sexual, or emotional abuse prior to their imprisonment. Zlotnick et al. (2003) also report that between 78 percent and 85 percent of incarcerated women have experienced at least one traumatic event in their lives, compared to 69 percent of the general female population. Childhood abuse is highly correlated with PTSD and is commonly reported by women offenders, with 23 percent to 48 percent of them reporting having been abused as a child (Zlotnick et al). In California prisons, approximately 80 percent of women inmates experienced some type of abuse, with 29 percent reporting childhood sexual abuse and 23 percent experiencing physical abuse as an adult; 40 percent reported emotional abuse as a child and 48 percent as an adult (Covington, 1998a).

As Marcus-Mendoza and Wright (2004) stated, abuse is frequently thought to be a "precursor to criminality." They cited findings that support the belief that abused girls were significantly more likely than nonabused girls to:

◗ Become runaways to escape from abuse

◗ Score lower on intelligence and reading tests

◗ Have substance-abusing parents

◗ Lack social and psychological resources, and

◗ Engage in criminal behavior

Also discussed by Marcus-Mendoza and Wright (2004) is a pattern among delinquent girls showing that childhood victimization results in running away, drug and alcohol abuse, prostitution, selling drugs, and, to support their drug or alcohol habit, robbery. Marcus-Mendoza and Wright point toward Zaplin's assertion that "this cycle of events leads to emotional stress, self-hatred, anxiety, depression, and aggressive and impulsive behaviors, with girls at risk of not being able to develop empathic or caring attitudes for themselves or others" (p. 251). In addition, those with the highest risk of recidivism reported more substance abuse, parenting problems, and mental health needs, all of which are consequences of physical, sexual, and emotional abuse. Zlotnick et al. (2003) concur, reporting that in addition to high rates of drug use, women prisoners have long histories of physical and sexual abuse. Marcus-Mendoza and Wright reinforce that abuse and traumatic early life experiences are the context from which women develop criminal behavior.

Female prisoners are reported to be five to eight times more likely to abuse alcohol than women in the general population, 10 times more likely to abuse drugs, and 27 times more likely to use cocaine (Zlotnick et al., 2003). Zlotnick et al. also reported that studies show the rate of women's drug possession convictions increased by 41 percent between 1990 and 1996. Further, a 1997 study showed that more than 40 percent of female inmates were under the influence of drugs at the time of their offence, compared to 32 percent of male inmates. Zlotnick et al. noted that the high rate of recidivism among women prisoners can be explained, in part, by their use of illegal substances along with high levels of physical and sexual abuse. Covington (1998a) asserts that traditional addiction treatment does not effectively deal with abuse issues, causing relapse to occur more often in these women.

ALLOSTASIS AND THE ALLOSTATIC LOAD FACTOR

Allostasis, meaning maintaining stability or homeostasis through change, was first introduced by Sterling and Eyer (1988) to describe the resting and active states of the cardiovascular system. Focal research by McEwen and associates at Rockefeller University has explored the relationship of the psychobiology of stress to allostasis and the allostatic load factor (McEwen, 1998, 2000, 2004). Wilson, Friedman, and Lindy (2001), having seen these concepts as important to the understanding of PTSD and its treatment, defined allostasis as "the body's effort to maintain stability through change when loads or stressors of various types place demands on the normal levels of adaptive biological function" (p. 9).

McEwen (1998, 2000, 2004) explained that allostasis is the psychobiological adaptation to the challenge of internal and external stress and is an essential component to maintain homeostasis. The moderators of the stress response are hormones and neurochemicals produced by the adrenergic and hypothalamic-pituitary-adrenocortical (HPA) systems, such as catecholamine and cortisol, that, in the short run, serve to meet the challenge of external and internal stressors. This allostasis response is inherent within the psychobiological system's effort to achieve stability and to adaptation through change. In a sense these are "first responders" to stress and provide short-term protection from potential damage due to stress.

The important part of this process is the "shutting down" or inactivation of the allostasis response, which allows the cortisol and catecholamine secretion to return to baseline levels. This is the normal response when the external threat or challenge is over and is the short-run benefit of allostasis. However, as McEwin explained, if each inactivation is "inefficient," or doesn't shut down to a normal level of hormones, and if, over the long run, this process is called upon frequently with repeated inefficiency, there is long-term exposure (over years) to the imbalance of stress hormones and this exposure can lead to an allostatic load and its wear and tear on the psychobiologic system (McEwin, 1998, 2000, 2004).

McEwin (2000) identified four dysfunctional allostatic conditions that can lead to allostatic load and result in impairment of the psychobiological system. These are

1. Frequent and repetitive activation of the stress response pattern due to exposure to multiple stressors

2. The breakdown of normal adaptation to stress due to the allostatic load's "wear" on the system

3. A persistent and prolonged stress response or responses resulting in a failure to turn off the responses or shut down the activation of the stress hormones in a timely manner

4. Inadequate response or system failure resulting in the inadequate production of hormone mediators or moderators of the stress response; this leads the system to produce other mediators that cause compensatory hyperactivity that is counterproductive to the mediation of stress

McEwen (2000) identified early childhood experiences of abuse and neglect as major risk factors for these conditions that can potentially lead to the increase of allostatic load in adulthood. There is a growing body of research to support the relationship between allostatic load and psychobiologic disorders, including cardiovascular disorders, depression, anxiety, aggression, and PTSD (e.g., Friedman, 2001; Glover, 2006 Kubzanski, Koenen, Spiro, Vokonas, & Sparrow, 2007; McEwen, 2004)." Friedman (2001) described eight psychobiological examples of allostatic load in PTSD and a rationale for PTSD pharmacotherapy based on allostatic load.

Wilson et al. (2001) see allostasis and the allostasic load as "fundamental to the understanding of stress-related psychobiological behaviors" (p. 9). Individuals with PTSD are vulnerable to sudden changes in their sense of well-being that, based on triggers or cues, internal or external, result in rapid switching back and forth between states of "relative calmness to states of hypervigilance, anxiety, anger, and extreme arousal" (p. 10). Wilson et al. see one of the "major challenges" of the treatment of PTSD is "to facilitate a reduction or 'switching off' of persistent hyper-arousal mechanisms associated with allostatic load that are readily reactivated and amplified by traumatic memories (conscious or unconscious) stored in the brain" (p. 10).

RECOVERY FROM TRAUMA

The recovery process discussed herein may be difficult at best and impossible at worst to apply to the female prisoner because of the controlled physical environment as well as the female prisoners' lack of trust for others. It is, however, an important aspect for understanding the rationale behind current treatment methodologies as well as the struggles a prisoner with PTSD will encounter. As Marcus-Mendoza and Wright (2004) point out, "Although helping women heal wounds from abuse in an abusive environment would seem impossible, scholars and practitioners are working, and must continue to work together to achieve this ambitious goal" (p. 115). It is with this in mind that the following is offered in order that the reader may understand the process women experience during their recovery from trauma.

Recovery from traumatic events is described by Herman (1997) as unfolding in three stages, the first being establishing safety. The second stage includes the tasks of remembrance and mourning, while the third stage encompasses reconnection with ordinary life. As with any abstract concept, the stages are not followed exactly, nor are they linear. Herman describes traumatic syndromes as "oscillating and dialectical in nature...defy[ing] any attempt to impose such simpleminded order" (p. 155). These stages are defined in an attempt to assist clients and clinicians alike in simplifying and gaining control of a seemingly uncontrollable process. While other writers identify five and some eight, we focus on Herman's three.

Safety

Survivors of victimization must shift their surroundings from that of unpredictable danger to reliable safety. This includes recognizing and naming the demon. As Herman (1997) discussed, some may feel relieved to learn that there is a name for their problems. Others, however, resist the diagnosis out of fear of the stigma associated with any psychiatric diagnosis; some may deny the condition out of a sense of pride. Many survivors of physical or sexual abuse do not connect the fact that their experience of abuse is directly related to their symptoms or behaviors. Herman went on to emphasize that the process of developing a framework that relates the client's problems with the traumatic history is beneficial, as it assists in developing a therapeutic alliance.

Establishing safety includes allowing the victim to regain control. While the female prisoner may have attempted to regain control through illegal acts, true control is accomplished when victims feel safe in relation to others as well as with their own thinking and feeling. As Herman (1997) suggested, gradually

developing a safe and trusting therapeutic relationship is key. In addition, family, friends, and lovers who were *not* involved in abuse of the victim should be mobilized to act as a support system. Further, any attachment to those involved in the victimization must be disconnected, as must use of illicit drugs or alcohol (assumed, in the case of incarcerated victims).

Herman (1997) has pointed out that the process of establishing safety may be hampered if the survivor is in a hostile or nonprotective environment. This may be the case within the prison system. The legal process is obviously outside of the victim's control, thus disrupting this initial stage of safety.

Remembrance and Mourning

After having regained a sense of control, developed a feeling of safety within and among others and self, and discontinuing self-destructive behaviors, trauma victims can gradually move on to stage 2: remembrance and mourning. This is the phase where victims verbally tell the whole, in-depth, sordid story. As Herman notes, the difference between remembering the trauma and retelling the trauma is likened to a series of still snapshots as opposed to full cinema movies with the inclusion of words and music.

Retelling the story must be repetitive; eventually, the story no longer will arouse such intense feelings (Herman, 1997). Eventually, it becomes only a part of the survivor's experience rather than the focus of it. The memory fades and grief loses its strength. The victim's life story begins to take on other aspects rather than only one. This, indeed, is a simple explanation of a complex process, but one that can be accomplished with a knowledgeable and trained clinician who can look past the anger and hatred that may accompany PTSD and its accompanying symptoms.

Reconnection

The third stage, reconnection, may not occur for inmates until their release; however, it is an important part of the process of recovering from trauma. After mourning the loss of the person they were before the trauma, they must create a new self and a new future. As quoted by Herman (1997), psychiatrist Michael

Stone described this task (specific to his work with incest survivors) thusly:

> All victims... have, by definition, been taught that the strong can do as they please, without regard for convention.... *Re-education* is often indicated, pertaining to what is typical, average, wholesome, and "normal" in the intimate life of ordinary people. Victims... tend to be woefully ignorant of these matters, owing to their skewed and secretive early environments. Although victims in their original homes, they are like strangers in a foreign country, once "safely" outside. (p. 196)

Herman (1997) believes the statement "I know I have myself" is the anchor of the third stage. No longer possessed by past trauma, the survivor understands the results of the damage done to her and now becomes the person she wants to be. Imagination and fantasy, desire and initiative are at the core of this stage, where hopes and dreams are weaved into reality.

Herman emphasizes that resolution of the trauma is never final and recovery is never complete; the impact of trauma will "reverberate throughout the survivor's lifecycle" (p. 211). While incomplete, recovery will allow the survivor to return to the normal tasks of life. Becoming more interested in the present and future than the past, a survivor of trauma overcomes her fear and opposition and gradually engages in new and healthy relationships.

In summary, as psychologist Mary Harvey has described, there are seven criteria for the resolution of trauma (Herman, 1997):

1. The physiological symptoms of PTSD have been brought within manageable limits.

2. The survivor is able to bear the feelings associated with traumatic memories.

3. The person has authority over the memories; for example, she can either remember the event or put it aside.

4. The memory is coherent and linked with feeling.

5. The survivor's self-esteem has been restored.

6. Important relationships have been reestablished.

7. A coherent system of meaning and belief concerning the trauma has been constructed.

CORE AREAS AND TREATMENT GOALS FOR POSTTRAUMATIC STRESS DISORDER

Before looking at specific approaches and modalities for addressing PTSD for women in corrections, it is helpful to look at the general core areas and goals that are addressed in the treatment of PTSD.

Wilson et al. (2001) described these in the context of and in relationship to allostatic load. As these goals relate to recovery as described by Herman (1997), they are as follows:

1. Identify and address the psychobiological alterations with the goal of reestablishing a normal (healthy) stress response. These psychobiological alterations include: hypervigilance, irritability, proneness to anger and depression, sleep disturbances, problems in concentration, dissociation, and exaggerated responses to external cues. As Herman (1997) noted, an important treatment component of establishing a stable and normal stress response is to provide an environment of safety. This safety factor will help mitigate the allostatic load and "wear and tear" on the system by helping to reduce the "repeated hits" (Wilson et al., 2001) by external multiple stressors.

2. Focus on traumatic memory including nightmares, affective memories, reliving the trauma, and so on, with the goal of helping clients identify the triggers for these memories and understand and change the cognitive appraisals of these memories that lead to pathological behavior. The allostatic load around these memories can be reduced through the client retelling her story in a way that there becomes an efficient "shutting down" to normal levels of hormones. *The goal* is to retrain the system to return to a normal response and level of hormones once the external or internal threat is over, that is, after her story is told. Additionally, identification of the triggers and management of them through cognitive reappraisal will prevent neurochemical and hormonal systems from cascading to a level where the allostatic load is compounded.

3. Numbing, avoidance, and denial can take on extreme states such as amnesia, withdrawal from others, and a variety of pathological responses including substance abuse and obsessive-compulsive responses. *The goal* is to help the client gain insight into the use of these defenses and establish a sense of

identity that includes seeing oneself as a person who is a survivor rather than a victim.

4. Another area to address is the trauma-producing damage to the ego process and structure, ego fragmentation, demoralization, engagement in dissociative thinking, helplessness, and vulnerability. These can all lead to depression, excessive guilt, and hopelessness. *The goal* is to restore personal integrity and energy, reduce the sense of injury to self, and replace faulty thinking about self and the world by promoting understanding of oneself within the process of change and growth as well as to help establish a renewed sense of vitality and hopefulness.

5. Trauma can lead to detachment, social isolation, difficulty in establishing intimacy, alienation, distrust, fear of abandonment, difficulty in establishing boundaries, and engagement in destructive relationships. *The goal* is to confront and change these relationships, replacing them with positive relationships that are based on healthy boundaries. As Wilson et al. (2001) pointed out, the critical factor in this goal is to "understand the connection between vulnerability states (e.g., fears, feelings, perceived threats) and dispositional tendencies in social encounters" (p. 23).

TREATMENT MODALITIES

Marcus-Mendoza and Wright (2004) pointed out how difficult and challenging creating treatment programs for women in prison can be. Because so many of these women have been hurt by those whom they have trusted in the past, they lack trust and respect for those in authority. Additionally, the authors point out the importance of a gender-specific, holistic approach that includes assessment and diagnosis and "supportive, educational, and custodial service" (p. 113). They note that by not utilizing a holistic approach when treating women prisoners, frustration and failure will follow.

Marcus-Mendoza and Wright (2004) stated that it isn't an option of whether or not to treat women prisoners for trauma and abuse; the question is *how* to do it. A variety of treatment styles have been utilized with survivors of extreme trauma who exhibit symptoms of PTSD. Outcome studies are infrequent, however, so intervention methods may rightly take the form of multimodal techniques. As Marcus-Mendoza and Wright (2004) state, it is important to treat each issue as if it were a part of the larger context of a woman's life. They continue:

> To effectively help incarcerated women, it is important to acknowledge that abuse and other life experiences are often the context in which these problems develop. Decontextualizing the problems of women prisoners leads to treatment that may only address the symptoms while ignoring the underlying experiences and psychological trauma. (p. 253)

Harrison, Jessup, Covington, and Najavits (2004) discuss gender-responsive treatment, an integrated approach to women's alcohol and drug programs that creates an environment and program content so as to understand the realities of women's lives. These authors describe the "Self-in-Relation" theory that was based on work in the mid-1970s by Jean Baker Miller. This model purports that the psychological development of women differs from that of men, namely, that relationships are the basis for women's psychological health. Pathologies, they propose, are often traced to "disconnections or violations within relationships, arising at personal/familial levels as well as at the socio-cultural level" (p. 58).

Cognitive-Behavioral Treatment for Co-Occurring Posttraumatic Stress Disorder and Substance Use Disorder: An Exemplary Model: *Seeking Safety*

The most-studied treatment model specifically for clients with PTSD and substance abuse is called "Seeking Safety" (Harrison et al., 2004). Najavits began developing this 25-session cognitive-behavioral therapy (CBT) model in 1993, when no published treatment studies or empirical evaluations for this population (PTSD and SUD) existed (Najavits, 1999).

Key Principles

Najavits describes the program title as expressing the program's philosophy, in that when an individual has substance abuse issues as well as PTSD, "the most urgent clinical need is to establish safety"

(p. 40). This is the *first* of the five key principles of the program. Najavits utilizes the term *safety* as relating to:

- Discontinuing substance use
- Reducing suicidality
- Minimizing HIV exposure risks
- Discontinuing dangerous relationships
- Controlling extreme symptoms such as dissociation, and finally
- Stopping self-harm behaviors

These behaviors are often reenactments of earlier trauma, particularly childhood abuse. This "first-stage" treatment of learning how to be safe is exhibited by teaching clients coping skills, by utilizing Safe Coping Sheets and a safety plan, and by reporting unsafe behaviors.

The *second* key principle of Seeking Safety is the integration of treatments for both PTSD and substance abuse. Despite the fact that most treatment programs do not treat disorders concurrently, it is the recommendation of clinicians and researchers that an integrated model is more likely to be effective, is more sensitive to clients' needs, and is more cost effective (Brown, 2000; Najavits, 1999). Even client surveys conclude that simultaneous treatment for both disorders is preferred. Najavits points to the example of one of her clients who had to lie in order to be enrolled in a PTSD treatment program because active substance abusers were not to be admitted.

Najavits (1999) emphasizes that while attention is given to both disorders at the first stage, it is done so in the present rather than detailing the past trauma, with the latter being done in second-stage treatment, which is outside of the realm of Seeking Safety. She explains that while exposure therapy for PTSD is efficacious, it is preferred that this not begin until there is a period of abstinence and stable functioning. Dwelling on past trauma may indeed trigger substance abuse in a continued effort to cope. Instead, clients are helped to understand why the two disorders frequently occur and are taught coping skills in order to decrease current symptoms of PTSD and substance abuse. In addition, the first-stage treatment focuses on explaining the relationship between the

two disorders as well as helping clients understand how becoming healthy will require attention to both disorders (Najavits).

The *third* key principle of Najavits's program involves the focus on ideals. Steps are taken to instill confidence and to restore clients' recognition of the potential for a better life. Having been so demoralized by childhood or adult victimization, clients have lost sight of values such as respect, care, integration, and healing. Through motivation and insight, clients take steps toward the hard work necessary to recover from both disorders.

The *fourth* key principle of Seeking Safety involves the addition of two issues to the original cognitive-behavioral focus, thus embracing four content areas: cognitive, behavioral, interpersonal, and case management. Because PTSD most commonly comes from trauma inflicted by others, whether childhood physical or sexual abuse, combat, or crime victimization, all revolve around interpersonal issues than can interfere with trust, expectations, and power. Substance abuse also is often associated with interpersonal relationships, since many of these clients grew up in homes with substance-abusing family members or may use substances to manage interpersonal conflicts. Case management was an added component, as the need was seen for helping clients with life problems such as housing, job counseling, HIV testing, domestic violence, child care, and other such issues (Najavits, 1999).

The *fifth* and final key principle is attention to the role of therapist processes. Najavits (1999) reports that research shows that the effectiveness of treatment for both substance abusers and those in psychotherapy in general is determined equally or more by the therapist than by the specific theoretical orientation or by patient characteristics. Effective therapy is difficult to provide to this "severe" or "extreme" population. Therefore, the following therapy skills are emphasized in Seeking Safety:

- Building an alliance with the client
- Compassion for the client's experience
- Using coping skills in one's own life so as to lead by example
- Giving the client as much control as possible

- Meeting the client more than halfway, doing as much as possible to help him or her succeed, and

- Obtaining feedback from the client about the treatment

Najavits (1999) warns of possible countertransference issues that can arise and interfere with effective treatment, particularly with severe or extreme clients. Problems that may arise include harsh confrontation, where the therapist insists on his or her own point of view, an inability to hold clients accountable because of misguided sympathy, becoming "victim" to the client's abusiveness, power struggles, and allowing a client to be a scapegoat in group settings.

Twenty-five session topics, each including a clinician guide and client handout, are broken down into four areas:

1. Interpersonal topics
   - Asking for Help
   - Honesty
   - Setting Boundaries in Relationships
   - Healthy Relationships
   - Community Resources
   - Healing From Anger
   - Getting Others to Support Your Recovery

2. Behavioral topics
   - Detaching From Emotional Pain: Grounding
   - Taking Good Care of Yourself
   - Red and Green Flags
   - Commitment
   - Coping With Triggers
   - Respecting Your Time
   - Self-Nurturing

3. Cognitive topics
   - PTSD: Taking Back Your Power
   - Compassion
   - When Substances Control You
   - Recovery Thinking
   - Integrating the Split Self
   - Creating Meaning
   - Discovery

4. Combination topics
   - Introduction to Treatment/Case Management
   - Safety
   - The Life Choices Game (Review)
   - Termination

Najavits (1999) indicates that a variety of treatment formats have been used, including group and individual, open and closed group, 50- and 90-minute sessions, singly and co-led, and outpatient and residential.

An uncontrolled pilot study of the effectiveness of Seeking Safety was conducted with 18 volunteers from a residential substance abuse treatment program in a minimum-security wing of a woman's prison, the goal being to evaluate its initial feasibility, acceptability, and efficacy (Zlotnik, Najavits, Rohsenow, & Johnson, 2003). It was to be used as an adjunct to "treatment as usual" for women with SUD and PTSD. It was expected that after Seeking Safety treatment, the inmates would report satisfaction with the program, an alliance with the providers, and decreased severity of PTSD symptoms and substance use. Najavits supervised the trained therapists throughout the study (Zlotnick et al., 2003).

Follow-up reports were available from 17 participants, with the data suggesting that Seeking Safety appears to be appealing to incarcerated women with SUD and PTSD and that the program has the potential to be beneficial, especially for improving PTSD symptoms, with 53 percent no longer meeting the criteria for PTSD diagnosis at the end of treatment and 46 percent no longer meeting the criteria at the 3-month follow-up. Thirty-five percent of the women reported use of illegal substances within 3 months after release. Unfortunately, a high recidivism rate was found, with 33 percent reoffending within 3 months (Zlotnick et al., 2003). These results are promising, particularly in light of the fact that PTSD is typically a chronic disorder and those who receive treatment require an average of 36 months to recover from their symptoms (Zlotnick et al., 2003). Najavits reported that four additional outcome studies have been completed and that all showed improvements in substance abuse as well as general psychiatric symptoms, suicidal thoughts and plans, problem-solving ability, sense of meaning, social adjustment, and depression. These studies also showed high treatment attendance and satisfaction. In the one randomized control trial by Hein, Cohen, Miele, Litt, and Capstick (2004), Seeking Safety was shown to be effective at relapse prevention, performing significantly better than treatment-as-usual. Najavits also notes that several other studies are currently underway, utilizing larger samples and control or comparison conditions.

Following are methods being used for treating PTSD that are not specific to women and particularly not appropriate for those who also exhibit substance abuse disorders.

Psychopharmacology

A variety of drugs have been used in the treatment of PTSD. These include selective serotonin reuptake inhibitors (SSRIs), other serotonergic agents, anti-adrenergic agents, tricyclic antidepressants, mono-amine oxidase inhibitors (MAOIs), benzodiazepines, anticonvulsants, and antipsychotics (see Friedman, 2001, pp. 94–124). Few randomized controlled trials have, however, been conducted with medications (Friedman, 2001; Herbert & Sageman, 2004). The general finding is that antidepressants such as SSRIs and MAOIs, antianxiety agents such as benzodiazepines, and anticonvulsants such as carbamazepine, all lead to general improvement of PTSD symptoms. However, due to the frequency of comorbidity among PTSD patients with depression or panic disorder, it is unclear which symptoms the drug therapy is addressing. In addition, only two drugs have been approved by the Food and Drug Administration (FDA) specifically for PTSD: the SSRIs sertraline and paroxetine. It is also important to note that subject selection for studies eliminates those involved in litigation or receiving compensation for PTSD so these important populations are not being studied. In addition, the potential harmful effects of these drugs have not been addressed (Herbert & Sageman, 2004). Friedman (2001) pointed out that no drugs specifically designed to target allostatic load (discussed previously) have been tested. He further expressed concern that since testing of older drugs such as tricyclics and MAOIs has been abandoned in favor of SSRIs and new anticonvulsants, the possible efficacy of older medications may be ignored.

Herman (1997) emphasizes the importance of informed consent when prescribing drugs to PTSD patients. She reminds readers that simply ordering the patient to take medication will again take away the necessary feeling of power so important to the recovering victim. In addition to assisting in building a client-therapist alliance, involving the client with decisions concerning the use of pharmaceuticals will enhance her general sense of efficacy and control.

Exposure

Exposure therapy is based on the natural tendency of humans to avoid distressing thoughts. Emotional avoidance is a key feature underlying much psychopathology, particularly PTSD. Borrowing principles from Buddhism, exposure therapy recognizes the importance of facing one's inner pain and tackling the damaging effects of avoidance (Herbert & Sageman, 2004). While Najavits (1999) resists using exposure as a treatment technique during the initial stages of treatment for PTSD when substance abuse is involved, it has been shown to be effective when used for PTSD alone (Marks, Lovell, Noshirvani, Livanou, & Thrasher, 1998; Herbert & Sageman, 2004). Studies do show exposure-based therapies are effective in traumatized populations, including victims of accidents, natural disasters, and, most important, *nonsexual* assault. Clients are assisted with imagining exposure to trauma memories by speaking in the first-person present tense about what they had undergone (imaginal exposure). They describe their response to the trauma, its meaning, what they smelled, heard, saw, felt, or tasted (*in vivo* exposure). This imagining of the trauma is held on to until distress levels drop, typically in about 20 minutes (Marks et al., 1998). Exposure interventions are often conducted as part of CBT, where cognitive restructuring and relaxation training is integrated into the program.

Herbert and Sageman (2004) reported that the precise mechanism by which exposure operates is unclear but that the client's expectancies are an important aspect of exposure. This was shown in a control study in which PTSD patients given an expectation of "treatment" demonstrated more rapid and greater improvement that those given the expectation of "assessment," hence suggesting the importance of maintaining optimistic therapeutic expectancies (Herbert & Sageman, 2004).

Hypnosis

Maldonado and Spiegel (1995) reported that therapists may use hypnotic methods as a simple tool to help clients access repressed and dissociated memories. Described as a "psychophysiological state of arousal," hypnotic phenomena are similar to many of the symptoms presented by victims of childhood sexual trauma, including dissociation and absorption.

Beall (1997) points out that in Maggie Phillip's *Healing the Divided Self: Clinical and Ericksonian Hypnotherapy for Post-Traumatic and Dissociative Conditions,* Phillip believes that failure to access unconscious memories may leave PTSD patients vulnerable to returning to problem symptoms and behaviors. In addition, it is reported that hypnosis reduces the length of treatment (Beall). Maldonado and Spiegel (1995), however, emphasize that hypnosis by itself is not therapy and that there is nothing a therapist can do with hypnosis that cannot be done without it, but they admit that the relaxing state one achieves can help create a safe environment for retrieving painful memories.

Eye Movement Desensitization and Reprocessing

Negative and/or mixed results from studies of eye movement desensitization and reprocessing (EMDR) have caused this complex treatment method to receive less than full acceptance by the scientific community. EMDR was devised by Francine Shapiro in 1995 and consists of manualized steps involving imaginal exposure exercises combined with visual stimulation in the form of tracking the back-and-forth motion of the therapist's finger across the client's visual field (Herbert & Sageman, 2004; Scheck, Schaeffer, & Gillette, 1998). Or as described by Friedman (2001), "it involves the elicitation of rapid, saccadic eye movements during the imaginal exposure sessions...." (p. 163).

After building rapport with the client and talking about the procedures, a relaxation exercise of envisioning a safe place is conducted. The client is asked to then focus on the trauma, to verbalize the event, and to identify associated feelings. Associated cognitions are also recognized. While maintaining a mental image of the traumatic event, the client follows the movement of the therapist's finger as it passes from left to right in front of the client (Scheck, et al., 1998).

As Herbert and Sageman (2004) report, EMDR has been found to be no more effective than standard exposure treatments and that the eye movements are superfluous to its effects. Studies that compare the EMDR protocol leaving out the eye movements to complete EMDR protocol with the eye movements show no difference in efficacy. Herbert and Sageman assert that there is no need for "unnecessary rituals" and that EMDR's effectiveness lies in the effects that are common to most psychotherapies, again emphasizing the importance of positive expectations leading toward improvement. Friedman (2001) concurs that EMDR use for chronic PTSD remains questionable.

THERAPIST CHARACTERISTICS

Recognizing the importance of therapist characteristics in working with populations with a dual diagnosis of PTSD and substance use disorder (SUD), Najavits (2002) looked at four issues that might shed light on the training of clinicians in delivery of services to this group. These issues are:

1. How difficult and how gratifying is treatment of clients with these diagnoses?

2. What are the characteristics of those who find this treatment most difficult?

3. What characteristics may explain clinician perception of treatment difficulty and gratification?

4. What are the most difficult dilemmas and emotions when working with these clients?

Najavits (2002) findings indicate that dual diagnosis is more difficult to treat than either alone; however, clinicians found higher gratification than perceived difficulty. Even those who found their work to be the most difficult were no less gratified than the others. (Respondents may have been biased toward gratification as they chose to attend the workshops and complete the survey, indicating they probably were positive about their work.)

Clinicians with a personal history of trauma and SUD (either singularly or concomitantly) were clearly influenced and had a more positive view of their work. Those reporting the most difficulty treating the dual diagnosis had a lower frequency of trauma, suggesting that therapists' personal experiences with these disorders allows them to have greater identification with their clients and to understand their often unpredictable affects.

It is often thought that it is a positive feature for SUD clinicians to have had a history of SUD. This does not appear to be a positive predictor of patient outcomes, as more than 50 studies have shown (Najavits, 2002). Najavits goes on to warn that while clinicians' perceptions of difficulty and gratification may be important to their work satisfaction, as yet there is no clear relationship to treatment outcome.

As opposed to the general thinking about clinicians' SUD history, a history of PTSD is rarely acknowledged among or thought to be of value to clinicians, probably due to the stigma or blame about traumatic events.

Najavits's work showed that those clinicians who were more positive about their work with PTSD were more likely to have a 12-step orientation, to work in a dual diagnosis setting, to be non-PhDs, to be younger, to feel more energized, and to *not* be in a mental health setting. She concludes that these characteristics likely reflect familiarity, training, and experience with the dual diagnosis. Many clinicians do not receive much, if any, formal instruction and supervision in the treatment of PTSD and SUD, particularly in the mental health field, which she finds distanced from the substance abuse field. Clients are often referred to deal with substance abuse before attempting treatment of co-occurring disorders. This leaves clinicians to struggle with dual diagnosis issues, not uncommonly resulting in a negative perception of SUD treatment.

The three major difficulties named by the surveyed clinicians were client's self-destructiveness, case

management needs, and dependency. One third of the respondents reported their work with dual diagnosis as extremely difficult. Najavits suggested that for this one third, attention is needed in training in handling client self-destructiveness and case management. She also noted that it is important to determine who those clinicians are, as they were not identified by other factors such as training, experience, or orientation or in their overall view of their work.

Clinicians reported their highest gratification was to be teaching new coping skills, developing expertise, and helping clients achieve abstinence. Najavits recognizes that these are action-oriented strategies as opposed to the lowest-rated gratifications, such as acting as a parent figure or listening to trauma histories, which are more passive activities. Najavits concluded that while this sample of clinicians reported high satisfaction with their work in general, a low burnout rate and a positive feeling about their work, difficulties treating those with the dual diagnosis are many.

Finally, Hein et al. (2004) reported that additional studies are needed to find out whether Seeking Safety therapy is feasible for community providers. Hein et al. is working with the National Institute on Drug Abuse (NIDA) Clinical Trials Network to conduct a study in which community drug abuse counselors will offer a modified form of Seeking Safety in typical patient populations and treatment settings. Patients are currently signing up to participate in this nationwide study.

CHAPTER REVIEW

This chapter began with a historical perspective of PTSD, explaining how conceptualizations of causality have evolved from organic explanations (for example, damage to brain or spinal chord) to psychobiological responses to such horrific events as natural disasters, rape, or exposure to war.

The chapter continues on to explore the symptoms of PTSD, which include reexperiencing the trauma, emotional numbing, avoidance, increased arousal, neurobiological changes, physiological changes, physical manifestations, and disturbances in psychological and social functioning. Complex PTSD is defined as a more severe form of the disorder, usually associated with more extreme problems with affect regulation, depersonalization, and difficulty assessing and receiving social support.

PTSD assessment is often complicated by the client not having full recall of trauma-related childhood events; however, clinicians who suspect a diagnosis of PTSD are encouraged to share this with the client. By giving the client words to describe and attach to her feelings and experiences, the client can feel not alone, not crazy, and can expect to recover as others have. Gender-sensitive assessment measures are discussed as means to gather data in two primary aspects of the disorder: (1) those that measure trauma history, and (2) those that measure symptom history. In addition to being twice as likely to suffer from PTSD as men, women experience more chronic forms of the disorder, with some differences in the appearance of co-occurring disorders: men are more likely to manifest alcohol dependence and antisocial personality disorder; women are more likely to experience depression, phobias, and more adverse medical conditions.

Treatment is discussed in the context of a gender-specific, holistic approach that includes assessment and diagnosis and a supportive, educational, and custodial environment. This chapter summarizes key principles from Seeking Safety, the most-studied treatment model for clients with PTSD and substance abuse.

Treatment effectiveness is attributed more to the qualities of the therapist than to the specific theoretical orientation or to patient characteristics. Additional strategies for treating PTSD are discussed such as psychopharmacology, exposure, hypnosis, and Eye Movement Desensitization and Reprocessing.

The chapter concludes by exploring the personal characteristics of therapists who find satisfaction in working with dually diagnosed clients and the relationships among personal experience with substance abuse, trauma, job satisfaction, and treatment outcomes.

SECTION II

ESSENTIAL ELEMENTS IN THE EDUCATION AND TREATMENT OF FEMALE JUDICIAL CLIENTS

CHAPTER 6: Assessment of Women in Correctional Settings

LEARNING OBJECTIVES

▶ To gain an overview of the assessment structure and process for female judicial clients

▶ To identify gender-specific factors in the assessment of women offenders

▶ To understand the initial screening process, the two types of screening, how screening enhances treatment, the intake interview and how motivational enhancements complements assessment and instruments used in screening

▶ To understand the concept and approach of in-depth and differential assessment

▶ To see how the client's master profile and master assessment plan fits into the assessment process, the SSC curriculum, and treatment matching

▶ To understand the importance of a collaborative relationship between the provider and client in the assessment process

▶ To see how the continuum of care fits into assessment

INTRODUCTION

A comprehensive presentation of the assessment concepts, structure, process, and instrumentation for both men and women *SSC* clients are found in Chapter 6 of the *Provider's Guide for Criminal Conduct and Substance Abuse Treatment: Strategies for Self-Improvement and Change (SSC)*. All of the methods and procedures for screening, comprehensive assessment, and progress and change evaluation are outlined in Chapter 6 of the *Provider's Guide* and in the *Progress and Change Evaluation (PACE) Handbook,* which is a supplement to the *SSC Guide* and to this *Adjunct Provider's Guide* (Wanberg & Milkman, 2008). All of the essential components and concepts of the *SSC* assessment program are described in Chapter 6 of the *Provider's Guide,* and the essential instruments used to implement that program are provided in the *PACE Handbook*. The provider should carefully review these two documents and become skilled in the utilization of the assessment instruments before conducting assessments with women *SSC* clients.

In this chapter, we briefly review some of the most salient components of the assessment process used in *SSC*. We then discuss some of the special assessment issues that need to be addressed for women in corrections, and more specifically, women in *SSC*.

OVERVIEW OF THE *SSC* ASSESSMENT PROGRAM

Multidimensional and comprehensive assessment using the convergent validation approach is a core strategy and a foundational model of *Strategies for Self-Improvement and Change*. This approach provides a specific operational assessment model used for evaluating the treatment needs, progress and change, and the treatment outcome of substance-abusing judicial clients entering *SSC*.

Objectives of Assessment

The overall goal of assessment for all components and levels of evaluation is to collect sufficient information in order to make intelligent decisions about the general and specific service needs of the judicial client. There are a number of common objectives that guide the process of assessment within each of the assessment components:

▶ To provide clients opportunity to disclose information about themselves or to tell their stories

▶ To gather information from other individuals associated with the client or from other sources of information

▶ To discern the level of openness or defensiveness of the client at the time of assessment

▶ To estimate the "true" condition of the client

▶ To make a referral and placement that match the presenting problems with appropriate services

▶ To evaluate progress and outcomes during treatment and at some point posttreatment

All of these objectives are viewed within the context of the partnership between the provider and client. The client is continually involved as a partner in determining the level of problems and service needs to address these problems.

Convergent Validation Approach

The *SSC* assessment program is based on the concept that there are two sources of information that are used in understanding, planning, and making decisions around the treatment needs of clients. These are self-report and other-report. Self-report provides clients with an opportunity to tell their stories. It is an essential component for assessment in that it provides a baseline understanding of where the client is at the time of assessment and the client's willingness to self-disclose. From this perspective, we see self-report as a valid representation of the client's openness and willingness to disclose and to take part in treatment. Thus, if this is our first objective of assessment, then all episodes of self-report are considered to be valid representations of where the client is and willingness to share. Other-report provides others the opportunity to disclose their perceptions of the client.

The discrepancy between self-report and other-report provides a basis for evaluating the level of defensiveness of the client. This is important, because the client's level of defensiveness gives us an understanding of where we should start treatment or intervention.

Both self-report and other-report provide the information that we use to estimate the client's "true" condition. We never know what that condition is—we always estimate it. Initially, self-report may not be a good estimate of that condition, particularly if the client is defensive and resistant. However, as rapport and trust are developed, the self-report information becomes more veridical or valid with respect to this true condition. This may mean that subsequent self-reports may make the client look worse, since there is more openness to disclosing past and current psychosocial problems, alcohol and other drug (AOD) use, and criminal conduct.

As time goes on in treatment, self-report information will become a better estimate of the client's true condition. As providers increase their knowledge of clients, their estimate of the client's condition also becomes more veridical or valid.

Thus, the convergent validation model uses these two sources of data to get the best assessment of where the client is at any point in assessment. This estimate changes at each assessment point. In this sense, the process of assessment—for example, monitoring this change in self-disclosure over time—is just as important as the content of assessment. However, the content of assessment, or the estimate of the client's condition, is also important. It provides the basis for developing the initial treatment plan of the client.

Women in corrections tend to be more self-disclosing and open than men (see Table A.1 in the Appendix) (Wanberg, 2008; Wanberg & Timken, 2008). Thus, the initial testing and interviews will tend to indicate that women clients are further along in the change process because of this openness and willingness to disclose. However, this may be deceiving with respect to willingness to change. Often, openness and willingness to disclose is a defense against change. Thus, when discerning motivation and readiness, other factors need to be considered than just the degree of openness.

One important factor is how congruent with actual evidence of change is the openness and willingness to self-disclose. Our experience is that there is often a large discrepancy between openness to self-disclose and commitment to change. One example is women who admit to having a serious problem with alcohol, openly discussing the negative consequences from drinking, yet proceeding to have episodes of drinking after being diagnosed with liver disease. One of the goals of treatment of women with AOD problems is to evaluate the degree of discrepancy between openness and commitment to change and then to use motivational approaches to close the gap between the two.

Summary of the Assessment Components

The *SSC* assessment program is identified as the *Progress and Change Evaluation (PACE) Monitor*. *PACE* is built around five components or tasks that provide the structure for evaluating the *SSC* client at various stages of *SSC* program. These are

1. Differential screening and intake

2. Differential and comprehensive assessment

3. Progress and change during treatment

4. Treatment closure and continuing care assessment

5. Follow-up assessment

These components are described in Chapter 6 of the *SSC Provider's Guide* and are a summarized here, particularly in reference to women in corrections.

COMPONENTS OF ASSESSMENT

Differential Screening and Intake

Initial screening involves determining the appropriateness of the client for *SSC*. It is recommended that evaluators and providers use the Adult Substance Use Survey-R (ASUS-R) and an initial brief interview. The guidelines for using the ASUS-R in helping to assess the appropriateness of the client for *SSC* is found in the *PACE Handbook*. Along with these instruments, a brief interview with the client to determine appropriateness should be conducted. For many *SSC* clients, the decision has been made to admit them to *SSC*. Thus the brief screening interview and intake interview are often merged.

The appropriateness for *SSC* is based on level of AOD use problems and degree of involvement in criminal thinking and conduct. For men, we look at selecting those clients that are higher risk with respect to criminal involvement. However, many women in *SSC* will not show the level of criminal involvement and risk for recidivism as do men. Evaluators will look for those issues with women that portend recidivism, such as strong associations and involvement with a male engaged in a criminal lifestyle, or the psychological factors in women that will increase the risk of recidivism as well as relapse, such as post-traumatic stress disorder (PTSD), history of physical and sexual abuse, depression, and other mental health co-occurring problems.

The admissions interview should explore the extent of AOD problems and extent of criminal conduct, but also other issues that may be more relevant to women in corrections. With respect to AOD involvement, the fourth edition of the *Diagnostic and Statistical Manual of Mental Disorders* (*DSM-IV;* American Psychiatric Association, 1994) criteria should be used in this process, but not as the sole criteria for determining the presence of AOD problems. Some and possibly many women clients may not meet the *DSM* criteria yet are appropriate for *SSC.* These are clients who do show evidence of a history of substance use problems but also fall into the medium- and high-risk categories of criminal conduct and recidivism. From the admissions interview and the self-report instruments, initial treatment needs are identified and an initial treatment plan is developed.

In addition to the admissions interview and the ASUS-R, the intake process involves the completion of other *PACE* instruments, including the Personal Data Questionnaire; the Status Evaluation Questionnaire (SEQ), which provides a baseline measure of the dynamic variables that represent targets of change in *SSC;* and the Adult Self-Assessment Questionnaire (AdSAQ), which provides guidelines for the client's readiness and motivation for treatment.

This initial contact actually begins the longer-range therapeutic process for both women and men in corrections (Kassebaum, 1999). Issues of trust or distrust that arise in the initial screening process can weaken or strengthen the potential for self-improvement and change. Women in corrections are particularly sensitive to these initial contacts. If they perceive that their personal concerns are not addressed, this may lead them to believe that this

experience is no different from those they've had in the past. This perception may produce resistance or indifference, which can prevent the building of trust and rapport, inhibit women's readiness for treatment, reduce their attentiveness to treatment goals, and weaken their commitment to change. If the initial assessment procedures can welcome a woman into a partnership with treatment and correctional staff for her eventual good, as well as the good of society, it will go a long way towards motivating readiness for treatment and a commitment to change.

At screening and intake, there are several areas that may need more attention with women in corrections because of the prevalence and seriousness of conditions found in women related to these assessment areas: (1) medical and physical problems and diseases, (2) mental health issues and concerns, (3) family responsibilities that may reveal a need for child care if treatment is to be negotiated, and (4) brief screening for a history of sexual and physical abuse and trauma. This screening must allow for a sensitive and gradual movement into these issues that will continue into the comprehensive and in-depth assessment. While questions regarding the history of these areas may be included in the initial assessment, it is advised that this initial screening not probe into these issues so as to prevent retraumatization at a point when clinical resources are not available to address them.

Whereas men are apt to be more matter of fact in their response to the initial assessment interview, women generally want to explain and discuss their answers to assessment questions. Thus, with women in corrections, initial assessment may need to be extended in the intake process (Kassebaum, 1999). Yet, some parameters should be set to limit time at this point, with the assurance that there will be opportunity to explore these issues later in assessment and treatment.

Finally, at the intake process and at points along the evaluation and treatment pathway, initial contact with women should convey an acceptance and a hope for improvement and change. Empathy is the basis for developing rapport and trust and is an important component of Miller's (2006) FRAMES concept: feedback, responsibility, advice, menu of options, empathy, and self-efficacy.

Comprehensive Multiple-Factor Assessment

This component of assessment is fully discussed in the *SSC Provider's Guide.* Multiple-factor assessment has a strong support in the literature as the basic approach to comprehensive assessment. The specific components of comprehensive assessment are briefly discussed.

Essential Multiple Factors to Address in Comprehensive Assessment

There are nine essential areas that multiple-factor assessment should address. These are (1) concerns about problems in childhood; (2) family, marital, and relationship problems; (3) mental health and psychological concerns; (4) employment and vocational adjustment; (5) involvement in antisocial behavior and history of criminal conduct; (6) AOD use and abuse problems and patterns; (7) motivation and readiness for change and treatment and perceptual defensiveness; (8) medical or physical health; and (9) client strengths and assets.

We recommend the Adult Clinical Assessment Profile, which is comprised of the Adult Self-Assessment Profile (AdSAP) and the Rating Adult Problems Scale (RAPS) (Wanberg, 1998, 2007) provided in the *PACE Handbook,* as the in-depth self-report and rater assessment of the major risk factors in women in corrections. Later in this chapter we will look at a comprehensive assessment and case planning model that uses all sources of information to generate a case management structure for women judicial clients.

As noted previously, assessment in the area of abuse and trauma will have greater focus and emphasis with women than with men in corrections. Instruments that are useful in this area are presented later in this chapter.

For specialty areas that go beyond the standardized comprehensive assessment, staff and personnel need to be trained and experienced. Yet *SSC* providers who do not have this specialized training need to know what to look for and to recognize the occurrence of these factors and know how to handle them until they can be addressed in specialized assessments and treatment.

Assessment of Cognitive-Behavioral Structures and Processing

The rationale behind cognitive therapy is that emotions and actions are determined by the individual's cognitive structures and processes. The task of assessment is to understand the way the individual organizes that world through various cognitive structures and cognitive processes that lead to emotional and behavioral outcomes. These structures and processes are discussed in detail in Chapter 4 of the *SSC Provider's Guide.* This area of assessment is also dealt with in some detail in Chapter 6 of the *Provider's Guide.*

What is important is that evaluators are sensitive to and identify those cognitive structures that are specific to women in corrections. Cognitive appraisals that are demeaning to self-confidence, self-efficacy, and psychological strengths and resiliency are often found with female clients.

As well, those cognitive structures unique to women in corrections that lead to criminal behavior need to be identified. These structures determine specific response to various life situations and lead to pathological or disruptive emotional or behavioral outcomes. The assessment starts with identifying the pathological or disruptive emotional and behavior responses and work back to those cognitive responses that lead to those emotions and behaviors. The treatment goal is then to help clients replace or learn new cognitive responses that lead to healthier and more positive emotional and behavioral outcomes. The selection of new cognitive responses is based on those most relevant to target emotions or behaviors.

A formal cognitive-behavioral (CB) assessment model is outlined in Chapter 6 of the *Provider's Guide* and in the *PACE Handbook.* It is congruent with the basic cognitive-behavioral approach to change that is used in the *Participant's Workbook,* and more specifically, with the *SSC CB Map.* Briefly, the specific tasks of this assessment model are

1. Identify the general and specific disturbed and pathological emotional and behavioral targets for change.

2. Identify the specific relevant internal and external events or situations that are part of these emotional and behavioral outcomes.

3. Identify the individual's cognitive structures (thoughts, attitudes, and beliefs) that are responses to these situations and that lead to the specific pathological emotional and behavioral outcomes, for example, depression, criminal conduct, substance abuse.

4. Identify the cognitive processes (for example, cognitive distorting, decision making, automatic thinking) through which the cognitive structures are expressed, errors in thinking, automatic thinking, etc.

5. Identify the specific emotional and behavioral outcomes that result from the cognitive structures and processes and that are targets for change.

6. Identify cognitive skills (thought restructuring, relaxation exercises) that can help replace, change, or manage maladaptive cognitive responses (thoughts, beliefs) with those that are predicted to produce healthy and more adaptive emotional and behavioral outcomes.

7. Identify the social and community responsibility skills congruent with the improved or changed cognitive responses that can lead to positive outcomes, for example, prosocial behaviors.

8. Identify and evaluate the expected outcomes of the new cognitive responses and the new interpersonal and community responsibility skills to determine their efficacy in producing positive outcomes.

The Cognitive Assessment Guide (CAG), found in the *PACE Handbook,* provides a structured outline for conducting cognitive assessments. The results from CAG can be used in developing the client's individual treatment plan, and the client can use CAG to complete her *Master Profile* and *Master Assessment Plan.* CB assessment continues throughout treatment.

Assessment of Motivation and Readiness for Treatment

As noted previously, women in corrections will often give an open message of willingness and readiness to self-disclose. Yet the commitment to change and the stick-to-it motivation may be lacking. The area of treatment motivation and readiness is not only assessed in the intake interview but is ongoing during intervention and treatment. For *SSC,* the following

are the most salient elements for assessing treatment readiness and motivation:

- Degree of problem awareness
- Acknowledgment of the need for help
- Acknowledgment of the perception that others also see a need for change and help
- Willingness to be involved in treatment
- Established thoughts about making changes in particular areas
- Whether changes have actually been made

The *SSC* instrument for this kind of assessment is the Adult Self-Assessment Questionnaire (Wanberg & Milkman, 1993, 2004). It provides six specific and two broad measures of readiness and change.

Assessment of Strengths

Those concerned about resiliency and strength assessment might conclude that the multiple-factor model described in Chapter 6 of the *SSC Provider's Guide* and in the *PACE Handbook* does not consider these areas of assessment as important. However, inherent in the previously identified problem factors are strengths. Persons who score low on job and economic problems indicate strengths in these areas. So is the case across all of the assessment factors. However, the direct measurement of strengths is also important. Thus, assessment needs to include a factor that measures the client's strength from both a self-report and other-report perspective. The ASUS-R and the AdSAP/RAPS provide both a self-report and other-report client strengths measure.

For women in corrections, the measurement of strengths is of particular importance. Again, the expectations of society are that women should be strong, resilient, moral, and good—like all mothers. This "strengths" expectation has high impact on women, whose criminal behaviors have greater cognitive dissonance in the minds of the community (and in their own minds), than it does with men. An initial strengths assessment provides an important platform for implementing treatment with women judicial clients. For example, women in corrections who score low on strengths measures will most likely experience greater dissonance with respect to these expectations of society. Such dissonance will increase guilt and shame and even anger, calling for therapeutic approaches to manage the negative behavioral and emotional outcomes resulting from this dissonance.

Assessment of Treatment Progress and Change

This area of assessment is most often addressed in treatment progress notes. However, these notes do not give a quantitative description of the progress and changes the clients make in treatment.

PACE is comprised of several instruments that allow for the discernment of progress and change. The results of these changes are graphed so that they can be compared across multiple testings. Chapter 6 of the *SSC Provider's Guide* and the *PACE Handbook* provide a detailed presentation of the progress and change instruments and process. These descriptions are not repeated here.

What is important is that the approach to providing feedback on the progress and change made by client will often differ between men and women. Although women may be generally more open to receiving feedback about their progress and change, they will be more sensitive to a perception that they are failing to reach certain benchmarks in the change process. Thus, feedback should be reflective, enabling, and avoid a confronting and critical approach. Because women often have strong defenses about perceiving and accepting their antisocial attitudes and behaviors in light of society's expectations that they are more morally responsible than men, every effort needs to be made to enhance their understanding of their antisocial thinking and conduct. Also, feedback about change in the sensitive areas of sexual abuse and trauma may need to be given in individual sessions rather within a group setting, even when delivering *SSC* in gender-specific groups.

Assessment of Outcome at Treatment Closure and Follow-Up

In essence, all of the components of the assessment process address treatment outcome. For example, the increase in the client's willingness to self-disclose from the time of initial screening to comprehensive assessment represents change and is a measure of treatment outcome. The decrease of cognitive preoccupation with criminal involvement or AOD use as measured by the Client Progress Ratings (CPR-C) completed by both the client (CPR-C) and provider (CPR-P) represents change and treatment outcome. These observed changes (clinically or psychometrically) during treatment are good predictors of posttreatment outcome. Again, the process and instruments are outlined in Chapter 6 of the *Provider's Guide* and in the *PACE Handbook*.

What is most important is how clients perceive their completion of the *SSC* program. Most judicial clients that complete *SSC* will feel a sense of accomplishment and strength. However, it is not uncommon for many who complete what can be described as a successful treatment experience to still feel and think they are unfulfilled and have not reached their desired level of accomplishment. Thus, women in corrections may not see completing *SSC* as a major milestone in their lives. Every effort should be made to reinforce the positive value of the completion of treatment.

AN ASSESSMENT AND CASE MANAGEMENT SERVICE PLANNING MODEL

Robinson and his associates (Van Dieten & Robinson, 2007) have developed an assessment and case management model for judicial clients using the Service Planning Instrument (SPIn). This model evaluates the major risk factors identified in the Comprehensive Multiple-Factor section of this chapter.

Evaluators and case planners use all of the available information in addressing the specific variables in SPIn. Although it uses client self-report as one source of data, it relies heavily on other-report and rater information. Thus, SPIn is based on a combined self-report (interview-based) and other-report database. As discussed previously, we see self-report as an essential component of the convergent validation model. In order to gain an understanding of the judicial client's current status with respect to openness and willingness to self-disclose, how the client sees herself at any particular point in assessment, and her level of defensiveness, it is essential that she be given an unencumbered opportunity to "tell her story" through a psychometrically based self-report instrument. Thus, both differential screening and in-depth self-report instruments should be used along with assessment instruments like SPIn (Van Dieten & Robinson, 2007).

SPIn has been adapted specifically for women in corrections. The Service Planning Instrument for Women (SPIn-W)(Van Dieten & Robinson, 2007) identifies, in a more comprehensive way, the areas that need special focus with women. Figure 6.1 provides a graphic representation of this instrument. The essential elements of SPIn-W are presented.

SPIn-W is a 100-item tool for assessing risk, need, and protective factors in women judicial clients. SPIn-W is suitable for use in probation, parole, custody, and other correctional settings where there is a requirement to assess risk of recidivism and identify service needs. The SPIn-W includes an abbreviated 35-item "prescreening" version used for making initial decisions about supervision levels. The longer "full-assessment" version is used for case-planning purposes. Based on a variety of assessment sources, SPIn-W provides a template for entering assessment information that has been collected by probation officers, classification officers, case managers, or other service practitioners. SPIn-W is designed to address need and responsivity issues that are particularly relevant for developing case plans for women.

While the content of the tool overlaps with traditional risk and need assessment protocols for general populations of male and female offenders, the SPIn-W includes additional content that is highly relevant for serving women clients. For example, there are a number of items related to child custody and parenting issues, domestic violence, mental health, social support, and community living. Items in assessment domains related to attitudes, aggression, interpersonal skills, and cognitive skills have been tailored to take into account how these areas of risk are manifested in female populations.

The full-assessment SPIn-W is comprised of the following domains:

▶ Criminal history (previous offenses and dispositions)

▶ Response to supervision (performance under criminal justice supervision in the past, for example, violations)

▶ Family and children (marital problems or satisfaction, relationships with children, parenting, custody, family of origin)

▶ Social network (positive and negative social influences, community participation)

▶ Substance use (frequency of use, severity of problems)

▶ Vocational/employment (employment or vocational service needs, employment stability)

▶ Attitudes (anti- and prosocial attitudes)

▶ Social and cognitive skills (interpersonal, problem-solving skills)

▶ Mental health (mental health conditions, previous abuse)

▶ Violence (history of violence, anger, or hostility)

▶ Community living (accommodation, finances, access to resources)

In addition to the gender-responsive content of the SPIn-W domains, the inclusion of protective factors or "strengths" is a key element of innovation in this assessment model. Rather than using overall ratings of broad categories (for example, family strength), strengths are measured at the item level using behavioral or attitudinal referents. Each domain (for example, family and children, social networks) includes strength or protective factor content. Both domain and overall level scoring is available for strengths. Hence, on reassessment, practitioners monitor for decreases or increases in both risk and strengths. Highly intuitive for case managers, the assessment of protective factors focuses on case plans to capitalize on strengths and helps develop resources for success. The incorporation of strengths grounds the model in a case-planning process that is mobilizing for both the women offenders and the professionals who must develop and monitor case plans. As such, the assessment tool helps move the practitioner toward a strength-based model of case planning and supervision that blends well with motivational interviewing methods.

Motivational components have also been included in the assessment model. At the domain level, assessment users are invited to consider the motivational elements that might need to be addressed in dealing with a

Figure 6.1 Service Planning Instrument for Women

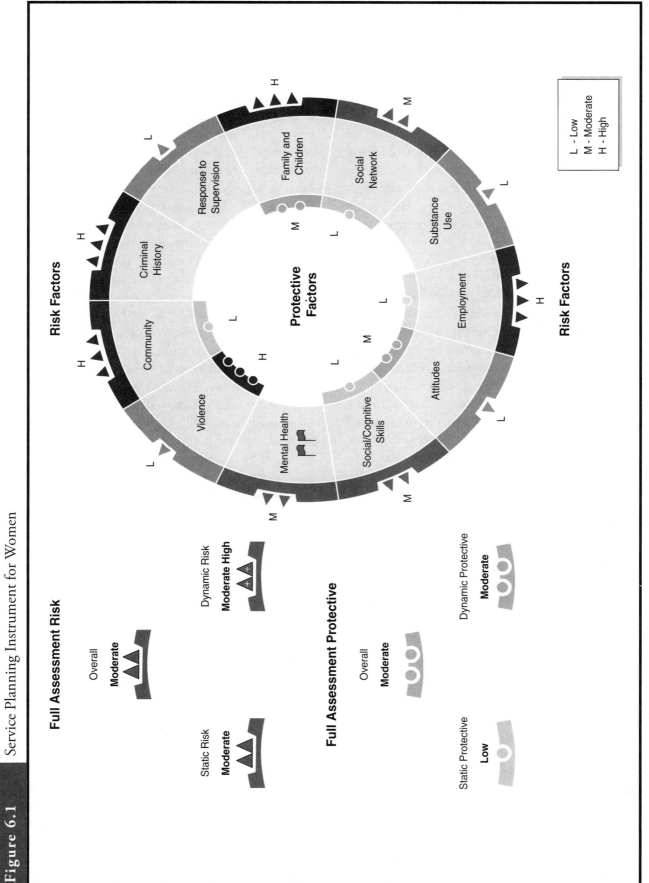

Source: Reproduced with permission of the authors (Van Dieten & Robinson, 2007).

particular area that places the woman at risk of ongoing criminal conduct (for example, family, substance use, social networks). The inclusion of motivational content in each domain (which is not scored as risk) keeps the case manager focused on the case-planning intent of the instrument. By focusing on motivational factors within the assessment, the case manager prepares for the work of debriefing with the woman and engaging her in the case-planning process. In addition to motivational items, the domains also include items that help assessment users review the resources (both external and internal) that the women can draw upon to reduce risk and increase or maintain strengths.

The SPIn-W is conducted using Web-based software through which the users enter information and achieve results through a browser interface (for example, Microsoft Internet Explorer). The software is easy to use and includes both assessment and case-planning components. The results are shown in a graphic format that displays both risk and protective factor scores on a wheel diagram. The interactive wheel diagram is then used as the starting point for the case-planning process. The software provides a step-by-step guided process for focusing on the issues that will become priorities in the case plan and delineating the goals and action plans to address the priorities.

SPECIFIC FACTORS IMPORTANT IN THE ASSESSMENT OF FEMALE JUDICIAL CLIENTS

Material in the previous chapters of this *Adjunct Provider's Guide* provides the basis for determining those areas of assessment that are gender specific and that are important focuses in assessment. These are summarized next.

Security Risk and Safety for Incarcerated Women Clients

Since the focus of this *Adjunct Provider's Guide* is to enhance assessment of female judicial clients for the purpose of presenting *Strategies for Self-Improvement and Change,* a detailed discussion of security risk assessment for women goes beyond the scope of this guide. However, some of the issues regarding assessment in this area are explored.

First, as discussed in Chapter 5, the safety and security of women in corrections (as well as men in correctional settings) has a direct bearing on the allostatic load factor that many women judicial clients with histories of PTSD carry into corrections. As discussed in that chapter, individuals with PTSD are vulnerable to sudden changes in the sense of well-being, based on triggers or cues, internal or external, resulting in rapid switching back and forth between states of "relative calmness to states of hypervigilance, anxiety, anger, and extreme arousal" (Wilson et al., 2001, p. 10). The treatment environment must foster safety and security so as to minimize these triggers that reactivate and amplify traumatic memories and to reduce the arousal mechanisms associated with allostatic load. Within a safe and secure treatment environment, controlled exposure to internal triggers can occur, allowing treatment staff to help clients learn self-control in managing these triggers, and to learn, when exposed to external or internal triggers or challenges, to return to a normal levels of stress hormones or allostasis. The literature indicates that the approaches and classifications used in determining security risk are often inadequate and even inappropriate for incarcerated women. Equal protection laws require that female and male offenders undergo the same security assessment and classification procedures. Whitaker (2000), however, asserts that "identical treatment is not necessarily equitable" (p. 5). As a result, most prison and jail systems have inadequate classification systems for women (Kassebaum, 1999). There is a trend toward developing specific diagnostic security procedures for women. For example, 26 percent of jail settings and 22 percent of state prisons now have specific diagnostic procedures for women.

A major element that must be considered in treatment with female judicial clients is that a far lower percentage of them require close custody and supervision. They are "less of a threat to each other, staff or property" (Kassebaum, 1999, p. 89). Classification systems based on the danger that male offenders pose lead to *over-restriction of women offenders,* which may contribute to retraumatization of these women within the correctional setting and could contribute to a setback in the treatment process (as discussed in Chapter 5 of this text). In addition to these psychological consequences, oversecurity of women is not a good use of correctional resources and produces no appreciable increase in safety for the public. It is for this reason and many others that advocates of gender-specific services advise keeping women in community correctional settings as an alternative to custody whenever possible (Kassebaum, p. 87).

Health and Medical Concerns

Previous chapters of this *Guide* have made it clear that many female judicial clients have unique medical problems and needs. It is important that these are assessed up-front as female clients enter the system. Clearly, they relate to gynecological problems, issues of pregnancy, assessment for sexually transmitted diseases, HIV and AIDS, malnutrition, and personal physical and medical care habits and patterns.

Assessment of Mental Health Problems and Co-Occurring Disorders

Because female offenders are apt to have more severe mental health problems than males, enhancement of this area of assessment is needed for most female judicial clients. This includes suicide risk, dual diagnosis and assessment of comorbidity, more in-depth assessment of depression, and the need for psychotropic medication. Levels of shame and guilt, self-image, sense of self, self-esteem, and self-efficacy around preventing recidivism and relapse have important gender-specific implications for assessment.

Because of the higher prevalence of co-occurring disorders (females with substance abuse and another major mental disorder) in the female judicial client population, this is an important component of both screening and in-depth assessment. Since the 1990s, there has been a trend toward including those with co-occurring disorders within the female-specific substance abuse treatment population. This appears to be more effective than separating them into a separate treatment population (Kassebaum, 1999). Such inclusion needs to consider that heavy correctional confrontation may go beyond the coping abilities of those women with co-occurring disorders and may precipitate relapse or recidivism. Thus, when there is a mixing of these populations, providers need to be sensitive to this possibility.

When assessing co-occurring issues with female offenders, it is important to determine the time of onset of these problems. Women who were depressed before the development of substance abuse problems or during a long period of abstinence, may have a primary depressive disorder requiring specific attention and treatment. Often, abstinence of drug use for as much as 6 months may be required before an adequate determination can be made as to whether a co-occurring disorder is primary or secondary to drug use. Unless the primary disorder is addressed (for example, major depression), the probability of relapse and recidivism increases.

As well, unless the environmental factors that contribute to triggering primary depression are addressed, the potential for relapse into depression, drug use, and criminal conduct is enhanced. There are many contributing factors to depression in women that may continue to cause depression even after addictive processes have been lifted. Failure to address this depression and its underlying causes will reduce treatment effectiveness for women with chronic depression (Blume, 1998).

The mood adjustment and psychological problems scales of the ASUS-R and the AdSAP/RAPS can provide effective screening for mental health concerns. However, as noted, for many women judicial clients, more in-depth assessment in this area may be needed. Certainly an interview-based mental status and clinical interview are essential. As well, there are a number of psychometric instruments that can be used to evaluate this area in a more in-depth manner. The Beck Depression Inventory (2006) is an excellent tool to determine the level of clinical depression. Instruments that provide a wider measurement of psychological and mental health problems include the Minnesota Multiphasic Personality Inventory II (Butcher et al., 1989), the Symptom Check List 90 (Derogatis, 2001), and the Millon Clinical Multiaxial Inventory III (Choca, 2004; Millon, Millon, & Davis, 2005). The Suicidal Behaviors Questionnaire (SBQ) evaluates frequency of self-injury, suicide attempts, and ideation (Linehan & Addis, 1990).

Parenting and Family Status

This area of assessment is most often unique to female judicial clients. The status of the woman's children, pending custody arrangements, need for parenting education, availability of child care, responsibility for other family members such as aging parents, needs for couples counseling, and family planning services are all important areas when discerning the female judicial client's treatment needs.

Assessment of Gender-Specific Relationships and the Relational Construct

The type and nature of the client's past and current intimate-partner relationships should be assessed. Female offenders who are trapped in an intense dependency relationship with a male partner should be identified. The degree of self-control and self-determination in relationship with the woman's male partner need to be assessed. Other areas of assessment unique to female offenders in the relationships area involve history of domestic violence. The FAMILY-MARITAL and INTERPERSONAL scales of the ADSAP can provide assessment information in this area. Again, these areas need to be explored in the clinical interview.

Assessment of Childhood and Adult Trauma

As discussed in previous chapters, this is a major issue with female offenders and needs special attention in assessment. Careful assessment of childhood and adult sexual and physical abuse is essential. An important part of this assessment is to determine the degree of trauma and posttraumatic disorder related to these childhood and adult experiences. Much of this assessment will be done in the interview process and during ongoing treatment contacts.

As a starter, the CHILDHOOD scale in the ADSAP will provide some indication of the degree of disruption clients report as having experienced in childhood. In addition to clinical interview data gathered in this area, there are several specific instruments that can assist the evaluator and provider in doing a more in-depth assessment. The Trauma History Questionnaire (THQ) assesses lifetime history of trauma, including physical or sexual, general disaster, and crime-related trauma (Green, 1996). The Childhood Trauma Questionnaire (CTQ) assesses emotional, physical, and sexual abuse as

well as motional and physical neglect (Bernstein et al., 1994). The Modified PTSD Symptom Scale (MPSSR) (Falsetti, Resnick, Resick, & Kilpatrick, 1993) evaluates both severity and frequency of symptoms. The Trauma Symptom Checklist 40 (TSC-40) assesses long-term symptoms of childhood trauma, such as "fear of men" (Elliot & Briere, 1990).

Lack of Social Unit and Community Support

Lack of social networking and support has been identified as a gender-specific issue. The client's perception of the degree of rejection by family members, including minor children, needs to be evaluated. This is a female-specific area given the stigma connected with women being involved in substance abuse and criminal conduct.

Assessment of Unique Substance Abuse Patterns

The special areas of AOD assessment that need to be attended to involve assessment of polydrug use patterns that involve prescription and over-the-counter medications. Regarding medical concerns, the history of drug use by injection, circumstances under which this has occurred, and the type of partners involved should be evaluated.

Part of this assessment is to determine the degree to which mental and physical deterioration has occurred due to AOD use. We have already presented evidence that female substance abusers have more rapid mental and physical deterioration than their male counterparts. Other unique patterns of female users such as episodic binge and solo patterns that may be more common among females need to be assessed. These patterns may relate to the stigmas associated with female AOD use and abuse. Just how strong this stigma cognition is should be determined. The Alcohol Use Inventory (Horn et al., 1990) is a valid and reliable self-report psychometric instrument that identifies use and disruption patterns related to the use of alcohol.

Type of Criminal Conduct

The kind of criminal conduct and the circumstances that surrounded that conduct determine how treatment is approached and the degree to which sanctioning is to be integrated into treatment. For example, possession of drugs that involve a male partner who is the primary determinant of possession will make a difference as to treatment approaches. A female judicial client convicted of check forgery will be treated differently than one convicted of prostitution. Of particular importance is to identify those criminal behaviors that are determined by the fact that the offender is female—for example, prostitution, and assault related to the female judicial client being self-protective, such as by anticipating and/or preventing rape.

Vocational Development and Education

Employment and employability are significant factors in recidivism and relapse. Very early on, employment was identified as a significant covariate of successful outcome in substance abuse treatment (for example, McLellan, 1983). Posttreatment social adjustment is significantly predicted by the degree of employment-focused services during treatment (McLellan et al., 1994). As well, work is related to lower levels of criminal activity (Inciardi, Surrat, Martin, & Hooper, 2002).

Each female offender should undergo a vocational skills and employability assessment and then engage in vocational development and education programs that enhance the probability of gainful employment that can support independent living. These assessment programs should be gender specific. As well, the vocational development programs in prison and community corrections settings should be gender specific (Vigdal, 1995).

Women in corrections, particularly those with substance use disorders, are, compared to men, less employable, more dependent on welfare and on a male partner, have poorer employment histories, and have fewer opportunities for employment at discharge (Peugh & Belenko, 1999). Vocational development programs are most often male oriented, for example, mechanic, electrician, truck driver (Baletka & Shearer, 2005). These vocational programs are often not available to women. Women judicial clients often have limited access to the higher-paying job and trade skills for which men are more apt to be

trained and that are most accessible for judicial clients reentering the community. It appears that correctional systems have not geared up to providing vocational and professional development programs for women that match the employment opportunities in the community.

Assessment of Economic Support and Living Situation

Related to vocational development and education programs are the issues of economic support and the woman offender's living situation. A careful assessment of financial support and the client's living situation should be done, particularly for women incarcerated and being released to the community. Housing is often a major problem for women in corrections who are being released from prison (Vigdal, 1995). Unless economic support and housing that allows the female offender to establish some degree of independent living is established, it will be easy for a woman judicial client to go back to the economic support and living conditions that were part and parcel of her involvement in criminal conduct, for example, returning to live with a male still involved in drug use or criminal activity.

Degree of Defensiveness in Perceiving or Admitting to Substance Abuse Problems

We have discussed the discrepancy between willingness on the part of women judicial clients to disclose emotional and behavioral problems and failing to demonstrate a commitment to change. The authors have extensive experience in working with both male and female clients whose substance use is physically deteriorative (for example, liver disease) and where evidence is provided to the client of this deterioration. Yet, many of these clients continue to drink and defend against integrating this evidence into conscious processing and/or a motivation to change. In-depth assessment in this area goes beyond determining the level of defensiveness to determining the nature of the defense system and specific defenses the woman judicial client is using that prevents change. As discussed previously, the client's perception of the expectations of women in society in general, and perception of the expectations of those close to the client will impact on this defense system. The self-identity defense of "I'm not that kind of person" will block a realistic appraisal of the reality of the client's manifested problems in the area of AOD use and abuse and criminal conduct. Therapeutic approaches must address the appraisal cognitive structures (automatic thoughts and core beliefs) that reinforce this sense of self-identity that blocks the reality of what is occurring in the client's life.

Barriers to Treatment

As some of the previous discussion indicates, there are many internal factors that become barriers to effective involvement in treatment, such as defensiveness, failure on the part of the client to have a realistic appraisal of her condition and problems, inner resistance to seek treatment, and so forth. Often, this resistance is based on the resistance of family members and intimate partners who may be invested in maintaining the woman's status quo position (Pollock, 1998). There are many external factors that also prevent effective involvement in treatment, such as transportation and lack of child care resources (McMahon, 2000). It is recommended that the provider develop a checklist that identifies specific external barriers preventing involvement in treatment and then provide services, when possible, to overcome those barriers.

THE CLIENT *MASTER PROFILE* AND *MASTER ASSESSMENT PLAN*

During Phase I of *SSC*, there is a strong emphasis on having clients complete their *Master Profiles* (MPs) and *Master Assessment Plans* (MAPs). The MP gives the client a graphic representation of the various areas of differential assessment described earlier. The MAP utilizes the MP and builds the client's Master Treatment Plan. The MAP is the client's guide for determining targets for self-improvement and change. Some enhancements and changes relative to the MP and the MAP for the female judicial client are discussed in Module 7 in Section III of this *Adjunct Provider's Guide*.

TREATMENT MATCHING

An important objective of both screening and in-depth assessment is to enhance the client's commitment to change. A second goal of in-depth assessment is to allow for appropriate matching of presenting problems with appropriate treatment options (Kassebaum, 1999; Pollock, 1998; Wanberg & Milkman, 1998). Treatment matching involves the following considerations:

- ▶ To identify, select, and engage clients who would most benefit from available treatment resources;
- ▶ To work along with the client to develop an individualized program of treatment;
- ▶ To assess treatment readiness and establish goals at each juncture of the treatment process;
- ▶ To specifically identify the most appropriate level of intervention.

In prisons where only one treatment program is available for women, screening is used primarily to determine a woman's appropriateness for treatment rather than treatment matching, which requires several treatment options. This is suitable, as prison populations tend to be more homogeneous than those in other correctional settings, and other factors such as anticipated date of release are less likely to interfere with necessary length of treatment (Kassebaum, 1999). Yet even in facilities that have only one treatment program, it is essential that the specific and unique problem areas of women in corrections, as described previously, be addressed (matched) with appropriate treatment methods and approaches.

COLLABORATIVE INVOLVEMENT IN ASSESSMENT AND THE DEVELOPMENT OF THE TREATMENT PLAN

Individual treatment must be developed in collaboration with the client (Wanberg & Milkman, 1998, 2008). This is especially important with a female client since disempowerment has often been a part of her life. A major goal of *SSC* treatment is to enable women to initiate proactive and healthy intrinsic cognition and behavior. Many females come from abusive and dysfunctional relationships in which they have not experienced a collaborative and participatory process in decision making. Female clients may need help in learning to initiate action in a proactive and collaborative manner.

Collaborative involvement in developing an individualized treatment plan throughout the continuum of treatment will help female judicial clients to develop thinking that supports self-control, self-esteem, and self-respect.

When the client takes ownership of the assessment process and engages in collaborative treatment planning, assessment becomes therapeutic and often leaves the client thinking that this is the first time anyone has ever addressed her seriously, one on one, as though her life matters. It may also be the first time anyone has addressed their problems in a non-judgmental way. Assessment is the beginning of the therapeutic experiences.

It is of major importance to involve the woman at each phase of assessment including providing her with feedback of the results of assessment. This means sharing with the client the profiles resulting from assessment and indicating where she stands in relationship to her peers. This normative feedback enhances the client's commitment to and ownership of treatment.

As well, an assessment process that allows the female judicial client to express her perception of treatment helpfulness may be useful in identifying potential problem areas before they have had time to develop into triggers for relapse. This kind of feedback from the client also reinforces the "ownership" phase of change.

THE CONTINUUM OF CARE

Continuing care, transitional planning, and reentry for women in corrections are discussed in some detail in Chapter 8 of this *Adjunct Provider's Guide*. The importance of continuing care and its efficacy in preventing relapse and recidivism are discussed in the *Resource Guide* (Wanberg & Milkman, in press), which is a companion to the *SSC Provider's Guide* (Wanberg & Milkman, 2008). Continuing care will involve transition planning and, for incarcerated

clients, prerelease planning. This plan will help clients identify obstacles to recovery and links current treatment to aftercare services in the community.

The relapse and recidivism prevention plans developed by clients in Session 16 should consider the resources in the community that clients can use to manage and deal with high-risk exposures for relapse and recidivism. Module 11 helps clients prepare for reentry and reintegration by developing a plan to establish a lifestyle balance.

In preparation for the development of the continuing care plan, a formal assessment should be done. This would include reassessment of the dynamic risk factors and a formal evaluation of services the client will need in reentry and reintegration. This formal assessment will address two questions: (1) What are the treatment goals and objectives that are still unmet and need to be worked on during the aftercare period? and (2) What resources do clients need to negotiate successful adjustment in the community?

PACE provides guidelines for the continuing care assessment process, which includes a brief continuing care interview guide and guidelines for reassessment of the dynamic risk scales of the Adult Self-Assessment Profile. The service needs checklist in the AdSAP is also readministered and providers need to look at the specific needs that clients indicate as being important at the time of this assessment. The dynamic risk scales in the AdSAP that clients should be retested on are

- Family-Marital Adjustment
- Interpersonal Adjustment
- Mental Health-Psychological
- Work and Job Productivity
- AOD Use Benefits
- Physical Health-Medical
- Motivation for Help
- Strengths-Resiliency
- Help Needs Checklist

A specific section in the *PACE Monitor Handbook* provides guidelines for doing the continuing care assessment.

Continued assessment and evaluation for service needs should be done by continuing care providers while the client is on probation or during the post-release period for those clients released from incarceration and who are on parole. This assessment process should involve:

▶ Monitoring of the treatment plan in close cooperation with the case manager to help women offenders identify and enhance and support recovery and crime-free living such as transportation to treatment, child care needs, and social support systems in the community; and

▶ Development of a strategy of specific and rapidly utilizable intermediate sanctions that can be used by the case manager as alternatives to reincarceration when the client violates the terms of probation or parole (Kassebaum, 1999).

Female clients coming out of an intensive residential facility or a community program or coming off probation require closure and transition planning to make it possible to maintain recovery and establish a constructive and crime-free life. The continuum of care serves to help female judicial clients to manage difficult challenges in the community environment that can lead to relapse and recidivism. It provides women with ongoing networking for resources and support that will help them to identify and meet these challenges.

The most important aspect of the continuum of care approach is to reinforce the client's effort to engage in behaviors that demonstrate moral responsibility and prosocial behavior in the community. We must always keep in mind that the goal of treatment, regardless of gender, is to prevent recidivism and reinforce the client's involvement in prosocial and responsible behavior. Probability of achieving this goal is increased when the client takes ownership of being a responsible member of society.

CHAPTER REVIEW

This chapter provides an overview of the many aspects of assessment that are useful in treatment with female clients. It begins with an overview of the assessment process and how this assessment fits into the overall *SSC* program and curriculum. The specific areas of assessment that are unique to female judicial clients are then delineated. The structure and process and importance of screening and in-depth assessment are discussed. Various assessment tools are identified that are designed to address specific areas of assessment unique to women. The assessment process is related to the *Master Profile* and *Master Assessment Plan* that are completed by clients during Phase I and reviewed in Session 20 of Module 7. The importance of the collaborative relationship between the provider and the female judicial client is discussed. The chapter concludes with looking at the importance and relevance of the continuum of care for the female client.

LEARNING OBJECTIVES

▶ To develop awareness and sensitivity to the broad diversity of backgrounds within the population of female judicial clients, including:
  - Gender
  - Ethnic and racial stereotyping and prejudice
  - Immigration and biculturalism
  - Sexual identity
  - Women with children
  - Pregnancy

▶ To develop sensitivity regarding the major socio-economic issues that confront women in criminal justice settings

INTRODUCTION

For the purposes of this chapter, the term *culture* refers to the context of values within which a person has lived and formed her primary experience of herself. In this way, we can speak of ethnic culture, lesbian culture, working-class culture, the "bar culture," the "drug culture," and so on. This broader view allows us to recognize that everyone is operating out of an interlocking network of cultures, within which their personal views of self as well as their environmental experiences and personal problems develop. The focus of this chapter is on considerations related to ethnicity, sexual orientation, motherhood, and socioeconomics. In-depth analysis of these factors is used to clarify how they may affect treatment strategies and outcome.

DIVERSITY CONSIDERATIONS IN WORKING WITH WOMEN JUDICIAL CLIENTS

A treatment provider who understands cultural differences and knows how to address them in treatment settings is more likely to achieve a positive outcome (Sue, 2006).

Women and Ethnicity

There are several methodological issues that should be taken into account when investigating multicultural research about female judicial clients. A major factor is the tendency for previous literature to lump a wide diversity of ethnic groups under the rubric of simplified labels, such as "Asian," "Latino," "African American," and "American Indian," or worse, under the rubric "nonwhite." This type of research fails to account for the wide range of diversity within each cultural group. In actuality, each cultural group is characterized by enormous heterogeneity—and it is as important to consider intracultural differences as it is to consider intergroup differences when investigating patterns of substance abuse and criminal conduct. Patterns of substance use, as well as types of criminal conduct, tend to vary markedly within groups due to a host of familial and geographic factors. These differences are related to a wide range of cultural traditions and values, socioeconomic issues such as poverty and malnutrition, health variables, ethnic

stereotypes, and encounters with racism that vary across cultural groups. These factors may serve to distort, and perhaps exaggerate, the degree of actual racial or ethnic differences between groups (Wilsnack, 1995).

Crosscultural Comparisons Among Female Judicial Clients

A number of statistical patterns have been determined across cultural groups. For example, African American women generally abstain from alcohol use more than do Anglo Americans and Hispanic or Latina women, but there is some evidence that when they do imbibe, they experience more severe alcohol-related problems, such as increased risk of fetal alcohol syndrome (Herd, 1989). This is believed to result from higher rates of malnutrition and lack of adequate health care (including prenatal) among African American women and men than is found in other groups. African American women, however, report a lower incidence of alcohol-related social problems than do women of European or Hispanic descent. This has been attributed to the many protective features of social life in the African American community, such as strong family bonds, a wide network of community (non-kin) relationships, and the role of black churches (Frances & Miller, 1998).

Although these factors refer to African American women's use of alcohol in the recent past, the rate of illicit drug use among African American women has crept above the rate of their European American counterparts (Markarian & Franklin, 1998). From even this brief analysis, it becomes clear that both strengths and nature of problems vary across and within cultural groups and may serve as important considerations in service delivery.

Alcohol and other drug (AOD) use among Latinas is currently on the increase among the young and the elderly, and especially among women of Mexican or Mexican American descent. Although these women may tend to abstain more than European American women, when acculturation is factored in, the rates of alcohol use and abuse tend to converge with mainstream culture. The longer a Mexican American woman's family has been in the United States, the more likely her substance use patterns will take on characteristics of the European American community (Gilbert, 1989). Other reports suggest that when Mexican American women do use alcohol, they are more likely to be heavy drinkers than are European American women (Markarian & Franklin, 1998). Additionally, pressures of conforming to the norms of mainstream society can lead to the abuse of drugs by Mexican American adolescents (Holleran & Jung, 2005).

Hohman and Galt (2001) investigated outcomes of substance abuse treatment for Hispanic women at a culturally specific residential facility. Although these women entered treatment with higher rates of poverty and employment, more prior arrests, and greater use of methamphetamine or heroin than average, they stayed more than a month longer in treatment than did those in nonculturally designed facilities. This is especially important in light of previous findings that length of stay in treatment is significantly correlated with improved outcome of treatment (Dodd, 1997). Moreover, it is shown that remaining active in a treatment program after official completion is imperative to reduce recidivism (Hser, Huang, Teruya, & Anglin, 2004).

Although alcohol abuse ranks high among social and medical problems in many Native American populations, there is much intertribal variation. The fallacy of stereotypical views of Native Americans is most clearly exposed by the high degree of variance found within this population. Native Americans differ across tribal groups, socioeconomic strata, age, and living environments.

For example, a study comparing a sample of Native Americans in an urban treatment setting with a reservation treatment setting, using the scales of the Alcohol Use Inverntory (AUI; Horn, Wanberg, & Foster, 1990), found that rural Native Americans showed significantly less alcohol-related problems and disruption. Moreover, no large-scale analysis of alcohol use has investigated differences in prevalence levels or dynamics across tribal groups or among Native American women (Lex, 1987). Thus, it may not be helpful to identify Native Americans as a single target population, and overgeneralizations should be cautiously avoided.

Bilingual Skills of Staff

A major problem in many treatment programs is the lack of bilingual staff members. In many instances, this barrier in communication may produce great difficulty for a provider in relating to the specific problems confronted by the Hispanic client. It is widely recognized that family—*la familia*—is of central importance to Hispanic culture. Most research points to the value of involving the strong networking systems of Hispanic families in the treatment process (Ruiz, 1995). Rapport and trust are secured as providers display respect for and comprehension of the individual roles of family members. Traditionally, each member of the Hispanic family has a special role: grandparents are respected for their wisdom; fathers for their authority; mothers for their commitment; children for their promise in the future; and godparents for their availability and support during times of crisis. It is important to consider using these family resources in treatment with Hispanic judicial clients (Ruiz).

Immigration and Biculturalism

As mentioned, a strong predictor of women's use of substances is acculturation, placing women who are in the process of acculturating at increased risk. This effect has been especially prominent in second- and third-generation Mexican American women; while only 25 percent of recently immigrated Mexican women engage in alcohol use, 62 percent of third-generation Mexican women were found to use (Gilbert, 1989). Similar results have been observed among Japanese American, Puerto Rican, and Cuban American women (Wilsnack, 1995). Some findings show an inverse relationship between ties to Hispanic countries and illicit drug use. U.S.-born members of Hispanic communities tend to have higher rates of substance use than Hispanics born outside of the United States (for example, 53 percent of U.S.-born versus 25 percent of Puerto Rico-born, and 11 percent born in other Hispanic countries) (Ruiz, 1995). A parallel finding is that 45 percent of Hispanics who speak primarily English had used illicit drugs, compared to only 8 percent who speak mostly Spanish. Clearly, values and responsibilities associated with traditional Hispanic cultures, especially family support, may be utilized toward the prevention of substance abuse and recidivism.

Geographic mobility and immigration often plays a negative role in substance abuse and crime. It can lead to breakdown of the family network, leaving family members who are without these bonds more vulnerable to deviant associates and escape-oriented activities. Without the support from family an immigrant may be accustomed to, turning to drugs with newfound friends may seem like the best option for her.

The Interface of Culture and Substance Use

The context of culture, specifically with regard to community, may play an important role in creating the ambience within which substance abuse occurs. It may influence what drugs are available, for example, the prevalence of crack cocaine among lower socioeconomic levels and pure cocaine among middle-class and wealthier communities. It may convey preferences regarding what types of substances are best to achieve what purpose. It may even shape expectations regarding the effects of a particular substance, as in previously discussed beliefs regarding the "sexual-enhancing powers" of alcohol in some communities. Clearly such expectations are important considerations in designing relevant intervention. Culturally aware counselors may develop insight into their client's expectancies about substance use, as well as specific triggers for recidivism and relapse. Expected outcomes following AOD use, such as relief from painful feelings, including anger over racism, homophobia, lack of adequate and affordable day care or housing, sexual harassment on the job, and so on, may then be addressed and brought into the context of therapeutic discussion.

BEYOND CULTURAL DIFFERENCES

Of significant relevance to working with women from a diversity of backgrounds involves going beyond potential differences in cultural values and/or patterns of substance abuse and crime. Perhaps more to the point are issues related to experiences of racism and economic discrimination experienced by many women who take drugs and commit crimes. A host of cognitive, emotional, and behavioral responses may follow in the aftermath of these experiences. The effects of internalized racism (the internalization of negative stereotypes of minorities

as "underachievers," "hostile and angry," "likely to fail," and so on) may undermine self-esteem and self-efficacy. The perception that these issues may be operating against them in the criminal justice system may have a profound effect on the achievement of program goals around prosocial adjustment.

African Americans, for example, may hold on to perceptions of systemic injustice, cruelty, and inevitable treatment failure in response to having been arrested and released without charge more frequently than other groups, having had a greater likelihood of being jailed before trial, having paid on average twice as much bail as European Americans, and having received heavier sentences for the same crime (Howard, 1996, p. 25). Although African Americans make up 12 percent of the American population, with 13 percent saying they used drugs in the past month, they account for 35 percent of arrests for drug possession, 55 percent of convictions, and 74 percent of prison sentences. Although African Americans apparently do not differ from other ethnic groups with respect to the consequences and symptoms of substance abuse (Wanberg & Horn, 1991), this ethnic group does receive differential and disproportionate criminal sanctioning. A provider who is sensitive to the potential for feelings of powerlessness, resentment, and/or anger at racism may be more effective in conquering resistance in treatment.

Service providers will be more effective if they are alert to these issues and are well-enough informed to engage in constructive dialogue with their clients. Crucial to these discussions should be helping the client to analyze ways in which experiences like those mentioned may fail to support their attempts to build a positive self-image. Key also is helping clients to identify strengths from their cultural heritage that enable them to transcend many of the problems they are experiencing.

Essential Elements of Cultural Awareness

A client's cognitive patterns and motivations to change are often defined within the context of cultural experience. Sensitivity to racial and cultural dynamics allows treatment providers collaboratively—with clients—to identify specific vulnerability factors for relapse and recidivism. Therefore, it is essential that providers embrace cultural awareness, so they can explore with their clients, in an open climate of sharing, specific considerations regarding culture or socioeconomic experience. To this end, basic elements of cultural sensitivity are described following:

▶ **Recognize universal ethnocentricity.** Humans generally tend to center on their own culture or group for definitions of reality, value orientations, and appropriate behavior. Cultural competence in service providers involves fostering a balance that allows clients to preserve their own cultural identity while identifying ways in which the client's interpretation of her culture may be at odds with the goals and constructive behaviors involved in reducing substance abuse and criminal behaviors. Usually these perceived conflicts are misinterpretations of cultural values that may have served as rationalizations for substance abuse and criminal conduct (for example, "Everyone I know does it"; "It's the only way to get ahead if you're a person like me"). In these circumstances, it may be helpful to ask the client to explore what she values about her culture or previous experience and to connect sobriety and abstinence, as well as restraint from criminal behavior, with being a responsible member of her community. Cultural pride is a powerful source of motivation for recovery when a person is able to come to understand these connections herself and is not lectured about them from the vantage point of a different cultural construction.

▶ **Recognize discrimination in economic and political power.** Many members of minority groups, including those from racial groups, single mothers, and lesbian and transgender people, have experienced limited access to economic and political power in mainstream society and, for the most part, have been hindered from influencing the structures that plan and administer therapeutic programs. These may have generated realistically pessimistic expectations regarding their "odds" at gaining legitimate employment that can provide them with livable wages and of being involved in their treatment program in meaningful ways. Sensitivity to these expectations and acknowledgment that they are founded in realities of the past (rather than arguing that they are merely "in the mind," "excuses," "feeling sorry for oneself," and so on) will go a long way toward building trust from which meaningful solutions to these real problems can be generated.

▶ **Separate ethnicity from poverty.** In our society, ethnic cultures are often confused with a "culture of poverty" or other socioeconomic conditions. Some believe that minority groups do not have cultures worth respecting or that the major culture of these groups is "hopelessness and helplessness" or "anger and entitlement" (common stereotypes of African Americans) or a "culture of alcoholism" (a stereotype of Native Americans) (Isaacs & Benjamin, 1991). Culturally aware treatment providers are able to distinguish culture from economic condition and understand that it is the cultural strengths and values within many ethnic groups that have allowed them to survive and grow in the midst of impoverished and hostile environments. Culturally competent providers are fully aware that alcoholism and poverty are not "cultures," but rather are parts of the struggle to adapt, for better or worse, to restrictive and often degrading interactions with the dominant society. It is important, therefore, to recognize and understand the cultural factors that have provided strength and sustenance to ethnic minority groups and to incorporate these strengths into treatment interventions and program designs.

▶ **Avoid stereotype substitutions.** In attempts to become more sensitive to another culture, and to incorporate its strengths into treatment, we must avoid substituting one set of stereotypes for another. Any stereotype or overgeneralization, whether positive or negative, reflects cultural insensitivity. Stereotypes strip us of being able to see unique individuals. This is a major factor that may undermine trust and effectiveness in a therapeutic context.

Effective treatment providers recognize that cultural understanding is multifaceted: it is a long and ongoing learning process that requires openness to new ways of thinking, the willingness to make mistakes and be told about it, and a nondefensive and collaborative searching for answers that fit a client's cultural identity as well as the goals of the criminal justice system.

The Culture of Counseling Versus the Values of Traditional Cultures

Psychotherapy and counseling have developed a set of values, many of which are rooted in European

American culture. These values represent underlying philosophical assumptions that may undermine counseling's effectiveness when working with clients from cultural traditions outside the American middle-class mainstream.

Sue and Sue (1990) have identified some of the characteristics of the culture of counseling: verbal emotional expressiveness, individual orientation, openness and intimacy, and a somewhat linear cause-effect orientation. Other characteristics include placing responsibility on the shoulders of the client and having the client take the lead in conversation. One of the most important components of the culture of counseling is self-disclosure. However, Antaki, Barnes, and Leudar (2005) found self-disclosure to be circumstantial, that is, taking place only when people are feeling it is necessary to perform socially.

Western society's service programs generally include a focus on individualism and competition, hierarchical power, communication controlled by authority, the Protestant ethic, Western notions of progress and history, Western views of nuclear family structure, religion and aesthetics, and a scientific orientation toward problem solving. Each of these values may at some point run counter to the values of many ethnic groups, as well as to the socialization of women in general. These values may put a client with a different cultural orientation at a distance and reduce appraisals of program relevance. For example, individualism and the scientific method are valued differently by a number of cultural groups, Asians and American Indians being distinct examples. In American Indian, Hispanic, and Asian cultures, a person's identity is generally more communal in nature (less individualized). Because cooperation (rather than competition) is tied into this orientation, a culturally traditional client may view appropriate behavior differently from that of Western culture. Additionally, within some cultures, self-disclosure to strangers is not acceptable. The culturally sensitive treatment provider is alert to the potential for these sources of alienation. Addressing the potential for these different values and perceptions can serve to communicate that the provider is interested in making the program relevant to the needs of the individual woman and can enhance rapport and sharing within the treatment group.

Effective treatment professionals develop an awareness that their values may vary from those of a minority client. Inherent differences may include such simple and routine issues as the importance of time schedules and keeping appointments. Making these expectations explicit through identification of these goals as mutual agreements can often improve treatment compliance.

Understanding a Client's Identity

A crucial element of therapeutic effectiveness involves understanding the nuances of a particular client's self-defined ethnic, racial, or sexual identity. Halliday-Boykins, Schoenwald, and Letourneau (2005) found strong evidence that ethnic similarity is important to treatment success. The group of adolescents treated by those similar in ethnicity showed greater progress in therapy than those treated by one dissimilar in ethnicity. This is not to say, however, a youth must receive treatment from one who is of the same race, but it does indicate the importance of understanding the client's ethnic background. This includes attention to the extent to which an individual woman perceives herself as a member of any given group, proclaims this identity to others, feels comfort or pride in being a member of this group, and/or understands the values, customs, and traditions of this group. It is extremely important to ask a client about her self-identification(s) and not to make assumptions based on physical or stereotypical characteristics. Just being asked often makes a person feel visible and important, while assumptions often engender resentment and feelings of invisibility as a person.

Recognition of cultural strengths is an important component of culturally sensitive services. Key Hispanic cultural values such as dignity, respect, and love (*dignidad, respeto, y cariño*) can all be beneficial in the therapeutic process. Clients who feel alone and disconnected may be encouraged to correspond with distant family members, perhaps reaching across years of little or no contact. Group discussions with a skillful focus on cultural themes may improve participant trust as well as treatment alliance. Efforts can be made to acknowledge a diversity of traditional celebrations, such as Cinco de Mayo, Kwanzaa (an African celebration about the time of Christmas and Chanukah), Gay

Pride, Mother's Day, and so on. Decorative images of Mayan women of Central America, strong women from the Ashanti tradition of Africa, a woman's council of elders from the Iroquois tradition... pictures of strong women of all colors and orientations, including lesbians, pregnant women, elderly women, and women with disabilities, may be safely placed around the group room in order to reflect back the diversity in the judicial population. These images of respect for each woman's identity may reflect the needed coherence, mutuality, and inclusiveness that can powerfully enhance group process.

Identity Testing

Identity testing (trying on a variety of roles, behaviors, and identity choices) is generally recognized as important to recovery for women offenders, as their former lives have often failed to grant them this opportunity. In general, conflict is viewed as grounds for change in a person's life (Kunnen & Wassink, 2003). The conflicting roles of who the woman was and who she is trying to become through therapy presents a conflict in lifestyle. Time spent within the criminal justice system may constitute a first opportunity for these women to explore and experiment with various aspects of their personalities, including trust, intimacy, and many other cognitive and behavioral factors, in a safe and nonthreatening environment. It is common that women may explore various aspects of their sexuality with each other, which may be understood as important in the process of identity development. In addition, women may experiment with being sassy, compliant, withdrawn, insulting, and a host of other emotional and coping responses. These should not be criticized, but rather seen as ways through which a woman may be feeling her way to an identity and manner of behaving within which she feels safe and comfortable. Instead of challenging her on these "outbursts" or shifts in behavior, facilitating exploration of why they are appealing at this time in life may prove beneficial for moving through them.

SOCIOECONOMIC ISSUES

Economic difficulties are involved in many aspects of women's criminal behavior, serving as motivators and sustainers of criminal conduct, as well as significant barriers to obtaining the treatment that might have prevented its development. Despite equal levels of education, women experience higher unemployment rates than men, and when employed, labor in lower-paying jobs. Women are more likely than men to be dependent on welfare, a spouse/ or partner, and/or prostitution than are men (Booth, Koester, & Pinto, 1995). These conditions place women at risk for poorer health care, poor medical insurance, if any, lack of affordable day care, and many other significant stressors in their lives.

The importance of addressing these issues is illustrated in a study that examined the relationship between economic factors and outcomes of substance abuse treatment with women (Gregoire & Snively, 2001). Reduced substance abuse was correlated with increases in economic self-sufficiency and the likelihood of achieving and keeping employment after treatment. In another study of drug treatment in a correctional setting, Hohman, McGaffigan, and Segars (2000) found that obtaining employment and a safe place to live before discharge reduced rates of relapse and recidivism.

Recessions in the late 1970s and early 1980s, reduction in government benefits paid to indigent people, and welfare reform legislation of the 1990s have all contributed to a culture of poverty in past decades. By 1982, social services programs were funded at about $9 billion less than funding allocations prior to 1981. During the 1980s, poverty affected between 12 percent and 15 percent of the population. "By 1989 about 31.7 million Americans lived below the official poverty level of $12,675 per year for a family of four" (Joseph, 1992, p. 876). In addition, there is a great imbalance in the racial distribution of poor people. From 1980 to 1989, levels of poverty vacillated between 30and 35 percent for African Americans, 25 and 30 percent for Hispanics, and 10 and 20 percent for Anglos. About 19.6 percent of children under 18 years of age and 22.5 percent of those under 6 years were being reared in poverty, usually in one-parent families headed by the mother (Pear, 1990).

It was conservatively estimated that in 1987 there were one-half million homeless persons living in the United States, of which 75 percent were male (Joseph, 1992). There is a significant correlation between substance abuse and homelessness. Estimates of alcoholism range from 35 to 40 percent of the homeless, with hard-core drug abuse estimated at 10–20 percent. Approximately 10–20 percent have a concurrent psychiatric disorder (Interagency Council on the Homeless, 1989). Additionally, severe psychiatric disorders and substance abuse in the homeless are strongly correlated. Seventy-eight percent of homeless prison inmates with a psychiatric disorder were found to have a substance abuse problem in conjunction (McNiel, Binder, & Robinson, 2005).

Combined effects of racism, poor education, and unemployment have undermined opportunities for African Americans, Hispanics, Native Americans, and women, leaving a large population entrenched in the dire conditions of inner-city squalor. Insufficient technical job skills in the current labor market, low wages in services industries, and unaffordable housing are reasons for poverty in the inner cities. The social consequences of these conditions include crime and violence, substance abuse, homelessness, and the spread of HIV infection. Essential ingredients of effective treatment programs for the culture of poverty, therefore, include vocational assessment and training and, most critically, job placement.

Women judicial clients are generally very familiar with inadequate housing, lack of decent job opportunities, low wages, and job discrimination. These experiences may generate maladaptive perceptions and cognitions (such as beliefs that dependence on a man—even an abusive man—and/or criminal behavior constitute the "only possible options" in making a living). The majority of women in corrections are poor, undereducated, and unskilled. More than 60 percent of women offenders were unemployed at the time of their arrest, compared to fewer than a third among their male counterparts (Collins & Collins, 1996, in Covington, 2000). Of women in prison, only 37 percent were found to be working at date of entry, 22 percent received public assistance, 16 percent were involved in drug selling, and 15 percent in prostitution, shoplifting, and other crimes (Bloom, Chesney-Lind, & Owen, 1994).

WOMEN JUDICIAL CLIENTS AND THEIR CHILDREN

As previously noted, two-thirds of women in criminal justice settings, versus 59 percent of men, have children (Covington, 2001). The Center for Substance Abuse Treatment (1999) found that 80 percent of the women in their treatment facilities had children. These women suffer an added burden of emotional difficulty. Many experience severe guilt over not being with their children or of losing custody (Phillips & Harm, 1997). They worry that they cannot be present while their child is growing up and feel deep shame and guilt for having imposed this burden on their child.

Currently, about 1 in 50 children is affected by incarceration of a parent (Curry, 2001). The percentages of incarcerated parents with children vary by ethnicity, with 50 percent black, 25 percent white, and 20 percent Hispanic. Fifty-one percent of nonparents are violent offenders, versus 44 percent of offenders with children.

Women with children who are restricted to correctional settings may be seriously affected by:

- Desire to see her child
- Fear she will not be able to sustain custody while in prison
- Guilt that she is not in her child's life
- Worry that she will lose custody once back on the outside
- Worry that she will not be a good mother upon reunification
- Worry about the effects of her incarceration on her child (Bloom & Steinhart, 1993)

Many women are unable to see their children while in a correctional facility. Prominent reasons for this separation are the isolated locations of prison facilities, lack of transportation for getting there, and family members or other caretakers who worry about the effects on the child of seeing their mother behind bars. Incarceration of mothers often relegates children to an irregular series of foster care arrangements, and the potential for creating a new generation of inmates is great (McQuaide & Ehrenreich, 1998).

Severity of the mother's substance abuse was found to be associated with the quality of parenting cognitions and mother-infant interactions. Substance-abusing women were found to:

▶ Be less sensitive to the needs of their babies

▶ Manifest subtle hostile behaviors when interacting with their infants

▶ Provide inappropriate developmental support (Goldman-Fraser, 1998)

Responsible Parenting

The factors mentioned fail to support a mother's ability to maintain ties with her children, and she may begin to lose sight of herself as a parent. It is important to help mothers maintain this identity, as it can serve as a powerful motivator for recovery and may serve to bring about better outcomes for the family as a whole.

Mothers in correctional placements should be advised that despite the hardship placed upon children when their parents are incarcerated, a warm and loving relationship between them can lessen some of this harm. A study investigating cognitive factors associated with effective parenting found key issues to be

▶ Knowledge about child development

▶ Sense of competence in the role of parent

▶ Positive perceptions of infant behavior (Goldman-Fraser, 1998)

Educating a woman in these areas may help her to maintain her identity as mother and to form bonds around a "culture of motherhood" with other women in the facility. Of course, women who have been engaged in child abuse should be given mandatory treatment in these areas.

Pregnant Women

As discussed earlier, 25 percent of women in jail or prison settings are either pregnant or in the months just following birth at the time of incarceration (McMahon, 2000). Substance abuse is listed among the most significant risks in childbearing, and yet statistics find that obstetricians and gynecologists are among the least likely to screen for substance abuse in their patients (Valente et al., 1992). Women judicial clients should be fully informed about fetal alcohol effects, fetal drug effects, and fetal alcohol syndrome (FAS). While full FAS is usually encountered among women who are heavy drinkers, even lower levels of drinking, cigarette smoking, and drug abuse increase risk of miscarriage, low birth weight, birth defects, and behavioral abnormalities (Valente et al., 1992). Substance abuse also may interfere with mother-infant bonding (Blume, 1998).

CHAPTER REVIEW

This chapter begins with an expanded view of culture to include the context of values within which a person has lived and formed her primary experience of herself. The existence of diversity within broad categories of ethnic groups is highlighted, with emphasis on the recognition of different patterns of AOD abuse and crime within subsets of major cultural groupings, for example, rural versus urban Native Americans, acculturated versus immigrant Hispanics. The importance of culture in determining the expectancies for certain drug effects is followed by a discussion of how the effects of "internalized racism" may undermine a client's willingness to participate and believe in the attainability of treatment goals, for example, gainful employment, freedom from drugs, or self-sufficiency.

The chapter then discusses essential elements of cultural awareness, including the proclivity for humans to assert their own cultural values and beliefs as definitions of reality and standards of conduct, the importance of recognizing discrimination in economic and political power, and the necessity to separate conceptions of ethnicity from the correlates of poverty. Counseling itself is discussed as a cultural identity with notable differences in values and expectations from traditional cultures, for example, keeping a schedule of appointments, self-disclosure, openness, and intimacy. The importance of being aware of the client's own self-definitions and culturally determined strengths is covered, followed by a discussion of the client's tendency to test out new identities in response to challenges posed by the treatment environment.

Economic difficulties are considered in the context of successful community reentry along with the importance of financial self-sufficiency in maintaining treatment goals of relapse and recidivism prevention. Treatment motivation and critical targets for intervention services are covered in terms of dealing with external circumstances such as poverty and housing; thoughts and feelings about taking care of children; disappointments and aspirations regarding pregnancy, children, and responsibilities of mothering.

CHAPTER 8: Gender-Specific Strategies and Models for Treatment

CHAPTER OUTLINE

INTRODUCTION

THE THERAPEUTIC ALLIANCE: WHAT MAKES AN EFFECTIVE COUNSELOR?

THE THERAPEUTIC ENVIRONMENT

GOALS OF TREATMENT WITH FEMALE JUDICIAL CLIENTS

THERAPEUTIC INTERVENTION WITH FEMALE JUDICIAL CLIENTS

Identification of Psychoeducational and Vocational Needs of Female Judicial Clients

Motivational Enhancement and Building Treatment Readiness

Important Cognitive Shifts

Exploration of Feelings

Women as Role Models

Awareness Principles for Male Counselors Working With Female Correctional Clients

INDIVIDUALIZED PLANS FOR REENTRY AND TRANSITION

Transitional Planning and Wraparound Services

SUPPORT FOR SERVICE PROVIDERS

Realistic Expectations

Resolving Disappointment in Treatment Failure

Vicarious Trauma

CURRENT TRENDS IN WOMEN-FOCUSED PROGRAMS: MODELS FOR TREATMENT

Incarcerated and Residential Models

Family-Oriented Services

CHAPTER REVIEW

LEARNING OBJECTIVES

▶ To develop a philosophical framework for gender-specific treatment programming, which includes conceptual approaches to education and therapy with women

▶ To explore factors that facilitate the establishment of a productive therapeutic alliance, addressing issues of confrontation, trust, and effective group process

▶ To examine ways in which cognitive-behavioral treatment can be adapted to include specific strategies of change for use with female judicial clients

▶ To identify and explain the major goals of treatment with women

▶ To emphasize the need for wraparound transitional services in generating realistic possibilities of women sustaining recovery after release into the community

▶ To review techniques being utilized in a range of gender-focused treatment programs

INTRODUCTION

This chapter provides a philosophical framework for gender-specific treatment and explores current psychoeducational models for female judicial clients. Female-focused treatment objectives, individualized treatment plans, wraparound services, and critical issues surrounding community reentry are discussed.

Women-only treatment programs produce positive outcomes and retention of therapy. This is because women perceive a same-sex treatment environment as one in which it is easier to disclose information about themselves, such as issues with children, sexuality, prostitution, sexual abuse, and physical abuse (Sun, 2006). Additionally, women-only settings eliminate the possibility of negative stereotyping and sexual harassment from male counterparts (Weisner, 2005). Conceptual approaches to effective treatment with women generally recognize the importance of both education and therapy. Because of the social context in which women's difficulties are initiated, develop, grow, and persist, education about this social context is critical (Covington, 2000; Crawford & Unger, 2000; Gergen & Davis, 1997; Kassebaum, 1999). Treatment will help a woman to recognize ways in which her behavior may:

- Meet social standards of appropriateness but work against positive outcomes

- Lead her to participate in situations and relationships that are bad for her, and

- Perpetuate the imposed powerlessness of women in society

Helping a woman to recognize how her personal psychology may both reflect and perpetuate processes that fail to empower her is a significant step in treatment (Covington, 2000; Crawford & Unger, 2000; Gergen & Davis, 1997).Research suggests that to be effective, treatment must take into consideration gender, demographics, and psychosocial behavioral patterns (Acharyya & Zhang, 2003). Many different fields have contributed to our present understandings, including the APA guidelines for therapy with women (American Psychological Association [APA], 1978); feminist therapy (Crawford & Unger, 2000; Gergen & Davis, 1997; Miller & Stiver, 1997); principles of nonsexist therapy (Matlin, 1996); and studies of female

criminality (Covington, 2000; Pollock, 1998). Each of these avenues of research has produced a surprisingly similar list of imperatives for effective therapy with women, leading to an interdisciplinary approach providing clear directives for effective intervention. Williams-Quinlan (2004) has outlined the following guidelines for treating women in psychotherapy:

- Effective treatment with women should be free of restrictions based on narrowly defined gender stereotypes.

- The empowerment process involves recognition that women are able to accomplish what they make a commitment to and that the female judicial client is no different from other women.

- Women who choose not to act in stereotypical ways and in nontraditional role choices should be respected. Marriage may not be a solution to women's problems.

- Consider that the "socially appropriate" ways women have been taught may not be ideal for mental health and adjustment (Crawford & Unger, 2000; Gergen & Davis, 1997; Matlin, 1996).

- It is important to use respectful language that communicates women's equal status to men (APA, 1978; Covington, 2000; Pollock, 1998; McMahon, 2000; Matlin, 1996).

- Service providers working with women should help women recognize the realities of sexism, racism, and economic discrimination and develop effective means of coping with them (APA, 1978; Matlin, 1996).

Treatment providers will understand that the source of many of women's problems are not only psychodynamic but can be social and cultural. Research suggests that one component of substance abuse may be violence in the female's domestic setting (Velez et al., 2006). Treatment that places the source of a woman's problems solely within herself can actually do damage to the recovery process by exacerbating already existing tendencies toward self-blame and feelings of powerlessness (APA, 1978; Covington, 2000; Crawford & Unger, 2000; Matlin, 1996; Pollock, 1998). Equally important is helping women to see that assuming a victim stance in response to social realities is not an excuse to avoid responsibility.

The treatment provider will want to understand the influence of gender roles on the development of female identity (APA, 1978; Miller & Stiver, 1997). Specifically, gender has been found to impact the roles women have in communication (Dow & Condit, 2005). A positive aspect of the "relational orientation" shared by many women is the ability to relate to female role models as important allies in developing a support system. Men, however, should not be cast as the enemy. Reverse discrimination is not a useful strategy of empowerment (Matlin, 1996).

Therapists will want to strive to involve women in decision making regarding treatment goals. Setting clear goals between the patient and the counselor produces improved therapy outcomes (Renik, 2002). Of therapeutic benefit is to expose women to egalitarian experiences in treatment in order to provide contrast from past life experiences of subordination (Matlin, 1996).

THE THERAPEUTIC ALLIANCE: WHAT MAKES AN EFFECTIVE COUNSELOR?

Establishment of an effective therapeutic alliance is challenged by many factors. Women, regardless of substance abuse or criminality, have a lower rating than men on scales measuring trust in others (Wang & Yamagishi, 2005). Because of this, the establishment of trust between client and the counselor is necessary to achieve the following treatment objectives:

- Understand healthy relationships
- Develop the motivation to end unhealthy relationships, thereby detaching from embedded triggers for relapse and recidivism
- Develop the skills to initiate and maintain healthy relationships after release
- Trust in the therapeutic relationship and the community of women to establish a base of social support, mutual aid, and role modeling that can help accomplish these goals

A second condition that poses a challenge for the treatment staff is women's frequent inability to

"perceive, establish, and defend their own personal boundaries" (Kassebaum, 1999, p. 99). Having had those boundaries violated so frequently, women may no longer recognize or protect them.

Poor coping skills may also interfere with a woman's ability to handle the conditions of incarceration; the loss of freedom, restriction of action, and strict procedures may pose serious triggers to retraumatization and further distrust. Therefore, the major steps in working with a woman who is first entering a treatment program are rapport building, building treatment readiness, and motivational enhancement (Kassebaum, 1999).

Another component of treatment that is extremely important at intake and throughout the entire therapeutic process is the use of accessible language (Najavits, Weiss, Shaw, & Muenz, 1998). Low rates of educational achievement among female judicial clients necessitate the assessment of a woman's level of language skills in general as well as English language comprehension in particular (Najavits et al., 1998). Atkinson, Thompson, and Grant (1993) cite language as a contributing factor that may undermine treatment with minority clients. Language that conveys differences in value orientation, or that makes attempted communication by staff incomprehensible to clients, creates a climate of difference, distance, and perhaps, irrelevance. The therapist and client may misinterpret each others' statements, creating dialogue that undermines positive expressions of a woman's identity. Therefore, the following may be essential toward establishing, and keeping, a productive therapeutic alliance:

Verbal Skills. Careful assessment of a woman's verbal and written skills should be undertaken. Language that is accessible and engaging should be used. Providers should recognize that some female clients may not have the verbal skills necessary to profit from extensive "talk" therapy. In these instances, the use of complicated or abstract concepts to facilitate change is ineffective. Terms like *cognitive restructuring* and *self-efficacy* should be replaced with *rethinking* (Najavits et al., 1998) and *self-confidence*.

Importance of the Client's Primary Language. Counseling must be done in the language of the client, especially if English is not her primary language (Sue & Sue, 1990). Understanding the content and syntax of different dialectical idioms (such as Ebonics in the

African American culture) is important in order to understand and work effectively with some African American clients.

▶ **Use of Psychological Jargon**. Counselors who are accustomed to the culture of counseling and its terminology may forget that this lingo and the conceptual categories behind it are not universally understandable, valued, nor appreciated. It has been found very important to speak in lay terms for reasons of clarity, in addition to refraining from sounding condescending (Allen, 2005). An example is the term *self-concept*, a crucial component of therapy with female judicial clients. Counselors should help female clients to understand the meaning of "self-concept" and why it is helpful for effective recovery. This can be empowering, because it communicates that the female judicial client is capable of understanding her own growth and change process. A lack of understanding of critical terms may undermine a woman's belief in her ability to change by making the change process seem abstract and unattainable.

▶ **A Crucial Note for Consideration.** Some language issues can be very subtle. A common error in thinking among service providers is to mistake "being like the client" for "being liked *by* the client." This may cause us to mimic the client's communication style by inserting what we project to be the client's jargon into our own speech patterns in an attempt to establish a sense of commonality. However, it should be noted that this kind of behavior is often experienced by clients as patronizing, may be subject to ambiguity and misinterpretation, and is not in line with the therapeutic purpose. Though we accept the client's jargon and have an obligation to understand the meanings conveyed therein, we must also maintain a professional role. The treatment alliance is built on information, empathy, and feedback, not on attempting to merge with a client's cultural identity (Wanberg & Milkman, 1998, 2008).

Multiple elements of therapist understanding that improve treatment effectiveness with women clients are listed in Table 8.1.

Table 8.1
Essential Elements of Gender-Focused Treatment
• Specialized training in gender-specific treatment in addition to training in addiction and criminality
• Knowledge of women's psychological development and gender identity formation
• Awareness of potential for shaming a woman and how this can contribute to already existing difficulties (self-blame)
• Skills to avoid shaming, replacing it with affirmation
• Recognizing that addressing intrapsychic conflicts is only part of the therapeutic process with women
• Assisting women in understanding environmental factors that may contribute to many of their difficulties
• Recognizing the existence and consequences of sex and race discrimination in the broader society and promote skills to deal with these practices
• Understanding the depth of psychological trauma that may occur in the aftermath of violent experiences as well as the use of strict procedures to avoid unnecessary "voyeuristic" probing into the details of this abuse
• Avoiding reinforcement of gender stereotypes that limit growth and empowerment
• Responding with respect toward a woman's decisions regarding explorations of her sexuality
• Respect for the client's confidentiality, especially with inquiring family members
• Helping a female victim of violence to see that she is a victim of a crime (abuse is so pervasive in many women's lives that they have difficulty recognizing that they are being abused)
• Recognizing that developing self-care, self-respect, and self-value are crucial to the healing process in women; this involves ownership of areas of strength, the power to survive, and the ability to solve problems
• Encouraging clients to develop the skills of self-sufficiency in order to break dependency on unhealthy and unequal relationships
• Recognizing how cultural differences may affect the conditions of a woman's life as well as how they may affect the therapeutic relationship

Sources: American Psychological Association (1978); Kassebaum (1999); Matlin (1996); Williams-Quinlan (2004).

THE THERAPEUTIC ENVIRONMENT

An unhealthy environment is detrimental to a woman's recovery. Once the living situation improves for a female, so do her chances of success in treatment (Grella, Scott, Foss, Joshi, & Hser, 2003). Bloom, Owen, and Covington (2005) stress the importance of recognizing the potential retraumatization that may occur when female judicial clients are sexually harassed by staff members, be they male or female. Most of the media attention has been focused on male staff members with female clients; however, female staff members have also been involved in serious misconduct. This retraumatization will undoubtedly affect the female judicial client's ability to heal. Bloom et al. also seek to set standardized procedures in the use of searches, restraints, and isolation, as these may also trigger traumatization.

Living with other women fosters growth of a female's self-concept and encourages healing and recovery. Therefore, women should be housed together, and, preferably, separate from the broader facility (Kassebaum, 1999). This type of living arrangement allows for development of a "supportive, family-type environment" (Kassebaum, 1999, p. 98) that is able to support women's recovery. Comfortable space of adequate size needs to be available for women to visit with their children and other family members. Classroom and meeting space must be available for group activities.

Scheduling issues must also be considered. Vocational programming and substance abuse programming must be coordinated, perhaps having treatment hours count toward the vocational requirement. "Part-time treatment schedules are less desirable than longer treatment hours, since the fewer hours may not be intense enough for the population of incarcerated women with severe substance abuse problems" (Kassebaum, 1999, p. 99). Outside resources may at times be required, especially for consultation regarding mental health, and especially trauma-related, issues. Those who may eventually serve in this capacity should be introduced to the women early, to establish a process of familiarity (Kassebaum, 1999).

GOALS OF TREATMENT WITH FEMALE JUDICIAL CLIENTS

An important goal of treatment with female judicial clients is empowerment (Chesney-Lind, 2000; Covington, 2000; Edwards & Pedrotti, 2004; Kassebaum, 1999), which therefore leads to less relapse and recidivism, the primary goal of judicial treatment. Empowerment provides a woman with the skills and self-confidence to escape former patterns of violent abuse, criminal behavior, and self-destructive use of substances. It is through empowerment that a woman can gain the self-esteem and self-efficacy she needs for a life characterized by self-sufficiency rather than financial dependence, self-awareness rather than self-sacrifice. Independence and self-reliance are necessary for a woman to withstand pressures from peers, partners, and family that set her up for relapse and return to criminal behavior. Creating a new life on the outside requires that a woman has the ability to trust herself, to take care of herself, and to find a support structure that is nurturing rather than defeating. Transition out of treatment presents an important opportunity for a woman to lead a substance- and crime-free life, but she will meet overwhelming odds in achieving this. Treatment must fortify her to deal with the complexities of reentry and the longer-term life difficulties that she will encounter.

Many of the specific goals with women substance-abusing clients have already been discussed. Priority is given to building the motivation to stop substance abuse, generating a sense of entitlement to self-care, and developing self-efficacy to achieve self-sufficiency. This shift in perception of herself, her gifts, and the potential for a quality of life sets the groundwork for the desire to gain legitimate means of self-support and develop healthy relationships. With the prospect of this better life a reality, she is more likely to cease criminal conduct, stay out of corrections, and proceed on a positive life course.

Throughout the course of treatment, a woman is best facilitated in resisting relapse and recidivism when she is guided through the following areas of focus.

Identifying and Responding to High Risk Situations. Clients become adept at identifying particular triggers for substance use and criminality.

Being alert to the potential occurrence of these triggers may provide an inoculating effect by being able to choose alternative routes of behavior before impulsively reacting. Crucial to this, of course, is having already been educated to what these alternative routes of behavior may be.

Identifying High-Risk Thinking. Learning to scrutinize self-talk, intercepting, and changing and managing thoughts that precede substance use and criminal conduct. Specifically, positive outcome expectancies for AOD use and criminal involvement should be explored and compared to actual experience. Alternatives such as reaching out for support, changing her environment, or contacting her case manager may break the downslide from negative thought and action to positive action.

Identifying Negative Thought Patterns. This refers to negative thought patterns that continue over time. Identifying these counterproductive thought patterns is often difficult because of their gradual development without a context for comparison to more constructive thought patterns.

Identifying Negative Feeling States. Women are given the opportunity to explore what it feels like when they are happy, content, comfortable, safe, and relaxed. Helping them to contrast these feelings from negative states is important, as many women have little experience with tuning in to their own bodies to understand internal signals of healthy living.

Identifying Changes in Self-Image and Internal Conflict. Self-talk is very important to a woman. If she suddenly feels bad about herself, finds that she is shaming herself, withdraws and isolates herself, or frantically seeks stimulation so that she doesn't have to think, she is likely to be experiencing a shift in self-image. Identifying the source of this shame and guilt may bring her to recognition of another person or situation that is contributing to this self-scolding. She is then presented with a choice: she might choose leaving the relationship or situation, rather than leaving herself (into a retreat with drugs and/or alcohol). At the same time, appropriate and constructive guilt that prevents criminal conduct and enhances prosocial thinking and behavior should be encouraged and strengthened.

Evaluating Action Choices in Terms of Outcome. Specific tools for resisting relapse and recidivism are essential for any realistic expectation of a woman's recovery. The obstacles are very large, and service providers should understand this thoroughly. They should also convey to the woman that they realize the profound strength and courage that she is using in her struggle. This positive appraisal and expectation may engender a self-fulfilling prophecy to boost the woman along. Social responsibility therapy (SRT) (Wanberg & Milkman, 2008) focuses on giving women judicial clients appropriate tools to enhance prosocial living.

Developing Insight Into Her Potential. The aim is for a woman to be self-reflective and to develop the ability to see her life in terms of her mistakes as well as her potential.

Intrinsic Motivation to Change. Phrases that show signs of an internal desire to improve life include "I'm tired of my life"; "I'm disgusted with myself"; "I want to change"; "I want to save myself"; "I want to be a better parent"; "I want a job" (Kassebaum, 1999, pp. 100–101). External motivation, indicated by phrases such as "I want to get the police out of my life" is a less optimistic sign.

THERAPEUTIC INTERVENTION WITH FEMALE JUDICIAL CLIENTS

Identification of the Psychoeducational and Vocational Needs of Female Judicial Clients

Table 8.2 provides an inventory of the psychoeducational and vocational needs of women in treatment for substance abuse and criminal conduct (Covington, 1999; Wanberg & Milkman, 2008).

Motivational Enhancement and Building Treatment Readiness

Initial contact with a woman client needs to convey a sense that she is accepted, that there is hope for an improved life, that treatment is the means for actualizing this hope into a reality (Kassebaum, 1999), and that there is an understanding of the background from which she comes (Velez et al., 2006). Women also

Table 8.2

Psychoeducational and Vocational Needs of Female Judicial Clients	
Building Self-Awareness	I am, I think, I need, I know
Building Body Awareness	Attending to internal cues
Skills Development	Understanding irrational thinking
	Parenting skills and accessing child care
	Problem solving
	Coping
	Stress management and relaxation
	Basic life management skills
	Resource utilization
	Learning to ask for help
	Seeing allies in other women
	Making contact and networking with community service organizations
	Developing motivation for community resource participation
Vocational Skills Development	Interest and skills evaluation
	Vocational training
	Job search and interviewing skills
	Job placement
Understanding Personal Power	Increasing agency/self-efficacy
	Understanding the processes of change
Engendering Feelings of Empowerment	Fostering a sense of entitlement
Relapse/Recidivism (RR) Prevention	Identifying potential triggers for RR upon reentry
	Proactive problem solving

need to recognize how life circumstances are deeply and negatively affected by substance abuse. The Miller FRAMES technique for motivational interviewing (Miller, 2006; Wanberg & Milkman, 2008) is useful for providing the woman with empathic feedback regarding her life situation and behavior. "Reflection and mirroring back" (Kassebaum, 1999, p. 99) helps the female judicial client to relate the costs of substance abuse to many of the conditions she currently experiences in life. Connecting behavior to consequence is a central goal of effective treatment as well as an important first step in establishing motivation to change. The Stages of Change Model is useful for helping to identify where a woman's motivation level is (see Wanberg and Milkman, 2008, for further discussion of this model).

Important Cognitive Shifts

Once the initial phase of building motivation and readiness for treatment has been established, the major therapeutic component of the program begins. At this point, a client can be helped to:

▶ Realize that she has a problem with substance abuse and that her alcohol and other drug (AOD) behaviors are significantly and harmfully affecting her life.

▶ Resolve her ambivalence about giving up substance use; an extremely daunting task, as it usually means changing an entire lifestyle and leaving behind much of what is familiar (and perceived as pleasant about her life)—including friends, activities, places, situations, long-standing relationships, habits, and so on. Her grief about these losses is real and profound, and it must be dealt with before she can move on to effective resolution of her substance abuse and criminal behavior.

▶ Identify personal barriers to recovery.

▶ Develop the ability to be introspective, to feel respect for her emotions, and feel empowered in her ability to change (Kassebaum, 1999, pp. 100–101).

Exploration of Feelings

Exploring and managing emotions and feelings is an especially important component for a female treatment program. An important part of therapy with women is for them to learn to express feelings appropriately as well as to contain feelings through self-soothing techniques. Females frequently become dependent on drugs to seek relief from painful emotional states, and therefore during recovery require an environment in which to understand their feelings and work through emotions. Because females are often raised to suppress their feelings and to be compliant, if a treatment program obliges them to act in that same way, it can feel like the original abusive environment in which they learned to keep silent and turned to alcohol or other drugs. Such silence encourages them to avoid dealing with issues that can lead to relapse (Pepi, 1998). As feelings emerge in early recovery, females may feel confused and return to a cognitive focus on their drug of choice unless they have a context in which to learn new ways of handling those feelings (Covington, 2000, p. 207).

Effective therapy allows women to explore their emotional responses stemming from previous traumatic experiences such as physical or sexual abuse, loss of child custody, racism, or sexism; evaluations of self as a daughter, mother, sister, spouse, partner, lover, or friend; previous substance abuse and criminal behavior; the idea of living a crime- and substance-free life; and resistance to recovery. They also need to carefully explore their involvement in criminal thinking and behavior.

Women as Role Models

Women who have role models have been found to have higher self-esteem than those without role models (Mack, Schultz, & Araki, 2002). Women-focused treatment programs generally use two major strategies for exposing clients to positive female role models. The first requires a culturally diverse staff of female treatment providers, some of whom may be former judicial clients, who can model effective styles of communication, conflict resolution, and empathy. The second involves associations between female judicial clients and others who are either farther along in the treatment process or have successfully completed a treatment program. These strategies are mutually reinforcing in that they provide a female judicial client with real-life illustrations of the skills of recovery. The contingency relationships that link constructive behavior with positive outcome may then become recognized, as outcomes from new and more constructive behaviors will inevitably vary from the negative outcomes with which she is familiar.

Awareness Principles for Male Counselors Working With Female Correctional Clients

As discussed previously, the literature recommends that gender-specific groups and all-female staff may be used for women in corrections, particularly when dealing with the issues of trauma and abuse in treatment (Bloom, Owen, Covington, & Raeder, 2003; Covington, 1999; 2000). This approach increases self-disclosure in these sensitive areas and also provides opportunity for female judicial clients to identify with positive female role models.

The reality, however, is that in many judicial settings, men counselors will work with female judicial clients. Because many of the negative and traumatic experiences of women judicial clients have occurred in interactions with men, male counselors need to be particularly aware of their role in relationship to these clients. Also, it can be argued that women in corrections need to experience healthy and prosocial men providers who show high regard and respect for the role of women in society, who can set clear ethical and moral boundaries with respect to the integrity of women, and who can show that men can have empathy for others.

In consideration of these concerns, and the treatment needs of women in corrections, Masters (2003) summarizes what she sees as some "awareness principles" for male counselors when working with female judicial clients (pp. 118–119). Following is a summary of these with some elaboration of these principles based on the clinical experience of the authors:

▶ The first priority is to make a connection.

▶ Work at establishing a common and equal level or position.

▶ Work at interactively cooperating with the client.

▶ Use consensus as a basis for decision making.

▶ Use reinforcers such as expressing appreciation.

▶ Demonstrate and model prosociality.

▶ Share problems.

▶ Interact around emotions and feelings.

▶ Elicit help and advice in problem solving.

▶ Work at understanding and showing empathy before giving advice.

INDIVIDUALIZED PLANS FOR REENTRY AND TRANSITION

An important component of the treatment plan is to identify situational factors that increase risk for relapse and recidivism within each judicial client's life. Identifying and preparing for the conflicts and challenges that she is likely to encounter in her family and community is an important component of treatment. In addition, establishing a regimen of practice while she is still in the correctional setting can aid in applying and maintaining the life and stress management skills that she has learned there.

At this stage of treatment, providers may address realistic aspects about the environment into which the woman will return. Helping her to realistically appraise her social environment and to identify basic assumptions, persisting conditions, and immediate triggers that may lead to relapse and recidivism are crucial at this juncture. It is then that she can enter in consideration of contingency planning for the probable lack of change in this environment. Once she has identified some specific options and alternatives for herself, in response to specific contingencies ("If he begins to hit me, I can…"; "If she takes away all of my money…"), she must identify how to access these alternatives. When she leaves, she should have more than just phone numbers. In-house visits from community service providers, so she has already begun to establish a relationship with them, and on-site visits at these agencies or shelters, so she may become familiar and comfortable with the environments there are extremely helpful for women at this time (Kassebaum, 1999). During this entire process, she can be aided through the use of imagery and role playing as a regimen of practice for the skills she has acquired in treatment.

Transitional Planning and Wraparound Services

Transition into the community is difficult for both women and men judicial clients. Unfortunately, these difficulties frequently become barriers to sustaining recovery and may develop into triggers for relapse and recidivism. Wraparound services are designed to provide a comprehensive continuum of care that will help a woman overcome trauma reminders, reoccurrence of abuse, physical and mental health issues for herself and her children, job placement difficulties, and difficulty in finding safe, affordable, and substance-free housing. Ongoing counseling services are provided to help a woman resolve excessive demands for care and caregiving responsibilities and for juggling these responsibilities with the realities of employment. Advocacy with a variety of community agencies may be involved for coordination of services and avoidance of conflicting demands and treatment goals. At times, the woman may need guidance in finding appropriate transportation and child care services. Fulfilling these and many other presenting needs of women in transition is vital to maintaining the goals of relapse and recidivism prevention.

Effective wraparound services involve coordination between the client and other members of the treatment staff to develop individualized, proactive case management. Client-specific teams are developed, consisting of the client, case manager, community corrections supervisor, medical personnel, concerned family members, and anyone else who may be of assistance during recovery. This team-based approach allows for available services in both meaningful and practical ways to provide a comprehensive continuum of care (Reed & Leavitt, 2000).

Contingency planning is done at the team level. In exchange for help in coordinating and maintaining cooperation across the various agencies with which the woman client will be involved, she is expected to proceed in full compliance with regulations requiring abstinence and absence of criminal conduct of any kind. Setting boundaries for clients and holding clients responsible for their own breach of this promise will be delineated and firmly held. Overall guidelines and meeting and reporting requirements should be clearly defined and presented in a written format so the information is clear to all parties concerned. Occasional case conferencing will be used to assess client progress and compliance and generate additional guidelines should the need arise.

It is at the transitional period between treatment and community reentry that a woman is most likely to relapse. Because of this, it is important that she surround herself with social support, such as friends, family, church, community activity, and the like. In comparison to men, when attempting abstinence, women are likely to respond better to social support and are more successful when utilizing the social support system (Kidorf et al., 2005).

At the beginning of transitional planning, both client-based needs assessment and systems assessment should be undertaken to match treatment need to available services. This involves identifying not only skills deficits but also the individual strengths and values of the transitioning female. Available resources are then implemented through referral and advocacy, and programs that are useful for meeting needs and developing strengths are located within the community where the woman will reside.

Table 8.3 shows agencies and community resources that should be enlisted as components of this continuum of care (Reed & Leavitt, 2000):

Monitoring of these agencies to assure that programs are both gender and culturally sensitive is important. Though this may be difficult, it is exceptionally useful to help the transitioning woman to understand what her options are, should contingencies of sex, race, or ethnic discrimination arise. Proactive planning in this regard may help to short-circuit the relapse or recidivism that these experiences may engender, as women may be undermined by encounters with indifference and oppression.

An active aftercare program that rigorously identifies and proactively problem solves is necessary for a realistic transition to a substance- and crime-free life. Transition out of a correctional setting presents extremely stressful challenges for a woman. She may experience grief from losing her substance-dependent lifestyle and losing her former friends and family members associated with that lifestyle. She may face a continuance of separation from her children due to custody arrangements that may exclude or limit her involvement with them. Alternately, if she resumes custody, the difficult prospect of trying to provide for her children both financially and emotionally may be complicated by shame and guilt over previous failures and unrealistic images of what it means to be a "good mother." Family, home, and many of the environments with which she is familiar have been recast as dangerous to her sobriety; finding and establishing new associations is an arduous and painstaking task. Becoming self-sufficient, when often all she has known was financial dependency, may seem impossible. All of these, and many other potential losses and difficulties, may test her endurance and serve as risk factors for relapse and recidivism. It is essential that an aftercare program be available to provide continuing support and guidance through this difficult transition. In this regard, the following services have been developed as part of the comprehensive treatment protocol for women:

- Drop-in services for counseling, which may involve family and close friends

- Advocacy with agencies for obtaining safe housing, reunion with children, and so on

- Facilitating resource utilization, by providing aid with transportation and child care

- Aid with locating opportunities for job training and placement

- Resource networking, for other needs as they arise

SUPPORT FOR SERVICE PROVIDERS

Realistic Expectations

It is important that service providers be realistic about the changes that can be brought about in a correctional treatment setting. Turnover, length of stay, court dates,

Table 8.3

Agencies and Community Resources in a Continuum of Care

- Primary health care services (including mental health care, care for dependent children, and gynecological services)
- Educational and job placement services
- Housing advocacy
- Continued substance abuse treatment and services
- Child welfare services
- Parenting training and support, including linkages to adequate child care services
- Family reunification and/or family strengthening services
- Domestic violence or rape awareness task forces
- Legal services
- Survival services, such as food stamps, emergency shelter programs, financial assistance
- Identification of "natural helpers" (recovery coaches, recovery mentors, community elders)
- Self-help recovery programs; faith-based support groups
- Self-help groups geared toward certain subpopulations of women, such as Black Women's Business Association or Latina's Health Care Association, Lesbian Coming Out groups and gay rights organizations, HIV support groups, and so on
- Recreational resources for meeting people living responsible, healthy lives; learning to play and have fun in healthy settings with constructive friends and role models

transfers, security measures, crowding, and limited resources can all pose limitations on the effectiveness of therapy (Kassebaum, 1999). In addition, women with substance abuse problems are often far along in the addiction process, have severe concurrent difficulties, and are resistant to leaving behind their substance of choice. Service providers should understand that relapse, when it occurs, does not mean failure of the client, therapist, or therapy; rather the process should be analyzed and integrated as an important part of the recovery process (Kassebaum, 1999). As Bloom, Owen, and Covington (2005) assert, staffing and training is an important issue in providing services for female judicial clients. They indicate that the perception exists among correctional staff that females are more difficult to work with than males. This emphasizes the importance of preparing staff members with the knowledge about and understanding of women as well as providing guidance to improve interpersonal skills when working with female judicial clients.

Resolving Disappointment in Treatment Failure

Because bonding is an essential part of treatment, providers and clients may be deeply impacted

by separation events that may occur in "family-like" communities. A woman leaving a program unexpectedly (especially following an episode of relapse or recidivism), a woman who loses custody of her child, a woman who is transferred to a lock-up facility—all commonly occurring events in the correctional world—can be tremendously upsetting for clients and providers. These are some of the challenges of gender-focused treatment, but ones that have tremendous potential for prosocial growth. Providing role models for effective response to sadness and pain may contribute enormously toward development of coping skills for use on the outside.

Providers have to deal with these stressors, especially because they are recurrent throughout their career. In-house supervision and support for dealing with a wide range of feelings, including anger, disappointment, frustration, and hopelessness due to the client's relapse or recidivism, should be provided.

Vicarious Trauma

Support should also be available to help providers deal with any vicarious trauma that they may experience through hearing the realities of their client's lives.

The Colorado Organization for Victim Assistance has issued several reports on a phenomenon they called "vicarious trauma" (Geissinger & Hill, 2000). By understanding these issues, service providers are better prepared to provide their women clients with the nonjudgmental acceptance that is crucial to a woman's recovery (Kassebaum, 1999). Vicarious trauma, or traumatic counter-transference, occurs when a treatment provider, while attempting to provide support services for a victim of trauma, experiences some of the same feelings that the victim may express. Rage at the perpetrator and/or non-interventionist bystanders, helplessness and despair at not having the skills or ability to help the victim, a sense of personal vulnerability, and cynicism may all be involved. As well, vicarious trauma may involve a triggering of the provider's trauma experiences or of guilt for causing the victim to relive her pain in the counseling session. These emotional responses can reduce treatment effectiveness by:

- The appearance of not believing the client's accounts of traumatic events (stemming from denial)

- Attempts to minimize the consequences of violent domination (to make them easier to deal with)

- Sleep disturbances, relationship problems, and other distress, which can compromise the provider's effectiveness

- Attempts to "rescue" the victim

- Feelings of inadequacy, grief, or burnout

- Conflict between coworkers concerning treatment recommendations

These cognitive-emotional responses can serve to work against effective treatment and disempower the client; when she sees someone she respects become overwhelmed by her experiences, her situation may appear all that much more hopeless. Geissinger and Hill (2000) suggest that treatment providers who work with trauma victims be given adequate time, opportunity, and support to express their own feelings, both with coworkers and administrative personnel, in order to avoid the deleterious effects that may occur through expression of these responses with the victim.

CURRENT TRENDS IN WOMEN-FOCUSED PROGRAMS: MODELS FOR TREATMENT

Successful treatment is measured by treatment retention, patient motivation, specified treatment elements, and cognitive-based treatment strategies (Simpson & Joe, 2004). Treatment programs are increasingly designed to meet the needs of female judicial clients (Drug and Alcohol Services Information System, 2006). The treatment recommendations presented in this *Adjunct Provider's Guide* incorporate many of the innovative solutions that have been developed within the context of these ongoing programs. The structure and scope of some exemplary female specific programs are described following.

Incarcerated and Residential Models

The Women's Prison Association (Conly, 1998) operates a number of innovative programs for female judicial clients in New York State, including:

- **Hopper House: Alternative to Incarceration Program.** Incorporates daytime services and evening workshops aimed at substance abuse issues and relapse prevention, counseling for trauma-related issues, as well as improving and expanding the women's sense of self through cultural events or attending community cultural opportunities such as concerts, plays, and museums. This program also focuses on developing an understanding of discipline and accountability and has developed a set of graduated sanctions, used as needed.

- **Sarah Powell Huntington House.** A renovated building in New York City that provides housing for homeless women and their children.

- **Steps to Independence Program.** Focuses on helping women to better their parenting skills, refine and utilize skills of independent living, and locate reasonable housing and job placement services. It also provides emergency services to help maintain women in independent living situations.

- **Transitional Services Unit.** Offers programming in both Spanish and English and focuses on specific needs in education and planning, such as medical care, housing issues, helping the women to gain financial assistance, stress reduction, parenting, and so on.

Providers at a therapeutic community in Denver, Colorado, The Haven, were particularly helpful in developing the material presented in this *Adjunct Provider's Guide*. The Haven's primary focus is to help women in corrections with substance abuse problems to learn skills for maintaining abstinence, achieve self-sufficiency, accept responsibility for their behaviors, and meet responsibilities to their family and to the program. It is classified as a half-way house, offering residential long-term treatment (more than 30 days) and outpatient services. Offering special programs such as one for persons with co-occurring mental and substance abuse disorders, pregnant or postpartum women, and criminal justice clients, The Haven offers low-cost, insurance-accepting services designed to rehabilitate women within the correctional system. Baby Haven is available for infants of the women, and counseling is provided for issues of attachment and mother-infant interactions. Health care services are also provided, including assistance with planning parenthood. These programs have been designed specifically to meet the needs of women in the areas of safe and adequate housing, health and mental health care, family reunification, and employment. These needs are addressed through individualized case management, including individual counseling. Clients are helped to prioritize what they want to get from the program and encouraged to advocate for themselves in achieving these goals.

Facilitators also help in networking with community services. Program representatives make official arrangements with many of these community services to increase efficiency in utilization of these services. Peer support is important, with the aim of helping women to construct healthy relationships with others.

Building on success as women move through the program is an important component that matches the strengths-based perspective used in the program presented in this *Adjunct Provider's Guide*. This involves recognizing small successes as they occur, encouraging the woman to develop a variety of responsibilities

that may accumulate to build a sense of self-efficacy. Treatment focuses on all areas of the living environment and encompasses such activities as:

▶ Work assignments

▶ Workshops and training sessions

▶ Support groups

▶ Recreational activities

▶ Updating and revising the individualized treatment plan, as necessary

Family-Oriented Services

Other programs of interest include those specifically designed to meet the needs of women and their children, such as:

▶ **The Rhode Island Women's Prison**. Provides for assessment of a woman's parenting behaviors and attitudes, parenting education classes, frequent visitation between mothers and their children, and counseling services (Blinn, 1997)

▶ **Women's and Children's Halfway House Program Model: NEON, Inc.** An innovative program that houses female judicial clients and their children in Connecticut (Blinn, 1997)

▶ **Summit House**. Operates in neighborhood settings for housing women and their children; its stated goals, in addition to the standard ones of substance abuse treatment, include strengthening the family system, preventing separation between mothers and their infants, assisting mothers to achieve education or vocational training, learn financial management and mediation skills, live cooperatively, and so on (Blinn, 1997)

Another substantial program designed to help women recover from substance abuse and criminal conduct may be found in Stephanie Covington's *Helping Women Recover: A Program for Treating Substance Abuse–Special Edition for Use in the Criminal Justice System* with accompanying *A Woman's Journal* (Covington, 1999). This program and facilitator's guide provide:

- Gender-specific services for women who abuse substances

- An integration of substance abuse treatment with issues of violent victimization and trauma

- A spiritual component to develop a woman's self-awareness and esteem

- Education regarding sexism in society, social practices regarding sexuality, and abuse

- Training in meditation and relaxation

The addictive process and personality, the effects of substances on the brain, and spirituality are discussed as important components of education and treatment for the female judicial client.

CHAPTER REVIEW

This chapter began with some important concepts to keep in mind when considering gender-specific treatment programs. The importance of forging a therapeutic alliance was discussed in terms of establishing healthy relationships, developing motivation to change, building trust in the treatment protocol, and a community of women who are united by a vision of comfortable and responsible living free of substance abuse and criminal conduct. Essential elements of therapist knowledge and skills were presented in relationship to female-focused treatment services. The therapeutic environment was discussed in terms of space requirements, safety, scheduling, and provisions for consultation on issues related to trauma and other mental health concerns.

The section on therapeutic intervention with female clients begins with psychoeducational and vocational needs, then moves on to motivational enhancement and building treatment readiness. Clients' cognitive shifts, such as resolving ambivalence and grief about giving up substance abuse and believing in her empowerment to change, are discussed. Treatment progress is enhanced through exploring cognitive-emotional factors and making connections with female role models, as means to get in touch with deeper thoughts and feelings.

The generic (for both genders) treatment goals of identifying thought and feeling triggers for relapse and recidivism are discussed in terms of female specific patterns and obstacles to change. Individualized plans for reentry and transition into community living are discussed in consideration of aftercare, wraparound services, and establishing a continuum of care from beginning of treatment through reentry and reintegration with family and the community. Support for service providers covers supervision and assistance in coping with such issues as vicarious trauma, frustration with poor treatment outcomes (that is, relapse and recidivism), and separation from caring relationships in the treatment community. Drawing on the experiences of a number of female-specific treatment programs, common themes are outlined for successful outcomes: safe and adequate housing, health and mental health care, family reunification, and opportunities for employment.

SECTION III

GENDER-SPECIFIC ADAPTATIONS FOR WOMEN

Criminal Conduct and Substance Abuse Treatment, Strategies for Self-Improvement and Change (SSC) is a generic program designed for both men and women in corrections. However, as Sections I and II of this *Adjunct Guide* illustrate, there are unique issues and problems that women in corrections need to address. This section provides adjunct and support information for each of the *SSC Participant's Workbook* modules and sessions that will help providers address and adapt the material to some of the unique issues for women in corrections.

Sections I and II offered important information for providers that will enhance the efficacy of delivering treatment services to women in corrections. It is important to note, however, that the *SSC* treatment program and its curriculum is a specific program that should be seen as nested within a broad spectrum of treatment services. Therefore, in the delivery of *SSC* to both men and women, providers should adhere closely to the curriculum and keep the focus of the group on the specific concepts, skills, and topics of each session.

A manual-guided program such as *SSC* is not designed to address the broad spectrum or the specific treatment needs of women or men in corrections. Providers will find that it is easy to divert from the focus of the *SSC* curriculum, particularly as specific issues and problems of clients arise in group discussions. When this happens, every effort should be made to address these issues within the context of the specific topic, skills, or content of the session. Within the context of this type of treatment model, it is not possible for individual clients to resolve their specific treatment needs.

Thus, treatment programs for men and women need to have the capability of providing individual treatment in order to address specific needs such as post-traumatic stress disorder (PTSD), history of trauma, depression, child care needs, and so forth. Providers are encouraged to keep the focus on session concepts and topics, limiting how much time is spent addressing individual issues and addressing those issues in the context of the session focus. Clients should have additional resources available to address their unique and specific needs.

PHASE I
challenge to change

Phase I sets the stage for self-improvement and change. The first step, self-disclosure, leads to self-awareness, which comes through feedback from others, learning what needs to be changed, and the skills to make change happen. Providers should keep in mind to reinforce the key mantra for Phase I: *Self-disclosure leads to self-awareness and self-awareness leads to change.*

Trust is an important facet of self-disclosure and self-awareness and building a therapeutic alliance and working partnership is an important part of Phase I. The therapeutic alliance provides the basis upon which the provider achieves the goals of Phase I and is the foundation of the *SSC* program. Building this alliance is an ongoing task. It is important to impress, however, that there are limits to keeping all information confidential, including any report of suspected child abuse or threat of harm to oneself or another person which would need to be reported to authorities.

Phase I inspires change. Through inspiration and motivation, change within the female judicial client can begin to form. Thinking and acting differently will work toward self-improvement, self-control, and change. Steps toward change are small and may occur like a spiral with slips back to earlier stages, so encouragement for the female clients to stay focused and to look forward is an important aspect of this Phase.

The counselor is encouraged to use the skills of attentiveness, encouragement to share, feedback clarification, and reflective communication.

MODULE 1

Orientation: How This Program Works

The material presented in Module 1 is crucial to treatment with both male and female judicial clients. Some additional or *alternative* issues, however, may arise for women, and therefore attention to them may be essential for developing an effective working relationship. The establishment of trust and rapport is essential in recovery and sets the stage for future responses to the treatment episode (Miller & Rollnick, 1991, 2002). However, for women in correctional settings, somewhat different procedures may be necessary to help clients develop trust.

SESSION 1: Getting Started: How *SSC* Works and Developing Trust and a Working Relationship

RATIONALE

A woman entering treatment within the judicial system should have experiences that affirm her as a *person* first (separate from her wrongful behavior), provide her with a warm welcome, and give her the time she needs to develop a sense of *safety* in this new environment. Thus, in addition to addressing the common emotional responses to treatment such as ambivalence, resistance, and anger, it is important to establish a feeling of safety (Bloom, Owen, & Covington, 2005; Hein, Cohen, Miele, Litt, & Capstick, 2004; Kassebaum, 1999) when working with women. Because developing a trusting relationship with women in a correctional setting may present particular difficulties, the following components of group focus may augment the therapeutic process:

▶ **Telling her own story.** Self-narrative is a major route for healing in women judicial clients. It helps them to develop a sense of self and begins orienting them to the many ways in which this self has been violated in their previous experience. Clients discover the injustices that they endured and begin to see the link with abuses they may have delivered to others through their antisocial or criminal behavior.

▶ **Positive self-image.** Allow the clients to develop healthy self-talk (their "inner voice") and to recognize this voice (and their inner feelings) as guides regarding healthy behavior and responsible conduct.

▶ **Safe boundaries.** Assist clients to understand that a healthy self involves appropriate boundary setting in relationships with other people.

▶ **Critical links.** Allow the clients to recognize relationships among their histories involving violence and abuse, their lack of voice (not being heard or attended to about their wishes and/or concerns), and their alcohol and other drug (AOD) use or criminal conduct.

▶ **Self-care and recovery.** Emphasize the link between self-care and recovery from AOD abuse and criminal conduct.

The treatment environment is critical in this regard. An atmosphere of safety may be expressed by using some very simple procedures, such as:

▶ Offering a warm welcome, beginning with the initial intake counselor, and remaining consistent across treatment providers and correctional personnel, especially the group leaders.

▶ Removing barriers—podiums, pillars, and such—from the treatment room; that is, group atmosphere is distinctly different from a classroom setting.

▶ Conducting group in a rectangle or other configuration in which the women can see each other and feel more like a prosocial family group.

▶ Addressing the group with a conversational style, rather than one that is formal and authoritative.

▶ Using everyday language; avoiding use of technical jargon or street talk.

▶ Helping women to name their own strengths in ways that are positive and affirming (rather than ways that denote deficits).

▶ Creating a safe treatment environment. Clients need a treatment environment free from threat of punishment and harsh or direct confrontation. The goal is to reduce allostatic load and not add to it.

▶ Approaching issues gently. Clients set the pace when dealing with traumatic history. This area is cautiously approached, and specific issues regarding personal-emotional needs, including unresolved trauma, should be dealt with in one-to-one sessions.

▶ Stay with the curriculum. As discussed previously, providers using manual-guided programs stay with the curriculum and do not let the group get diverted into dealing with or trying to resolve specific issues. These should be dealt with in individual treatment or in specialized groups.

Combined, these procedures initiate a process of communication intended to convey to the woman that, in addition to the context of accountability and restitution, this program is designed to *help* her. By placing their experiences alongside those of other women, clients feel less isolated and begin forming an "in-group identity" with the *Strategies for Self-Improvement and Change (SSC)* program.

Learning Self-Care Parallels the Motivation for Women to Change

By offering respect, by allowing her time to speak her life, by listening to her (all likely to be unfamiliar experiences), the program gradually can convey to the client that she matters, that her life matters, and that this program can help her reach better health, a better life for her children, and enhanced well-being. Learning self-care is a critical aspect of treatment with women, as self-care generally provides the motivation to correct self-destructive behaviors such as substance abuse, criminal activity, and the damaging relationships that often induce trauma. Readiness improves as she realizes that this program might help her improve her life as well as reduce her likelihood of returning to a criminal lifestyle.

Failing to act from a position of self-care often contributes to a woman's participation in substance abuse and criminal activity (that is, self-abuse). Fulfilling the expectations of a woman's social role frequently demands that she put the needs of others in front of her own. As the task of caring for others' needs can never be fulfilled, she may feel pressure to escape from such a burden into AOD use and criminal conduct (CC). This may also contribute to negative cycles of anger at others for not recognizing (and appreciating) her sacrifice. In response, this anger may cause her to aggress against loved ones; their reaction may be to denigrate and further abuse her in the aftermath. And when the victim of her abuse is her children, she further jeopardizes her relationship with them, both emotionally and legally.

The Commonality of Women's Experience

Women in correctional settings benefit from understanding that in many ways their individual lives and reactions are not unique. They are shared with others, many of whom have experienced similar injustices along with destructive counteractions from others. This facilitates release from maladaptive cycles of self-blame and "emotional paralysis" frequently developed in the aftermath of abuse. Consequent to recognizing these experiential, emotional, and behavioral commonalities, women become oriented to:

▶ **Personal rights.** Injustices imposed upon her were wrong, were not her fault, and were counter to the development of a self that knows how to lead a healthy, noncriminal lifestyle.

▶ **Non-negotiable responsibilities**. Responsibilities are necessary to preserve these rights.

This process of understanding commonalities may help a client look toward other women who are achieving these ends as role models for resisting the thoughts and emotions that trigger substance abuse and criminal conduct. A priority for orientation to this program, then, will be to allow sufficient time for all of the women who wish to speak to do so, so that the themes of commonality may arise.

In sum, this commonalities aspect of Session 1, whether in a group or one to one in an individual session with the orientation counselor, encourages a woman to share the general nature of her life in a "getting-to-know-you" fashion. The spirit of the *SSC* Orientation is to draw program participants into a state of treatment readiness, that is, into an attitude that allows for a gradual increase in trust and openness to the possibility for change and social support. These aims should not be pushed, as the client will need time to test the limits of this new setting. However, an atmosphere that invites each client to voice her perspectives and concerns, while not pressuring those who are not yet ready to participate, may initiate a breakthrough into a group environment characterized by openness, mutuality, and safety.

Healthy Boundaries

The provider is reminded to avoid personalizing women's problems. Despite this open environment that encourages free sharing, treatment providers are reminded that they need to maintain **healthy boundaries,** and to gently but definitively model effective boundary setting themselves (Gartner & Kruttschnitt, 2004). Part of effective boundary setting by a treatment provider during this initial encounter is to:

▶ Show interest in the female client's experiences and avoid inappropriate curiosity or boredom.

▶ Encourage women to express the details of their lives in a matter-of-fact manner, but communicate that there will be plenty of time provided later in the program for deeper exploration of inner emotions and conflicts.

▶ Nearly all women's programs consider the use of harsh language, direct confrontation, expressions of hostility, and physical restraint by staff as detrimental to client recovery, because these actions recreate an abusive interpersonal situation similar to those experienced by many of the clients when they were in the community (Peters & Wexler, 2005, p. 97). These approaches merely exacerbate the allostatic load of clients.

Note: In some cases, there may be a hazard of overdisclosure, as the newness of the treatment orientation may provide women in correctional settings an audience for hearing about their pain for the first time. Providers are encouraged to allow some expression of emotion, while informing clients that these initial sessions are not designed to probe deeply into painful emotional issues, lest more difficult conflicts be exposed without adequate time for resolution. Clients are assured that deeper reflection will occur throughout the treatment process. Women are protected from sharing too much of their lives too quickly (for example, details regarding incest, sexual assault, and so on), while gently reminding them that the program will provide time for these experiences to come out and be explored in a safe setting. Providers are advised to refrain from challenging a woman's negative self-talk too soon or too abruptly, lest the client withdraw because she feels cut off or invalidated. A client must first be allowed to express her feelings (Covington, 2000), as well as her perception of reality, and feel heard in doing that. There is time later for therapeutic challenges and confrontation when the need arises. Module 1 helps clients explore their resistance to recovery as well as their hesitations about living a crime-free life. Again, these in-depth issues should not be dealt with in *SSC* sessions.

Orientation counselors and treatment providers are encouraged to review earlier chapters in this *Adjunct Provider's Guide:* Chapter 3, Mental and Physical Health Issues in Female Criminal Justice Clients, and Chapter 5, Understanding Posttraumatic Stress Disorder. These chapters provide a grounding in the contextual issues involving abuse that are often part and parcel of a woman's personality, life experience, and treatment needs.

PRESENTATION GUIDELINES

The Participant's Workbook: A Growth Orientation

The *Participant's Workbook* may be most effective in supporting the treatment process if it is given personal meaning in the context of a woman's growth and change. Referring to it as a place in which she can explore her own history and pathways to change will enhance its meaning for her. Encourage her to see the workbook as a place to record her personal feelings and opinions, to express her own voice. Helping a woman to recover her voice and develop a sense of internal authority from which to speak is an important part of the change process. It initiates a process whereby a woman can learn to name her experience from the perspective of her own best interest as well as the interests of others in her life. This is crucial for her to develop the motivation for self-care that may propel her into constructive and responsible behavior toward herself and others. The *Participant's Workbook* is a valuable place for her to initiate this process.

It is essential that this "growth orientation" (rather than a deficit orientation) be utilized. Initiating a woman on a "journey of self-improvement" is far more likely to work than implying she needs to change her basic personality or flawed sense of self. Female clients often bear the burden of multiple experiences with family members, spouses, children, and so on, trying to do just that: remake her damaged self. Motivation for antisocial behaviors such as substance abuse and criminal activity may stem from a woman's desire to "be her own person," disconnected from the demands of others, albeit in a misguided manner. A treatment provider working with women in the criminal justice system should protect against further reactance and resistance to treatment by focusing on positive growth and change rather than on deficits.

Thus, therapeutic messages should not echo "This program will help you get back in line" (likely to be heard by the women client as to stop being "selfish," stop being "bad"); rather, "This program will help provide you with the tools you need to better solve the problems you encounter in life," or "This program will help you grow into a more satisfying expression of yourself, " or "This program will help you have a positive relationship with others and the community in order to be prosocial." This shift in orientation can effectively circumvent negative self-appraisal and desperate searching for avenues (such as AOD or CC) to escape from self-destructive feelings.

Confidentiality on the Part of Participants and Staff

Facilitators should explain the safety element involved in confidentiality. Clearly explain that workbook entries will **not** be shared without the client's permission, nor will they become part of a woman offender's official record. This "personal journaling" element of the *SSC* program is readily integrated into the client's treatment along with keeping a journal of thoughts, feelings, and experiences.

Note: It should also be made clear that personal sharing is not expected to follow a "confessional" format and that information concerning specific criminal activity may be outside the realm of confidentiality and is thus not being solicited. The aim of personal sharing is attainment of healing and growth, for the mutual benefit of individual participants and the entire group; it is not a platform for self-serving attention or releasing nonproductive anger toward the correctional system. At the same time, as required by law, if personal sharing is judged by the provider to indicate imminent harm to self or others, then the provider must respond in such a manner to protect the client and others.

GENDER-FOCUSED OBJECTIVES FOR SESSION 1

▶ Begin to develop a feeling of safety in treatment, develop trust that the *SSC* program is designed to help her improve her life (and the lives of her children), as well as to develop community responsibility.

▶ Begin to experience affirmations of self-worth.

▶ Begin to recognize the relationship of self-care to the avoidance of self-destructive behaviors such as AOD use and criminal conduct.

▶ Begin to recognize recurrent (and frequently destructive) themes and experiences in the thoughts, feelings, and lives of other women criminal justice clients.

▶ Begin to recognize the relationship between negative life experience and the thoughts and feelings that invoke substance abuse and criminal conduct.

▶ Begin to develop a support group.

Introducing the Cognitive-Behavioral Map

When introducing the Cognitive-Behavioral (CB) Map, it is helpful for clients to distinguish between thoughts and emotions, since the map clearly delineates between these two psychological entities. This certainly is important for both men and women judicial clients, and most people have difficulty differentiating between these psychological structures and processes. However, it is particularly important for women, since there tends to be a popular view that women have stronger emotional responses to both internal and external events than do men. And, we have presented evidence that women offenders score higher on the Adult Substance Use Survey—Revised (ASUS-R) Mood Adjustment scale. Our CB theory holds that thoughts lead to both emotional and behavioral responses, and that control of emotional and behavior responses is maintained through our thought structures and underlying core beliefs.

This differentiation is not always easy. Therapists often fail to make this distinction; a common therapeutic question is, "How do you feel about that?" rather than, "What do you think about that?" Or a common therapeutic reflection is, "You feel really…about that," rather than, "You're thinking . . . about that!" If our goal is to have our thoughts control and monitor our emotions and behaviors, then this distinction is important. All emotions are associated with thought structures. The emotion of feeling depressed or feeling sad is associated with depressed thinking.

It is important to validate the authenticity of a woman's emotions while introducing the concept of using thinking to better manage negative emotional states. A negative thought may not necessarily represent a distortion of reality; however, through effective use of cognitive-behavioral treatment (CBT), it may be diffused among an array of other (less pejorative) thoughts, rendering the resultant emotional state more comfortable and manageable.

Exercise. Have clients briefly discuss whether women are more emotional than men, or whether women have stronger emotional responses to life experiences than men. Then discuss the difference between thoughts and feelings. Have clients practice making statements that express an emotional thought versus showing feelings and emotions. Example: Stating an angry thought versus showing an angry feeling or being angry. Discuss the importance of validating one's emotions while using the CB Map to change or more effectively manage negative emotional states.

RATIONALE

This session presents guidelines for successful participation in the *SSC* program. Providers continue building trust by exhibiting empathy and patience throughout the orientation phase. Women are encouraged to explore the *tools for change* with the understanding that there will be ample opportunity to increase their understanding of these elements of the program. The orientation presents an "overture to the symphony," introducing critical themes and concepts that will be further elaborated and explored in the weeks and months that follow. The *change rules,* as listed, are important for anyone engaged in the process of transforming their lives. In this session, however, the change rules are additionally interpreted within a framework of group process and interpersonal relationships to make them more relevant to women's experience.

Regarding the establishment of ground rules, women's compliance will be enhanced if focus is placed on the function of rules within the group process and interpersonal relationships. Women generally are not oriented to rules in the same way that men are; rules presented as "dictates" or abstract "standards" are unlikely to engage women offenders and are more likely to produce anxiety, resentment, and/or distancing. Women should be invited into a process of caring and sharing that will initiate motivation to adhere to rules out of a sense of responsibility to each other and to group success (Gilligan, 1982).

PRESENTATION GUIDELINES

Abstinence

Facilitators should help the client understand how each client's abstinence aids in successful completion of the program by everyone. This may initiate a process of taking responsibility for her own recovery as well as helping others to succeed around her. As women's motivations are often relationally based, this may also start a process of improving self-image, as the client recognizes the importance of her individual contribution as a role model to aid in the success of others. Community responsibility initiated in the treatment group may later transfer to being prosocial and responsible in the broader society upon her release.

Gender Focus for Teaching Rules, Tools, and Targets for Change

Change Rule 1: Your thoughts, attitudes, and beliefs—not what happens outside you—control your emotions, actions, and behavior.

When expressing Change Rule 1, it is important to acknowledge that many of the things that "happen outside of you" (such as family environment, physical and sexual abuse, racism, poverty, and so on) in fact do have a profound effect on your life and thoughts, but it is how you learn to cope and adapt to these events that matters in the long run in terms of recovery.

Patterns of CC and AOD abuse are determined in part by how the client thinks and feels about herself, her relationships, and her world. For example, a client who perceives herself to be of little worth is not likely to think or act in her own best interest, that is, is not likely to feel concern for herself or others. Thus, the self-destructive nature of AOD use and criminal conduct may become "invisible" to her, increasing her tendency to use them as substitutes for more productive means of behaving, such as caring for herself and her family and assuming responsibility to the community.

The continuing interaction of AOD abuse and CC contributes to a self-perpetuating cycle of decline. Negative thoughts like "I'm not very good at anything" may be generalized into global "self put-downs" (such as "I'm worthless"). These negative thoughts about self frequently underlie depression and despair. Depression, in turn, frequently generates a desire for escape by engaging in AOD use, which then sets up a need for money to get more of the preferred substance. CC may follow to accomplish this end. Finally, engaging in criminal activity may create fear and anxiety at the prospect of getting caught as well as at the real possibility of criminal sanction. This may feed more substance abuse, more negative thoughts, and so on.

Change Rules 2 and 3:

Change Rule 2: We resist or fight changing our thinking, attitudes, and beliefs.

Change Rule 3: We have mixed thoughts and go back and forth about change.

Regarding ambivalence about change, it is important that clients are informed that relapse often occurs in relation to ambivalence in thinking and feeling. Clients are advised that although they are required to self-report any violations of their judicial requirements, for example, abstinence, they will be supported in their commitment to regain lost ground. Many clients are quite sensitive to shaming, hence, excessive disapproval by the group or group leader for rule violations may further contribute to relapse and recidivism.

The open climate of acceptance should be extended even into these circumstances, with clear distinction between behavior that will not be tolerated and the worth of the person who may engage in this behavior. Such differentiated feedback will help the client to better see herself, to separate what she likes and dislikes in herself, what she wants and wants not to change. Intrinsic motivation is the eventual goal for sustaining recovery.

Attendance

When *SSC* is offered in a community setting, treatment providers and program administrators recognize that there are many obstacles to simply *attending* a group session, especially if the client has care of small children. A program that acknowledges these obstacles and offers suggestions, referrals, and alternatives is far more likely to engender consistent attendance and completion rates. Consider the following gender-related obstacles to satisfactory attendance at group meetings.

▶ A woman standing alone on a bus stop at night is not safe in ways a man may be in a similar position. Especially if she has trauma-related issues, this experience may place her in psychological as well as physical danger, which may serve as justification for failing attendance. Suggestions for acquiring and/or provision of safe transportation will enable women to concentrate on their commitment issues when considering attendance, rather than other, highly valid, reasons for avoidance. Suggestions may include living on a bus line near to the program; accessing a taxi; obtaining transportation vouchers (if available), and so on.

▶ Trudging across town at rush hour with kids in tow is a daunting task for any mom, and a female client will benefit from being acknowledged in this. Again, suggestions regarding nearby (and affordable) day care would be helpful, or ideally, provision of day care at the treatment facility during group sessions.

If there is time, treatment providers may want to engage the client in brainstorming what obstacles to attendance and their solutions might be. Clear acknowledgment that these barriers do exist and are understood, and that the program will assist (by providing referrals and so on), may help a woman to feel that her (and her children's) welfare matters and that the program actually sees her. As the program may facilitate attendance, the woman must also be informed that it is her responsibility to follow up on these solutions and that these obstacles will not be accepted as excuses for noncompliance with the program.

Specific alternatives and referrals that may aid a woman's attendance at group sessions include:

- Displaying a bus map, and helping her to read it, locating relevant stops near her home and the program

- Having bus schedules on hand, for routes relevant to accessing the program

- Suggesting a buddy system for women in the group who may live near each other and who can accompany each other on trips to the program. (Note: Some jurisdictions do not allow offenders to relate to each other in the community.)

- In some instances, teaching a woman how to ride a bus; some women will be unfamiliar and/or hesitant about doing this for a variety of reasons

- Suggesting alternative means of transportation (as applicable)

- Providing referrals for safe and affordable day care options that are on the route to the program, and so on

Change Rule 4: We choose the thoughts we have about ourselves and about the outside world that lead to our actions.

Women clients in correctional settings frequently have had little real choice in their lives; experiences with abuse and coercion are far more often the rule. Therefore, women clients may benefit from exploring feelings concerning the exercise of choice as well as skills building in both confidence and decision making. Exploration of potential resentment and anger at the suggestion that she may have had the capacity to take control or make choices in the past (which she didn't use) may also be necessary.

Exercise. Have clients discuss and make a distinction between choices they made and situations that were forced upon them that resulted in abusive and coercive relationships.

As presented in Chapter 1, Women and Crime, and Chapter 2, Connecting Female Substance Abuse, Cognition, and Crime, women often develop thoughts about their own deviant activity that reflect a perception that "there is no choice," for example:

- **Relationship issues**. Belief that AOD use will relieve shyness, make it easier for them to perform socially, and improve their sexual function

- **Psychological issues**. The need to numb feelings associated with self-blame and low self-esteem, or to "deal with" anger, expecting that AOD use will relieve depression and make them feel more "happy"

- **Trauma-related issues**. The need for escape, especially from the pain of psychological and physical trauma; entitlement to inflict harm on others is justified by the harm inflicted upon them

- **Skills deficits**. Report and manifest poor coping skills, believing there are no options to AOD use and crime

Because of You

As I look at you glaring back at me
Exchanging words of silence for eternity
Buried feelings of disappointment creates a civil war within
A battle of faded hopes lost shadows and what could have beens
Speechless I remain a lost spirit in the wind
Left with memories of the past and a broken heart to mend
Anger raging inside me and it is you I have to blame
Ever since the day you left and my life has never been the same
So many questions
Only you hold the answers
My past remains untold
A temporary high
A false sense of security
Was it worth the life you sold?
The longer I look at you before me the more frightened I am to see
That these eyes into which I stare
These eyes belong to me

Annie H.

MODULE 2

Cognitive-Behavioral Approach to Change and Responsible Living

The key to changing thoughts, feelings, and actions is the knowledge of how change happens. These concepts are universal among male and female judicial clients. The cognitive-behavioral model for learning and change explains the rules of thinking that lead to action outcomes. These are explored via the CB Map showing how thoughts are reinforced and strengthened and then behavior is learned and strengthened. Use of the CB Map can result in positive outcomes and prevent relapse and recidivism.

As mentioned in the *Provider's Guide* the distinction between Sessions 3 and 4 is subtle regarding the CB Map. Session 3 focuses only on how the model applies to thinking and how thoughts are reinforced and strengthened. Session 4 describes the combination of how thinking and behavior are learned and strengthened. Use of the CB Map will assist in changing thoughts resulting in prosocial and responsible behavior.

The concepts and skills in this module form the basis of subsequent sessions. The goals of this module include:

▶ Helping female clients understand how thinking and emotions fit into self-improvement and change

▶ Helping female clients understand how behavior and actions are learned and changed

▶ Facilitating the application and practice of the CB model to help make changes in their lives

SESSION 3: How Our Thinking, Attitudes, and Beliefs Control Our Actions

Providers are reminded that while women must assume full personal responsibility for managing and controlling their thoughts, feelings, and actions, they are also supported in seeing a broader social context in which female substance abuse and criminal conduct (CC) occurs. In addition to the generic knowledge base about how thinking, attitudes, and beliefs control our actions, this session can be broadened to help women begin to recognize and change gender-specific thoughts, attitudes, and beliefs that may perpetuate negative life choices, such as alcohol and drug use (AOD) and CC.

The gender focus of this session is designed to facilitate growth and change in the following areas of cognition and affect:

▶ Providers should help clients explore specific thoughts, attitudes, and beliefs that lead to low self-esteem and the role these may play in negative thought and behavior patterns (that is, *what specific core beliefs lead to low self-esteem*).

▶ Providers need to understand the external events and environmental sources of many of the female judicial client's problems, such as toxic family environments (those that model AOD or CC behaviors), the unrealistic demands of relationships, low salaries and job discrimination, violent assault, and so on.

▶ Clients should be assisted in identifying self-blame thinking and core beliefs that are responses to the critical environmental factors as stated earlier.

▶ Clients are encouraged to develop a sense of possibility with regard to alternatives.

▶ Clients should be helped to continue to develop and utilize their "inner voice" or "self-talk" in the service of positive change, that is, learn to use thought structures that lead to positive outcomes.

The objectives and content of Session 3 remain the same when working with female clients, with some *shifts in focus.*

While the recovering and changing client is seen as a potentially independent self, choosing thoughts and actions in terms of personal best interest, this individual orientation (self-as-separate), depicting the individual as largely acting alone, may not fully resonate with many women who generally experience more of a relational self.

Women's motivation to change may be significantly enhanced through coming to appreciate the important connection between regaining a life free of substance abuse and crime and regaining their health, family, friends, and community. This session therefore should be enhanced to help women to recognize the close association between self-sufficiency and acting in one's *own* best interest and interdependence with others. Indeed, change and the demonstration of self-sufficiency may be necessary preconditions for the continuation of supportive relationships.

It may be useful here to review the concept of ambivalence and resistance to changing dependent, anxious, and depressive thoughts and behaviors, as well as antisocial and addictive patterns in behavior. Female clients are encouraged to see the connection between resistance to change and the disruptive cycles in their life. This involves:

▶ Establishing a sense of appreciation and understanding for the power of individual choice, as well as the power of working together, in the process of change

▶ Clarifying the distinction between "working together" for someone else's gain and working together for mutual gain

▶ Helping the client to perceive the connection between abstinence and reunification with family, friends, and a healthy support network

Additionally, several areas of focus may be helpful in educating women about thinking, feeling, behavior, and the change process. This includes discussion of:

▶ **Feelings of grief and loss.** These may occur when giving up familiar thoughts, feelings, or behaviors. Recognize that these loses may trigger additional grief over more profound losses they have experienced in their lives.

▶ **Perceived lack of alternatives to substance abuse and criminal conduct**. Women's recognition that they have alternatives must be reinforced, along with the message that they can change. This statement is critical in working with women. A major purpose of treatment with women must be to broaden their perception of options, as well as to supply them with suitable educational opportunities to build the basic skills needed to actualize these options. After all, restrictive relationships, social policies, and social pressures may provide messages to women, especially poor women, that life is dismal, no improvement is possible, and one must get by any way one can (including criminal activity).

Women's social position places them in situations that generally restrict their options while providing barriers to expanding possibilities (such as finding affordable child care, safe and affordable housing and transportation, good jobs with decent pay, and so on). Domestic, secretarial, or day care work, areas where working-class women are most likely to obtain jobs, are notorious for their low pay, low status, and repetitiveness. Workplace participation is therefore likely to be perceived as unrewarding and insufficient to provide for herself and her children. With perception of few alternatives for living healthy lives with legitimate opportunities, criminal conduct may seem a reasonable way to make ends meet. Marriage, partnership and family, and the dependence (and potential abuses) each of these relationships may invoke may seem the only desirable and/or available routes for living. While a woman does have the option to live without a partner, in doing so, especially if she has children, she is likely to experience greater poverty, which may serve to motivate criminal behavior.

While a woman theoretically has the option to go out alone wherever and whenever she wants (for example, to meet the demands of night shifts or transportation delays), utilizing this option places her in danger of assault and may put her in the position of social sanctions should something happen to her: "What did she *expect* walking alone at night?" Additionally, the internalization of gender norms into a woman's self-concept can be associated with a restricted view of self as well as perceived limits to the range of her potential. Indeed, self-definition for women generally stems from their social relationships and bonds; in a real sense, without those relationships, women may be without any sense of self. Together, these can be barriers that may limit a woman's perception or belief in alternatives to her former lifestyle, including AOD abuse and criminal conduct.

REFLECTION POEM

Trapped

I feel trapped in my thoughts
My past won't let me go.
It won't let me move on.
He betrayed me, turned out the lights on me.
Now I'm lost and can't find my way out of the darkness.
Betrayal is black and mysterious.
It slithers through the darkness
Alongside unspoken words and hatred.
I regret every word I have forgotten to say.
I use my imagination to take me away
So I don't have to face reality.
I'm lost in a world I created and can't find my place,
I failed . . .
I failed everyone.
I failed myself.

Kenzie F.

SESSION 4: How Behavior Is Learned and Changed

RATIONALE

The gender focus of this session addresses ways in which experiences with gender expectations, as well as sexism, racism, poverty, and so on, may have contributed to the behavior patterns a woman has learned and how these patterns of thinking, feeling, and acting interfere with her present functioning. It also addresses how coming to understand these social forces may increase her motivation to change. Specifically, this involves coming to terms with:

▶ Ways in which social structures of gender may have left her "powerless" in some situations, and understanding that she is not responsible for this

▶ Recognizing the negative influence of significant others who may have contributed to her developing patterns of AOD use and CC

▶ Leaving the past behind, perhaps giving up much of which has been familiar to her

▶ Facing the future with renewed hope and positive expectation for what she can accomplish and how she can improve her life

▶ Recognizing ways in which role models within the *SSC* program (staff and counselors as well as others in the recovery process) may aid in reducing these AOD and CC cycles

PRESENTATION GUIDELINES

The previous discussion points should be considered in light of the three rules of learning as presented in Session 4. What behaviors (for example, crime, substance abuse, accepting abuse) were learned to turn on short-term positive events (for example, euphoria) or turn off negative events (for example, anger, guilt, shame)? What thoughts might now be enlisted to result in positive (prosocial) outcomes?

Gender Roles and Change in Women

Recognizing one's own best interests and the consequences of behavioral choices is central to prosocial change for both women and men. In this context, a particularly potent area for women is related to the performance of women's roles. In addition to discovering how cognition, feelings, and behavior comply to the laws of learning as stated in the *SSC Workbook for Session 4,* this segment may be enhanced by addressing how gender norms may keep women stuck on the immediate short-term needs of a situation (for example, meeting goals of appeasement, harmony, and caretaking) to the detriment of their own long-term needs and interests.

Women in the criminal justice system benefit from learning to distinguish between short-term and long-term goals. This is achieved by asking questions about the different trajectories that a situation might take when different choices and behaviors are utilized. It is helpful to understand the concept of "tough love" when dealing with others who put inappropriate demands on time, energy, and, most important, behavioral choices, especially when this includes being pressured into criminal activity to "show their love." Many women have entered the life of AOD use and criminal activity through attempts to please others (especially men) in their lives. Understanding the long-term consequences of these choices is essential to a woman's recovery.

Exercise. Have clients identify behaviors they have learned and that were strengthened and reinforced because of being female and that led to positive events for them, but resulted in maladaptive and negative society outcomes. For example, engaging in drug use or criminal conduct with a male companion because it strengthened the need to be accepted and loved by that companion.

REFLECTION POEM

Protector (NOT!)

When I was a child
She taught me to fear the wild...
You need a protector...
Need a protector...
You need a protector
From the BIG BAD WOLF.
And when I was bad (or not)
I was punished by the dad (or what)...
He's our protector...
He's our protector...
But he's also the BIG BAD WOLF.
And when I was grown
I wanted out on my own.
Not without a protector...
You need a protector...
Need a protector
From the BIG BAD WOLF.
And so I was married
And tradition carried...
I had a protector...
Had a protector...
I had a protector
Who turned into the BIG BAD WOLF.
LEARN TO PROTECT YOURSELF.

Ree H.

MODULE 3

AOD Use Patterns and Outcomes

Prior to the delivery of the four sessions covered in Module 3, facilitators should read and familiarize themselves with the material covered in Chapter 3, Mental and Physical Health Issues in Female Criminal Justice Clients, of this *Adjunct Provider's Guide.* Chapter 3 provides background information on specific mental and physical issues pertaining to AOD abuse that differ between men and women. These female-focused issues include:

▶ Trauma from physical and sexual abuse, both historical and ongoing, which contributes to PTSD, interactive with substance abuse and criminal conduct

▶ High rates of dual diagnosis, with symptom patterns often different from those found in males, including chronic depression and suicide, other mood disorders, anxiety disorders, and borderline personality disorders

▶ Health problems including sexuality issues, hepatitis, cancer, fetal alcohol syndrome (FAS), and HIV/AIDS

▶ Different patterns of AOD disruption in women

▶ Ethnic issues in health care

SESSION 5: Alcohol and Other Drugs: How Do the Facts Fit You?

RATIONALE

This workbook session is adapted to include information regarding the differences in AOD metabolism and the physiological effects of substance abuse in women. Facilitators are asked to explain the differences in women's and men's physiological response to various substances and the ways in which these differences place women at greater risk for a variety of health and reproductive problems. Paying particular attention to negative influences of AOD usage on the developing fetus during pregnancy is important.

PRESENTATION GUIDELINES

It is important to convey that given equal doses of alcohol (even if corrected for body weight), women reach higher blood alcohol levels than men (Blume, 1998; Wilsnack, 1995), because:

▶ Women have less total body water than men.

▶ Men have higher levels of an enzyme needed to metabolize alcohol (thus, in women, more gets into the bloodstream).

▶ Women have, on the average, 30 percent more body fat than men.

A higher proportion of body fat in women allows certain drugs (such as diazepam) to remain in women's systems for a longer period of time than in men's. Although AOD abuse is linked to serious medical problems in both sexes, these problems tend to develop more rapidly in women and reach a greater level of severity, even at lower levels of alcohol intake.

Women who abuse alcohol are at greater risk than men for contracting alcohol-related liver disease and gastric ulcers. The risk of developing breast cancer is higher in women who drink two or more drinks per day. Alcohol-related mortality rates are higher in women than in substance-abusing men. The rate of mortality from alcohol-related medical problems is 3 times that of men, and 5.2 times that of women in the general population (Blume, 1998).

When discussing alcohol use with females, it is important to include an accurate portrayal of the effects of alcohol on sexual functioning. Contrary to the popular misconception that alcohol is an aphrodisiac, alcohol actually inhibits female sexuality, including interest, arousal, and orgasmic function and may lead to reproductive problems (Blume, 1998).

Exercise. When having the group work on Table 2 from *The Participant's Workbook* (how blood alcohol content (BAC) is related to the number of drinks and body weight) and Table 3 (the time it takes for the BAC to reach zero, depending on number of drinks and weight), have each group member compare her findings about herself with those of a past or current male drinking companion. This will help women clients understand the danger of "trying to keep up" with a male companion's alcohol consumption with respect to number of drinks and time over which drinking occurs.

SESSION 6: Understanding AOD Use Patterns: How Do They Fit You?

RATIONALE

This session is adapted to provide education regarding social definitions of gender that may be implicated in women's AOD use patterns. This includes:

▶ The association between AOD use and social relationships (relational orientation) in women, specifically women's frequently stated motivations for engaging in alcohol and drug use to "loosen up," "please others," "join in," "forget my troubles," and so on

▶ Errors in thinking and the "cheerful, helpful me" trap—the association between AOD use and internalization of social images of womanhood, especially the image of the "cheerful, helpful" woman, who never has any needs and is always ready to help others

PRESENTATION GUIDELINES

It is helpful for clients to see the connection between clients' yielding to the demands of social relationships with others who engage in AOD abuse and their own substance-abusing behaviors. It is important to explore reasons why female clients might choose to engage in self-destructive behaviors within the context of these relationships. Facilitators can help clients explore the social definitions of gender expectations for women's behavior in relationships (especially primary relationships) that encourage them to yield to the needs and best interests of others.

The relational connection between gender roles and substance abuse are explored and involve the following:

▶ Social functions that are served by substance abuse in creating, managing, and maintaining the social relationships in their lives

▶ Long-term results that may belie the usefulness of apparent short-term "gains" in relationships

▶ Alternative, more constructive avenues toward meeting these social functions (remind female clients that skill building, such as assertiveness training and communication skills building, is included later in the SSC program)

Of particular importance is the identification of the solo versus the gregarious (social) drinking pattern. Although earlier studies (Wanberg & Horn, 1970) indicated women scored lower on the gregarious-solo pattern, this differentiation has been less prominent in recent research (Wanberg, 2008).

Exercise. When having the group work on the various exercises in this session, for example, describing alcohol or other drug use pattern, the quantity-frequency-prediction pattern, and the worksheets on identifying social-gregarious and solo patterns, have clients relate their patterns to the actual or potential harmful outcomes related to these patterns. Have each client share with the group whether she is a solo or social-gregarious drinker, and how this pattern reinforces her involvement in criminal conduct.

SESSION 7: AOD Impaired Control Cycles: Pathways to Problem Outcomes and Addiction

RATIONALE

Both men and women will identify with the two impaired control cycles (ICCs): mental-behavioral and mental-physical. Yet, we have cited evidence that women may experience a more rapid escalation in these cycles than men. Women judicial clients benefit from identifying how they fit these cycles, how being female affects their entry into and entrenchment in the cycles, and how these cycles lead to involvement in criminal conduct. It is also useful to understand how their physical and emotional trauma contributed to their involvement in these ICCs. Equally important is that women clients understand how other factors related to their gender contributed to their involvement in these ICCs.

PRESENTATION GUIDELINES

Female clients tend to be more sensitive to and affected by disruptive and traumatic family experiences, which are correlated with a high degree of mental health problems. Recognition of the connection between these family disruptive factors and trauma and the occurrence of substance abuse and criminal activity can be facilitated by discussing the following:

▶ Many women who have experienced abuse in their lives use substances to manage the pain of their memories.

▶ While the use of substances may provide short-term relief from painful memories, it actually contributes to a worsening of symptoms in the long run.

▶ Symptoms related to traumatic and disruptive histories include anxiety, deeper fear, more frequent and more traumatic memories, and possible impairment of rational thinking.

Exercise. Have each client share how she fits the two ICCs and how being female may cause her to differ with respect to her involvement in the cycles.

Exercise. Have the group share how their histories of trauma and disruptive relationships, either within their families or in intimate relationships, impacted on their involvement in AOD-impaired control. Then, have them look at how other factors in their lives, other than their history of trauma, lead to their involvement in the ICCs.

SESSION 8: AOD Problem Outcomes: Patterns of Misuse and Abuse: How They Fit You

RATIONALE

This session is about helping clients identify what kind of AOD disruption pattern they fit:

1. AOD use problems

2. Problem drinker or AOD problem user

3. Problem user: Substance abuse

4. Problem user: AOD dependence

As discussed in other parts of this *Adjunct Provider's Guide,* although women are more disclosing and less defensive about sharing their AOD use history and negative consequences, there is a tendency for women clients to put up barriers (defend against) making changes in their lives that prevent further disruptive and destructive involvement in AOD use and abuse. Thus, as female judicial clients identify the specific type of AOD problem pattern they fit, have them look at how they might resist making clear-cut changes to intervene in these patterns.

PRESENTATION GUIDELINES

Exercise. Have clients discuss how congruent is their degree of openness around admitting to being involved in a disruptive and even destructive AOD use pattern with the degree of their commitment to a lifestyle of total abstinence from AOD use. What are the barriers to this commitment?

Note: Upon culmination of the four sessions in Module 3 (ideally clients complete all sessions of this module in sequence; that is, new admissions do not occur between Sessions 5 and 8), providers address the following concerns of group members, providing individual sessions and referrals to medical, counseling, and mental health specialists as necessary:

▶ Ethnic considerations

▶ Fetal alcohol syndrome

▶ Pregnancy

▶ Cancer

▶ Health and overcrowding

▶ Hepatitis

▶ HIV and AIDS

▶ Psychoses

▶ Anxiety disorders

▶ Depression, suicidal thoughts, and other mood adjustment problems

My Own Prison (excerpt)

...

But today reality slapped me across the face

Opening my eyes to how f—ed up I've become

If only I knew why I can't seem to live life sober

What am I so scared of?

What is so painful that I only feel protected behind these glazed eyes?

Too much has never been in my vocabulary

I welcome...

Actually I prefer

To fill my body with as many drugs as I can get my hands on

Challenging death to come upon me one more time

But again I beat the odds

How sad for me

I take pride in my ability to tolerate an amount of drugs what would kill most people

But for whatever unfortunate reason

Not me

Annie H.

Spinning

Spinning,

Spinning,

Spun

How many lines 'til I come undone

Blast after blast

Past after past

I swear this time I'll be sober

Like every twieker

You'll eventually find

These lines on your mirror

Have control of your mind

So rack what you will

It's your soul you will kill

But there is no morning after

Annie H.

MODULE 4

Understanding Criminal Thinking and Behavior

One of the main purposes of this *Adjunct Guide* is to assist female judicial clients to have a clear understanding of how their female identity contributes to their involvement in alcohol and other drug (AOD) abuse and criminal conduct. There is a strong cultural emphasis on gender identity. Billions of dollars are spent each year on advertisements that first focus on identifying who women are and then associating products to that identity. The fashion and cosmetic industries are examples of this focus of economic expenditure.

It is seldom that we see advertisements showing how the identity of being female relates to the involvement in disruptive and destructive behaviors and outcomes in the lives of women. Unless this piece of the picture is clarified, it will be difficult for women to have a clear understanding of their involvement in maladaptive behaviors that lead to negative outcomes for the individual and for society.

Thus, the adaptation of the sessions in this module is to help female judicial clients have a clear understanding of how their gender and society's expectations for them contribute to their involvement in criminal conduct.

Note: Chapters 1 and 2 of this *Adjunct Provider's Guide for Women in Correctional Settings* are prerequisite reading prior to delivery of Module 4. Chapter 1 describes the crimes that women generally commit, presents theories of female crime, and explores the interaction between substance abuse and female criminal behavior. Chapter 2 explores the connections between acquired cognitive sets and criminal conduct in women. Together, these chapters provide a rich conceptual framework from which to facilitate examination of cognitive-behavioral alternatives to substance abuse and criminal conduct in women judicial clients.

REFLECTION POEM

Regret

I can't see the sun anymore.
Come to think of it, I can't see much of anything at all.
My world seems to be falling apart.
My once strong grip on life seems to be slipping through my fingers.
I feel like a puppet.
Unable to lead the life I desire because I'm controlled...
By an unseen entity...regret.
My once strong ground seems to be crumbling beneath my feet.
Where do I go from here?
How do I escape the fate life has chosen for me?
How do I unsay the hurtful words I've said?
How do I say the words I now regret leaving unsaid?
How do I deal?
How do you deal?

Kenzie F.

SESSION 9: Prosocial, Antisocial, and Criminal Thinking and Behavior

RATIONALE

Physical and emotional trauma in a woman's life, particularly at an early age, can impact her susceptibility toward AOD use and criminal activity. As discussed in Chapter 4 of this *Adjunct Provider's Guide,* 46 percent of women who have been convicted for criminal activities report that their first arrest occurred before the age of 18 (Acoca & Austin, 1996). Leve and Chamberlain (2004) found the mean age of first arrest for females to be somewhat younger than for males, at 12.5 years of age. The authors identify two main predictors that may account for early onset of female substance abuse and crime: (1) parental transitions (regarding family environment) and (2) the criminality of the biological parents.

This session is enhanced by placing examples of antisocial behavior and attitudes into the contexts of women's lives. In addition to the primary focus of identifying and taking personal responsibility for criminal thinking and behavior, women are encouraged to discuss gender-relevant vulnerability factors. Criminal conduct and substance abuse in women are often led by relational issues interactive with maladaptive cognitions influenced by gender expectations and learned patterns of maladaptive coping. Risk and need factors leading to criminal conduct by women differ from men's in that relational and environmental factors such as assault, poverty, job discrimination, and so on are more likely to impact them.

PRESENTATION GUIDELINES

In addition to taking an honest inventory of past and present risk factors, as well as antisocial behavior and attitudes that lead to substance abuse and criminal conduct, facilitators can emphasize the following:

- Effective coping in demanding environments
- Building of healthy relationships
- Improvements in self-image
- Detection of the factors that make relationships unhealthy, as well as the ways they may undermine a woman's recovery and resistance to recidivism
- Continued building of self-efficacy
- Vocational rehabilitation and job placement to provide realistic assistance for her ability to earn a legitimate living on the outside
- Developing skills of moral responsibility in the community

SESSION 10: Thinking Errors and the Criminal Conduct Cycle

RATIONALE

This session is enhanced by including female-focused examples of distorted thinking that serve as triggers for antisocial or criminal behavior. It presents a balanced coverage of both rights and care orientations in moral reasoning. The identification of cognitive risk factors for AOD abuse in women is important, as substance abuse commonly is a major factor underlying criminal conduct in women.

PRESENTATION GUIDELINES

Discussion of common thinking errors and distortions among women may include:

- Putting herself down and feeling totally out of control
- Seeing her way as the only way
- Blaming herself for everything bad that happens
- Blaming others for negative outcomes of her own actions
- Thinking of herself as inferior to others, giving others the power to define her reality
- Defining reality at the expense of others
- Being overly concerned for how others are affected, resulting in neglecting herself
- Expecting that no one trusts her
- Refusing to do things because she is afraid
- Making irresponsible commitments
- Giving to others and not herself
- Allowing others to lean excessively on her
- Putting off stopping things that make her a victim
- Minimizing the truth about negative events in her life
- Making others the victims of her criminogenic needs

MODULE 5

Sharing and Listening: Communication Pathways to Self-Awareness and Other-Awareness

Once again, keep in mind the mantra that "self-disclosure leads to self-awareness and self-awareness leads to change." The purpose of this module is to have clients learn and practice the skills of self-oriented communication and other-oriented communication. This represents the foundation of engaging in meaningful, positive, effective, and responsible social and interpersonal relationships. These are the focus of Sessions 11 and 12 and the basis of much of the work throughout SSC.

Typically, females are more likely to self-disclose than males. Females also will appreciate the opportunity to more deeply explore their personal and emotional experiences as they relate to substance use problems and criminal conduct. The challenge of this module is to engage in honest and open sharing and to take the risk of receiving feedback from others.

Providers are reminded that focusing on thoughts and emotions rather than on specific details about life experiences is important. It is critical to be aware that some female clients may need individual specialized sessions to work through issues that may arise in group. Seeking appropriate therapy for these women is important.

SESSION 11: Pathways to Self-Awareness: Skills of Active Sharing

RATIONALE

This session is intended to help women enter the process of empowerment through developing healthy ways to share thoughts, feelings, and reflections on their life. As illustrated in the Johari Window (*Participant's Workbook,* p. 99), self-disclosure and being open to feedback are the critical elements of growth and change. Sharing with others may help the client to begin:

- Developing self-awareness: to identify what she likes, feels, wants, and knows

- Exploring her own responses when she makes the declaration: "I am me"

- Developing body awareness: to interpret internal body signals

- Recognizing the difference between power or domination over others versus personal power within oneself

- Taking initiative in developing her treatment

- Developing a feeling of safety within the group

PRESENTATION GUIDELINES

Women are typically comfortable with self-disclosure. Giving female judicial clients the opportunity to tell their stories and feel they are being heard is an important aspect of treatment. In relation to the focus of this session on nonverbal communication, facilitators are also urged to discuss how women's body language may communicate power and confidence or advertise low self-confidence and vulnerability. Examples of nonverbal cues that communicate responsible power, strength, self-confidence, and self-awareness include:

▶ Standing erect with a straight back and head held high

▶ An open posture

▶ Appropriate eye contact

▶ Leaning forward to express interest in the other person

Examples of nonverbal cues expressing lack of power or low self-esteem include:

▶ Slumped back and rounded shoulders

▶ Closed posture with folded arms

▶ Legs held tightly together, tentatively situated

▶ Diminished eye contact

▶ Looking into one's own lap

▶ Cowering

Facilitators may ask the clients to role-play the cues listed and discuss the messages that are being sent and how they are received. Focusing on the dimensions of power and control, how might these behaviors be used by others to manipulate a woman's behavior?

Facilitators should help female judicial clients explore the automatic thoughts and expectations that underlie their use of these cues, how they may stem from their attempts at self-protection by making themselves as threatening or as invisible as possible, and how this may play into their means of self-defense or manipulating others to gratify needs around power and control.

It is also important to address how aggression and hostility may serve as means for self-protection. While this behavior may sometimes be successful, it can actually undermine the women's safety in the long run by impeding the formation of safe, trusting relationships. Facilitators should explore with the women whether they have learned to protect themselves by "being small" or "being large" and discuss the advantages and disadvantages of each.

Clients are urged to examine the nonverbal aspects of their speech, including the tone, volume, and speed. While shouting by men (often at women, albeit destructive) may satisfy certain needs, shouting by women is generally received negatively. Shouting by women is often interpreted as a sign of imbalance, thereby undermining any attempt at communication. Helping the female judicial client to recognize the gender bias of this communication style will help them more effectively meet their needs.

The following may be used as a starting point for discussion concerning this gender bias:

Ronald and Susan are involved in an argument around the issue of their daughter. Susan wants to attend parenting classes with her newborn, Sarah, but Ronald accuses her of wanting to "go out with the girls and gossip about him behind his back." Susan feels overwhelmed with her new responsibilities of child care and shouts at Ronald, accusing him of being a jerk and rushing through all the reasons why she needs help with Sarah. During her outburst, Ronald, in a calm and congenial manner, accuses her of being a "hysterical, irrational female" and walks away, telling her that he'll talk to her when she is "reasonable." He threatens that if she leaves the house and goes to the class, "she will have hell to pay."

Homework assignments around the use of "I" messages may be augmented by asking clients to develop an opinion concerning an important issue of their choice. Alternately, a variety of issues may be written on scraps of paper and the clients may choose a topic at random, for example, *Should parents allow their underage teens to drink at home in a safe setting?* Ask them to think about this issue for 5 minutes each day until the next session, imagining themselves expressing their opinion to their peers. At the next session, ask them to use "I" messages to express what they are thinking and feeling. Are they proud of being confident in expressing themselves? How does their body language express that confidence?

Exercise. Using the Johari Window in the *Workbook,* have clients put in the Free Area those aspects that, for a woman, it is easy to share with others, particularly an intimate partner; and put in the Hidden Area those aspects that, as a woman, it is most difficult to share with others, particularly an intimate partner.

Exercise. In the total group, using a wagon wheel–round robin method, have each client tell another client across from her something she wants to say to someone close but has not been able to share. Use only "I" messages, and have clients completely avoid the use the use of the word *you.* The "receiver" (person opposite) reflects back what was said, and then the person to the left of the "sharer" continues the process until everyone has had the opportunity to share and reflect.

SESSION 12: Pathways to Other-Awareness: Skills of Active Listening

RATIONALE

One of the most effective ways to establish a sense of empowerment is to use the skills of active listening. Rather than attempting to control a relationship, these skills give self-control and self-confidence within relationships. Even though social norms often encourage women to listen to others at the expense of being listened to, or listening to themselves, the reality is that few individuals effectively use the skills of active listening. Thus, the challenge is to put to work these skills to increase a sense of empowerment of women within their relationships. Remind female clients that when asking others about feelings and opinions, it should not interfere with their own right to have and express feelings and opinions.

Methods of active listening follow the pattern of inviting others to share, maintaining eye contact, giving feedback, and accurately reflecting what was said—or not said, via expressions, postures, or tone—to encourage the speaker to continue on her course of sharing.

Feedback from others is instrumental in helping people understand the need to change behavior, because it provides information about how they may be affecting others without realizing it. Effective feedback is neither judgmental nor condemning. Constructive criticism is an important skill to learn and includes the following:

- Positive as well as negative

- Specific as opposed to general (avoid "you always" or "you never" and replace with "sometimes it seems like …")

- The use of "I" statements, taking ownership of opinions and reactions

PRESENTATION GUIDELINES

As a sequel to the exercises on active listening and active sharing as presented in the *Participant's Workbook* (p. 104), providers may ask women clients to form pairs and share their impressions of each other with each other but not with the larger group. This exercise fosters positive "in-group" identity and relational strength, while reinforcing the use of positive feedback as an essential element for growth and change.

> ▶ My first impression of you was...

> ▶ My impression of you now is...

> ▶ You helped me to understand...

> ▶ I admire you because...

After returning to the whole group, clients may be asked to disclose their feelings and insights gained from the experience of sharing. Questions may include:

> ▶ How did this experience make you feel?

> ▶ What were your thoughts as you listened to your partner?

> ▶ Were you surprised by what you heard?

> ▶ What did you learn from this experience?

Exercise. Explain that the skill of reflecting what others say means that the person puts aside her own agenda and focuses completely on the other person. In the total group, using a wagon wheel–round robin method, have each client share when it is the most difficult to use the reflection skill in an intimate or close relationship.

SESSION 13: Deeper Sharing of Your AOD Use and Emotions

RATIONALE

This session is conducted with mindfulness of the ways in which sharing may be hampered in mixed-sex groups. Female-only sessions are indicated for discussion of posttraumatic stress-related symptoms that may be revealed in the context of "deeper sharing."

Prior to presenting this session, treatment facilitators are strongly encouraged to review Chapter 5, Understanding Posttraumatic Stress Disorder, of this *Adjunct Provider's Guide* to increase their professional understanding of the causes, consequences, and treatment approaches for posttraumatic stress disorders (PTSDs) and related symptoms.

PRESENTATION GUIDELINES

It is important that this session be adapted for the likelihood that deep-seated emotions will be brought to the surface. A structure must be built to help women talk about feelings without further increasing their vulnerability. Current thinking among researchers is that, for successful treatment outcome among women, trauma-related issues as well as AOD use must be treated in tandem. Any in-depth sharing or discussion of these issues are, however, beyond the scope of a manual-guided program. Providers are reminded to limit the processing of these issues to the scope of this program and referral to a trained provider should be made when appropriate.

During this session, clients should be helped to:

▶ Understand deep feelings that stem from previous trauma and recognize that:
  • Children are not responsible for any abuse that occurred.
  • Children cannot understand the meaning of sexual behavior nor defend themselves appropriately.

▶ Recognize ways that these feelings contribute to substance abuse

▶ Realize that substance use does not resolve these feelings, but rather covers them up

▶ Recognize other areas of counterproductive feelings and behaviors associated with body image, low self-esteem, sexual choices, and relationship issues

Appropriate questions to ask female judicial clients include:

▶ Do you become distrustful when someone is nice to you?

▶ Do you find yourself feeling guilty? What myths or thinking errors surround this feeling?

▶ Do you feel responsible for the actions of others?

Correctional treatment providers are advised to refer direct treatment for PTSD to qualified PTSD treatment facilitators (Harrison, Jessup, Covington, & Najavits, 2004). However, all treatment providers for women in correctional settings are strongly advised to adhere to the following principles for attaining successful outcomes with PTSD-affected women who have co-occurring substance abuse patterns (Najavits, 1999).

1. The most critical clinical need is to assure safety. *Safety* applies to:
   • Discontinuing the substance use
   • Minimizing HIV exposure risks
   • Discontinuing dangerous relationships
   • Controlling extreme symptoms such as dissociation
   • Stopping self-harm behaviors

2. Integrate treatments of PTSD and substance abuse.

3. Instill confidence and restore clients' recognition of the potential for a better life.

4. Treatment embraces four content areas: cognitive, behavioral, interpersonal, and case management.

5. Attend to:
   • Building an alliance with the client
   • Understanding the client's experience
   • Using coping skills in one's own life so as to lead by example
   • Giving the client as much control as possible
   • Meeting the client more than halfway, doing as much as possible to help her succeed, and
   • Obtaining feedback from the client about the treatment

SESSION 14: Deeper Sharing of Your Criminal History

RATIONALE

Providers should be especially attuned to the connections between criminal acts and negative thoughts and corresponding emotional states that are often rooted in past experiences of trauma and abusive relationships. This session is one that may trigger emotional revelations and sadness. Providers are encouraged to review Chapter 5 of this *Adjunct Provider's Guide,* Treatment for Posttraumatic Stress Disorder, and the guidelines provided for Session 13. Session 14 should be delivered in tandem with the Session 13 (that is, new clients should not be admitted at this session, Deeper Sharing of Your Criminal History, without having first completed Session 13, Deeper Sharing of Your AOD Use and Emotions).

Providers are encouraged to help women begin the process of sharing thoughts and feelings regarding their criminal history. This session provides a forum to discuss trauma-related thoughts and feelings from a manageable distance. **Probing into details of the actual events is unnecessary and inappropriate.**

Through this session, clients may be helped to understand how relationships with others may have been implicated in their criminal histories and how to find alternatives to these influences.

While men frequently engage in criminal conduct on their own or with male peers, women more often engage in criminal conduct in response to the demands of their relationships. These may include:

- A male partner who wants her help in carrying out his crime

- Families in which drug dealing and/or other types of criminal behaviors are a way of life

- Dependent parents or children who require care beyond current financial resources

Female judicial clients may benefit from understanding how attempts to meet the needs of others may place them at risk for criminal activity. Being able to identify when these situations occur is an important part of the change process and can serve as an important component to prevent recidivism.

PRESENTATION GUIDELINES

Discussion of the meaning of love as a commitment to the well-being of the loved one may be useful here. Providers may help the female judicial client understand that it is not a loving thing for others to expect or demand that she should engage in criminal behavior for their benefit.

Prior to completing Worksheets 35 and 36 of the *Participant's Workbook,* which are designed to establish client recognition and ownership of all the problems and costs engendered by their criminal conduct, it is important that providers encourage recognition of socialization factors (including endurance of destructive relationships and economic difficulties) that may drive a woman's criminal conduct, perhaps including prostitution. Facilitators are reminded that these discussions should ideally occur in female-only groups.

To Be Heard

I lay alone in the darkness as the cold brisk wind crawls through my window
Sending chill all over my naked body
I close my eyes and blinded by the whiteness that surrounds me
Desperate for someone
Anyone to hear me
I open my mouth
But the sound is silent
And my voice remains buried beneath the emptiness that consumes me
Confusion is the state of mind
Helpless is the reality
And a familiar pain seeps into my heart
Releasing new tears which trickle slowly down my gaunt cheeks
I hear a faint whisper
A soft voice echoing in the night
But as I reach out into darkness
My starving hand remains empty and I am scared
A fear sets in
As I realize the numbness is gone
And I am forced to feel once again

Annie H.

MODULE 6

Understanding and Preventing Relapse and Recidivism

The sessions included in Module 6 (Sessions 15, 16, and 17) should be delivered in sequence, avoiding the entry of new clients between sessions. Prior to the delivery of Module 6, facilitators should read and familiarize themselves with the material covered in Chapter 2 of this *Adjunct Provider's Guide,* Connecting Female Cognition, Substance Abuse, and Crime. Chapter 2 explores vulnerability factors for substance abuse and criminal conduct in women and describes gender-related addiction cycles.

As earlier described in the Introduction to this *Adjunct Provider's Guide,* women can develop an internal process to recognize the sequencing of events, thoughts, feelings, and actions that precipitate relapse and recidivism. Conversely, participants can develop appreciation for the little steps that initiate change, feel a sense of accomplishment in making these small changes, and see how small changes become large as they accumulate over time. Sometimes just helping a woman to mail a letter to her child, and receive a response, can provide a basis for building the sense that things can change.

In order to prevent relapse and recidivism, clients need an environment with support structures to accomplish their goals, encouraging and reinforcing of abstinence. Women who receive treatment in correctional settings often return to an environment that is disrespectful and abusive, to relationships that reinstate the expectations of a "women's role," and to the demands of those close to them. Additional obstacles to successful reentry include inadequate housing, an indifferent social response for regaining custody of her children, a work world in which a decent wage is difficult to attain, and the added stigma of being a "woman offender." The positive contribution to preventing relapse and recidivism is awareness that clients have an opportunity to change and recover and live a prosocial life.

For recovery to succeed, women must be specifically fortified to deal with these aspects of their life situations, as they will almost undoubtedly arise during reentry. But also, women can learn to capitalize on the positive opportunities afforded to them. Alongside these difficult experiences, there is need for support and rekindling of what they have learned. Aftercare as an integral part of treatment can support management of these experiences in an ongoing manner. Support structures that can successfully advocate for a woman's needs in transition must be available in the community, to help her avoid relapse and recidivism. She must be informed of and taught how to use these community resources (Kassebaum, 1999).

Note: A helpful exercise that facilitators may use throughout the three relapse prevention sessions (15, 16, and 17) that comprise Module 6 is encouraging clients to create a collage that is designed to reflect a vision of recovery. This collage will reflect the positive opportunities in their lives. It can be constructed in one of two ways: materials can be pasted on a poster board or placed in a box. The box allows for greater privacy and selectivity in who sees the contents, whereas the poster can convey an attitude of willingness to take on a challenge for others to see. Both are acceptable methods to meet the clients' individual needs. Sources for materials that can be used include:

- Magazines, newspapers, postcards, greeting cards, photos
- Drawings
- Stones, trinkets, charms, mementos
- Stickers

This collage activity allows the clients to create a visual structure that represents where they are at this stage in life. It should evoke a sense of self, the present stage of change, as well as prominent emotions. Symbols that represent attitudes toward involvement with alcohol, drugs, crime, or the prison system may be included. Discussion of the symbols that evoke thoughts, feelings, and concepts may assist the clients to become creative and expressive.

In secure settings, some of the materials listed (for example, scissors) must be substituted with those allowed under regulations. Stickers, precut pieces of construction paper, and/or precut images from magazines can be selected and placed in a readily accessible file folder. The key to success with this exercise is to give women a chance to represent themselves in a visual manner that can be referred back to later in treatment for comparison, insight, and signs of change.

Specific to the issue of relapse and recidivism, group participants can use a collage activity to answer the following questions:

▶ What will recovery look like for you?
  • Collect images and objects that represent your personal understanding of relapse.
  • Use images that are relevant to your own particular life and self.

▶ What obstacles and barriers do you see in recovery?

▶ What new thoughts and behaviors will allow you to resist these dangers and challenges?

▶ Who is present in your life?
  • Include actual others with photos; potential others with magazine images to depict roles and relationships that may be filled by others but not yet met.

▶ How do others react to you in recovery?
  • Consider nonverbal cues (dancing, smiling, and so on)

▶ What does it feel like to be on the road to self-sufficiency?
  • Imagine being at a rehab facility learning a new skill.
  • Imagine getting a job and a paycheck.

▶ What do you see in recovery that you may have wished for?

SESSION 15: Pathways to Relapse and Recidivism

RATIONALE

This session is adapted to include woman-centered examples of high-risk thinking. Motivation for substance abuse and criminal behavior and the context in which it occurs often vary between women and men. Therefore, in discussing the triggers for relapse and recidivism, a woman-centered perspective is needed.

PRESENTATION GUIDELINES

Although clients are asked in Worksheets 37 and 38 of the *Participant's Workbook* to identify their personal examples of high-risk exposures and high-risk thoughts for relapse and recidivism, the examples following may be used to set the tone for a gender-focused perspective.

High-risk thinking that can lead to relapse and recidivism may include the following:

- ▶ Conflict with another person
  - I'm powerless to change anything.
  - I can't leave this relationship.
  - I can't make it on my own.
  - He won't listen to me anyway.

- ▶ Social or peer pressure or hanging out with criminal peers
  - I must be a good caretaker, even if I have to sacrifice my sense of right and wrong.
  - A good mother would not let this happen.
  - I must be loved by everyone or I'm worthless.

- ▶ An unpleasant feeling
  - I'm worthless; my needs don't matter.
  - No one sees me; I'm invisible.
  - I'm all alone.
  - He or she doesn't like me.
  - I feel overwhelmed.

- ▶ Experiences with social stigma that stems from:
  - Sexism: sex discrimination, the need to be beautiful and thin
  - Racism: being denied the opportunity for jobs or education

Have each client share her thoughts around this question: As a woman making an effort to change and prevent relapse and recidivism, *What is the most high-risk exposure that you will face? And, what specific skills will you use to manage that high-risk exposure?*

SESSION 16: Pathways and Skills for Preventing Relapse and Recidivism

PRESENTATION GUIDELINES

Worksheets 41 and 42 of the *Participant's Workbook* (pp. 130–131) provide the basis for developing relapse and recidivism prevention plans, which will be modified and become more refined as treatment proceeds. Female clients will benefit from completing their relapse and recidivism prevention worksheets by choosing alternative patterns of thinking, feeling, and acting in consideration of the importance of:

- ▶ A sense of positive self-worth
- ▶ The ability to stand firmly in her own self-awareness and best interests
- ▶ A commitment to value herself equally with other people
- ▶ A commitment to engage in healthy behaviors, that is, to learn and practice techniques of healthy self-care

Prior to completing Worksheets 41 and 42, facilitators may reflect on the collage exercise (described in the introduction to Module 6) or otherwise assist women participants in answering the following questions:

- What will change look like for you?

- What are your personal goals for avoiding relapse and recidivism?

- What obstacles and barriers do you see in change?

- What new thoughts and behaviors will allow you to resist these dangers and challenges?

- Who is present in your life (actual others and potential others)?

- How do these people react to you while you are making changes? Include nonverbal as well as verbal cues.

- What does it feel like to be on the road to self-sufficiency?

- What do you see as possibilities that you may have wanted for a very long time?

SESSION 17: Preventing Relapse and Recidivism: Urges and Cravings and Learning Refusal Skills

RATIONALE

In this session, women practice skills to avoid and manage high-risk situations that may trigger relapse and recidivism. This involves helping clients to:

- Develop feelings of self-efficacy

- Further explore self-esteem issues and the importance of healthy boundaries

- Learn and practice skills to manage cravings and urges, and

- Develop strong refusal skills in order to recognize and overcome the difficulties in saying "No" to loved ones and friends

The focus of this session includes a heightened awareness of how to institute changes in cognitive structures and processes, environmental and affective support systems, and social situations.

There are two types of broad social influences for which refusal skills are needed:

1. **Informational influences.** Provided by society and by one's peers. Cues are provided regarding how to interpret the world, how to understand the acts and behaviors of others, and what behaviors make the most sense. These may often be misleading or wrong, but they are usually presented as if they are embedded in reality, without question. Examples may include:
   - The world is an unsafe place.
   - People are out to get you.
   - People are out to use you.
   - Get them before they get you.

2. **Normative influences.** Communicated by one's peers. Subtle messages regarding acceptable behavior are communicated through body language, attention and praise, liking and acceptance, subtle changes in voice

tone, and so on. Since being liked is a powerful motivator for most people, particularly women, normative social influences are very strong. Each subculture (including the drug culture, the tavern culture, the criminal world, and so on) defines its own norms for acceptable and appropriate behavior. It is difficult to maintain harmonious relationships within a culture without accepting and enacting these basic rules.

Problems arise in the criminal, drug, and alcohol subculture because many of the normative behaviors within it are self-destructive. Since all are involved in a "mutual destruction of self," no one wishes to take responsibility for understanding this or to taking steps to change. Denial operates on a consensual basis, reinforcing self-destructive behaviors by labeling them as "fun," "partying," "having a good time," "letting it all hang out," and "releasing tension." Subculture members rarely risk pointing out that other labels could be applied, such as "slow suicide," "neglect of self," "setting oneself up for failure," and "danger for relationships." The "happy-go-lucky" demeanor of people associating in these subcultures generates the supposition that "all is well." Examples of normative influence include:

▶ Getting drunk-out-of-your-mind is a reasonable form of recreation.

▶ Substance use is necessary to keep friends.

▶ It's not a party if we aren't partying.

These may translate into self-talk such as:

▶ I'm more likable when I'm stoned.

▶ I need a drink to loosen me up and relax.

▶ I'm uncomfortable at a party without a glass of wine in my hand.

▶ Alcohol makes me sexy.

A number of approaches may be taken in order to encourage change:

▶ **Cognitive change.** Understand social images and peer pressures that impact the woman's view of reality.

▶ **Environmental choices.** Recognize that the best defense against urges, cravings, and social influence is prevention; that is, staying out of the situations that accept negative behavior as normal and natural.

▶ **Affective strengthening.** Utilize her developing sense of self and self-acceptance in decision making. Self-care skills and self-soothing techniques can assist in reinforcing that only she can make choices that will affect how she lives her life.

▶ **Support system.** Accept alternative ways of interpreting the world and her place in it, especially learning to value and structure access to a prosocial support network. Having a warm and supportive experience in this treatment setting, where information and norms are vastly different from what she has known in the past, is powerful in helping her see the possibilities of change. Careful attention should be paid to the processes of group interaction so that healthy boundaries, encouragement for self-care and care from others, and the right to assert personal needs and feelings are provided.

▶ **Social learning interventions.** Use of role playing, behavioral rehearsal, and conditions of reinforcement.

PRESENTATION GUIDELINES

After covering the content included in this session, as time allows, treatment providers may facilitate some of the role plays described. This exercise will set the tone for completion and discussion of Worksheets 43, 44, and 45 in the *Participant's Guide* from a female-focused perspective. Participants are urged to discuss: *How are the skills for managing cravings and urges and refusal skills for managing high-risk exposures used to accomplish the positive outcomes attained in the role plays that follow?*

Role-play a situation in which you:	Outcome goal of this role play:
Let others choose something for you	Choose for yourself
Are self-denying and inhibited	Are direct and self-respecting
Feel helpless and manipulated	Feel confident and goal oriented
Feel anxious or ignored	Feel valued and accomplished
Feel frustrated	Feel valued and respected
Feel guilty	Feel correct and self-accepting
Feel humiliated and defensive	Feel proactive and strong
Feel "pushed over"	Know where you stand
Watch others achieve their goals at your expense	Negotiate a win-win situation

Exercise. Using the Highway Map on page 136 of the *Participant's Workbook*, have each client give specific examples of each of the "highway signs" that apply to being a woman in the process of taking the road to the "city of responsible living" or "collapse city."

REFLECTION POEM

My Own Prison (excerpt)

Each day I awake hoping to see the sun shine once again
Wanting to escape the darkness that surrounds me day and night
Too scared to feel the emotions fighting to be released inside me
I no longer recognize the stranger looking back at me
And I refuse to accept this reflection is who I've become once again
I've found my old friend in the state of intoxication
Sober days have become just a memory to me
I now share the days with the poisons running ramped through my veins
Each spirit adding something different to my world
Slowly pushing reality further and further away
I choose to ignore the voice in the back of my head
Finding shelter behind a wall of denial
Refusing to entertain the possibility that I have lost control
Gambling with my life each day
In order not to feel

Annie H.

MODULE 7

The Process and Skills for Self-Improvement and Change

As discussed in the *SSC Provider's Guide,* the three sessions of this module (Sessions 18, 19, and 20) are designed to clarify how the sequential process of change is made possible through self-disclosure, openness to feedback, and taking responsibility for control of our thoughts, feelings, and actions. Throughout Phase I, clients are engaged in the complementary processes of self-disclosure and receiving feedback. This is accomplished through instruments designed for differential screening and in-depth assessment, along with group discussions, worksheets, role playing, and experientially based exercises. Through this process, clients increase their self-awareness and develop increased self-efficacy as they experience more understanding and control over the course of their lives.

The provider goals for this module are

- ▶ Give clients an understanding of the steps and stages of change and their current stage of change in specific areas.
- ▶ Facilitate understanding of the barriers to change.
- ▶ Facilitate the identification of the targets for change and developing a plan for change.
- ▶ Assist clients in identifying their strengths that support change.

All of the content, exercises, and worksheets of these sessions are critical to successful completion of Phase I of this program. The information following reviews female-focused topics, the discussion of which will enhance client comprehension and skills development in the areas of:

1. Stages, steps, and roadblocks to change
2. Skills for changing thinking and beliefs
3. Developing a plan for change: The Master Profile (MP) and Master Assessment Plan (MAP)

The collage activity described for Module 6, Understanding and Preventing Relapse and Recidivism, may be utilized in furthering clients' understanding of the three sessions that comprise Module 7. A new collage can be constructed, or an overlay on the previous one may assist in developing the theme of change.

Topics that are useful to cover include:

- ▶ A commitment to value themselves on par with other people
- ▶ A commitment to engage in healthy self-caring and healthy caring about others
- ▶ A willingness to be open to suggestions from others regarding needed areas to change
- ▶ Acceptance that change takes time, that it will not happen overnight, but with perseverance it will occur
- ▶ The wisdom to set small, realistic goals
- ▶ A commitment to stop searching for quick and easy solutions to life's problems

- A willingness to take small risks, such as asking for what is wanted and expressing feelings in order to build the confidence for bigger risks, such as applying for a job and asserting their needs

- The ability to accept that not everyone will like them

- Acceptance that one will not always get what one wants

- The wisdom to know that although change takes time, effort, and practice, eventually the gains will make it more than worth it

Providers are reminded to include the following issues when discussing these topics:

- Self-efficacy

- Self-esteem

- Body image

- Healthy boundaries

- Realistic expectations

- Healthy self-care

- Prosocial responses

For the benefit of new clients entering the program at this juncture, the meaning and purpose of the collage is reviewed with the group. New clients are asked to add to the collage based on where they are at this point in their stage of change.

SESSION 18: Stages, Steps, and Roadblocks to Change

SESSION 19: Skills for Changing Thinking and Beliefs

RATIONALE

Roadblocks to change are both cognitive and emotional. Some barriers relate to the women's experiences in judicial institutions. Some stem from abuse, trauma, and powerlessness in past relationships and within society. These realities and challenges still exist. Thus, it is important to help women judicial clients understand how to manage their thoughts that are related to these past and current experiences. Memories from these experiences need to be dealt with insofar as they prevent making real progress around present choices. These memories may include abuse and traumatic experiences in childhood and in their adult relationships. This session will help women clients explore how these past and current experiences present barriers to change.

PRESENTATION GUIDELINES

Providers may want to share with the group some of the specific barriers to change that women in corrections face, such as allowing their past negative experiences of rejection, trauma, or powerlessness get in the way of generating positive thoughts for change.

Exercise. Have clients briefly share some of the barriers and roadblocks to change that are specifically related to being a woman in corrections making an effort to change patterns of AOD abuse and criminal conduct. Then, as clients complete Worksheets 46 and 47, have them put a plus sign (+) by those items that are easier to change because of being female, and a minus sign (-) by those items that are more difficult to change because of being female.

Many women in the process of change will be faced with thoughts and feelings that they have denied or repressed with the use of substances or involvement in criminal activity. Providers are urged to focus on managing and changing the thoughts surrounding external events or internal memories so as to allow for better outcomes.

Female judicial clients should be made aware that this is a building-block process; changing thought structures and processes will not make traumatic memories disappear. However, learning the skills of cognitive restructuring will help empower the female judicial client to manage those memories, leading to better choices and positive outcomes.

For those clients who have been diagnosed with PTSD, the skills for changing thinking and beliefs as presented in Session 19 of the *Participant's Workbook* (pp. 144–149) are not meant to provide actual therapy for these symptoms and the provider should make sure the group does not become enmeshed in resolving the issues of any one client. **Referral to a specialist is required for the treatment of PTSD.** However, the mental-cognitive skills as described in Session 19 may help the women deal with these issues as they impact present functioning and provide them with tools to help remove potential roadblocks to recovery and change

SESSION 20: Plan for Change: Your Master Profile and Master Assessment Plan

RATIONALE

Successful completion of all sessions in Phase I, culminating in the client's presentation of the Plan for Change to her treatment group, are required for graduation from Phase I of *SSC*. Operational guidelines for how to develop the material for the Plan for Change are detailed in the *SSC Provider's Guide* and *Participant's Workbook*. Providers may include additional assessment inventories that have been designed and/or normed for use with women to their battery of assessment and feedback inventories. Prior to completing the Master Assessment Plan (MAP) with clients, treatment providers should review Chapter 6 of this *Adjunct Provider's Guide*, Assessment With Women Judicial Clients. In addition to summarizing female-specific assessment tools, Chapter 6 examines all phases of the assessment process, including:

▶ Objectives of assessment

▶ Convergent validation approach

▶ The assessment components

- Differential screening and intake

- Comprehensive multiple-factor assessment

- Assessment of cognitive-behavioral processing

- Assessment of motivation and readiness for treatment

- Assessment of strength

- Assessment of treatment progress and change

- Assessment of outcome at treatment closure and follow-up

PRESENTATION GUIDELINES

Earlier sessions have fostered a sense of personal responsibility and commitment to change: "I am, I feel, I like, I want, I know, I need" (Covington, 1999). This discovery will have initiated the development of true recovery and change within the female judicial client. The following concepts will help understand the change process:

- An important part of "addiction is a chronic neglect of self in favor of something or someone else…so recovery is a process of finding, knowing and caring for the self" (Covington, 1999, p. 48).

- Neglect of self in favor of something or someone else is one foundation of criminal conduct.

- Ultimately, it is the client herself who makes the commitment to change.

- Criminal conduct is the failure to connect a positive regard for self with a positive and prosocial regard for others and the community.

Prior to graduation from Phase I, there are several important questions for the client and provider to answer:

- Has the client begun to display a clearer sense of self, including a better connection to her own needs and feelings? Is she using body signals to do this?

- Has the client recognized the importance of developing the ability to express her needs and feelings, values and goals? Is she integrating this with a commitment to grow and change?

- Has the client begun to connect to this "developing self" as a friend or an ally? Does she recognize this self as a friend who has the power to change long-standing self-destructive behaviors?

The essential decision as to whether clients have successfully completed the requirements for entry to Phase II of *SSC: Commitment to Change* is based on staff assessment that the client has developed a credible relapse prevention plan and demonstrated understanding of Phase I concepts.

Exercise. The content and objectives of this session are generic. However, it may be useful for clients to review their problem identification areas and then identify what strengths as women they bring to resolving the major problem areas and targets for change and then share the most important parts of their MAP with the group.

I Swear

I write these words with the utmost sincerity,

With heart and soul, I commit to this.

I will trust in my strength and ability to stand on my own two feet.

I will no longer call upon you no matter what excuse I invent.

You have no place in my life anymore.

You no longer keep me from all that awaits.

I will no longer justify your presence, nor will I believe your lies.

I will no longer promise empty words in desperation.

I'm stronger than you!

I've beaten you once and I'll do it again.

I'll do whatever it takes to get rid of you.

I swear this time is real.

If I had a penny for every time I promised myself this was it,

I'd be rich.

I'm tired of the battle your presence brings.

I surrender.

Annie H.

PHASE II
commitment to change

In Phase I, clients were prepared to make a commitment to change through the development of core knowledge about critical areas (for example, how thinking affects emotions and behaviors; patterns and cycles of substance abuse and criminal conduct) and by learning the rules, tools, and targets for change. There was strong emphasis on self-disclosure and increasing self-awareness of the clients' unique problems. Clients learned the Cognitive-Behavioral (CB) Map and specific skills to change thoughts, beliefs, and attitudes. Clients also learned the basis for improved communication skills, discovered roadblocks to change, learned the pathways to relapse and recidivism, and how to counter past patterns by learning new pathways to relapse and recidivism prevention. Phase I culminated in the development of each client's individual plan for change: the Master Assessment Plan (MAP).

As stated in Section III of the *Provider's Guide,* Phase II, which represents the clients' commitment to change, is action-oriented treatment based on two important processes:

1. Enhancing commitment to change through more intensive feedback using both therapeutic and correctional confrontation

2. Enhancing cognitive self-control and prosocial attitudes and actions toward others and the community

Phase II is structured around strengthening skills in three focal areas:

1. Cognitive or mental self-control and change

2. Social and interpersonal relationships

3. Prosocial and community responsibility

Thinking and behavior changes in these areas are practiced and reinforced.

Section III of the *Provider's Guide* presents a thorough discussion of the following topics, which are germane to successful program delivery:

▶ Provider skills and treatment strategies for Phase II

▶ Provider goals and objectives of Phase II

▶ Focus on positive actions and outcomes: The STEP approach

▶ Preparing clients for Phase II

MODULE 8

Self-Control: Managing Thoughts and Emotions

The basic purpose of the eight sessions that comprise Module 8 is to help clients further develop and put into action cognitive skills that facilitate change and self-control over thoughts, feelings, and behaviors.

As stated in Presentation Logistics for Module 8 in Section III of the *Provider's Guide,* the ideal presentation strategy for this module is to present the eight sessions in sequence, starting with Session 21. For agencies that are running Phase II open groups presented on a once-a-week basis, this would not be practical, as a client would have to wait as long as 7 weeks to start Module 8. Thus Module 8 is designed so there are only two no-entry points: Sessions 23 and 26. Sessions 22 and 23 are presented in sequence, as are Sessions 25 and 26.

A critical element of effective treatment with women in correctional settings is professional and steadfast attention to the symptoms of anxiety, depression, substance abuse, and criminal conduct that may occur within a context of mistreatment, neglect, abuse, and trauma. Providers are reminded that, for women who have a diagnosis of posttraumatic stress disorder (PTSD), the sessions of this module are **not designed as the primary treatment** for this disorder. Clients should receive specialized individual or group treatment for these issues. However, because of the abuse and trauma experiences of female judicial clients, treatment providers are encouraged to include proactive strategies for helping clients understand and manage the thoughts, feelings, and actions associated with these negative life experiences.

Providers are directed to Chapter 5 of this *Adjunct Provider's Guide* for a discussion of PTSD, trauma, and the female judicial client, again remembering that PTSD symptoms should be addressed by professionals with expertise in this field. Whatever limited time can be spent on these individual issues within the *SSC* manual-guided approach, the provider's task is to help clients learn and apply the concepts and skills of Phase II in order to prevent relapse and recidivism. Providers should closely follow the *SSC* manual in integrating important techniques for establishing self-control through effective management of thoughts and emotions. Care should be taken, however, to gear the discussion toward the realities of women's lives.

Two factors to include are

1. Feelings of low self-esteem, pain, and shame are common in the aftermath of trauma. Women need to acknowledge those feelings and reassure themselves that their response is normal. Moving on is the important next step.

2. The resurfacing of memories and pain during the recovery process is normal. The healing process includes the return and/or worsening of symptoms. Eventually, these feelings will lessen and be replaced with positive ones.

In *SSC* groups, it is important to look for common reactions to powerlessness, especially as it occurs from sexual abuse. The following list of reactions is adapted from Kunzman (1989), *Healing From Childhood Sexual Abuse: A Recovering Woman's Guide:*

▶ Isolation and inability to trust; feeling alone and "not good enough," incapable of being loved and respected

▶ Unhealthy boundaries and problems with intimacy, including confusion over rights to privacy as well as the right to say no to others

- Confusion of sex and affection, feeling that sexual attention, even if it feels bad, is better than no attention

- Disassociation or "spacing out," feeling of "leaving one's body" is often used as a coping mechanism to deal with the pain of violation and injustice

- Problems with body image, feeling ugly and/or repulsively seductive

- Flashbacks or finding oneself responding to past situations by projecting them into the present, thereby confusing lovers and friends with abusers and antagonists

- Being easily hurt or angered

- Being overly sensitive

- Being fearful

When these reactions are observed to be overt and disruptive, clients should be referred for evaluation for additional treatment. Providers can review these symptoms within the group, but only for the purpose of helping clients determine the need for treatment. Female clients may be guided to take the following steps toward deescalating dysfunctional thoughts and feelings in response to traumatic memories of abuse:

- Share feelings with others who have had similar experiences.

- Recognize that abstinence from substance abuse is the most important factor in recovery.

- Build a support group of those who feel positively about themselves and are not abusing substances.

- Establish personal boundaries:
  - Within your body
  - Within your wants, needs, desires, and willingness to help others, and
  - Don't make boundaries too rigid or too weak.

Female judicial clients should be assisted in making the following assertions (Kunzman, 1989):

- I have a right to say "No" without feeling guilty.

- I will not tolerate abuse of any type.

- I have a right to privacy.

- I have a right to share what I want and with whom I want.

- I have a right to expect mutuality in relationships.

Other crucial elements involved in healing from trauma resulting from oppressive circumstances include recognizing the following:

- The tremendous strength involved in surviving these experiences

- Moving from being a "victim" to being a "survivor"

- The specific strengths such as endurance, wit, creativity, and making do, that have characterized past functioning and will continue to provide aid in the future

- The necessity of grieving before moving on

- The need to develop an inner dialogue to provide support, advice, and nurturance

- The right to one's own sexuality, with boundaries and limitations

- The need to utilize stress reduction and self-care techniques to soothe and strengthen inner resources

SESSION 21: Practicing Mental or Cognitive Self-Control Skills

RATIONALE

In addition to the general objectives of Module 8 as stated earlier, and more specifically this session, clients should be assisted to further develop and put into action cognitive skills that facilitate change and self-control over thoughts, feelings, and behaviors. The female-focused treatment agenda for this session is

- ▶ Helping women clients develop the strength to acknowledge and accept past instances of powerlessness

- ▶ Helping women clients to understand that they were not responsible for abuse perpetrated on them, but they are responsible for managing their current cognitive-behavioral responses to their past abuse

- ▶ Facilitating the ability to leave the past behind, looking forward to the future with the hope of renewal and a different pattern of responses and experiences

- ▶ Developing specific skills related to understanding and managing traumatic feelings and ways to accept and transcend them

- ▶ Helping clients to understand that their past experiences of abuse and trauma are not justifications for criminal conduct or behaviors that harm or violate the rights of others in the community

PRESENTATION GUIDELINES

Female-focused treatment providers are encouraged to utilize the following guidelines in order to promote a sense of internal authority among women clients. In using Table 6, Mental Self-Control and Change Skills (*Participant's Workbook,* p. 160), a sense of self-directedness should govern the content of changes in thought and belief.

- ▶ Begin using her *self* as a source of opinion and expression.

- ▶ Help develop a sense of *internal authority* about what she wants and needs.

- ▶ Help recognize the *rights and responsibilities* that come with self-improvement and responsible living.

- ▶ Further explore *boundary issues* with regard to the preceding points.

Exercise. Female judicial clients should be assisted in exploring the Five Freedoms that were espoused by renowned therapist and author Virginia Satir (Brenner, 2007). The Five Freedoms are

1. The freedom to perceive what is here and now, rather than what was, will be, or should be

2. The freedom to think what one thinks, rather than what one should think

3. The freedom to feel what one feels, rather than what one should feel

4. The freedom to want, and to choose what one wants, rather than what one should want

5. The freedom to imagine one's own actualization rather than playing a rigid role

SESSION 22: Recognizing and Being Aware of Negative Thinking

RATIONALE

This session is enhanced by placing examples of negative thinking into the contexts of women's lives. Clients learn to recognize irrational thoughts, self-blaming effects, and destructive behavioral responses.

Areas and examples of negative thinking that are common among women include:

▶ Parenting
  - I'm not a good mom. I can't make my children happy all of the time.
  - I have to lie in order to keep my family together.
  - I must constantly try to make peace with everyone.
  - My kids are a mess. I'm a total failure.

▶ Relationships
  - I'm a bad partner and he drinks because of me.
  - If I were a better wife, he would spend more time with me and come home earlier.
  - Being alone is awful and I hate it.
  - I'm the only person in the world who can't find a good partner.

▶ Evaluations of self
  - I can't pay bills, keep the house clean, fix dinner, and take care of the kids all at once. I'm totally worthless.
  - My mother-in-law disapproves of me; I'm always wrong.
  - I'm a total slob and feel like crap.

▶ General life situations
  - Anger is bad and destructive.
  - My needs are selfish and wrong. I hate myself.
  - Everything bad happens to me. I can't win.

▶ Toward the world in general
  - You can't trust anyone, particularly men.
  - Everything that has happened to me is bad.

PRESENTATION GUIDELINES

Facilitators may assist women to write some of their irrational thoughts on the board or poster paper. The group may then be asked to free-associate feelings and behaviors that are likely triggered by these thoughts. Helping them to discuss insights into recognizing the immediate responses may help. When discussing their irrational thoughts, providers can explore how these thoughts

▶ Privatize the source of all problems
▶ Are a set-up for relapse and recidivism
▶ Attack a developing sense of self, and
▶ Undermine the development of self-love and self-esteem

SESSION 23: Managing and Changing Negative Thinking and Beliefs

This session continues the work of Session 22, which is a prerequisite to this session on managing and changing negative thinking and beliefs—that is, new clients do not enter *SSC* at Session 23. As in the previous session on recognizing and being aware of negative thinking, Session 23 is predicated upon understanding how gender norms may lead women to engage in thinking and behavioral processes that orient her toward servicing others, to the neglect of herself (for example, aiding others in criminal behavior while placing herself and loved ones at risk). The negative schemas and the thoughts that emanate from them (for example, expecting the worst: "I know it won't work out") listed in Session 22 are helpful to develop discussion within this session.

SESSION 24: Recognizing and Changing Errors in Thinking

RATIONALE

As stated in the *Provider's Guide* review for this session, "thinking errors" are cognitive distortions that are a critical focus in the treatment of substance abuse, antisocial thinking, and criminal conduct. They are "self statements that operate as permission-givers for engaging in offensive behaviors, and that function to bring the client from trigger or cue to a high-risk situation" (Brunswig, Sbraga, & Harris, 2003, p. 324).

In relation to the injustice and abuse experienced by many women, the "entitlement trap" as presented in this session is an important focal point of self-disclosure, feedback, and personal growth. It is perhaps equally important, however, to explore the "helpful me" trap, whereby women believe that by helping others—often at their own expense—they will be loved and appreciated, can assist dysfunctional family and friends, and their lives will be worthwhile. Following is a list of some thinking errors that strengthen the "entitlement trap."

- Because I have been so abused, I'm right and the world is wrong.
- Because of being shortchanged as a women, I deserve more than what I have.
- I can be in control of others by being passive and withholding what they want and need from me.
- If you had happen to you what has happened to me, you'd want revenge.

Other female-focused errors in thinking center on ways in which they have been influenced by society's images and ideals of femininity. In addition to issues of beauty and attractiveness, other messages include:

- The stigma associated with women who drink or use drugs
- Images of the "fallen woman," the "whore" or the "slut"
- Images of the female criminal as a "monster"
- Images of the "good mom," "good daughter" or "good wife"
- Images of the nice, always helpful, smiling woman

PRESENTATION GUIDELINES

Specific references can be made toward helping the female judicial client to understand the nuances of female socialization and the many experiences and messages that orient women toward pleasing and taking care of others before themselves, or paying the price with low self-esteem, disrespect, rejection, low feelings of self-worth, and punishment by others.

Objectives for this session that are specific to women include recognition of the following:

 ▶ How trying to live up to social norms of "womanhood" may underlie tendencies toward self-blame, admonishment, and neglect of self

 ▶ How trying to live up to gender norms may discount authentic needs, thoughts, and feelings when they are different from others'

 ▶ How the need to "drown sorrows" with alcohol and drugs follows these tendencies

 ▶ How the "helpful me" trap connects to engagement in criminal conduct when asked by a significant other, or if it seems necessary, to obtain drugs or money, and

 ▶ The extent to which an adoption of this orientation has contributed to self-destructive behaviors

 ▶ How past history of abuse can give the woman judicial client justification for her criminal conduct—the *entitlement trap*

Have clients share their own examples of entitlement based on their past experiences. This can provide information on implementing the following exercise. Providers need to be supportive and reflective in this process and let clients take their own pace without probing or confronting. Most clients should be able to handle this kind of sharing, since they have gained self-confidence and strength through their work in Phase I of *SSC*.

Exercise. Have clients role-play examples of the entitlement trap using examples they share as to how they may justify their criminal thinking and conduct. Only ask for volunteers. If no one volunteers, then a role play can be structured around the examples given earlier at the hypothetical level.

SESSION 25: Understanding Stress, Its Causes and Roots

RATIONALE

Sessions 25 and 26 are presented in sequence—that is, clients must enter the sequence at Session 25 (no entry at Session 26). Session 25, Understanding Stress, Its Causes and Roots, presents the basis for comprehending stress from the interaction of psychological, biological, and social influences. The session is organized in accordance with the following content areas and exercises:

 ▶ Understanding stress: Review of the automatic thought structures that determine emotional and behavioral outcomes

 ▶ Roots and sources of stress: Internal and external stressors

 ▶ Stages and effects of stress on the body

- ❯ Signs of stress and efforts to cope: Homeostasis
- ❯ How problems come from the reaction to stress
- ❯ How stress triggers the relapse and recidivism cycle
- ❯ Looking at our stress: Self-assessment

PRESENTATION GUIDELINES

All of the material is this session is applicable to the female judicial client. When doing Worksheet 56, after clients list the stressful events, have them identify those that may be more specific to being a woman. This can be an important step as they begin to reintegrate and reestablish stability in their lives. It is important that they begin to develop some understanding and empathy for men in their lives, since many will continue in a relationship with a male. Positive interpersonal relationships are based on having appropriate sympathy and empathy for their intimate partners. The goal is for women to begin to see how they can establish healthy intimate relationships. This is dealt with more in Modules 9 and 10.

Have the group discuss how stress may differ in men than in women. For example, when men are under stress, are they more apt to withdraw or to get aggressive? Mindfulness and acceptance of these differences are important steps in establishing positive relationships with intimate partners.

SESSION 26: Managing Stress and Emotions

RATIONALE

This session integrates contemporary relaxation and stress management techniques with evidence-based strategies for managing negative thoughts and emotions, intrusive memories of trauma, and associated feeling states. For some women, traditional relaxation exercises elicit feelings of vulnerability and anxiety because of the associations between relaxation and "letting down one's guard."

Women judicial clients should be encouraged to experiment with, discover, and cultivate their "relaxation methods of choice." The technique of "grounding" as described in Table 7 (Participant's Workbook, pp. 181), Session 26, appears to be particularly useful for women who require a present focus when inundated with disturbing memories, thoughts, and feelings associated with past events.

Note: As stated in the *Provider's Guide* notes for these sessions, *SSC* facilitators are cautioned to adhere to the following guidelines when dealing with trauma-related topics:

- ❯ Providers should give, and facilitate the group to provide, reflective support when traumatic events are being discussed

- ❯ Appropriate cognitive and emotional closure should be brought to such discussion (that is, affirmation and confirmation of the importance of what the client has shared, and that others in the group may have had similar experiences).

- ❯ *SSC* group sessions should not examine, and providers are cautioned to avoid, opening "the window" into the details of specific situations and associated thoughts and feelings that may emanate from a traumatic life event (for example, the what, where, how, and why of such and event).

Addressing and treating the thoughts and emotions associated with past traumatic events are done in a specialized therapy setting by counselors and therapists with training and experience in this area. Providers should evaluate whether these clients need further specialized resources.

Facilitators are directed to Chapter 5 of this *Adjunct Provider's Guide,* for a thorough discussion of techniques that may be utilized, including CBT, psychopharmacology, exposure, hypnosis, and eye movement desensitization and reprocessing (EMDR).

PRESENTATION GUIDELINES

Exercise. The "Strings" exercise can help individuals experience physically and emotionally how stress affects them. First, have a volunteer client identify four our five stressors in her life. Then, using a ball of string, have the volunteer hold on to four or five strings, each representing one of the stressors, and have volunteers represent those stressors and tug on each of the strings, while verbalizing each of the stressors. It is important that the volunteer client hold on to the strings and feel the tug. What is significant is that she has control as to whether she lets go of the strings. Most clients will cling to the stressor strings and then realize they can let go if they want. But have the client hold on to the strings and feel the tugging. Then, before letting go, have the client identify a skill that she can use to manage the stressor. Once that is done, she lets go of each string, one at a time, after using the skill. Note which stressor does she let go last? Have the group discuss the experiences.

SESSION 27: Managing and Regulating Anger

RATIONALE

This session is enhanced with the realization that anger may be expressed differently in women than in men. It begins by shifting focus to help women recognize and safely express their anger as an important component of mental health and healthy living. In addition, recognition of depression and the relationship between unexpressed anger and depression are discussed.

Before presenting this session on anger and anger management and the next session that covers managing guilt and depression, providers should review the principles and concepts covered in this *Adjunct Provider's Guide* in Chapter 3, Mental and Physical Health Issues in Female Criminal Justice Clients (particularly the sections on dual diagnosis, women and violent trauma, and the specific causes of violent trauma) and Chapter 5, Understanding Posttraumatic Stress Disorder.

PRESENTATION GUIDELINES

This session should include discussion of how socialization experiences frequently leave women with a need to learn to manage and then appropriately express their anger (rather than to how to control it as is often the difficulty with men). Research suggests that women manage their anger through depression, substance abuse, suicidal gestures, and other self-destructive behaviors, including criminal conduct.

Therefore, sessions on anger will facilitate a woman's ability to:

▶ Identify the source of her anger within her personal life experience

▶ Explore healthy and effective ways to express that anger

▶ Recognize that the healthy expression of anger is not the same as aggression or selfishness

▶ Develop the ability to channel her anger away from self-destructive pursuits

▶ Recognize that anger turned inward can lead to criminal conduct

Not all women turn their anger inward. Some—particularly those who have borderline personality features—act it out directly toward others. When doing the anger scale, have clients identify whether they turn their anger inward or outward. Also have them discuss the question, *How can anger turned inward lead to criminal conduct?* Improved means to manage and appropriately express anger is addressed in this *Adjunct Provider's Guide* for Session 33, It's Your Right: Developing Assertiveness Skills.

SESSION 28: Managing Guilt and Depression and Increasing Positive Emotions

RATIONALE

This session continues the work on managing anger begun in Session 27. A shift in focus provides greater emphasis on depression as an underlying source of anger or as a way to manage anger in female judicial clients' lives. Nineteen percent of females in correctional settings are diagnosed with a depressive disorder. It is especially useful for a woman to see how many of the stresses and difficulties in her individual life reflect the general social position of women.

PRESENTATION GUIDELINES

Providers should help clients look at the source(s) of their depression and assist them in creating practical steps to relieve depressive symptoms and prevent depression from becoming a chronic contributor to cycles of AOD use and CC. Female judicial clients are encouraged to consider the following thought patterns as sources of depression:

▶ I am alone, as if no one notices me.

▶ I am neglected, no one cares.

▶ I am taken for granted and treated as a "doormat."

▶ I am being used for sexual gratification.

▶ I am worthless and unworthy.

▶ I am a bad mother, sister, daughter, friend, or partner.

▶ I am a victim.

▶ Life has never offered me a chance to succeed.

Other areas to be included in this session are helping the female judicial client to

▶ Become aware of depressed thoughts and pay attention to body signals

▶ Know the difference between sadness, which is normal and healthy, and feeling depressed, which may undermine constructive functioning

▶ Recognize the thoughts that led to the sadness or a depressed feeling

▶ Recognize the destructive signs of depression, such as sleeplessness or oversleeping, difficulty getting out of bed, having no appetite or overeating, or boredom with things that previously provided great joy

▶ Recognize the constructive things that can be done when feeling depressed
  • Call a friend or stop by the treatment center
  • Exercise
  • Become absorbed in a task
  • Learn how to change depressed thoughts and use positive self-talk: "I'm strong; I'll get through this; this is a minor setback."

When the immediate feeling has passed, female judicial clients should be encouraged to ask themselves what a good friend would ask:

▶ What were you depressed about?

▶ Why were you really depressed?

▶ What positive action can you take to remove the source of negativity and to build coping skills to avoid it in the future?

Exercise. Have clients look at how their depression and guilt can lead to criminal conduct.

Exercise. Too often, clients focus on the negative and not the positive. Have clients take one specific thought that leads to depression, and then use STEP to change that thought to get a positive outcome.

Exercise. When discussing the positive faces of our moods, have clients identify, as women, how some of the negative moods such as depression and guilt can lead to strength and resiliency.

MODULE 9

Social and Relationship Skills Building

The focus of Module 8 was to develop the self-control skills to manage thoughts and emotions related to anger, depression, guilt, and negative thinking, particularly as they affect the female judicial client's movement toward or away from relapse and recidivism (RR). Another category of triggers for RR is interpersonal and relationship problems and stress

Although self-control skills are certainly related to more or less satisfying and functional relationships, there is a specific set of skills that are associated with healthy relationships. The specific skill sets that we have included in Module 9 are the following:

▶ Refusal training

▶ Communication skills, which include conversation building and giving and receiving praise

▶ Assertiveness training

▶ Interpersonal problem solving

▶ Managing anger and other emotions in relationships

▶ Building and maintaining close and intimate relationships

▶ Conflict resolution

As described in the *Provider's Guide,* the ideal presentation strategy for this module is to present the seven sessions in sequence. Since this is not practical for agencies using the open group approach, Sessions 29 and 30 are presented in sequence (no entry at Session 30) and the remaining sessions can be presented as stand-alone.

SESSION 29: Strengthening Communication Skills

RATIONALE

As stated in Section IV of the *Provider's Guide,* communication skills training (CST) is considered to be the foundation for all of the specific areas of social and relationship skills training (SRST), for example, problem solving, assertiveness training, starting conversations, refusal skills, managing emotions in relationships, enhancing intimacy, and so on. CST involves the specific learning and practice of the core communication skills of **active sharing** and **active listening**.

PRESENTATION GUIDELINES

Sometimes communication skills do not work. Clients can make every effort to be reflective and engage in active listening, and the other persons involved do not respond or they see the use of these skills as a threat.

Women often have greater ability to engage in active listen, whereas men will often want to get to the point and problem-solve without listening or reflecting. There is a risk for women clients that they will get discouraged when the core communication skills do not work. At this point, the client then needs to engage in cognitive change skills that will lead to a good emotional outcome even though the relationship outcome is negative.

Exercise. Role-play a situation in which the client engages in active listening and the other individual is a male who plays the role of not responding to the use of active listening skills. Have one or two group members double for the client and reflect out loud self-talk that will keep the client in a positive poise and get positive emotional outcomes. For example, to the client's internal talk, "He's just not responding to these active listening skills. What's the use of using them?" a group member could respond, "I'm doing the best I can, and I feel good about that, regardless of where these skills are not working right now." Have group discuss the outcome of the role play.

SESSION 30: Starting and Keeping a Difficult Conversation Going

RATIONALE

Both male and female judicial clients often lack the skills to initiate a conversation, particularly around a difficult topic. This can be especially important for the female judicial client who needs to approach a difficult topic with someone who is a dominating figure or with whom she has played a submissive role in the past. Therefore, the gender relevant enhancement of Sessions 29 and 30 focus on communication of "strength versus helplessness," that is, "power or pushover."

PRESENTATION GUIDELINES

Carefully review the steps in handling a difficult conversation as outlined in the *Workbook*, p. 199.

Exercise. Have clients utilize these suggestions and role-play starting a conversation about a difficult topic with someone they feel dominated by. Providers may discuss the results by having the group look at how the woman's sense of self, self-esteem, and body image played into the conversation and the feelings that followed the discussion.

SESSION 31: Giving and Receiving Positive Reinforcement

RATIONALE

The female judicial client is most likely to find it difficult to receive compliments, particularly if she has an unattractive self-image. Self-esteem and body image are important topics to again discuss during this session. In addition, compliments, especially from males, may be tied to past negative memories. Fear and anxiety surrounding past experiences may interfere with the female judicial client from being open to receiving positive reinforcement or praise.

PRESENTATION GUIDELINES

The following exercise may be used as means to defuse defensiveness and anxiety around receiving compliments.

Exercise. The group may be split into pairs for a 5-minute conversation, ending with each individual writing down a compliment about her partner. The compliments may then be read anonymously by the facilitator and written on the board. Then, each person is asked to choose which compliment they would like as their own and to explain why. (Including the facilitator in this process would be an added dimension.) Each person should then orally or in writing express a statement of thanks for the compliment of her choice.

SESSION 32: Skills in Problem Solving

RATIONALE

There is a general view in the literature that women have more cultural skills then men with respect to negotiating daily living tasks. In relationships, women are more apt to do the shopping, write the checks, pay the bills, make phone calls to get house repairs, report problems with bills or with household services, and so on, because they have, on the average, greater command of verbal-language-spelling skills than do men, who have greater difficulty negotiating these tasks. For example, because women are better spellers than men, they can spell out the amount of money—$140.00 (one hundred and forty dollars and 00/100 cents)—more easily than can men. In fact, many men will have problems spelling *hundred*. Thus, this often puts women in a position of power with respect to problem solving. Yet, this very position can create problems in relationships.

On the other hand, men have, on the average, greater skills in solving logistic and mechanical problems, such as how to fix the sink drain, how to repair equipment, how to change the furnace filter, and so on. This can also create power conflicts in relationships.

Positive relationships result when strengths are reciprocated and combined in problem solving rather than become diametrically opposed and creating power struggles.

PRESENTATION GUIDELINES

Pose the following questions to the group:

▶ What conflict might arise if a woman takes ownership of the five-step model (*Participant's Workbook,* p. 207) for problem solving because she has the verbal skills to do so?

▶ What conflict might arise when the man takes ownership of the five-step model for problem solving because he has the mechanical skills to do so?

▶ Are there gender differences in how women and men analyze and resolve problems?

Exercise. Briefly role-play a situation in which the woman has the skills to problem-solve yet the man wants to have control and dominance. Then, do another role play where the situation is reversed. Discuss results in group.

SESSION 33: It's Your Right: Developing Assertiveness Skills

RATIONALE

As stated in the *Provider's Guide,* this session contrasts three nonproductive ways that people use to solve problems, deal with conflicts, and get their needs met and that often lead to bad outcomes: (1) avoidance (flight), (2) aggression (fight), (3) being passive-aggressive (fake). These approaches often result in outcomes in which the needs of neither party are met, or the needs of one party are met at the expense of the other. The outcomes are either lose-lose or win-lose.

By developing assertiveness skills, women move toward empowerment, thereby mitigating much of the anger related to suppression of the female voice. Female judicial clients typically have limited access to role models in the use of assertiveness skills. In addition to pointing out the differences among assertiveness, aggression, and passivity, a deeper level of belief about self and entitlement must be addressed in this session.

Clients are assisted in recognizing ways in which they participate in giving up their own rights, such as staying in relationships with people who abuse these rights or by engaging in criminal behavior that endangers the freedom to enjoy these rights. Discuss ways in which women's assumptions about their own unimportance are a set-up for staying in these destructive relationships.

PRESENTATION GUIDELINES

Providers should explore the goals of assertiveness:

▶ **Self-expression:** You do not need to manipulate other people into doing what you want, but to make your opinions known, without feeling guilty, and then to feel good about yourself.

▶ **Choice:** It is not necessary to always be assertive. Women need to understand when to be proactive, not reactive, and to effectively choose when and how to be assertive or not to engage in a situation.

Discussion may also center on what specific areas in the female judicial client's life would benefit from assertiveness. These may include

▶ **Oneself:** To help change self-destructive habits and criminal behavior

▶ **One's body:** To monitor feelings and needs that can then be expressed and to prioritize self-care

▶ **One's behavioral changes** that will create changes in self-image and thought processes

▶ **Difficult situations**: To express oneself clearly so as to improve the outcomes and consequences of situations and result in recognizing self-competence and effectiveness

Discussion should also be geared toward recognizing what barriers exist against becoming assertive. Long-standing beliefs and thinking errors may include "Being assertive is selfish"; "An assertive woman is an aggressive woman"; "My assertiveness interferes with my relationships with loved ones."

It is important to remember that significant others may react negatively toward the client's newfound assertiveness. This makes it difficult for a woman who is going through positive changes and attempting to build healthier skills. Clients should be allowed to see that, while in the short term assertiveness may be upsetting to others, ultimately being stronger and more capable is in everyone's best interest.

Examples of questions that may be asked of female judicial clients to assist in assertiveness training include

- ▶ What are a woman's rights? The same as every person's.
- ▶ When my husband is being unfair, I...
  - Withdraw
  - Lovingly call it to his attention
  - Get back at him
- ▶ When I am afraid of embarrassment, I...
  - Avoid the situation
  - Give myself affirmations
  - Try to embarrass someone else first
- ▶ I am confident in my own decisions
  - Most of the time
  - Some of the time
  - Rarely
- ▶ When a salesperson pressures me to buy something, I...
  - Buy it, even if it's not what I want
  - Thank the salesperson and move on
  - Accuse him or her of pushing me around
- ▶ When friends or coworkers are having a discussion, I...
  - Join in and voice my opinions
  - Sit silently, unable to decide who is right
  - Verbally attack the person I don't agree with
- ▶ When I need help with a task, I...
  - Ask a friend or family member to help me
  - Wish I had someone to help me and do it myself
  - Leave the task incomplete
- ▶ When my friend asks me for a favor, I...
  - Gladly comply if it's workable
  - Consider the favor and compromise with another idea
  - Wish I could say "No," but comply to avoid feeling guilty

SESSION 34: Managing Anger in Relationships: The Guilt-Anger Cycle

RATIONALE

Anger is a fundamental and primary driving force behind both male and female substance abuse and criminal conduct. However, because females manage their anger very differently than men, Sessions 34 and 35 are expanded to include Supplementary Sessions 34-A and 35-A. These session supplements should be presented as additional 2-hour sessions, each following female-focused delivery of Sessions 34 and 35.

While Session 27 looked at what triggers anger and the skills to manage anger, Session 34 develops skills to manage anger in relationships. Often, women's response to aggression is not productive in preventing it or escaping from it.

PRESENTATION GUIDELINES

Providers should first present Session 34 from the *Workbook*. Then, adjunct session 34-A, which addresses dealing with aggression, can be presented.

SUPPLEMENTARY SESSION 34-A: Managing Anger in Relationships

RATIONALE

Women are often the victims of aggression and violence. After having reviewed in Session 27 the signs and triggers for the expression of anger and developing adaptive coping skills in the context of relationships, the critical focus of this session is dealing with aggression from others and keeping oneself safe.

PRESENTATION GUIDELINES

Group members should be asked to share how they have been aggressive or violent in the past, in order to determine the balance of how much of the session will focus on managing anger emanating from the self versus anger emanating from significant others.

Important objectives of this session include allowing female judicial clients to

- Recognize her rights to a life free from violence
- Understand when to leave rather than participate in a situation that may erupt into violence
- Avoid violent situations by recognizing the characteristics of relationships that may proceed toward violence
- Explore alternatives to use when in a potentially violent situation
- Recognize who around her is violent
- Understand her increased vulnerability to violence when entering high-risk situations such as prostitution, the drug culture, or bars

Exercise. Discuss methods that may be utilized to avoid or escape violent situations. Discussion may focus on the causes and dynamics of violent trauma and how similar or different the processes and occasions may be among group members.

Community services should be discussed and offered, including

- ❱ Battered women's shelters and counseling services
- ❱ Rape crisis services, including victim assistance programs and long-term counseling
- ❱ Suicide hotlines
- ❱ Assistance with sexual harassment on the job
- ❱ Self-defense classes

Having representatives from local agencies available to meet with clients would be helpful. Telephone numbers for these agencies should be provided by the facilitator. Clients should understand that there is a network of helpful people to turn to for assistance in freeing themselves from a life of violence. The necessity of confidentiality should be confirmed and reinforced in that these agencies are not associated with corrections facilities, but are advocacy groups for women and their children.

Female judicial clients should be encouraged to utilize these resources, and providers should assuage feelings of apprehension and stigma that may be associated with contacting these agencies.

Exercise. Role-play having a woman call one of the organizations to explore her options with them. She can describe a previous experience with violence or one she knows of within her family or group of friends and ask what she can do if she should find herself in a similar position. Facilitators may assist in this process by making previous arrangements with the agency to expect the call.

Exercise. Have the group develop a plan for what to do in the case of violence. Having a plan in advance is helpful during times of crisis when thinking logically may be hindered by terror and fear. Ask each small group to share their plans with the other members.

Discussions may also revolve around ideas surrounding the fusion of anger and sexuality in the following contexts:

Most rapes involve people who know each other and include

- ❱ Date and acquaintance rape
- ❱ Marital rape
- ❱ Recreation (bars, clubs, drug scene, and so on)
- ❱ Substance use and sexual availability

Providers should emphasize that the perpetrator is responsible for controlling his (or her) own behavior. However, it is important for women to make wise choices about where they go and with whom, as well as the possibility of taking self-defense classes to give an added measure of protection. Discussions may revolve around common patterns of power, including

- ❱ Fear and intimidation through threats or assault (both psychological and physical)
- ❱ Child abuse, sibling abuse, elder abuse, and pet abuse

- Rigid definitions of female and male roles
- Demeaning attitudes, such as treating a woman like a servant
- Minimizing or denying the abuse
- Blaming the woman for the abuse
- Forcing the woman to engage in criminal conduct or substance abuse to "prove her love"

Women should be alert to occasions when abuse may intensify

- Newborn children are taking away attention.
- Financial resources are scarce.
- Jobs require additional time.
- Friends request time for fun or camaraderie.

Women should be alert to situations of manipulation, including

- Control of financial resources
- Undermining of getting or keeping a job
- Surveillance of daily activities and isolation from family members and friends
- Accusations of cheating and resulting jealous rages
- Destruction of property
- Threats of suicide or calling the police
- Threats to harm children, pets, or other relatives
- Attacks to produce guilt or a sense of psychological imbalance

Other sources of a display of violence against women may include

- Obscene phone calls
- Inappropriate remarks or threats by coworkers or bosses
- Unnecessary medical procedures
- Pornographic modeling and sexual favors in return for money or drugs

Reactions that may occur after trauma may include

- Perceived inability to live alone
- Fear and diminished coping skills
- Attempts to please others to reduce the threat of violence
- Loss of independence
- Loss self-esteem and feelings of worthlessness
- Self-doubt

SESSION 35: Developing and Keeping Close and Intimate Relationships

RATIONALE

The objectives of Session 35 are to learn skills for developing and keeping healthy close relationships and to understand the basic human conflict between our needs for closeness and for separateness.

Because relationality is often a central focus of a woman's life, Session 35 is first presented and then followed by Adjunct Session 35-A, Developing and Keeping Close and Meaningful Relationships, to provide some basic education about the significant relationships in women's lives, including mother-daughter, children, work supervisors and associates, spouses, and partners. The stages of change in relationships—*enmeshment, detachment,* and *balance*—are critical aspects of relationship skills training. Session 35 lays the foundation for exploring and expanding healthy and meaningful relationships in addition to those with a "significant other." An important gender focus for Session 35 is exploration of when and when not to pursue an intimate relationship.

PRESENTATION GUIDELINES

After Worksheets 70 and 71 (*Participant's Workbook,* p. 224) have been completed, the proactive resolution of relationship conflicts identified in Sessions 34 and 35 is to recognize the difference between situations to *avoid and leave* and those in which to *stay and cope.*

We *do* create our own realities. Our choices about how we interpret and react to what happens to us are deeply bound up in the quality and consequences we experience in our lives and minds as a result. However, it is difficult to see the power of these choices, much less learn to utilize them, when we are confronted with physical or psychological assault and the other kinds of manipulations described in Section I. There appears to be a clear distinction between the two levels of processing of this lesson.

The following example may be used to illustrate how relationships may play a critical role in thinking associated with female substance abuse and criminal conduct:

> *Mona's boyfriend says that "if she doesn't help him in getting drugs to make this one big score," he "will leave her and turn her in to the police for her drug use." She thinks, "I have to do this; he's the only one I have to depend on" (appraisal and decision). During the transport of these drugs (maladaptive behavior), she is apprehended and arrested for possession (negative consequences). This example provides a female-focused exploration of the rules of thinking and change, clearly showing the relationship among thought, decision, action, and consequence.*

ADJUNCT SESSION 35-A: Developing and Keeping Close and Meaningful Relationships

RATIONALE

Specific areas that are important to cover include:

- ▶ Understanding that self-sufficiency and acting in her own best interest can exist along with interdependence with loved ones

- Understanding that motivation to change does not require abandoning significant others in her life
- Understanding the "other side" of feelings of grief and loss through recovery

This session discusses the characteristics of healthy relationships as well as the warning signs of dysfunction and destruction. The ability to recognize and choose healthy relationships is often difficult for female judicial clients due to the fact that most of them rarely had positive relationships when growing up. Their relationships may have involved violence, argument, violation of boundaries, and disrespect.

Female clients should be assisted in recognizing how societal attitudes may blame women for problems in relationships. In response to this perceived blame, women often respond with rationalization strategies such as

- Our family is normal. There's just a lot of stress.
- It's not that bad. My sister has it much worse.
- I'm okay. I can handle it.

Women often assume the role of approval seeking in their relationships. Disapproval, on the other hand, triggers thoughts and feelings surrounding failure, incapacity to be loved, and worthlessness. This often leads to poor judgment in interactions with others and reasons to "loosen-up to be liked," be "more sexually available," or to engage in criminal conduct to be accepted. Female judicial clients need to be assured that these behaviors are not goal enhancing and are self-destructive. This **approval-seeking** behavior cycle needs to be broken in order to allow female judicial clients to engage in a more healthy and productive lifestyle.

PRESENTATION GUIDELINES

Discuss the following warning signs for problems in a relationship and the potential for abuse:

- Constant criticism
- Distrust and jealousy
- Having to report in for all activities
- An atmosphere of tension
- Feeling manipulated or controlled
- Strict rules, for example, "We don't talk about that here"
- Threats of physical or psychological harm
- Excessive dependency for daily needs

The signs of a good and meaningful relationship include

- Trust and honesty
- Open communication and expressions of feelings
- Sharing of hopes and expectations
- Open discussion of rules that have been mutually agreed upon
- Respect for each other's individuality

- Commitment to each other's well-being

- Feeling of freedom to move

- Flexibility to change

- Fun and relaxation

- Support for each other's change and growth

This session may also address issues of major concern for women surrounding sexuality, sexual choices, and sexual identity. Specifically, this session is adapted to help women to

- Recognize that healthy sexual function is part of an integrated wholeness of self

- Gain comfort with the need to talk about sexual needs and wants

- Debunk myths regarding substance use as an enhancement of sexual performance

- Explore sexual preferences and decide on future options

MODULE 10

Skills in Social and Community Responsibility

Whereas the goals of the seven sessions that comprise Module 9 focused on developing and maintaining positive social and interpersonal relationships, the focus of Module 10 is on learning the concepts and skills of community responsibility. Module 10 specifically focuses on the goal of helping clients develop and strengthen character and prosocial attitudes and behaviors through Responsibility Skills Therapy (RST).

As stated in Chapter 2 of this *Adjunct Provider's Guide,* many of the women in criminal justice settings had disruptive and traumatic experiences during their developmental and adult years. However, this fact cannot be used to justify inflicting harm on innocent victims. An important part of treatment is understanding the cycle of victimization; that is, being a victim often leads to the victimization of others. In the case of women in correctional settings, this takes the form of criminal behavior. A vital aspect of RST is helping the client to understand her role in being the perpetrator of victimization and in facilitating the knowledge, awareness, motivation, and skills to learn and practice morally responsible behavior in the community. This component of cognitive-behavioral treatment—the development of social and moral responsibility towards others and the community—is of equal importance to that of helping clients develop self-control through cognitive restructuring and control in relationships through interpersonal skill building.

SESSION 36: Strengthening Character and Prosocial Attitudes and Behaviors

RATIONALE

This session builds on the work that clients did in Module 4, Understanding Criminal Thinking and Behavior. As indicated in the *Participant's Workbook,* after reviewing the concepts and redoing the worksheets associated with Session 9, Prosocial, Antisocial, and Criminal Thinking and Behavior; and Session 10, Thinking Errors and the Criminal Conduct Cycle, clients use the STEP method to explore how prosocial thinking can change the course of negative emotional states and consequent criminal conduct.

PRESENTATION GUIDELINES

Providers may elicit autobiographical examples of how real-life events trigger developing patterns of negative thinking, emotional distress, and antisocial behavior. The 10 ways to strengthen moral character and prosocial behavior (*Participant's Workbook,* pp. 227–228) should be discussed in terms of women-focused themes, for example

▶ Criminal conduct and substance abuse in women led by relational issues entangled with maladaptive cognitions engendered by gender expectations and learned patterns of maladaptive coping

  • Effective coping in demanding environments

  • Building of healthy relationships

▶ Vocational rehabilitation and job placement to provide realistic assistance for her ability to earn a legitimate living on the outside

It is suggested that providers review the example of Mona that was described earlier in this *Adjunct Provider's Guide* in Session 35. This vignette may be used to illustrate how relationships play a critical role in the thinking associated with female substance abuse and criminal conduct. The example of Mona serves as an introduction as to how the 10 ways to strengthen moral character may be personally applied by women clients (*Participant's Workbook*, pp. 227–228.)

> *Mona's boyfriend says that "if she doesn't help him in getting drugs to make this one big score" he "will leave her and turn her in to the police for her drug use." She thinks, "I have to do this; he's the only one I have to depend on"* (appraisal and decision). *During the transport of these drugs* (maladaptive behavior), *she is apprehended and arrested for possession* (negative consequences). *This example provides a female-focused exploration of the rules of thinking and change, clearly showing the relationship among thought, decision, action, and consequence.*

SESSION 37: Understanding and Practicing Empathy

RATIONALE

This session is adapted to include components of parenting skills in order to allow women to

- Explore common dynamics of parent-child relationships
- Apply empathy training to the context of child development
- Develop skills of effective parenting

Many female judicial clients are mothers, and an important use of empathy is with their children. Providers should give clients the opportunity to explore situations in which empathy may provide them the ability to focus on the real-life pain or joy of others and that can ultimately help them better understand themselves and have empathy toward others and the community.

There is often value in exploring a woman's relationship with her own mother, where much of the foundation of empathy is formed. Through this exploration, the female judicial client may be motivated to explore her own mistreatment, neglect, or lack of attention by her mother and to build a foundation of more effective parenting skills.

PRESENTATION GUIDELINES

Share with clients these areas that are crucial to empathy in parenting:

- Healthy bonding
- Appropriate discipline
- Maintaining or rebuilding trust
- Helping children to deal with their feelings
- Appropriate play
- Effective communication
- Impact of abuse and neglect

Providers may use the following scenarios as starting points for discussion:

▶ You have been dealing all day with your colicky baby. Your boyfriend wants to watch a movie and chill out. He demands that you "shut the kid up." What is he thinking and feeling? What do you think your baby is experiencing?

▶ You are tired and worried about paying the rent. Your 5-year-old son is unmanageable, getting into everything, throwing things, and making a mess. What do you think he is thinking and feeling?

▶ Your 15-year-old daughter resents that you have been in jail. She thinks you don't care about anyone but yourself and that you have neglected her all her life. What is she thinking and feeling?

▶ You see your 9-year-old and he is sad. He's been in foster care while you've been serving your sentence. How do you help him cope with the sadness?

▶ Your daughter is refusing to talk to you. You think it may be because of your assault. Her grades have dropped, and she is sulking when she comes home. What are her thoughts behind her sulking?

These scenarios are helpful for evaluating the health and well-being of the child. The child's teachers should be aware of the mother's situation and assist in encouraging and providing the child with a stable and nurturing environment at school.

Female judicial clients should also be helped to explore the thoughts and feelings of their children.

The following questions may be asked and explored with the clients:

▶ Do you understand and accept the thoughts and feelings of your children?

▶ Do you realize that their feelings aren't wrong or bad?

▶ Are these thoughts and feelings similar to those you felt with your parents?

▶ How did your parents respond?

▶ How will you change the way you respond with your children?

In addition to the exercises presented in Worksheet 72 (Practicing Empathy) and Worksheet 73 (Persons Affected by Your AOD Abuse and Criminal Conduct), homework assignments may include practicing empathy with others, particularly their children, and reporting back to the group as to what changes they may have made since recognizing the others' feelings.

SESSION 38: Understanding Aggression, Abuse, and Violence

SESSION 39: Preventing Aggression, Abuse, and Violence

RATIONALE

Sessions 38 and 39 are presented in sequence, and new clients do not enter at Session 39. *SSC* devotes four sessions to dealing with anger. Session 27, Managing and Regulating Anger, focuses on managing anger at the intrapersonal level (that is, anger within the self, usually in response to life experiences involving abuse or neglect). Clients are given a two-phase skills approach that involves first becoming **mindful** of angry thoughts, feelings, and triggers, then using **mental self-control skills** to express constructive anger, problem-solve, and use self-reward. Session 34, Managing Anger in Relationships: The Guilt-Anger Cycle, focuses on the relational aspects of anger. Building on the self-control skills presented in Session 27, clients learn and practice specific skills for managing relationship anger. Our discussion of these sessions in this *Adjunct Provider's Guide* includes the following gender focus:

▶ Developing means for healthy expression of anger (Session 27)

▶ How client can deal with aggression that is directed toward her and how to remain safe (Session 34-A)

Before presenting these sessions on anger and anger management, providers should review the principles and concepts covered in this *Adjunct Provider's Guide* in Chapter 3, Mental and Physical Health Issues in Female Criminal Justice Clients (particularly the sections on dual diagnosis, women and violent trauma, and the specific causes of violent trauma) and Chapter 5, Understanding Posttraumatic Stress Disorder.

PRESENTATION GUIDELINES

The provider is asked to review topics in Sessions 27 and 34 before presenting Sessions 38 and 39. In programs using open groups, some clients may not have had Session 27 or 34. Thus it is important to review the concepts and skills covered in those two sessions prior to covering Sessions 38 and 39.

The goal of Sessions 38 and 39 is to help clients (1) understand aggression, violence, and abuse and (2) learn and apply skills to prevent aggression, abuse, and violence. It is often common to view women as not being aggressive, abusive, or violent. Although women may become abusive and violent under different circumstances, women judicial clients are susceptible to these behavioral responses. Thus, women clients should receive Sessions 38 and 39 as they stand.

However, this *Adjunct Provider's Guide* has presented clear evidence that many women judicial clients have been subjects of abuse and violence. Thus, these sessions are adapted to cover issues of violence against women and help women psychologically and physically with strategies to reduce and avoid violence that is directed toward them as victims. Certainly, this protective approach is facilitated by helping women understand abuse, aggression, and violence through the material and concepts covered in Session 38. This understanding is enhanced by presenting the following concepts:

▶ Challenging some of the myths regarding danger in women's lives (for example, by educating her regarding the statistics that show most violence against women occurs in the context of family and other personal relationships rather than by "crazy men on the streets")

▶ Defusing the tendency for women to blame themselves for the abuse they have experienced

▶ Teaching women to identify the signs of impending violence

▶ Helping women to explore avenues of escape from such situations (that is, to identify family and community resources that they may contact for help)

▶ Learning strategies for self-defense

The key concepts of Supplemental Session 34-A should also be reviewed, since this directly focuses on the protective approaches that women judicial clients need to take regarding abuse and violence. The following concepts should be reviewed:

▶ The option to leave an abusive situation

▶ The role that previous trauma may play in relapse

▶ Distorted thinking that may encourage an obligation to stay in an unhealthy relationship

- The difference between healthy exercise of personal power from within versus dominating or having power over someone else

- The importance of self-valuing

- The impact of gender norms on women's feelings of powerlessness

- Empowerment and choice, and

- Assertiveness and refusal skills

SESSION 40: Settling Conflicts and Getting to a Win-Win Situation

RATIONALE

Improved means for female clients to settle conflicts and arrive at a win-win solution are addressed in Session 33: It's Your Right: Developing Assertiveness Skills. Providers should review the three nonproductive ways of dealing with conflict (fight, flight, and fake) and the assertiveness skills involved in finding win-win solutions (fair) in the *Provider's Guide* (pp. 210–213).

In conjunction with the material covered in Session 33, this session on conflict resolution fosters the critical treatment component *assertiveness skills development*. Women's orientation is likely to be focused on yielding too much rather than too little. This yielding is often at the heart of her anger and resentment, which may be part of her alcohol and drug abuse and criminal behavior. This session is adapted to help women to explore:

- Their rights as a person

- Goals and barriers to assertiveness

- Important areas where assertiveness may be necessary in a woman's life

- How assertiveness aids the process of win-win negotiation

At the same time, a healthy resolution to conflict and achieving a win-win solution must not only consider the egocentric dimension, for example, "What do I get out of this?" but a sociocentric dimension, "What does the other person need to get from this and what do I need to yield to get this win-win outcome?" This model for conflict resolution is the metaphor for preventing recidivism. Criminal conduct is egocentric: "What can I get out of this?" Preventing recidivism and getting a win-win for the client and community are sociocentric: "What good can I and others get out of this?" Or, "What do I need to yield to the community?"

Thus, even though a women's orientation may have been on "yielding" or giving, the actual fact of women committing crimes has gone against this very orientation. Thus, this orientation is a healthy component of any conflict resolution and win-win situation. It may be that women have a head start on this, since they do have a good sense of "yielding" and giving that men may not have.

PRESENTATION GUIDELINES

Discussion topics may include the barriers that stand against assertiveness among women. Thoughts such as "Being assertive is selfish," "An assertive woman is an aggressive woman," and "My assertiveness comes at the expense of my loved ones" are links to defeating behaviors that can be discussed along with ways to overcome them.

Also, have clients discuss the idea that women tend to be more "yielding" and "giving" and whether part of women being involved in criminal conduct has to do with their losing this orientation?

SESSION 41: Values and Morals for Responsible Living: The Moral Dilemma

SESSION 42: Giving to the Community and the Good of Society

Sessions 41 and 42 continue the process of developing empathy and prosocial strengths begun in Session 36, Strengthening Character and Prosocial Attitudes and Behaviors, and Session 37, Understanding and Practicing Empathy. Critical points from these sessions should be reviewed.

In addition to the gender focus of Session 37, in which clients developed improved understanding of their thoughts, feelings, and behavioral reactions to care (or lack of) from female caretakers, female judicial clients should be encouraged to discuss relationships with their fathers by considering empathy toward him, exploration of pain at the possible lack of attention from him, and how this extends to her own attitude toward her children. Session 41 should include a balanced coverage of both rights and care orientations in moral reasoning.

In addition to the focus of this session on developing ways to reach out to the community and enhance public safety through driving with care, considerable time in this session may be given to the reciprocal relationship between support of one's community and sources of community support and services.

It is important to express the importance of reaching out to others and how that reciprocal relationship increases empathy and prosocial responding in the community. Daily living that balances a sense of entitlement to comfort, safety, and moral responsibility with the satisfaction found through helping others can be a major influence in avoiding relapse and recidivism. Providers may suggest avenues within the community through which female judicial clients can offer their skills and interests to others less fortunate than them.

PHASE III
ownership of change:
lifestyle balance and
healthy living

As stated in the *Provider's Guide*, Phase III of *Strategies for Self-Improvement and Change (SSC)* prepares clients for reentry and integration into the community and for the restoration of a positive relationship with society. It builds on the client's increased self-awareness and the coping and change skills learned and practiced in Phase II. Providers help clients tie together thoughts, feelings, and behaviors that have emerged in their overall treatment experience. Treatment experiences are designed to reinforce and strengthen established changes. Phase III strengthens the client's skills to prevent relapse and recidivism by developing strategies for a balanced lifestyle.

Phase III is adapted to provide transitional services in keeping with women's primary needs during reentry into the community. The *wraparound model* of treatment is used.

MODULE 11

Relapse and Recidivism Prevention: Review and Strategies for Healthy Living

Before delivering Module 11, providers should review the basic relapse and recidivism prevention concepts and approaches used in the *SSC Provider's Guide* in Chapter 5 and in the introduction section to Module 6. If possible, the three sessions that comprise this module should be presented in sequence, that is, no new admissions at Session 44 or Session 45.

This module is a review of the RR concepts and the skills of RR prevention. Clients review their RR prevention plan and the prevention skills that work best for them. They examine how lifestyle imbalances can lead to RR and then enhance their RR prevention plans by focusing on community support and critical reasoning. Prior to delivering the content and exercises of this module, providers should review with clients the understandings, skills, and attitudes developed in Phase I, Module 6, Understanding and Preventing Relapse and Recidivism (Session 15, Pathways to Relapse and Recidivism; Session 16, Pathways and Skills for Preventing Relapse and Recidivism, and Session 17, Preventing Relapse and Recidivism: Urges and Cravings and Learning Refusal Skills).

SESSION 43: Strengthening Your Relapse and Recidivism Prevention Skills

SESSION 44: Strengthening Your Relapse and Recidivism Prevention Plan

SESSION 45: Strengthening Relapse and Recidivism Prevention: Critical Reasoning

RATIONALE

These sessions are adapted to facilitate exploration of barriers to change that are likely to occur upon female clients' reentry into their communities and to proactively problem-solve in order to prevent these difficulties from becoming triggers for relapse or recidivism. The treatment provider is asked to supply female clients with information regarding the importance of community networking. They may also arrange on-site visits to places clients are likely to encounter upon reentry into the community. These include

- Safe and affordable housing
- Safe and affordable child care services, such as day care and child health services

This should also include information regarding parks and playgrounds and other areas to encourage healthy play with their children.

- Emergency assistance programs that may supply food stamps and other sources of financial aid

- Emergency assistance programs for potentially dangerous or abusive situations

- Transportation alternatives, such as bus routes, taxis, and so on

PRESENTATION GUIDELINES FOR SESSIONS 43, 44, AND 45

Women are asked to ponder the relationships among *restraint, respect, responsibility,* and *transformation* (Poitier, Niliwaambieni, & Rowe, 1997). They are asked to explore specific ways in which they can achieve these objectives as a part of managing and maintaining recovery and crime-free living. The explicit purpose of Session 45, Strengthening Relapse and Recidivism Prevention: Critical Reasoning, is to help the judicial client develop a logical and critical "eye" for any attempts to be persuaded by others or to take part in activities that "do not make sense" from the standpoint of being responsible, free, and healthy (that is, restraint, respect, responsibility, and transformation).

The exercises provided in the *SSC* workbook are utilized to encourage exploration of these objectives of Module 11, essentially "relapse and recidivism prevention through lifestyle balance and healthy living."

Gender Adaptation to Worksheet in Session 43

One of the themes of this *Adjunct Provider's Guide* is that women in corrections are confronted with different high-risk exposures to relapse and recidivism than men. This implies that they will need to use skills more appropriate to their gender when managing these high-risk exposures. When doing Worksheet 83 in the *Participant's Workbook*, have clients focus on skills that are appropriate to their gender when dealing with these high-risk exposures.

Gender Adaptation to Worksheets in Session 44

When doing the work on Figure 30 of this session (*Participant's Workbook,* p. 262), have clients again be cognizant of their gender when identifying skills and strategies for maintaining a lifestyle balance in the effort to prevent RR. Worksheets 84 and 85 should also be completed within a gender-specific context. For a woman judicial client, what are the immediate and long-term positive benefits of being drug free and crime free, and what are the immediate and long-term benefits of continuing using drugs and engaging in criminal conduct? For example, making the decision to no longer engage in criminal conduct for many women in corrections may mean that they must decide to no longer engage in any relationship with a man who is using drugs or engaging in criminal activity. For some women, this will be a major shift in lifestyle.

Gender Adaptation to Worksheet 86 in Session 45

Many women in corrections have experienced excessive pressure from individuals in their lives, that is, their male companions, to continue in a drug-use and crime-involvement lifestyle. Many of these pressures are based on the strong suasions that are similar to the approaches used in the field of advertising and propaganda, as outlined in this session of the *Participant's Workbook.* When clients complete Worksheet 86, have them be very specific with respect to how these advertising and propaganda ploys to continue using drugs and continue to stay in a crime-involved lifestyle target them specifically as women. As a preparatory exercise to this worksheet, some providers will have clients cut out newspaper advertisements that match the various propaganda approaches outlined in this session. Make that exercise gender specific.

MODULE 12

Strengthening Ownership of Change: Skills for a Healthy Lifestyle

As stated in the *Provider's Guide*, the purpose of this module is to give substance to the lifestyle balance of clients and look at integrating and strengthening five healthy lifestyle alternatives to AOD use and criminal behavior:

1. Meaningful involvement in one's work and job as an expression of healthy productivity

2. Participating in healthy play and leisure time, integrating relaxation into daily living

3. Establishing a pattern of healthy eating

4. Personal care and physical activity

5. Participating in the receiving and giving of help and support in maintaining a healthy and productive lifestyle

The sessions in this module can stand alone; that is, new clients can enter at any session. However, it is most effective to present the five sessions in sequence. For clients who learn this module prior to Module 11, it is helpful to provide a summary of Module 11 to show how Modules 11 and 12 are tied together. Prior to the delivery of Module 12, providers should review the sections of this *Adjunct Provider's Guide* in Chapter 8, Gender-Specific Strategies and Models for Treatment, on Individualized Plans for Reentry and Transition and Transitional Planning and Wraparound Services.

SESSION 46: Managing Work, Job, and Time

RATIONAL

This session brings in the following work-related topics and helps the woman to:

▶ Explore a variety of traditional and nontraditional work opportunities

▶ Process feelings regarding previous experiences with discrimination

▶ Provide specific job training, or (if not possible), referral to job training opportunities in the community

▶ Understand some of the action that may be taken to relieve some of the pressures involved in dual roles (such as caretaker-worker, and so on)

PRESENTATION GUIDELINES

The female judicial client should be assisted in developing new job skills and the means for obtaining the training. Some women may find that the word *work* carries a negative connotation, as something unpleasant and obligatory. Some may find the word *job* or *career* more positive. When doing Worksheets 87 through 89, clients should be very gender specific.

SESSION 47: Healthy Leisure Time

RATIONALE

This session is expanded to explore the bind that women fall into when they care for others at the expense of caring for themselves. This functions to prevent women from engaging in healthful leisure activities that would encourage self-growth. For women, leisure activities often start with self-care, including tending to and taking good care of themselves. This session is adapted to address the areas of self-care so that the female judicial client recognizes the degree to which substance abuse and criminal conduct undermine self-care.

Self-care is important throughout this *Adjunct Provider's Guide.* This session is specifically geared to assist the female judicial client in developing body awareness, which will lead toward increased feelings of self-esteem. It is also important to recognize that these activities are deeply personal for each woman; the activities chosen by each of them may reflect the circumstances of their own lives and may not be universally appreciated.

The basis for self-care is to help the female judicial client:

▶ Manage stress

▶ Remain focused

▶ Accomplish her goals

▶ Deal with risks to relapse and recidivism, and

▶ Create self-efficacy and empowerment, contributing to the ultimate goal of recovery

Self-care, however, is an egocentric orientation to treatment and change and is only part of the picture. It must be balanced with a healthy caring about others and the communities in which they live. Certainly, caring about others at the expense of self is not healthy. Yet, a woman's engagement in criminal conduct is unhealthy self-care and is egocentric. Thus, the theme of self-care must be balanced with the theme of being prosocial and morally responsible toward others and the community.

PRESENTATION GUIDELINES

When doing Worksheet 90, have clients again be gender specific. Then, have clients ask an individual they are close to—for example, intimate partner, significant other—to complete Worksheet 91, the Personal Pleasure Inventory. Then, as homework, have them compare their own scores with their partner's scores. Have them discuss the differences. Are the differences so great that they will have a difficult time meeting their own personal pleasures with their partner's? How can they find common ground in achieving personal pleasure with their partner?

SESSION 48: Relaxation Skills for a Healthy Lifestyle

RATIONALE

Prior to the delivery of this session, clients should review the content and exercises pertaining to relaxation and stress management as presented in Session 25, Understanding Stress, Its Causes and Roots, and Session 26, Managing Stress and Emotions. These sessions provide an excellent foundation for this session, the primary goal of which is to develop a "daily program of relaxation."

SESSION 49: Healthy Eating and Physical Activity

RATIONAL

This session is designed to help women in corrections learn basic concepts about healthy eating, clarify their own goals about personal care, and understand the value of exercise. There is considerable societal pressure for women to meet certain expectations around physical appearance and body weight. In no way should this session reinforce this pressure. Rather, the goal is for women to take a close look at how they can engage in a healthy diet, personal care, and physical activity that meets their lifestyle expectations and goals.

For some women, drug abuse, particularly methamphetamine abuse, had its inception in the "benefits" of weight loss and self-concept related to slimness. The topic of how certain drugs and their harmful actions (for example, anorexia and bulimia) may contribute to self-harm should be addressed in this session. The relapse plan should be reviewed with reference to high-risk situations, thoughts, feelings, and positive changes necessary to maintain a lifestyle characterized by healthy eating and optimal physical activity.

PRESENTATION GUIDELINES

When doing Worksheet 94, have clients generate their "healthy menu" in reference to the image they have of themselves and how they want to be and the goal of eating in a healthy way. It may be that healthy eating is not necessarily compatible to the image they want of themselves. This relates to the use of weight loss medication to look a certain way versus adhering to a healthy diet.

When doing Worksheet 95, have clients establish a Weekly Activity Plan based on their own goals and expectations, and not on the goals and expectations others have of them.

SESSION 50: Receiving and Giving Support for Change and Responsible Living

RATIONALE

As stated in the *Provider's Guide,* this session represents one of the most important lifestyle alternatives in the substance-abusing judicial client's life: receiving support from and giving support to others. This session is designed to help women build a bridge of support from the treatment program into the community. Each woman is encouraged to find sources of strength within herself, within the treatment group, from an ongoing alumni group, by serving as a role model or mentor for new clients, and in associations with prosocial, non-using, and recovering women.

PRESENTATION GUIDELINES

Have each client discuss and make a plan for contacting one or two supportive family members or a friend who will assist in her reintegration into the community. These client advocate resources who "stand in support" of community reentry may include neighbors, church members, social workers, former counselors, teachers, housing managers, or a member of the treatment staff who can assist in the next step of the client's treatment and reentry. These people will help to build both a symbolic and real bridge between *SSC* and the community. Providers should encourage each client to tell these supportive persons how important this support will be in her effort to make a positive reentry into the community. One of the best resources for this is an Alcoholics Anonymous (AA) or Narcotics Anonymous (NA) sponsor.

Exercise. Have clients discuss specific strategies to maintain their self-development and change. Discuss and explore the various self-help groups and other community support programs. Clients can work together, with the help of the provider, in getting together information on these resources, such as brochures, Web sites, and Internet links. It is suggested that the group work together in constructing a poster or even a PowerPoint presentation of these various resources. This will assist clients in taking ownership of this process and enhance the probability of clients engaging in community reinforcement resources.

Exercise. Have clients discuss their sense of confidence and goals with respect to giving support and mentoring others. Some clients may not be comfortable or even ready for such mentoring and support giving. Encourage clients to be open and honest about this.

Explore what *spirituality* means to clients and what experience they have had within their meaning of spirituality. It may also be useful to discuss ways that this can bring people together and feel connected. Experiences and stories from various traditions and activities that represent spirituality may be provided in the discussion. Some providers and clients may not feel comfortable exploring this area. Get group consensus before proceeding.

CONTINUING YOUR JOURNEY OF RESPONSIBLE LIVING

The provider is asked to follow the guidelines provided in the *Strategies for Self-Improvement and Change (SSC) Provider's Guide* (p. 329) and the *Participant's Workbook* (p. 290) for this closure session. For closed groups, closure will be done as a group. Most agencies, however, use an open group model. In this case, clients may be completing *SSC* during any of the Phase III sessions (except for those where there is no entry for new clients). In the open group delivery model, in the final group session, a short period of time is allotted to make closure with the group. Guidelines for this are found in the *Provider's Guide* and the *Workbook* on the pages referenced. A certificate of completion is given to the client. Some agencies also have a graduation exercise to which family and friends are invited.

Exercises for Closure. Each woman is asked to identify imminent and long-range challenges, including

▶ The personal qualities she pledges to maintain

▶ The relationships she pledges to maintain or dissolve

▶ The healthy activities she will engage in that assist in preventing relapse and recidivism

Discuss the following four concepts that can help the client in her efforts to change and engage in a drug-free and crime-free lifestyle:

1. Restraint

2. Respect

3. Responsibility

4. Transformation

Completion of *SSC* will also involve bringing closure to the interpersonal feelings and relationships that have developed during treatment, both for the group and provider. During *SSC,* clients have been encouraged to look to each other as sources of respect, support, and feedback, and it is likely that strong bonds have developed among them. This bonding often develops with greater strength among women clients than with men. Also, women may have a more difficult time reestablishing supportive relationships in the community than will their male counterparts. Thus, losing the group and relationship with the group and provider may create a great sense of loss. Every effort should be made to help clients establish healthy and positive connections in the community. This is one of the main goals of Session 50.

Helpful in this process is the client advocate resource that was discussed in Session 50. This advocacy model is designed to facilitate the following termination objectives:

▶ Reach a feeling of closure on the process of SSC

▶ Acknowledge the importance of relationships developed within treatment

▶ Understand ways of establishing similar relationships in the community

- Understand that all relationships cannot be continued, but where "one door closes, another will open" with respect to healthy relationship opportunities

- Identify ways to symbolically draw upon the relationships they have had

- Keep the group alive in spirit as ways to energize and invigorate.

- Celebrate the completion of a major step toward the attainment of a meaningful and drug-free and crime-free life

Closure will involve an individual session as well. Guidelines for this session are spelled out in the *Provider's Guide*. Prior to that session, clients complete the final treatment phase PACE Monitor instruments, and providers complete the charting of the Client Program Response-Client (CPR-C) and Client Program Response-Provider (CPR-P) instruments. The *SSC* Cognitive-Behavioral Map and the Cognitive-Behavioral STEP method are reviewed. The continuing care plan is also completed.

APPENDIX
Gender Comparisons Across Offender Samples

RATIO OF MALE TO FEMALE CRIMINAL JUSTICE CLIENTS

As shown in Table A.1, females represent approximately 26 percent of the presentenced probation group, approximately 20 percent of the postsentenced probation group, and approximately 13 percent of those incarcerated. Another large sample of prisoners, not included in this study ($N = 1668$), was represented by 6.1 percent females. These findings are congruent with reports in the literature. Frost, Green, and Pranis (2006) report that nationally, women comprise about 7 percent of the prison population. Most important is that as we move from lower levels of judicial involvement (presentenced probation) through postsentenced probation to prison settings, the percentage of females declines significantly. A study by Wanberg (2008) indicates a similar finding among juveniles. The percentage of females in a large juvenile probation sample was 23.8, and among committed juvenile, 18.7 percent. Thus, as we move from less severe criminal involvement to greater involvement, the percentage of females declines.

Antisocial and Criminal Conduct. Table A.2 clearly shows that, across all 10 samples, males report higher levels of antisocial attitudes and behaviors on the Adult Substance Use Scales (ASUS). This finding is generally supported in the literature. Two of the 10 samples did not have Level of Supervision Inventory-Revised (LSI-R) scores. Of the eight that did, the six probation samples showed males scoring higher on the crime scale. However, for the two incarcerated samples, there was no gender differentiation. This indicates that crime involvement in male and female group tends to equal out as they become more entrenched in criminal behavior and the judicial system.

Psychological and Mental Health Problems. Across all 10 samples, females score higher on the ASUS scale measuring psychological and mood adjustment problems and on the LSI-R mental health scale. These findings, supported by other research summarized earlier, clearly indicate that females have higher needs in the areas of mood adjustment, psychological problems, and mental health concerns.

General Drug Involvement. Male and female judicial clients do not differ with respect to the extent of general alcohol and other drug (AOD) involvement. Scores on the ASUS AOD INVOLVEMENT scale did not differ in 9 of the 10 groups. This scale measures the extent of AOD use across 10 basic drug use categories. High scores indicate polydrug involvement. This does not support some studies in the literature suggesting that female judicial clients are more apt than males to be involved in multiple drug use. What is most important is that, across all drug categories, females are just as involved in drug use as are males.

Specific Drug Involvement. As shown in Table A.2, there is a clear pattern of differences regarding the reported lifetime use of specific drugs. The drug item data were available for only 6 of the 10 samples. Male judicial clients clearly show greater involvement in the use of alcohol and marijuana (they scored higher in all six samples), whereas females show greater involvement in cocaine and amphetamines, scoring higher in five of the six samples. Generally, these findings would suggest that females use drugs that will enhance their sense of power and energy in relationship with others (cocaine and amphetamine involvement). Males may be more apt to use those drugs that will mitigate anxiety and fear of engaging in criminal conduct and fear of getting caught (alcohol and marijuana) and in enhancing their sense of power over others (alcohol). Although there are mixed findings with respect to the other drug categories, there is a trend for males in the judicial system to have a history of greater involvement in hallucinogens and females to have a greater involvement in tranquilizers.

Extent of Drug Disruption and Symptoms. Female judicial clients reported greater *disruption* and *symptoms* related to AOD use across 8 of the 10 samples. Thus, even though there is no gender differentiation across the general INVOLVEMENT scale, females report having *greater life disruptions* resulting from AOD use. This would suggest that female judicial clients may have more psychophysical problems associated with AOD use. A study of the PSYCHOPHYSICAL subscale of the DISRUPTION scale clearly showed that, across all of the six samples that had ASUS item data, female judicial clients scored higher on scales that measure symptoms of psychological and physical disruption related to AOD use.

Level of Defensiveness. Male criminal justice clients across all 10 samples had a higher score on the DEFENSIVE scale. This scale is comprised of items that measure desirable psychological characteristics ("never get angry," "never cry," "never lie," "never frustrated with a job," "never unhappy," "never hold things in," and "never unkind or rude"). A very high score on this scale is interpreted to indicate that such respondents are trying to look good or desirable, or are defending against admitting to or perceiving themselves as having personal problems. Since females score higher than males on the PSYCH PROBLEMS scale, it would be expected that females would score lower on the DEFENSIVE scale. This suggests that women are more open to reporting symptoms of a psychological and emotional nature. It also suggests that men attenuate their responses or are more defensive across all of the self-report scales. Yet, as shown in Table A.1, males score higher on antisocial attitudes and behavior, there is no difference on the INVOLVEMENT scale between the two groups, and males report greater involvement in marijuana and alcohol. Thus, even though men may attenuate their responses across the ASUS-R scales, they are so much more into antisocial and rebellious behaviors or into alcohol and marijuana use, compared to women, they still end up scoring higher in these areas. What is important is that women see themselves as having more psychological symptoms and men see themselves as having more antisocial behaviors. At the clinical level, men or women with very high DEFENSIVE scores (for example, say "no never" or "hardly at all" to all of the items in the scale) are presenting a guarded posture with respect to openly disclosing life adjustment problems (drug abuse, mood problems, antisocial behavior, and so on).

Education and Employment. Female criminal justice clients scored higher on the LSI-R EDUCATION/EMPLOYMENT scale on six of the eight samples where the LSI-R data were available. This supports the previous findings that women in corrections are more economically disrupted and are undereducated and unskilled.

Family and Marital Disruption. Females have higher scores on the six probation samples for which the LSI-R data were available, again supporting general findings in the literature. Most interesting, this differential effect was not present in the two prison samples. Again, we tend to see some leveling of problems between genders with those who are more entrenched in criminal conduct and the judicial system.

Table A.1

Descriptions and Distributions by Gender for Samples in Table A.2

Sample No.	Description of Sample	Total N	Percentage Male	Percentage Female
1	State A: Probation presentence	4,000	72.6	27.4
2	State A: Probation presentence	4,000	73.4	26.6
3	State A: Probation presentence	4,000	73.5	26.5
4	County A: Probation presentence	1,183	74.8	25.2
5	State B: Probation postsentence	1,383	80.4	19.6
6	State C: Probation presentence	2,604	75.6	24.4
7	State D: Probation presentence	2,070	76.2	23.8
8	State D: Probation presentence	2,079	76.6	23.4
9	State D: DOC*: incarceration	2,739	87.5	12.5
10	State D: DOC*: incarceration	2,652	86.6	13.2
Total N = 15,910				

*DOC = Department of Corrections

Table A.2

Comparison of Male and Female Offenders Across the Adult Substance Use Scales and on Level of Supervision Inventory-Revised on the Crime, Mental Health, and Total LSI-R Scales* for 10 Judicial Samples

ASUS SCALE NAME	1	2	3	4	5	6	7	8	9	10
ASUS: INVOLVEMENT	NS	NS	NS	NS	NS	F2	NS	NS	NS	NS
ASUS: DISRUPTION	NS	F1	F2	F2	F2	F1	F1	NS	F1	F1
ASUS: PSYPHY DISRUPT	F1	F1	F1	F1	F2	F1	—	—	—	—
ASUS: ANTISOCIAL	M1	M1	M1	M1	M1	M1	M1	M1	M1	M1
ASUS: PSYCH PROB	F1	F1	F1	F1	F1	F1	F1	F1	F1	F1
ASUS: DEFENSIVE	M1	M1	M1	M1	M1	M1	M1	M1	M2	M2
ASUS: MOTIVATION	M1	NS	NS	NS	NS	NS	—	—	—	—
ASUS: GLOBAL	NS	NS	NS	NS	NS	F1	F1	NS	F1	F1
ASUS: EVAL. RATE	M2	NS	M1	NS	NS	NS	—	—	—	—
ASUS: ALCOHOL	M1	M1	M1	M1	M1	M1	—	—	—	—
ASUS: MARIJUANA	M1	M1	M1	M1	M1	M1	—	—	—	—
ASUS: COCAINE	F1	F1	F1	NS	F1	F2	—	—	—	—
ASUS: AMPHETAMINES	F1	F1	F1	NS	F1	F1	—	—	—	—
ASUS: HALLUCINOGENS	M1	NS	M1	M1	NS	NS	—	—	—	—

(Continued)

(Continued)

ASUS SCALE NAME	1	2	3	4	5	6	7	8	9	10
ASUS: INHALANTS	NS	M1	NS	M2	NS	NS	—	—	—	—
ASUS: HEROIN	NS	NS	NS	NS	NS	F1	—	—	—	—
ASUS: OTHER OPIATES	NS	NS	NS	NS	F1	F1	—	—	—	—
ASUS: BARBITURATES	NS	NS	NS	NS	NS	F1	—	—	—	—
ASUS: TRANQUILIZERS	NS	F2	F1	NS	F2	F1	—	—	—	—
LSI-R CRIME	M1	M1	M1	—	M1	—	M1	M1	NS	NS
LSI-R: EDUC/EMPLOY	F1	F1	F1	—	NS	—	F2	NS	F1	F1
LSI-R: FAMILY	F1	F1	F1	—	F1	—	F1	F1	NS	NS
LSI-R: MENTAL HEALTH	F1	F1	F1	—	F1	—	F1	F1	F1	F1
LSI-R: TOTAL SCORE	F1	F1	F1	—	NS	—	NS	NS	F1	F1

Statistical significance levels:

NS = Statistically nonsignificant

F1 = Females score higher with probability < .009

F2 = Females score higher with probability < .05

M1 = Males score higher with probability < .009

M2 = Males score higher with probability < .05

*The cells with the dashed lines (--) indicate that data were not available for those scales. These findings show a consistent and clear trend across the ASUS and LSI-R scales.

References

Acharyya, S., & Zhang, H. (2003). Assessing sex differences on treatment effectiveness from the Drug Abuse Treatment Outcome Study (DATOS). *American Journal of Drug and Alcohol Abuse, 29,* 415–444.

Acoca, L. (1998a). Defusing the time bomb: Understanding and meeting the growing health care needs of incarcerated women in America. *Crime & Delinquency, 44*(1), 49–69.

Acoca, L. (1998b). Outside/inside: The violation of American girls at home, on the streets, and in the juvenile justice system. *Crime & Delinquency, 44*(4), 561–589.

Acoca, L., & Austin, J. (1996). The hidden crisis: Women in prison. San Francisco: National Council on Crime and Delinquency.

Acoca, L., & Dedel, K. (1998). *No place to hide: Understanding and meeting the needs of girls in the California juvenile justice system.* Washington, DC: National Council on Crime and Delinquency.

Adler, F. (1975). *Sisters in crime: The rise of the new female criminal.* New York: McGraw-Hill.

Alexander, M. J. (1996). Women with co-occurring addictive and mental disorders: An emerging profile of vulnerability. *American Journal of Orthopsychiatry, 66*(1), 61–70.

Allen, D. M. (2005). The clinical exchange. *Journal of Psychotherapy Integration, 15,* 67–68.

American Psychiatric Association. (1980). *Diagnostic and statistical manual of mental disorders* (3rd ed.). Washington, DC: Author.

American Psychiatric Association. (1987). *Diagnostic and statistical manual of mental disorders* (3rd ed., rev.). Washington, DC: Author.

American Psychiatric Association, (1994). *Diagnostic and statistical manual of mental disorders* (4th ed.). Washington, DC: Author.

American Psychological Association. (1978). Guidelines for therapy with women: Task force on sex bias and role stereotyping in psychological therapeutic practice. *American Psychologist, 33,* 1122–1123.

American Psychological Association (1978). Task force on sex bias and sex role stereotyping in psychotherapeutic practice. *American Psychologist, 33,* 1122–1123.

American Psychological Association. (2000). *Diagnostic and statistical manual of mental disorders* (4th ed, text revision).Washington, DC: Author.

Ames, G., Schmidt, D., Klee, L., & Saltz, R. (1996). Combining methods to identify new measures of women's drinking problems. Part I: The ethnographic stage. *Addictions, 91*(6), 829–844.

Andrews, D. A., & Bonta, J. (2003). *The psychology of criminal conduct* (3rd ed.). Cincinnati: Anderson.

Anooshian, L. J. (2005). Violence and aggression in the lives of homeless children: A review. *Aggression and Violent Behavior, 10*(2), 129–152.

Antaki, C., Barnes, R., & Leudar, I. (2005). Self-disclosure as a situated interactional practice. *British Journal of Social Psychology, 44,* 181–199.

Armstrong, J. G., & High, J. R. (1999). Guidelines for differentiating malingering from PTSD. *National Center for Posttraumatic Stress Disorder Clinical Quarterly, 8*(3),46–48.

Arnkoff, D. B., & Glass, C. R. (1992). Cognitive therapy and psychotherapy integration. In D. K. Freedheim (Ed.), *History of psychotherapy: A century of change* (pp. 657–694). Washington, DC: American Psychological Association.

Arrigo, B. A., & Griffin, A. (2004). Serial murder and the case of Aileen Wuornos: Attachment theory, psychopathy, predatory aggression. *Behavioral Sciences and the Law, 22,* 375–393.

Ashley, O. S., Marsden, M. E., & Brady, T. M. (2003). Effectiveness of substance abuse treatment programming for women: A review. *American Journal of Drug and Alcohol Abuse, 29,* 19–53.

Atkinson, D. R., Thompson, C. E., & Grant, S. K. (1993). A three-dimensional model for counseling racial/ethnic minorities. *Counseling Psychologist, 21,* 257–277.

Bachman, R., & Saltzman, L. E. (1995). *Violence against women: Estimates from the redesigned survey.* Washington, DC: U.S. Department of Justice, Bureau of Justice Statistics.

Baillargeon, J., Ducate, S., Pulvino, J., Bradshaw, P., Murray, O., & Olvera., R. (2003). The association of psychiatric disorders and HIV infection in the correctional setting. *Annals of Epidemiology, 13*(9), 606–612.

Baletka, D. M., & Shearer, R. A. (2005). Assessing program needs of female offenders who abuse substances. In B. Sims (Ed.), *Substance abuse treatment with correctional clients: Practical implications for institutional and community settings* (pp. 227–242). New York: Haworth.

Bartol, C. (2002). *Criminal behavior: A psychosocial approach.* Upper Saddle River, NJ: Prentice Hall.

Bayse, G. (1998). *Introduction to PTSD*. Retrieved on April 8, 2006, from http://campus.houghton.edu/orgs/psychology/ptsd/introduction/htm

Beall, L. S. (1997). Posttraumatic stress disorder. *Choice, 34*(6), 917–930. Retrieved February 20, 2007, from http://www.lib.auburn.edu/socsci/docs/ptsd.html

Beck, A. T. (1963). Thinking and depression. *Archives of General Psychiatry, 9,* 324–333.

Beck, A. T. (1976). *Cognitive therapy and the emotional disorders.* New York: International Universities Press.

Beck, A. T. (2006). *Beck Depression Inventory—BDI.* San Antonio, TX: Psychological Corporation.

Beck, A., Wright, F., Newman, C., & Liese, B. (1993). *Cognitive therapy of substance abuse.* New York: Guilford.

Beck, J. (1995). *Cognitive therapy: Basics and beyond.* New York: Guilford.

Becker, M. A., & Gatz, M. (2005). Introduction to the impact of co-occurring disorders and violence on women: Findings from the SAMHSA women, co-occurring disorders and violence study. *Journal of Behavioral Health Services & Research. Special Issue: The Impact of Co-occurring Disorders and Violence on Women, 32,* 111–112.

Belknap, J. (1996). *The invisible woman: Gender, crime and justice.* Belmont, CA: Wadsworth.

Belknap, J., & Holsinger, K. (1998). An overview of delinquent girls: How theory and practice have failed and the need for innovative changes. In R. T. Zaplin (Ed.), *Female crime and delinquency: Critical perspectives and effective interventions* (pp. 31–64). Gaithersburg, MD: Aspen.

Belknap, J., Holsinger, K., & Dunn, M. (1997). Understanding incarcerated girls: The results of a focus group study. *Prison Journal, 77*(4), 381–404.

Bem, D. J. (1996). Exotic becomes erotic: A developmental theory of sexual orientation. *Psychological Review, 103*(2), 320–335.

Bem, S. L., & Bem, D. (1971). Training the woman to know her place: The power of a nonconscious ideology. In M. H. Garskof (Ed.), *Roles women play: Readings toward women's liberation* (pp. 84–96). Belmont, CA: Brooks/Cole.

Bender, E. (2004). Chronic health problems often accompany PTSD in women. *Psychiatric News, 39*(17), 36.

Bernstein, D. P., Fink, L., Handelsman, L., Foote, J., Lovejoy, M., Wenzel, K., et al. (1994). Initial reliability and validity of a new retrospective measure of child abuse and neglect. *American Journal of Psychiatry, 151*(8), 1132–1136.

Blinn, C. L. (1997). *Maternal ties: A selection of programs for female offenders.* Lanham, MD: American Correctional Association.

Bloom, B., Chesney-Lind, M., & Owen, B. (1994). *Women in California prisons: Hidden victims of the war on drugs.* San Francisco: Center on Juvenile and Criminal Justice.

Bloom, B., & Covington, S. (1998). *Gender-specific programming for female offenders: What is it and why is it important?* Paper presented at the 50th annual meeting of the American Society of Criminology, Washington, DC.

Bloom, B., Owen, B., & Covington, S. (2005). *Gender responsive strategies for women offenders: A summary of research, practice, and guiding principles for women offenders.* Washington, DC: U.S. Department of Justice, National Institute of Corrections.

Bloom, B., Owen, B., Covington, S., & Raeder, J. (2003). *Gender responsive strategies: Research, practice, and guiding principles for women offenders.* Washington, DC: U.S. Department of Justice, National Institute of Corrections.

Bloom, B., & Steinhart, D. (1993). *Why punish the children? A reappraisal of the children of incarcerated mothers in America.* San Francisco: National Council on Crime and Delinquency.

Bloom, S. L. (2000). The sanctuary model. *Therapeutic Communities, 21*(2), 67–91.

Blume, S. B. (1990). Alcohol and drug problems in women: Old attitudes, new knowledge. In H. Milkman & L. Sederer (Eds.), *Treatment choices for alcoholism and substance abuse.* New York: Lexington Press.

Blume, S. B. (1991). Sexuality and stigma: The alcoholic woman. *Alcohol Health and Research World, 15*(2), 139–146.

Blume, S. B. (1998). Addictive disorders in women. In R. J. Frames & S. I. Miller (Eds.), *Clinical textbook of addictive disorders* (2nd ed., pp. 413–429). New York: Guilford.

Bonta, J., & Hanson, R. K. (1994). *Gauging the risk for violence: Measurement, impact and strategies for change* (User Report No. 1994–09). Ottawa, Canada: Department of the Solicitor General of Canada.

Booth, R. E., Koester, S. K., & Pinto F. (1995). Gender differences in sex-risk behaviors, economic livelihood, and self-concept among drug injectors and crack smokers. *American Journal on Addictions 44*(4), 313–322.

Boyd, C., Guthrie, B., Pohl, J., Whitmarsh, J., & Henderson, D. (1994). African-American women who smoke crack cocaine: Sexual trauma and the mother-daughter relationship. *Psychoactive Drugs, 26*(3), 243–247.

Bremner, J. D. (2002). *Does stress damage the brain?* New York: Norton.

Brennan, T. (1998). Institutional classification of females: Problems and some proposals for reform. In R. T. Zaplin (Ed.), *Female offenders: Critical perspectives and effective intervention* (pp. 179–204). Gaithersburg, MD: Aspen.

Brennan, T., & Austin, J. (1997, March). *Women in jail: Classification issues*. Washington, DC: U.S. Department of Justice, National Institute of Corrections.

Brenner, R. (2007). *Ethical Influence: Part I.* Cambridge, MA: Chaco Canyon Counseling. Retrieved August 29, 2007, from http://www.chacocanioncounseling.com/pointlookout/070704.shtml

Brown, P. J. (2000). Outcome in female patients with both substance use and posttraumatic stress disorder. *Alcoholism Treatment Quarterly, 18*(3), 127.

Brown, T. G., Kokin, M., Seraganian, P., & Shields, N. (1995). The role of spouse of substance abusers in treatment: Gender differences. *Journal of Psychoactie Drugs, 27*(3), 223–231.

Brunswig, K., Sbraga, P., & Harris, T. (2003). *Relapse prevention.* Hoboken, NJ: Wiley.

Bugental, D. B., & Shennum, W. (2002). Gender, power, and violence in the family. *Child Maltreatment, 7,* 56–64.

Bureau of Justice Statistics. (2006). *Prison statistics.* Washington, DC: U.S. Department of Justice. Retrieved August 29, 2007, from http://ojp.usdoj.gov/bjs/prisons.htm

Bush-Baskette, S. (2000). The war on drugs and the incarceration of mothers. *Journal of Drug Issues, 30*(4), 919–928.

Butcher, J. H. N., Dahlstrom, W. G., Graham, J. R., Tellegan, A. M., & Kaemmer, B. (1989). *MMPI-2: Manual for administration and scoring.* Minneapolis: University of Minnesota Press.

Butler, S. (1978). *Conspiracy of silence: The trauma of incest.* San Francisco: New Glide.

Bylington, D. (1997). Applying relational theory to addiction treatment. In S. L. A. Straussner & E. Zelwin (Eds.), *Gender and addictions: Men and women in treatment* (pp. 33–45). Northvale, NJ: Jason Aronson.

Campbell, A. (1993). *Men, women, and aggression.* New York: Basic Books.

Carten, A. J. (1996). Mothers in recovery: Rebuilding families in the aftermath of addiction. *Social Work, 41*(2), 214–223.

Casswell, S., Pledger, M., & Hooper, R. (2003). Socioeconomic status and drinking patterns in young adults. *Addiction, 98,* 601–610.

Chen, X., Tyler, K. A., Whitbeck, L. B., & Hoyt, D. R. (2004). Early sexual abuse, street adversity, and drug use among female homeless and runaway adolescents in the Midwest. *Journal of Drug Issues, 34,* 1–21.

Chesney-Lind, M. (2000). Women and the criminal justice system: Gender matters. *Topics in Community Corrections Annual Issue 2000: Responding to Women Offenders in the Community, 7*–10.

Chesney-Lind, M., & Sheldon, R. G. (1998). *Girls, delinquency, and juvenile justice* (2nd ed.). Belmont, CA: West/Wadsworth.

Choca, J. (2004). *Interpretive guide to the Millon Clinical Maltiaxial Inventory* (3rd ed.). Washington, DC: American Psychological Association.

Clark, D. A., & Steer, R. A. (1996). Empirical status of the cognitive model of anxiety and depression. In P. M. Salkovskis (Ed.), *Frontiers of cognitive therapy* (pp. 75–96). New York: Guilford.

Coll, C. G., Miller, J. B., Fields, J. P., & Matthews, B. (1997). The experiences of women in prison: Implications for services and prevention. *Women and Therapy, 20*(4), 11–28.

Collins, W. C., & Collins, A. W. (1996). *Women in jail: Legal issues.* Washington, DC: National Institute of Corrections.

Conly, C. (1998). *The Women's Prison Association: Supporting women offenders and their families.* Program Focus. Washington, DC: National Institute of Justice.

Cook, L. S., Epperson, L., & Gariti, P. (2005). Determining the need for gender-specific chemical dependence treatment: Assessment of treatment variables. *American Journal on Addictions, 14,* 328–338.

Courtois, C. A. (1995). Scientist-practitioners and the delayed memory controversy. *Counseling Psychologist, 23,* 294–299.

Covington, S. S. (1998a). The relational theory of women's psychological development: Implications for the criminal justice system. In R. T. Zaplin (Ed.), *Female offenders: Critical perspectives and effective intervention* (pp. 113–131). Gaithersberg, MD: Aspen.

Covington, S. S. (1998b). Women in prison: Approaches in the treatment of our most invisible population. *Women Therapy 21*(1), 141–155.

Covington, S. S. (1999). *Helping women recover: A program for treating addiction.* San Francisco: Jossey-Bass.

Covington, S. S. (2000). Helping women to recover: Creating gender-specific treatment for substance-abusing women and girls in community corrections. In M. McMahon, (Ed.), *Assessment to assistance: Programs for women in community corrections* (pp. 171–234). Lanham, MD: American Correctional Association.

Covington, S. S. (2001). Creating gender-responsive programs: The next step for women's services. *Corrections Today, 63*(1), 85–87.

Covington, S. S., & Surrey, J. L. (1997). The relational model of women's psychological development: Implications for substance abuse. In R. W. Wilsnack & S. C. Wilsnack (Eds.), *Gender and alcohol: Individual and social perspectives* (pp. 335–351). New Brunswick, NJ: Rutgers Center of Alcohol Studies.

Cox, D., Hallam R., O'Connor, K., & Rachman, S. (1983). An experimental study of fearlessness and courage. *British Journal of Psychology, 74,* 107–117.

Crawford, M., & Unger, R. (2000). *Women and gender: A feminist psychology* (3rd ed.). Boston: McGraw-Hill.

Crime in the United States. (2005). Washington, DC: Department of Justice, Federal Bureau of Investigation. Retrieved March 2, 2008, from http://www.fbi.gov/ucr/05cius/data/table_33.html

Curry, L. (2001). Tougher sentencing, economic hardships and rising violence. In P. Herman (Ed.), *The American prison system* (pp. 126–129). New York: H. G. Wilson.

Davis, W. R., Johnson, B. D., Randolph, D., & Liberty, H. J. (2005). Gender differences in the distribution of cocaine and heroin in Central Harlem. *Drug and Alcohol Dependence, 77,* 115–127.

Dawson, J. M. (1994). *Murder in families* (Bureau of Justice Statistics Special Report). Washington, DC: U.S. Department of Justice, Bureau of Justice Statistics.

Dean-Gaitor, H., & Fleming, P. (1999). Epidemiology of AIDS in incarcerated persons in the United States, 1994–1996. AIDS13: 2429–2435. In National Institute of Justice (2001), *Health status of soon-to-be released inmates,* Vol. 1. Washington, DC: National Institute of Justice.

Demaris, A., & Kaukinen, C. (2005). Violent victimization and women's mental and physical health: Evidence from a national sample. *Journal of Research in Crime and Delinquency, 42,* 384–411.

Denmark, F., Rabinowitz, V., & Sechzer, J. (2000). The world of work. In *Engendering Psychology* (pp. 197–227). Needham Heights, MA: Allyn & Bacon.

Derogatis, L. R. (2001). *SCL-90 administration, scoring and procedure manual.* Bloomington, MN: Pearson Assessments.

Ditton, P. M. (1999). *Mental health and treatment of inmates and probationers.* Washington, DC: U.S. Department of Justice, Bureau of Justice Statistics.

Dixon, A., Howie, P., & Starling, J. (2005). Trauma exposure, posttraumatic stress, and psychiatric comorbidity in female juvenile offenders. *Journal of the American Academy of Child and Adolescent Psychiatry, 44,* 798–806.

Dodd, M. H. (1997). Social model of recovery: Origin, early features, changes and future. *Journal of Psychoactive Drugs, 29*(2), 133–139.

Dow, B. J., & Condit, C. M. (2005). The state of the art in feminist scholarship in communication. *Journal of Communication, 55,* 448–478.

Drug and Alcohol Services Information System (DASIS). (2006). *Facilities offering special programs or groups for women: 2005* (Report issue 35). Washington, DC: U.S. Department of Health and Human Services.

Dryden-Edwards, R., & Stoppler, M. C. (2007). *Posttraumatic stress disorder (PTSD).* MedicineNet.com. Retrieved March 4, 2008, from http://www.Medicinenet.com/posttraumatic_stress_disorder/article.htm

Dyer, O. (2003). Suicide among women prisoners at a record high. *British Medical Journal* (7407), 122. http://www.bmj.com/cgi/content/full/327/7407/122

Edwards, L. M., & Pedrotti, J. T. (2004). Utilizing the strengths of our cultures: Therapy with biracial women and girls. *Women and Therapy, 27,* 33–43.

Ehrmin, J. T. (2002). "That feeling of not feeling": Numbing the pain for substance-dependent African American women. *Qualitative Health Research. Special Issue: Culture and Health, 12,* 780–791.

El-Bassel, N., Gilbert, L., Schilling, R. F., Ivanoff, A., Borne, D., & Safyer, S. F. (1996). Correlates of crack abuse among drug-using incarcerated women: Psychological trauma, social support, and coping behavior. *American Journal of Drug and Alcohol Abuse, 22*(1), 41–56.

Elliott, D. M., & Briere, J. (1990, August). *Predicting molestation history in professional women with the Trauma Symptom Checklist (TSC-40).* Paper presented at the meeting of the Western Psychological Association, Los Angeles, CA.

Ellis, A. (1975). *A new guide to rational living.* Englewood Cliffs, NJ: Prentice Hall.

Ellis, A., & Harper, R. A. (1961). *A guide to rational living.* Englewood Cliffs, NJ: Prentice Hall.

Eronen, M. (1995). Mental disorders and homicidal behavior in female subjects. *American Journal of Psychiatry, 152*(8), 1216–1218.

Falck, R. S., Wang, J., Carlson, R. G., & Siegal, H. A. (2001). The epidemiology of physical attack and rape among crack-using women. *Violence and Victims, 16*(1), 79–89.

Falsetti, S. A., Resnick, H. S., Resick, P. A., & Kilpatrick, D. G. (1993). The Modified PTSD Symptom Scale: A brief self-report measure of posttraumatic stress disorder. *Behavior Therapist, 16*(6), 161–162.

Fals-Stewart, W., & Kennedy, C. (2005). Addressing intimate partner violence in substance abuse treatment. *Journal of Substance Abuse Treatment, 29,* 5–17.

Fickenscher, A., Lapidus, J., Silk-Walker, P., & Becker, T. (2001). Women behind bars: Health needs of inmates in a county jail. *Public Health Report, 116*(3), 191–196.

Finkelhor, D., Ormrod, R., Turner, H., & Hamby, S. L. (2005). The victimization of children and youth: A comprehensive national survey. *Child Maltreatment: Journal of the American Professional Society on the Abuse of Children, 10,* 5–25.

Finkelstein, N., Kennedy, C., Thomas, K., & Kearns, M. (1997). *Gender specific substance abuse treatment.* Alexandria, VA: National Women's Resource Center for the Prevention and Treatment of Alcohol, Tobacco, and Other Drug Abuse and Mental Illness.

Fletcher, B. R., Shaver, L. O., & Moon, D. G. (1993). *Women prisoners: A forgotten population.* Westport, CT: Praeger.

Frances, R. J., & Miller, S. I. (1998). *Clinical textbook of addictive disorders* (2nd ed.). New York: Guildford.

Franks, C. M., & Wilson, G. T. (1973). *Annual review of behavior therapy: Theory and practice* (Vols. 1–7). New York: Brunner/Mazel.

Franzek, E., & Beckmann, H. (1992). Sex differences and distinct subgroups in schizophrenia: A study of 54 chronic hospitalized schizophrenics. *Psychopathology, 25*(2), 90–99.

Friedman, M. J. (2001). Allostatic versus empirical perspectives on pharmacotherapy for PTSD. In J. P. Wilson., M. J. Friedman, & J. D. Lindy (Eds.), *Treating psychological trauma and PTSD* (pp. 3–27). New York: Guilford.

Frost, N. A., Greene, J., & Pranis, K. (2006, May). Hard hit: The growth in the imprisonment of women, 1977–2004. *Institute on Women and Criminal Justice, Women's Prison Association.*

GAINS Center. (1997). *Women's program compendium: A comprehensive guide to services for women with co-occurring disorders in the justice system.* Delmar, NY: GAINS Center/Policy Research Associates.

Galbraith, S. (1991). Women and legal drugs. In P. Roth (Ed.), *Alcohol and drugs are women's issues* (pp. 150–154). New York: Scarecrow.

Gartner, R., & Kruttschnitt, C. (2004). A brief history of doing time: The California Institution for Women in the 1960s and the 1990s. *Law & Society Review, 38*(2), 267–304.

Geissinger, C. J., & Hill, M. M. (2000). *Vicarious trauma debriefing groups: Getting started.* Denver: Colorado Organization for Victim Assistance.

Gergen, M. M., & Davis, S. N. (Eds.). (1997). *Toward a new psychology of gender: A reader.* New York: Routledge.

Gilbert, M. J. (1989). Hispanic Americans: Alcohol use, abuse and adverse consequences. In T. D. Watts & R. Wright (Eds.), *Alcoholism in minority populations* (pp. 55–75). Springfield, IL: Charles C Thomas.

Gilligan, C. (1982). *In a different voice: Psychological theory and women's development.* Cambridge, MA: Harvard University Press.

Glover, D. A. (2006). Allostatic load in women with and without PTSD symptoms. *Annals of the New York Academy of Science, 1071,* 442–447.

Goldfried, M. R., Decenteceo, E. T., & Weinberg, L. (1974). Systematic rational restructuring as a self-control technique. *Behavior Therapy, 5,* 247–254.

Goldman-Fraser, J. (1998). Cognitive influences on mother-infant interaction: A focus on substance-dependent women in treatment during pregnancy and postpartum. *Dissertation Abstracts International, 58*(12), 6844B. (UMI No. 9818337)

Gomberg, E. (1986). Women: Alcohol and other drugs. In B. Segal (Ed.), *Perspectives on drug use in the United States* (pp. 75–106). New York: Haworth.

Goodman, L. A., Dutton, M. A., & Harris, M. (1995). Episodically homeless women with serious mental illness: Prevalence of physical and sexual assault. *American Journal of Orthopsychiatry, 65*(4), 468–478.

Grant, K., Grace, P., Trujillo, J., Halpert, J., Kessler-Cordeiro, A., Razzino, B., & Davis, T. (2002). Predicting desire for a child among low-income urban adolescent girls: Interpersonal processes in the context of poverty. *Journal of Primary Prevention, 22,* 341–359.

Green, B. L. (1996). *Trauma History Questionnaire (THQ).* Washington DC: Georgetown University.

Greenfield, L., Burgdorf, K., Chen, X., Porowski, A., Roberts, T., & Herrell, J. (2004). Effectiveness of long-term residential substance abuse treatment for women: Findings from three national studies. *American Journal of Drug and Alcohol Abuse, 30,* 537–550.

Gregoire, T. K., & Snively, C. A. (2001). The relationship of social support and economic self-sufficiency to substance abuse outcomes in a long-term recovery program for women. *Journal of Drug Education, 31*(3), 221–237.

Grella, C. E., Scott, C. K., Foss, M. A., Joshi, V., & Hser, Y. I. (2003). Gender differences in drug treatment outcomes among participants in the Chicago target cities study. *Evaluation and Program Planning, 26,* 297–310.

Gunter, T. D. (2004). Incarcerated women and depression: A primer for the primary care provider. *Journal of the American Medical Women's Association, 59*(2), 107–112.

Halliday-Boykins, C. A., Schoenwald, S. K., & Letourneau, E. J. (2005). Caregiver-therapist ethnic similarity predicts youth outcomes from an empirically based treatment. *Journal of Consulting and Clinical Psychology, 73,* 808–818.

Harper, R. L., Harper, G. C., & Stockdale, J. E. (2002). The role and sentencing of women in drug trafficking crime. *Legal and Criminological Psychology, 7,* 101–114.

Harrison, A., Jessup, M. A., Covington, S. S., & Najavits, L. M. (2004). Weaving the vision: Research-to-practice strategies for women's recovery. *Counselor: The Magazine for Addiction Professionals 5*(4), 57–63.

Harrison, P. M., & Beck, A. J. (2005). *Prisoners in 2004.* Washington, DC: U.S. Department of Justice, Bureau of Justice Statistics. 10:8.

Haywood, T. W., Kravitz, H. M., Goldman, L. B., & Freeman, A. (2000). Characteristics of women in jail and treatment orientations: A review. *Behavioral Modification, 24*(3), 307–324.

Hein, D. A., Cohen, L. R., Miele, G. M., Litt, L. C., & Capstick, C. (2004). Promising treatments for women with comorbid PTSD and substance use disorders. *American Journal of Psychiatry, 161*(8), 1426–1432.

Hellard, M. E., & Aiken, C. K. (2004). HIV in prison: What are the risks and what can be done? *Sex Health, 1*(2), 107–113.

Henskens, R., Mulder, C. L., Garretsen, H., Bongers, I., & Sturmans, F. (2005). Gender differences in problems and needs among chronic, high-risk crack abusers: Results of a randomized controlled trial. *Journal of Substance Use, 10,* 128–140.

Herbert, J. D., & Sageman, M. (2004). "First do no harm": Emerging guidelines for the treatment of posttraumatic stress reactions. In G. M. Rosen (Ed.), *Posttraumatic stress disorder issues and controversies* (pp. 213–232). Chichester, West Sussex, UK: Wiley.

Herd, D. (1989). The epidemiology of drinking patterns and alcohol-related problems among U.S. blacks. In *Alcohol use among U.S. ethnic minorities* (National Institute on Alcohol Abuse and Alcoholism Research Monograph no. 18. DHHS Pub. No. [ADM] 89–1435, pp. 3–50). Washington, DC: U.S. Government Printing Office.

Herman, J. (1992). *Trauma and recovery: The aftermath of violence—from domestic abuse to political terror.* New York: Basic Books.

Herman, J. (1997). *Trauma and recovery: The aftermath of violence—from domestic abuse to political terror* (2nd ed.). New York: Basic Books.

Hidalgo, R. B., & Davidson, J. R. (2000). Selective serotonin reuptake inhibitors in post-traumatic stress disorder. *Journal of Psychopharmacology, 14*(1), 70–76.

Hohman, M. M., & Galt, D. H. (2001). Latinas in treatment: Comparisons of residents in a culturally specific recovery home with residents in non-specific recovery homes. *Journal of Ethnic and Cultural Diversity in Social Work 9*(3–4), 93–109.

Hohman, M. M., McGaffigan, R. P., & Segars, L. (2000). Predictors of successful completion of a postincarceration drug treatment program. *Journal of Addictions and Offender Counseling, 21*(1), 12–22.

Holleran, L., & Jung, S. (2005). Acculturative stress, violence, and resilience in the lives of Mexican-American youth. *Stress, Trauma, and Crisis: An International Journal, 8,* 107–130.

Horn, J. L., & Wanberg, K. W. (June, 1973). Females are different: On the diagnosis of alcoholism in women. In *Proceedings of the First Annual Alcoholism Conference of the National Institute on Alcohol Abuse and Alcoholism* (pp. 332–354). Washington, DC: U.S. Department of Health, Education, and Welfare.

Horn, J. L., Wanberg, K. W., & Foster, F. M. (1990). *Guide to the Alcohol Use Inventory (AUI).* Minneapolis, MN: National Computer Systems.

Howard, M. (1996, June 8). In defense of prisons. *Economist,* pp. 25-72.

Hser, Y. I., Huang, D., Teruya, C., & Anglin, M. D. (2004). Diversity of drug abuse treatment utilization patterns and outcomes. *Evaluation and Program Planning, 27,* 309–319.

Hubbard, R. L., Craddock, S. G., Flynn, P. M., Anderson, J., & Etheridge, R. M. (1997). Overview of 1-year follow-up outcomes in the Drug Abuse Treatment Outcome Study (DATOS). *Psychology of Addictive Behaviors, 11,* 261–278.

Huling, T. (1991). *Breaking the silence.* Albany: Correctional Association of New York.

Inciardi, J. A., Surratt, H. L., Martin, S. S., & Hooper, R. M. (2002). The importance of aftercare in a corrections-based treatment continuum. In C. G. Leukefeld, F. Tims, & D. Farabee (Eds.), *Treatment of drug offenders: Policies and issues* (pp. 204–216). New York: Springer.

Interagency Council on the Homeless. (1989). *The 1989 annual report of the Interagency Council on the Homeless.* Washington, DC: Author.

Isaacs, M., & Benjamin, M. (1991). *Towards a culturally competent system of care (Vol.2): Programs which utilize culturally competent principles*. Washington, DC: Georgetown University, Child Development Center, CASSP Technical Assistance Center.

Jacobson, E. (1938). *Progressive Relaxation* (2nd ed.). Chicago. University of Chicago Press.

Johnson, P. B., Richter, L., Kleber, H. D., McLellan, A. T., & Carise, D. (2005). Telescoping of drinking-related behaviors: Gender, racial/ethnic and age comparisons. *Substance Use and Misuse, 40*(4), 1139–1151.

Jordan, B. K., Schlenger, W. E., Fairbank, J. A., & Caddell, J. M. (1996). Prevalence of psychiatric disorders among incarcerated women. *Archives of General Psychiatry, 53*(6), 513–519.

Jordan, J. V. (1991). Empathy and self boundaries. In J. V. Jordan, A. G. Kaplan, J. B. Miller, I. P. Stiver, & J. L. Surrey (Eds.), *Women's growth in connections* (pp. 67–80). New York: Guilford.

Jordan, J. V., Kaplan, A. G., Miller, J. B., Stiver, I. P., & Surrey, J. L. (1991). *Women's growth in correction: Writings from the Stone Center*. New York: Guilford.

Joseph, H. (1992). Substance abuse and homelessness within the inner cities. In J. H. Llowinson, P. Ruiz, R. B. Millman, & J. G. Langrod (Eds.), *Substance abuse: A comprehensive textbook* (pp. 875–889). Baltimore, MD: Williams & Wilkins.

Kanfer, F. H. (1970). Self-regulation: Research, issues and speculations. In C. Neuringer & J. L. Michael (Eds.), *Behavior modification in clinical psychology* (pp. 178–220). New York: Appleton-Century-Crofts.

Kassebaum, G., & Chandler, S. M. (1994). Polydrug use and self control among men and women in prisons. *Journal of Drug Education, 24*(4), 333–350.

Kassebaum, P. (1999). *Substance abuse treatment for women offenders: Guide to promising practices* (DHHS Publication no. SMA 99–3303). Washington, DC: U.S. Government Printing Office.

Keeney, B. T., & Heide, K. M. (1994). Gender differences in serial murderers: A preliminary analysis. *Journal of Interpersonal Violence, 9*(3), 383–398.

Kerr, D. (1998). Substance abuse among female offenders: Efforts to treat substance-abusing women offenders must address underlying reasons for use. *Corrections Today, 60*(7), 114–120.

Kidorf, M., King, V. L., Neufeld, K., Stoller, K. B., Peirce, J., & Brooner, R. K. (2005). Involving significant others in the care of opioid-dependent patients receiving methadone. *Journal of Substance Abuse Treatment, 29,* 19–27.

Kilpatrick, D. G., Resnick, H. S., & Freedy, J. R. (1991). *The potential stressful events interview.* Charleston: Medical University of South Carolina, Department of Psychiatry, Crime Victims Research and Treatment Center.

Kimerling, R., Prins, A., Westrup, D., & Lee, T. (2004). Gender issues in the assessment of PTSD. In J. P. Wilson & T. M. Keane (Eds.), *Assessing psychological trauma and PTSD* (2nd ed., pp. 565–602). New York: Guilford.

Kinchin, D. (2005). *Post traumatic stress disorder: The invisible injury.* Oxfordshire, UK: Success Unlimited.

Knight, M., & Plugge, E. (2005). The outcomes of pregnancy among imprisoned women: A systematic review. *BJOG: An International Journal of Obstetrics and Gynecology, 112*(11), 1467–1474.

Knox, G. W. (2004). Females and gangs: Sexual violence, prostitution, and exploitation. *Journal of Gang Research, 11,* 1–15.

Koss, M. P., & Dinero, T. E. (1989). Discriminant analysis of risk factors for sexual victimization among a national sample of college women. *Journal of Consulting and Clinical Psychology, 57,* 242–250.

Krause, E. D. (2004). Role of feminine personality style, stereotyping, and self-discrepancy in women's recovery from childhood abuse. *Dissertation Abstracts International: Section B: The Sciences and Engineering, 64,* 4620.

Kubany, E. S., Haynes, S. N., Leisen, M. B., Owens, J. A., Kaplan, A. S., Watson, S. B., & Burns, K. (2000). Development and preliminary validation of a brief broad-spectrum measure of trauma exposure: The Traumatic Life Events Questionnaire. *Psychological Assessment, 12,* 210–224.

Kubiak, S. P. (2004). The effects of PTSD on treatment adherence, drug relapse, and criminal recidivism in a sample of incarcerated men and women. *Research on Social Work Practice, 14,* 424–433.

Kubzansky, L. D., Koenen, K. C., Spiro, A., Vokonas, P. S., & Sparrow, D. (2007). Prospective study of posttraumatic stress disorder symptoms and coronary heart disease in the normative aging study. *Archives of General Psychiatry, 64,* 109–116.

Kunnen, E. S., & Wassink, M. E. K. (2003). An analysis of identity change in adulthood. *Identity, 3,* 347–366.

Kunzman, K. (1989). *Healing from childhood sexual abuse: Recovering woman's guide.* Center City, MN: Hazelden.

Lange, A. J., & Jakubowski, P. (1976). *Responsible assertive behavior: Cognitive behavioral procedures for trainers.* Champaign, IL: Research Press.

Leahy, R. L. (1997). Cognitive therapy interventions. In L. Leahy (Ed.), *Practicing cognitive therapy: A guide to interventions* (pp. 3–20). Northvale, NJ: Jason Aronson.

Lee, L., Harkness, K. L., Sabbagh, M. A., & Jacobson, J. A. (2005). Mental state decoding abilities in clinical depression. *Journal of Affective Disorders, 86,* 247–258.

Lerner, B. G. (2001). BEAT IT!: Booster Efficacy Awareness Therapy Intervention Treatment: HIV prevention for severe mental ill alcohol/drug adult abusers (Immune deficiency). *Dissertation Abstracts International, 61*(10), 5570B. (UMI No. 9991530)

Leve, L. D., & Chamberlain, P. (2004). Female juvenile offenders: Defining an early-onset pathway for delinquency. *Journal of Child and Family Studies, 13,* 439–452.

Lewis, D. C. (1997). The role of the generalist in the care of the substance-abusing patient. *Medical Clinics of North America, 81*(4), 831–843.

Lex, B. W. (1987). Review of alcohol problems in ethnic minority groups. *Journal of Consulting and Clinical Psychology, 55*(3), 293–300.

Lightfoot, L. (1997). *What works in treating the correctional substance abuser?* Paper presented at the ICAA Fifth Annual Research Conference, Cleveland, OH.

Linehan, M. M., & Addis, M.E. (1990). *Screening for suicidal behaviors: The Suicidal Behaviors Questionnaire.* Unpublished manuscript. University of Washington, Seattle.

Longshore, D., & Teruya, C. (2006). Treatment motivation in drug users: A theory-based analysis. *Drug and Alcohol Dependence, 81,* 179–188.

Lorber, J. (1994). *Paradoxes of gender.* New Haven, CT: Yale University Press.

Macalino, G. E., Hou, J. C., Kumar, M. S., Taylor, L. E., Sumantera, I. G., & Rich, J. D. (2004). Hepatitis C infection and incarcerated populations. *International Journal of Drug Policy, 15,* 103–114.

Mack, M. G., Schultz, A. M., & Araki, K. (2002). Role models in self-esteem of college women. *Psychological Reports, 90,* 659–664.

Maldonado, J. R., & Spiegel, D. (1995). Using hypnosis. In C. Classen & I. D. Yalom (Eds.). *Treating women molested in childhood* (pp. 163–186). San Francisco: Jossey-Bass.

Marcus-Mendoza, S., & Wright, E. (2004). Decontextualizing female criminality: Treating abused women in prison in the United States. *Feminism & Psychology, 14*(2), 250–255.

Marecek, J., & Hare-Mustin, R. T. (1991). A short history of the future: Feminism and clinical psychology. *Psychology of Women Quarterly, 14,* 521–436.

Markarian, M., & Franklin, J. (1998). Substance abuse in minority populations. In R. J. Frances & S. I. Miller (Eds.), *Clinical textbook of addictive disorders* (2nd ed., pp. 397–412). New York: Guilford.

Marks, I. M., Lovell, K., Noshirvani, H., Livanou, M., & Thrasher, S. (1998). Treatment of posttraumatic stress disorder by exposure and/or cognitive restructuring: A controlled study. *Archives of General Psychiatry, 55,* 317–325.

Martin, J. A., Hamilton, B. E., Sutton, P. D., Ventura, S. J., Menacker, F., Kirmeyer, S., et al. (2007). Births: Final Data for 2005. *National Vital Statistics Reports, Centers for Disease Control 56*:6, 1–104. Retrieved March 5, 2008, from http://www.cdc.gov/hcds/data/nvsr56/nvsr56_06.pdf

Masters, R. E. (2003). *Counseling criminal justice offenders* (2nd ed.). Fresno: California State University Press.

Mathew, P., Elting, L., Cooksley, C., Owens, S., & Lin, J. (2005). Cancer in an incarcerated population. *Cancer, 104*(10), 2197–2204.

Matlin, M. W. (1996). *The psychology of women.* Fort Worth, TX: Harcourt Brace.

McEwen, B. S. (1998). Protective and damaging effects of stress mediators. *New England Journal of Medicine, 338,* 171–179.

McEwen, B. S. (2000). Allostasis and allostatic load: Implications for neuropsychopharmacology. *Neuropsychopharmacology, 22,* 108–124.

McEwen, B. S. (2004). Protection and damage from acute and chronic stress: Allostasis and allostatic overload and relevance to the pathophysiology of psychiatric disorders. *Annals of the New York Academy of Science, 1032,* 1–7.

McLellan, A. T. (1983). Patient characteristics associated with outcomes. In J. R. Cooper, F. Altman, B. S. Brown, & D. Czechowicz (Eds.), *Research on the treatment of narcotic addiction: State of the art* (DHHS Publication No. ADM 87–1281, pp. 500–529). Rockville, MD: U.S. Department of Health and Human Services.

McLellan, A. T., Alterman, A. L., Metzger, D. S., Grissom, G. R., et al. (1994). Similarity of outcome predictors across opiate, cocaine, and alcohol treatment: Role of treatment services. *Journal of Counseling and Clinical Psychology, 62,* 1141–1158.

McMahon, M. (Ed.). (2000). *Assessment to assistance: Programs for women in community corrections.* Lanham, MD: American Correctional Association.

McNeil, D. E., Binder, R. L., & Robinson, J. C. (2005). Incarceration associated with homelessness, mental disorder, and co-occurring substance abuse. *Psychiatric Services, 56,* 840–846.

McQuaide, S., & Ehrenreich, J. H. (1998). Women in prison: Approaches to understanding the lives of a forgotten population. *Affilia, 13*(2), 233–246.

Meichenbaum, D. (1985). *Stress inoculation training.* New York: Pergamon.

Mertens, D. J., (2001). Pregnancy outcomes of inmates in a large county jail setting. *Public Health Nursing, 18*(1), 45–53.

Mesrian, P. (1998). Analytical description of psychological constructs of women who drink alcohol during pregnancy. *Dissertation Abstracts International, 58(10), 5633B.* (UMI No. 9813153)

Messina, N., Burdon, W., Hagopian, G., & Prendergast, M. (2006). Predictors of prison-based treatment outcomes: A comparison of men and women participants. *American Journal of Drug and Alcohol Abuse, 32,* 7–28.

Messing, J. T., & Heeren, J. W. (2004). Another side of multiple murder: Women killers in the domestic context. *Homicide Studies: An Interdisciplinary & International Journal,* 123–158.

Miller, B. A., & Downs, W. R. (1986). *Conflict and violence among alcoholic women as compared to a random household sample.* Paper presented at the 38th annual meeting of the American Society of Criminology, Atlanta.

Miller, E. M. (1986). *Street woman.* Philadelphia: Temple University Press.

Miller, D. (1994). *Women who hurt themselves: A book of hope and understanding.* New York: Basic Books.

Miller, J. B. (1990). *Connections, disconnections, and violations.* Work in progress no. 22. Wellesley, MA: Wellesley College, Stone Center.

Miller, J. B., & Stiver, I. P. (1997). *The healing connection: How women form relationships in therapy and in life.* Boston: Beacon Press.

Miller, W. R. (2006). Motivational factors in addictive behaviors. In W. R. Miller & K. M. Carroll (Eds.*), Rethinking substance abuse: What the science shows, and what we should do about it* (pp. 134–150). New York: Guilford.

Miller, W. R., & Rollnick, S. (1991). *Motivational interviewing: Preparing people to change addictive behavior.* New York: Guilford.

Miller, W. R., & Rollnick, S. (2002). *Motivational interviewing: Preparing people for change.* New York: Guilford.

Millon, T., Millon, C., & Davis, R. (2005). *Millon Clinical Multiaxial Inventory-III.* Minneapolis, MN: Pearson Assessments.

Mulder, R. T., Wells, J. E., Joyce, P. R., & Bushnell, J. A. (1994). Antisocial women. *Journal of Personality Disorders, 8,* 279–287.

Najavits, L. M. (1999). Seeking Safety: A new cognitive-behavioral therapy for PTSD and substance abuse. *National Center for Post-traumatic Stress Disorder Clinical Quarterly, 8*(3), 40–45.

Najavits, L. M. (2002). *Seeking safety: A treatment manual for PTSD and substance abuse.* New York: Guilford.

Najavits, L. M., Weiss, R. D., & Shaw, S. R. (1997). The link between substance abuse and posttraumatic stress disorder in women: A research review. *American Journal on Addictions, 6(4),* 273–283.

Najavits, L. M., Weiss, R. D., Shaw, S. R., & Meunz, L. R. (1998). "Seeking safety": Outcome of a new cognitive-behavioral psychotherapy for women with posttraumatic stress disorder and substance dependence. *Journal of Traumatic Stress, 11*(3), 437–456.

National Campaign to Prevent Teen & Unplanned Pregnancy. (2007). Retrieved March 4, 2008, from http://teenpregnancy.org/America/statisticsDisplay.asp?ID=48sID=28

National Center for Health Statistics. (1997). *Death rates for selected causes, by 5-year age groups 1997.* Retrieved January 28, 2007, from http//www.nccev.org/violence/statistics/statistics-community.html

National Center for Posttraumatic Stress Disorder. (2007). Washington, DC: U.S. Department of Veterans Affairs. Retrieved August 29, 2007, from http://www.ncptsd.va.gov/ncmain/ncdocs/fact_shts/fs_how_common_is_ptsd.html

National Center on Addiction and Substance Abuse at Columbia University. (1998). *Behind bars: Substance abuse and America's prison population.* New York: Author.

National Institute of Justice. (2004). *Arrestee drug abuse monitoring (ADAM) program in the United States, 2003.* Washington, DC: U.S. Department of Justice.

National Survey of Substance Abuse Treatment Services (N-SSATS). (2005). *Data on substance abuse treatment facilities.* Washington, DC: U.S. Department of Health and Human Services (SAMHSA).

Nemeroff, C. B., Bremner, J. D., Foa, E. B., Mayberg, H. S., North, C. S., & Stein, M. B. (2006). Posttraumatic stress disorder: A state-of-the-science review. *Journal of Psychiatric Research, 40,* 1–21.

Ness, C. D. (2004). Why girls fight: Female youth violence in the inner city. *Annals of the American Academy of Political and Social Science, 595,* 32–48.

Niehoff, D. (1999). *The biology of violence: How understanding the brain, behavior and environment can break the vicious cycle of aggression.* New York: Free Press.

Nolen-Hoeksema, S. (2004). *Women who think too much: How to break free of overthinking and reclaim your life.* New York: Holt.

Norris, F. H., & Hamblen, J. L. (2004). Standardized self-report measures of civilian trauma and PTSD. In J. P. Wilson & T. M. Keane (Eds.), *Assessing psychological trauma and PTSD* (2nd ed., pp. 63–102). New York: Guilford.

Nuffield, J. (1989). The SIR Scale: Some reflection on its application. *Forum on Corrections Research, 1,* 19–22.

Oliver, S. J., & Toner, B. B. (1990). The influence of gender role typing on the expression of depressive symptoms. *Sex Roles, 22*(11–12), 775–790.

Ostermann, J., Sloan, F. A., & Taylor, D. H. (2005). Heavy alcohol use and marital dissolution in the USA. *Social Sciences and Medicine, 61,* 2304–2316.

Ouimette, P. C., Wolfe, J., & Chrestman, K. R. (1996). Characteristics of posttraumatic stress disorder—alcohol abuse comorbidity in women. *Journal of Substance Abuse, 8*(3), 335–346.

Owen, B., & Bloom, B. (1997). *Profiling the needs of young female offenders: A protocol and pilot study* (Final report) (NCJ 179988). Washington, DC: U.S. Department of Justice.

Palacios, W. R., Urmann, C. F., Newel, R., & Hamilton, N. (1999). Developing a sociological framework for dually diagnosed women. *Journal of Substance Abuse Treatment, 17*(1–2), 91–102.

Palermo, G. B. (2003). Editorial: Female offenders in a changing society. *International Journal of Offender Therapy and Comparative Criminology, 47,* 493–495.

Pear, R. (1990, September 26). United States reports poverty is down but inequality is up: Report of the census bureau. *New York Times,* p. A14.

Pelissier, B., & Jones, N. (2006). Differences in motivation, coping style, and self-efficacy among incarcerated male and female drug users. *Journal of Substance Abuse Treatment, 30,* 113–120.

Pepi, C. (1998). Children without childhoods: A feminist intervention strategy utilizing systems theory and restorative justice in treating female adolescent offenders. In J. Harden & M. Hill (Eds.), *Breaking the rules: Women in prison and feminist therapy* (pp. 85–101). Binghamton, NY: Haworth.

Peters, R. H., & Wexler, H. K. (2005). *Substance abuse treatment for adults in the criminal justice system.* Treatment Improvement Protocol (TIP) 44. Rockville, MD: Center for Substance Abuse Treatment.

Peugh, J., & Belenko, S. (1999). Substance-involved women inmates: Challenges to providing effective treatment. *Prison Journal, 79*(1), 23–44.

Phillips, S. D., & Harm, N. J. (1997). Women prisoners: A contextual framework. *Women and Therapy, 20*(4), 1–9.

Pike, K. M., & Striegel-Moore, R. H. (1997). Disordered eating and eating disorders. In S. J. Gallant, G. P. Keita, & R. Royak-Schaler (Eds.), *Health care for women: Psychological, social, and behavioral influences* (pp. 97–114). Washington, DC: American Psychological Association.

Poehlmann, J. (2005). Incarcerated mothers' contact with children, perceived family relationships, and depressive symptoms. *Journal of Family Psychology, 19,* 350–357.

Poitier, V. L., Niliwaambieni, M., & Rowe C. L. (1997). A rite of passage approach designed to preserve the families of substance abusing African-American women. *Child Welfare League of America, 76*(1), 173–195.

Pollock, J. M. (1998). *Counseling women in prison.* Thousand Oaks, CA: Sage.

Primm, A. B., Osher, F. C., & Gomez, M. B. (2005). Race and ethnicity, mental health services and cultural competence in the criminal justice system: Are we ready to change? *Community Mental Health Journal, 41,* 557–569.

RachBeisel, J., Scott, J., & Dixon, L. (1999, November). Co-occurring severe mental illness and substance abuse disorders: A review of recent research. *Psychiatric Services, 50*(11), 1427–1434.

Rasting, M., & Beutel, M. E. (2005). Dyidic affective interactive patterns in the intake interview as a predictor of outcome. *Psychotherapy Research, 15,* 188–198.

Rau, D. R. (2002). Personality pathology, criminal careers, and disciplinary problems of women in a county jail. *Dissertation Abstract International: Section B: The Sciences and Engineering, 62,* 4801.

Reed, B. G., & Leavitt, M. E. (2000). Modified wraparound and women offenders in community corrections: Strategies, opportunities, and tensions. In M. McMahon (Ed.), *Assessment to assistance: Programs for women in community corrections* (pp. 1–106). Lanham, MD: American Correctional Association.

Renik, O. (2002). Defining the goals of a clinical psychoanalysis. *Psychoanalytic Quarterly, 71,* 117–123.

Resnick, H. S., Falsetti, S. A., Kilpatrick, D. G., & Freedy, R. (1996). *Potential Stressful Events Interview (PSEI)*. Charleston, SC: National Crime Victims Research and Treatment Center.

Richardson, L. (2002). Substance abusers' friendships and social support networks in the therapeutic community. *Therapeutic Communities: International Journal for Therapeutic and Supportive Organizations, 23,* 85–104.

Richie, B. E. (1996). *Compelled to crime: The gender entrapment of battered black women.* New York: Routledge.

Root, M. P. P. (1992). Reconstructing the impact of trauma on personality. In L. S. Brown & M. Ballou (Eds.), *Personality and psychopathology: Feminist reappraisals* (pp. 229–265). New York: Guilford.

Ross, C. E., & Mirowsky, J. (2002). Age and the gender gap in the sense of personal control. *Social Psychology Quarterly, 65,* 125–145.

Rotter, J. (1966). Generalized expectancies for internal versus external control of reinforcement. *Psychological Monographs, 80*(1), 1–28.

Rubinstein, G. (2004). Locus of control and helplessness: Gender differences among bereaved parents. *Death Studies, 28,* 211–223.

Ruiz, P. (1995). Assessing, diagnosing and treating culturally diverse individuals: A Hispanic perspective. *Psychiatric Quarterly, 66,* 329–341.

Sadker, M., & Sadker, D. (1994). *Failing at fairness: How America's schools cheat girls.* New York: Scribner's.

Salekin, R. T., Rogers, R., & Sewell, K. W. (1997). Construct validity of psychopathy in a female offender sample: A multitrait-multimethod evaluation. *Journal of Abnormal Psychology, 106*(4), 576–585.

Salekin, R. T., Rogers, R., Ustad, K. L., Sewell, K. W. (1998). Psychopathy and recidivism among female inmates. *Law & Human Behavior, 22*(1), 109–128.

Salkovskis, P. M. (1996). The cognitive approach to anxiety: Threat beliefs, safety-seeking behavior, and the special case of health anxiety and obsessions. In P. M. Salkovskis (Ed.), *Frontiers of cognitive therapy* (pp. 48–74). New York: Guilford.

Sandrine, P., Sharon, E., Kang, S. K., Angarita, G. A., & Gastfriend, D. R. (2005). Prevalence of physical and sexual abuse among substance abuse patients and impact on treatment outcomes. *Drug and Alcohol Dependence, 78,* 57–64.

Saunders, D. G. (1994). Child custody decisions in families experiencing woman abuse. *Social Work, 39*(1), 51–59.

Saunders, D. L., Olive, D. M., Wallace, S. B., Lacy D., Leyba, R., & Kendig, N. E (2001). Tuberculosis screening in the federal prison system: An opportunity to treat and prevent tuberculosis in foreign-born populations. *Public Health Report, 116*(3), 210–218.

Scheck, M., Schaeffer, J. A., & Gillette, C. (1998). Brief psychological intervention with traumatized young women: The efficacy of eye movement desensitization and reprocessing. *Journal of Traumatic Stress, 11,* 25–44.

Schmidt, G., Klee, L., & Ames, G. (1990). Review and analysis of literature on indicators of women's drinking problems. *British Journal of Addiction, 85,* 179–192.

Seedat, S., Stein, D. J., & Carey, P. D. (2005). Post-traumatic stress disorder in women: Epidemiological and treatment issues. *CNS Drugs, 19,* 411–427.

Seligman, M. (1975). *Helplessness.* San Francisco: Freeman Press.

Sharp, S. F. (2003). *Incarcerated women: Rehabilitative programming in women's prisons.* Upper Saddle River, NJ: Prentice Hall.

Simon, R. J. (1975). *Women and crime.* Lexington, MA: Lexington Books.

Simpson, D. D., & Joe, G. W. (2004). A longitudinal evaluation of treatment engagement and recovery stages. *Journal of Substance Abuse Treatment, 27,* 89–97.

Smith, A., Krisman, K., Strozier, A. L. & Marley, M. (2004). Breaking through the bars: Exploring the experiences of addicted incarcerated parents whose children are cared for by relatives. *Families in Society, 85,* 187–195.

Smith, D. W., Davis, J. L., & Fricker-Elhai, A. E. (2004). How does trauma beget trauma? Cognitions about risk in women with abuse histories. *Child Maltreatment, 9,* 292–303.

Smith, E. M., & Cloninger, C. R. (1981). Alcoholic females: Mortality at 12-year follow-up. *Focus on Women, 2,* 1–13.

Smith, M., Jaffe, J., & Segal, J. (2008). *Post-traumatic stress disorder (PTSD): Symptoms, types and treatment.* Helpguide.org. Retrieved March 3, 2008, from http://www.Helpguide.org/mental/post-traumatic-stress-disorder-symptoms-treatment.htm

Snell, T. L. (1994). *Women in prison: Survey of state prison inmates, 1991* (BJS Special Report, NCJ 145321). Washington, DC: U. S. Department of Justice, Bureau of Justice Statistics.

Snyder, H. N. (1997). *Juvenile Arrests 1996* (NCJ 167578). Juvenile Justice Bulletin, November 1997. Washington, DC: U. S. Department of Justice, Office of Juvenile Justice and Delinquency.

Snyder, H. N., & Sickmund, M. (1999). *Juvenile Offenders and Victims: 1999 National Report.* Washington, DC: U.S. Department of Justice, Office of Juvenile Justice and Delinquency.

Sommers, I., & Baskin, D. R. (1993). The situational context of violent female offending. *Journal of Research in Crime & Delinquency, 30*(2), 136–162.

Sorbello, L., Eccleston, L., Ward, T., & Jones, R. (2002). Treatment needs of female offenders: A review. *Australian Psychologist, 37,* 198–205.

Spivack, G., & Shure, M. B. (1974). *Social adjustment of young children: A cognitive approach to solving real-life problems.* San Francisco: Jossey-Bass.

Staton, M., Walker, R., & Leukefeld, C. (2003). Age differences in risk behavior among incarcerated substance-abusing women. *Journal of Addictions Nursing, 14,* 3–9.

Steele, C. T. (2000). Providing clinical treatment to substance abusing trauma survivors. *Alcoholism Treatment Quarterly, 18*(3), 71–81.

Stenius, V. M. K., Veysey, B. M., Hamilton, Z., & Anderson, R. (2005). Social roles in women's lives: Changing conceptions of self. *Journal of Behavioral Health Services and Research. Special Issue: The Impact of Co-occurring Disorders and Violence on Women, 32,* 182–198.

Sterling, P., & Eyer, J. (1988). Allostasis: A new paradigm to explain arousal pathology. In S. Fisher & J. Reason (Eds.), *Handbook of life stress, cognition and health* (pp. 629–649). New York: Wiley.

Stewart, A. J. (1994). Toward a feminist strategy for studying women's lives. In C. E. Franz & A. J. Stewart (Eds.), *Women creating lives: Identities, resilience and resistance* (pp. 11–35). Boulder: Westview.

Strauss, S. M., & Falkin, G. P. (2001). Social support systems of women offenders who use drugs: A focus on the mother-daughter relationship. *American Journal of Drug and Alcohol Abuse, 27*(1), 65–89.

Substance Abuse and Mental Health Administration. (2006). *Results from the 2005 National Survey on Drug Use and Health: National Findings* (NSDUH Series H-30, DHHS, Publication No. SMA 06-4194). Rockville, MD: Office of Applied Studies.

Sue, D. W., & Sue, D. (1990) *Counseling the culturally different* (2nd ed.). New York: Wiley.

Sue, S. (2006). Cultural competency: From philosophy to research and practice. *Journal of Community Psychology, 34,* 237–245.

Sun, A.P. (2006). Program factors related to women's substance abuse treatment retention and other outcomes: A review and critique. *Journal of Substance Abuse Treatment, 30,* 1–20.

Taylor, C. (1993). *Girls, gangs, women and drugs.* East Lansing: Michigan State University Press.

Teplin, L. A., Abram, K. M., & McClelland, G. M. (1996). Prevalence of psychiatric disorders among incarcerated women: Pretrial jail detainees. *Archives of General Psychiatry 53*(6), 505–512.

Timco, C., Finney, J. W., & Moos, R. H. (2005). The 8 year course of alcohol abuse and gender differences in social context and coping. *Alcoholism: Clinical and Experimental Research, 29*(4), 612–621.

Tsai, J., Floyd, R. L., & Bertrand, J. (2007). Tracking binge drinking among U.S. childhood-bearing age women. *Preventive Medicine, 11* 298–302.

Valente, C. M., Duszynski, K. R., Smoot, R. T., Ferentz, K. S., Levine, D. M., & Troisi, A. J. (1992). Physician estimates of substance abuse in Baltimore and Cumberland: 1991. *Maryland Medical Journal, 41*(11), 973–978.

Van Dieten, M., & Robinson, D. (2007). *Service planning instrument.* Ottawa, Canada: Orbis Partners.

Veysey, B. M., DeCou, K., & Prescott, L. (1998). Effective management of female jail detainees with histories of physical and sexual abuse. *American Jails, 12*(2), 50–54.

Velez, M. L., Montoya, I. D., Schweitzer, W., Golden, A., Jansson, L. M., Walters, V., Svikis, D., Jones, H. E., Chilcoat, H., & Campbell, J. (2006). Exposure to violence among substance-dependent pregnant women and their children. *Journal of Substance Abuse Treatment, 30,* 31–38.

Vigdal, G. L. (1995). *Planning for alcohol and other drug abuse treatment for adults in the criminal justice system: TIP 17.* Rockville, MD: U.S. Department of Health and Human Services, Center for Substance Abuse Treatment.

Vitale, J. E., Smith, S. S., Brinkely, C. A., & Newman, J. P. (2002). The reliability and validity of the Psychopathy Checklist—Revised in a sample of female offenders. *Criminal Justice and Behavior, 29,* 202–231.

Vogt, D. (2007). *Women, trauma and PTSD.* National Center for Posttraumatic Stress Disorder Fact Sheet. Washington, DC: U.S. Department of Veterans Affairs.

Volpe, J. S. (2005). *Traumatic stress: An overview.* Commack, NY: The American Academy of Experts in Traumatic Stress.

Walker, L. E. (1989). Psychology and violence against women. *American Psychologist, 44*(4), 695–702.

Walker, L. E. (1994). *Abused women and survivor therapy: A practical guide for the psychotherapist.* Washington, DC: American Psychological Association.

Wanberg, K. W. (1992a). *A user's guide for the Adolescent Self Assessment Profile.* Arvada, CO: Center for Addictions Research and Evaluation.

Wanberg, K. W. (1992b). *A user's guide to the Adolescent Substance Use Survey—SUS: Differential screening of adolescent alcohol and other drug use problems.* Arvada, CO: Center for Addictions Research and Evaluation.

Wanberg, K. W. (1996). *A user's guide for the Adult Substance Use Survey—Revised (ASUS-R).* Arvada, CO: Center for Addictions Research and Evaluation.

Wanberg, K. W. (1997). *The Adult Substance Use Survey (ASUS).* Arvada, CO: Center for Addictions Research and Evaluation.

Wanberg, K. W. (1998, 2007). *The Adult Clinical Assessment Profile (ACAP): The Adult Self Assessment Profile (AdSAP) and Rating Adult Problems Scale (RAPS).* Arvada, CO: Center for Addictions Research and Evaluation.

Wanberg, K. W. (2006). *The Adult Substance Use Survey—Revised (ASUS-R).* Arvada, CO: Center for Addictions Research and Evaluation.

Wanberg, K. W. (2008). *Differences in men and women in judicial populations.* Arvada, CO: Center for Addictions Research and Evaluation.

Wanberg, K. W., & Horn, J. L. (1970). Alcoholism symptom patterns of men and women: A comparative study. *Quarterly Journal of Studies on Alcohol, 31,* 40–61.

Wanberg, K. W., & Horn, J. L. (1991). *The Drug Use Self-report: User's Guide.* Arvada, CO: Center for Addictions Research and Evaluation.

Wanberg, K. W., & Knapp, J. (1969). Differences in drinking symptoms and behavior of men and women. *British Journal of the Addictions, 64,* 1–9.

Wanberg, K. W., & Milkman, H. B. (1993, 2004). *The Adult Self-Assessment Questionnaire (AdSAQ).* Arvada, Co: Center for Addictions Research and Evaluation.

Wanberg, K. W., & Milkman, H. B. (1998). *Criminal conduct and substance abuse treatment: Strategies for self-improvement and change, The provider's guide.* Thousand Oaks, CA: Sage.

Wanberg, K. W., & Milkman, H. B. (2006). *Criminal conduct and substance abuse treatment: Strategies for self-improvement and change, The participant's workbook* (2nd ed.). Thousand Oaks, CA: Sage.

Wanberg, K. W., & Milkman, H. B. (2008). *Criminal conduct and substance abuse treatment: Strategies for self-improvement and change, The provider's guide* (2nd ed.). Thousand Oaks, CA: Sage.

Wanberg, K. W., & Milkman, H. B. (in press). *Criminal conduct and substance abuse treatment: History, research and foundational models: A resource guide.* Thousand Oaks, CA: Sage.

Wanberg, K. W., & Timken, D. (1998). *The Adult Substance Use and Driving Survey.* Arvada, CO: Center for Addictions Research and Evaluation.

Wang, F., & Yamagishi, T. (2005). Group-based trust and gender differences in China. *Asian Journal of Social Psychology, 8,* 199–210.

Watkins, K. E., Shaner, A., & Sullivan, G. (1999). Addictions services: The role of gender in engaging the dually diagnosed in treatment. *Community Mental Health Journal, 35*(2), 115–126.

Way, B. B., Miraglia, R., Sawyer, D. A., Beer, R., & Eddy, J. (2005). Factors related to suicide in New York state prisons. *International Journal of Law and Psychiatry, 28*(3), 207–221.

Weisner, C. (2005). Substance misuse: What place for women-only treatment programs? *Addiction, 100,* 7–8.

Weizmann-Henelius, G., Viemero, V., & Eronen, M. (2004). Psychological risk markers in violent female behavior. *International Journal of Forensic Mental Health, 3,* 185–196.

Whealin, J. (2003). *Child sexual abuse. National Center for Posttraumatic Stress Disorder. Fact Sheet.* Washington, DC: U.S. Department of Veterans Affairs. Retrieved August 30, 2007, from http://www.ridalaskaofchildabuse.org/csa_ptsd.html

Whitaker, M. S. (2000). Responding to women offenders: Equitable does not mean identical. *Topics in Community Corrections Annual Issue 2000: Responding to Women Offenders in the Community,* 4–6.

White, A. M. (2001). *Alcohol and adolescent brain development.* Durham, NC: Duke University Medical Center.

Wilke, D. J. (2001). Reconceptualizing recovery: Adding self-esteem to the mix. *Dissertation Abstracts International, 61(12),* 4950A. (UMI No. 9996821)

Williams-Quinlan, S. L. (2004). Guidelines for treatment women in psychotherapy. In G. Koocher, J. Norcross, & S. Hill (Eds.), *Psychologists' Desk Reference* (2nd ed.). New York: Oxford University Press.

Willis, K., & Rushforth, C. (2003). The female criminal: An overview of women's drug use and offending behaviour. In *Australian Institute of Criminology.* Retrieved August 30, 2003, from http://aic.gov.au

Wilsnack, S. C. (1995). Alcohol use and alcohol problems in women. In A. L. Stanton & S. J. Gallant (Eds.), *Psychology of women's health: Progress and challenges in research and application* (pp. 381–443). Washington, DC: American Psychological Association.

Wilsnack, S. C., Vogeltanz, N. D., Klassen, A. D., & Harris, T. R. (1997). Childhood sexual abuse and women's sexual abuse: National survey findings. *Journal of Studies on Alcohol, 58*(3), 264–271.

Wilson, J. P., Friedman, M. J., & Lindy, J. D. (2001). Treatment goals for PTSD. In J. P. Wilson., M. J. Friedman, & J. D. Lindy (Eds.), *Treating psychological trauma and PTSD* (pp. 3–27). New York: Guilford.

Wilson, M. K., & Anderson, S. C. (1997). Empowering female offenders: Removing barriers to community-based practice. *Affilia, 12*(3), 342–358.

Wolfe, J., & Kimerling, R. (1997a). Gender issues in the assessment of posttraumatic stress disorder. In J. Wilson & T. M. Keane (Eds.), *Assessing psychological trauma and PTSD* (pp. 192–238). New York: Guilford.

Wolfe, J., & Kimerling, R., (1997b). *Life Stressor Checklist—Revised (LSC-R).* Menlo Park, CA: Education Division National Center for PTSD.

Wolpe, J. (1958). *Psychotherapy by reciprocal inhibitors.* Stanford, CA: Stanford University Press.

Women's Prison Association. (2003). *The population of women in prison increases rapidly.* Retrieved from http://www.wpaonline.org

Wu, Z. H., Baillargeon, J., Grady, J. J., Black, S. A., & Dunn, K. (2001). HIV Seroprevalence among newly incarcerated inmates in the Texas correctional system. *Annals of Epidemiology, 11*(5), 342–6.

Yarkin, K. L., Town, J. P., & Wallston, B. S. (1982). Blacks and women must try harder: Stimulus persons' race and sex attributions of causality. *Personality and Social Psychology Bulletin, 8*(1), 21–24.

Zilberman, M. L., & Blume, S. B. (2005). Domestic violence, alcohol and substance abuse. *Brazilian Journal of Psychiatry, 27,* 51–55.

Zins, M., Guegen, A., Leclerc, A., & Goldberg, M. (2003). Alcohol consumption and marital status of French women in the GAZEL cohort: A longitudinal analysis between 1992 and 1996. *Journal of Studies on Alcohol, 64,* 784–789.

Zlotnick, C., Najavits, L. M., Rohsenow, D. J., & Johnson, D. M. (2003). A cognitive-behavioral treatment for incarcerated women with substance abuse disorder and posttraumatic stress disorder: Findings from a pilot study. *Journal of Substance Abuse Treatment, 25,* 99–105.

Index